Emerging Applications of FPGAs and Reconfigurable Computing System

Emerging Applications of FPGAs and Reconfigurable Computing System

Guest Editor

José V. Frances-Villora

MDPI

Basel • Beijing • Wuhan • Barcelona • Belgrade • Novi Sad • Cluj • Manchester

Guest Editor
José V. Frances-Villora
School of Engineering
University of Valencia
Burjassot
Spain

Editorial Office
MDPI AG
Grosspeteranlage 5
4052 Basel, Switzerland

This is a reprint of the Special Issue, published open access by the journal *Electronics* (ISSN 2079-9292), freely accessible at: https://www.mdpi.com/journal/electronics/special_issues/5923EM72V7.

For citation purposes, cite each article independently as indicated on the article page online and as indicated below:

Lastname, A.A.; Lastname, B.B. Article Title. *Journal Name* **Year**, *Volume Number*, Page Range.

ISBN 978-3-7258-7917-5 (Hbk)
ISBN 978-3-7258-7918-2 (PDF)
https://doi.org/10.3390/books978-3-7258-7918-2

Contents

About the Editor

José V. Frances-Villora

José V. Frances-Villora received his M.Sc. and Ph.D. degrees in physics from the Universitat de Valencia, Valencia, Spain, in 1994 and 2000, respectively. From 1995, he was a Part Time Lecturer at the Faculty of Physics, the University of Valencia. In 1997, he switched to a Full Time Lecturer at the Polytechnic University of Valencia, Department of Informatics Systems and Computation. He subsequently returned to the University of Valencia as an Assistant Professor in 1998. He is currently an Associate Professor and Researcher at the Department of Electronic Engineering, the University of Valencia, Spain. His research interests include hardware implementation of signal processing and machine learning algorithms into embedded systems and reconfigurable logic, seeking to achieve on-chip learning in real-time applications, neuromorphic systems, event-based systems and spiking neural networks.

electronics

MDPI

Editorial

Emerging Applications of FPGAs and Reconfigurable Computing Systems

Jose V. Frances-Villora

Department of Electronic Engineering, School of Engineering (ETSE), University of Valencia, 46100 Burjassot, Spain; jose.v.frances@uv.es

1. Introduction

Field-programmable gate arrays and reconfigurable computing have moved beyond their earlier role as convenient prototyping platforms. In modern computing systems, they are increasingly occupying a strategic position between the flexibility of software and the efficiency of fixed-function hardware [1,2]. This role has become especially important as many application areas are demanding combinations that are difficult to achieve with conventional architectures alone, including acceleration, deterministic low latency, high-throughput streaming, low energy consumption, and the ability of rapid adaptation to changing algorithms and standards [3,4]. Thus, FPGA and reconfigurable computing have become central not only to embedded and industrial systems, but also to edge AI, wireless communications, cryptographic processing, scientific instrumentation, and other data-intensive environments [3–6].

The evolution of these devices reflects that growing importance, incorporating richer memory hierarchies, abundant DSP resources, hardened interfaces, embedded processors, and, in some cases, direct-RF capabilities. It enables these devices to function as heterogeneous computing systems rather than as standalone logic fabrics [2,7].

At the same time, the field faces a number of persistent challenges. These include the trade-off between development productivity and hardware efficiency, the difficulty of mapping irregular or control-dominant workloads, the cost of data movement and synchronization, the need to balance area, throughput, latency, and power, and the increasing importance of resilience, security, and maintainability in critical deployments [8–11]. Emerging research trends address these issues through high-level synthesis and software–hardware co-design, custom arithmetic and approximation methods, more scalable multi-FPGA organizations, and design methodologies that better connect algorithmic intent with hardware implementations [2,10,12,13].

Against this background, the Special Issue "Emerging Applications of FPGAs and Reconfigurable Computing System" offers a timely cross-section of current directions in the field. The nine papers collected here reflect both the breadth of application domains and the diversity of abstraction levels at which innovation is taking place. Taken together, they show that progress in reconfigurable computing depends not only on faster devices, but also on advances in design flows, arithmetic structures, control architectures, resilient data processing, and hardware-aware machine learning. The contributions range from methodological and architectural studies to concrete deployments in power electronics, high-energy physics, spaceborne systems, wireless testbeds, and edge inference. Overall they illustrate the continuing expansion of reconfigurable solutions into technically demanding and scientifically relevant contexts.

https://doi.org/10.3390/electronics15091905

2. Summary of the Contributions

The review by Kaur et al. broadens the perspective of the Special Issue by examining scheduling techniques for efficient deep learning computations on GPUs. Although its immediate focus is not FPGA implementation, the paper addresses a problem that is highly relevant across heterogeneous accelerator platforms: how to translate massive parallelism into effective throughput under constraints imposed by memory behavior, execution imbalance, and resource contention. By organizing the literature around strategies such as dynamic load balancing, workload partitioning, memory-access scheduling, prefetching, hybrid scheduling, or pipelined execution, the review provides a useful map of the accelerator-scheduling landscape. Its contribution to this Special Issue lies in situating reconfigurable computing within a larger systems context and in highlighting future directions—energy-aware operation, adaptive scheduling, interoperability, and fault tolerance—that are equally pertinent to FPGA-based platforms.

A closely related concern, addressed from the standpoint of hardware compilation, appears in the work of She et al., who tackle the long-standing limitations of static scheduling in High-Level Synthesis (HLS). Conventional HLS tools remain highly effective for regular, compute-dominant designs, but they are often very conservative when loops contain runtime-dependent control flow. In this work, the authors respond to this problem with a source-to-source compiler that converts untimed code into a Pseudo-Cycle-Accurate (PCA) model, exposing useful dynamism while remaining compatible with existing static HLS backends. This is a significant contribution because it seeks to preserve the mature optimizations of commercial tools—such as resource sharing and datapath optimization—without incurring in frequency and area penalties commonly associated with dynamic or tool-specific hybrid flows. The reported improvements in wall-clock time and in the overall area–frequency–latency balance make this work particularly relevant for broadening the practical reach of HLS in reconfigurable computing.

Where She et al. focus on compilation, Salauyou and Klimowicz draw attention to a lower, but no less important, layer of the design process: the HDL description of finite state machines. FSMs remain fundamental building blocks of digital systems, and their quality directly affects the efficiency of larger architectures. The paper shows that a careful use of default assignments in Verilog/SystemVerilog can substantially improve the synthesized implementation of FSM circuits. Rather than replacing established techniques such as state minimization or encoding, the proposed styles complement them by optimizing the coding stage itself. This practical emphasis is one of the paper's strengths. Across benchmark studies, the most effective style yields strong reductions in area and clear performance gains, while also delivering measurable savings in another synthesis environment. The broader significance of the contribution is that it reminds designers that implementation quality is shaped not only by algorithms and architectures, but also by the descriptive discipline with which hardware intent is expressed.

At the arithmetic level, Magyari and Chen revisit modular reduction, a core operation in modern cryptographic and residue-based computation. Because modular reduction is both frequent and expensive, its hardware realization has direct implications for performance, power, and resource allocation in FPGA systems. The proposed Hardware-Optimized Modular Reduction (HOM-R) method replaces multiplier- and divider-dependent approaches with a structure based on calculated reduction cycles, addition, and configurable look-up tables. This matters because many emerging security-oriented workloads, including post-quantum cryptography and related modular-arithmetic applications, require implementations that are not only fast but also resource-conscious. The results show that HOM-R reduces power and logic costs relative to a conventional implementation while offering stronger timing margins. Particularly notable is its ability to

https://doi.org/10.3390/electronics15091905

condense a 256-bit input to a 4-bit base in a single 250 MHz cycle, illustrating how carefully specialized arithmetic can simultaneously reduce latency and free DSP resources for the rest of the design.

A different but equally important form of specialization is presented by Bonanno, who addresses the delay limitations of digital pulse-width modulation in power-electronics control. In such systems, phase delay can degrade closed-loop performance and restrict achievable bandwidth, making the problem both practical and technically significant. The proposed enhanced Digital PWM (eDPWM) architecture introduces zero phase delay, or a programmable derivative action, while retaining a structure suitable for commercial FPGA implementation. Its relevance lies in the way it combines control-theoretic benefit with implementation simplification: the architecture removes several sources of complexity present in earlier approaches, avoids burdensome fractional-slope counter structures, and inherently generates a synchronization signal useful for ADC triggering in power-electronics applications. This paper therefore exemplifies a recurring strength of reconfigurable computing: the capacity to embed refined control functionality in hardware structures that remain implementable, configurable, and efficient in real systems.

The contribution by Perticaroli et al. demonstrates the role of FPGAs in one of the most demanding real-time scientific environments: online event selection in high-energy physics. Their FPGA-RICH system is designed for the NA62 experiment and aims to bring part of the particle-identification capability of the Ring Imaging Cherenkov detector into the experiment's low-level trigger chain. The challenge is severe, since meaningful classification must be performed under a throughput requirement of roughly 10 MHz and a latency on the order of 1 μs. The authors address this by combining a streaming preprocessing pipeline with a compact neural-network classifier developed through an HLS and hls4ml workflow. The result is an implementation that reaches sub-microsecond pipeline latency and throughput compatible with the trigger environment, while producing richer trigger primitives than the baseline scheme. Beyond the immediate application, the paper shows how machine learning can be integrated into tightly constrained firmware pipelines and points toward more elaborate detector-level inference in future trigger systems.

Reliability under harsh operating conditions is the central theme of the paper by Li, Zhou, and Zhu, who focus on the implementation of an RS(255,223) encoder for spaceborne storage systems. Here, the challenge is twofold: the encoder must meet increasing throughput demands imposed by modern storage interfaces, while also improving tolerance to radiation-induced faults. The authors respond with an interleaved pipelined architecture that embeds interleaving directly into the pipeline rather than treating it as a separate stage. This structural decision enables a 36-stage implementation that raises performance substantially while also dispersing upset patterns across sequences, thereby enhancing radiation resilience. Implemented on a Xilinx platform, the encoder reaches a throughput of 3.043 Gbps with an 8-bit symbol size. Equally important is the study's attention to the fault recovery behavior and its discussion of future physical radiation testing, which place the work squarely at the intersection of high-performance design and dependable reconfigurable computing for space applications.

The paper by Gayanath et al. advances the discussion from single-device acceleration to scalable heterogeneous systems for RF and AI workloads. Their work addresses a problem of growing importance in next-generation wireless experimentation: how to combine direct-RF acquisition, large-scale digital signal processing, and higher-level AI functions within a unified and expandable framework. The proposed solution interconnects RF-SoC and downstream FPGA platforms through high-speed Aurora-based SerDes links, enabling sustained data rates of up to 50 Gbps per ADC–DAC channel and supporting real-time matrix–vector computation at the tera-MAC scale. The system is demonstrated in wireless-testbed configurations that perform beamforming and polyphase filterbanking over 1.0 GHz bandwidth, while also providing a path toward integration with external AI compute resources. This contribution is especially relevant because it illustrates how reconfigurable computing is evolving from isolated acceleration blocks into distributed, application-specific infrastructures for communications, sensing, and AI-native RF systems.

Finally, the article by Sadheerthan et al. turns to one of the most active frontiers in embedded intelligence: efficient on-device inference for large language models. In low-power neural processing units (NPU), softmax remains a costly component because transcendental operations are expensive and direct exponential support is often absent. The authors address this bottleneck with an attention distribution-aware approximation strategy that uses particle swarm optimization to derive non-uniform segmentation and variable polynomial degrees, while snapping the resulting boundaries to a 128-bin look-up structure for constant-time, branch-free access. The importance of the work lies in its careful balance between numerical fidelity and implementation efficiency. On TinyLlama, the method reduces the cycle cost of the exponential kernel relative to uniform baselines while preserving ranking fidelity and keeping end-to-end language-model quality nearly unchanged. This paper is a strong example of hardware-aware approximation design for edge AI and reflects the growing convergence of reconfigurable and accelerator-oriented thinking in practical inference systems.

3. Conclusions

The papers gathered in this Special Issue highlight several key directions in current FPGA and reconfigurable computing research. One is the continuing improvement of design productivity through better abstractions, coding practices, and compilation flows, as seen in the works on HLS scheduling and FSM description. A second is the refinement of domain-specific hardware structures (arithmetical, control-oriented, or approximate) that allow designers to achieve meaningful gains in latency, power, and area without sacrificing implementability. A third is the expansion of FPGA-based solutions into environments where real-time behavior, reliability, and system-level integration are crititcal, including particle-physics instrumentation, spaceborne data protection, high-bandwidth wireless testbeds, and edge AI inference. The review contribution further reinforces this picture by showing that performance is increasingly determined not by raw hardware capacity alone, but also by the quality of the scheduling and orchestration strategies that govern heterogeneous systems.

Overall, this Special Issue shows that the emerging applications of FPGAs are shaped by a capacity for co-optimization across multiple levels: algorithms, arithmetic, architecture, design flow, and deployment context. This capacity will remain central as future systems demand not only higher performance, but also stronger resilience, greater adaptability, and shorter development cycles. The contributions presented here provide a valuable snapshot of this evolution and, at the same time, point towards a future in which reconfigurable computing will continue to expand its role in both advanced research infrastructures and high-impact practical systems.

Funding: This research received no external funding.

Acknowledgments: The Guest Editor of this Special Issue thanks all researchers who submitted their articles, the reviewers for their time and valuable feedback, and the Editorial Board Members and Editors of Electronics for their support.

Conflicts of Interest: The author declares no conflicts of interest.

https://doi.org/10.3390/electronics15091905

List of Contributions

1. Sadheerthan, S.; Hsu, M.-J.; Huang, C.-H.; Wang, Y.-T. Attention Distribution-Aware Softmax for NPU-Accelerated On-Device Inference of LLMs: An Edge-Oriented Approximation Design. *Electronics* **2026**, *15*, 1312. https://doi.org/10.3390/electronics15061312.
2. Salauyou, V.; Klimowicz, A. Optimizing Digital Systems Implemented in FPGA Through Effective Description of Finite State Machines. *Electronics* **2026**, *15*, 831. https://doi.org/10.3390/electronics15040831.
3. Gayanath, B.; Rathnasekara, G.; Karunanayake, K.; Madanayake, A. Scalable AI + DSP Compute Frameworks Using AMD Xilinx RF-SoC ZCU/VCU Platforms for Wireless Testbeds for Scientific, Commercial, Space, and Defense Applications. *Electronics* **2026**, *15*, 445. https://doi.org/10.3390/electronics15020445.
4. She, Y.; Huang, Y.; Liu, J.; Cheung, R. C. C.; Yan, H. A Source-to-Source Compiler to Enable Hybrid Scheduling for High-Level Synthesis. *Electronics* **2025**, *14*, 4578. https://doi.org/10.3390/electronics14234578.
5. Li, X.; Zhou, L.; Zhu, Y. Enhancing Radiation Resilience and Throughput in Spaceborne RS(255,223) Encoder via Interleaved Pipelined Architecture. *Electronics* **2025**, *14*, 2447. https://doi.org/10.3390/electronics14122447.
6. Perticaroli, P.; Ammendola, R.; Biagioni, A.; Chiarini, C.; Ciardiello, A.; Cretaro, P.; Frezza, O.; Lo Cicero, F.; Martinelli, M.; Piandani, R.; Pontisso, L.; Raggi, M.; Rossi, C.; Simula, F.; Turisini, M.; Vicini, P.; Lonardo, A. Achieving Low-Latency, High-Throughput Online Partial Particle Identification for the NA62 Experiment Using FPGAs and Machine Learning. *Electronics* **2025**, *14*, 1892. https://doi.org/10.3390/electronics14091892.
7. Bonanno, G. An Innovative Digital Pulse Width Modulator and Its Field-Programmable Gate Array Implementation. *Electronics* **2025**, *14*, 1522. https://doi.org/10.3390/electronics14081522.
8. Magyari, A.; Chen, Y. Hardware Optimized Modular Reduction. *Electronics* **2025**, *14*, 550. https://doi.org/10.3390/electronics14030550.
9. Kaur, R.; Asad, A.; Al Abdul Wahid, S.; Mohammadi, F. A Survey of Advancements in Scheduling Techniques for Efficient Deep Learning Computations on GPUs. *Electronics* **2025**, *14*, 1048. https://doi.org/10.3390/electronics14051048.

References

1. Ottimo, A.; Mencagli, G.; Danelutto, M. Boosting general-purpose stream processing with reconfigurable hardware. *J. Supercomput.* **2024**, *80*, 13048–13078. [CrossRef]
2. Samayoa, W.F.; Crespo, M.L.; Cicuttin, A.; Carrato, S. A Survey on FPGA-Based Heterogeneous Clusters Architectures. *IEEE Access* **2023**, *11*, 67679–67706. [CrossRef]
3. Cordova-Cardenas, R.; Amor, D.; Gutierrez, A. Edge AI in Practice: A Survey and Deployment Framework for Neural Networks on Embedded Systems. *Electronics* **2025**, *14*, 4877. [CrossRef]
4. Alam, S.; Yakopcic, C.; Wu, Q.; Barnell, M.; Khan, S.; Taha, T.M. Survey of Deep Learning Accelerators for Edge and Emerging Computing. *Electronics* **2024**, *13*, 2988. [CrossRef]
5. Abdulsamad, A.A.; Répás, S.R. Application of FPGA Devices in Network Security: A Survey. *Electronics* **2025**, *14*, 3894. [CrossRef]
6. Khan, L.; Isanaka, S.P.; Liou, F. FPGA-Based Sensors for Distributed Digital Manufacturing Systems: A State-of-the-Art Review. *Sensors* **2024**, *24*, 7709. [CrossRef] [PubMed]
7. Zhang, Q.S.; Chen, M.Z.; Li, J. General heterogeneous real-time baseband backend system scheme applied to QTT based on RFSoC+GPU. *Front. Astron. Space Sci.* **2024**, *11*, 1420066. [CrossRef]
8. Kose, H.T.; Nunez-Yanez, J.; Piechocki, R.; Pope, J. A Survey of Computationally Efficient Graph Neural Networks for Reconfigurable Systems. *Information* **2024**, *15*, 377. [CrossRef]
9. Almomany, A.; Jarrah, A.; Sutcu, M. Exploring memory synchronization and performance considerations for FPGA platform using the high-abstracted OpenCL framework: Benchmarks development and analysis. *PLoS ONE* **2024**, *19*, e0301720. [CrossRef] [PubMed]

10. Lahti, S.; Hämäläinen, T.D. High-Level Synthesis for FPGAs—A Hardware Engineer's Perspective. *IEEE Access* **2025**, *13*, 28574–28593. [CrossRef]
11. Ahmed, Q.A.; Wiersema, T.; Platzner, M. Post-configuration Activation of Hardware Trojans in FPGAs. *J. Hardw. Syst. Secur.* **2024**, *8*, 79–93. [CrossRef]
12. Barbareschi, M.; Barone, S.; Mazzocca, N.; Moriconi, A. FPGA approximate logic synthesis through catalog-based AIG-rewriting technique. *J. Syst. Archit.* **2024**, *150*, 103112. [CrossRef]
13. Birath, B.; Ernstsson, A.; Tinnerholm, J.; Kessler, C. High-Level Programming of FPGA-Accelerated Systems with Parallel Patterns. *Int. J. Parallel Program.* **2024**, *52*, 253–273. [CrossRef]

electronics

MDPI

Review

A Survey of Advancements in Scheduling Techniques for Efficient Deep Learning Computations on GPUs

Rupinder Kaur [1,*], Arghavan Asad [2], Seham Al Abdul Wahid [1] and Farah Mohammadi [1]

1 Electrical, Computer and Biomedical Engineering Department, Toronto Metropolitan University, 350 Victoria St, Toronto, ON M5B2K3, Canada; salabdulwahid@torontomu.ca (S.A.A.W.); fmohamma@torontomu.ca (F.M.)
2 School of Computer Science and Technology, Algoma University, Brampton, ON L6V1A3, Canada; arghavan.asad@algomau.ca
* Correspondence: rupinder.kaur.ece@torontomu.ca

Abstract: This comprehensive survey explores recent advancements in scheduling techniques for efficient deep learning computations on GPUs. The article highlights challenges related to parallel thread execution, resource utilization, and memory latency in GPUs, which can lead to suboptimal performance. The surveyed research focuses on novel scheduling policies to improve memory latency tolerance, exploit parallelism, and enhance GPU resource utilization. Additionally, it explores the integration of prefetching mechanisms, fine-grained warp scheduling, and warp switching strategies to optimize deep learning computations. These techniques demonstrate significant improvements in throughput, memory bank parallelism, and latency reduction. The insights gained from this survey can guide researchers, system designers, and practitioners in developing more efficient and powerful deep learning systems on GPUs. Furthermore, potential future research directions include advanced scheduling techniques, energy efficiency considerations, and the integration of emerging computing technologies. Through continuous advancement in scheduling techniques, the full potential of GPUs can be unlocked for a wide range of applications and domains, including GPU-accelerated deep learning, task scheduling, resource management, memory optimization, and more.

Keywords: deep learning algorithms; deep neural networks (DNNs); energy-efficient scheduling; performance optimization; heterogeneous computing; machine learning (ML)

1. Introduction

Deep learning has emerged as a powerful technique for solving complex problems and has achieved remarkable success in various domains, including computer vision, natural language processing, and autonomous systems. Graphics processing units (GPUs) have played a pivotal role in accelerating deep learning computations due to their parallel processing capabilities and high memory bandwidth. However, harnessing the full potential of GPUs for deep learning requires efficient scheduling techniques that optimize resource utilization and minimize latency [1–5].

The efficient execution of deep learning algorithms on GPUs faces several challenges. Firstly, deep learning computations often involve massive amounts of data and complex neural network architectures, resulting in high computational demands. Secondly, GPUs consist of numerous parallel processing units known as warps, which execute threads in parallel. However, the inefficient scheduling of these warps can lead to the underutilization of GPU resources and suboptimal performance. Moreover, memory latency, caused by data movement between the GPU and memory, can significantly impact overall system performance [6–16].

To address these challenges, researchers have been actively developing advanced scheduling techniques specifically tailored for deep learning computations on GPUs. These techniques aim to maximize the efficiency and throughput of deep learning algorithms by effectively managing the execution of parallel threads, optimizing memory access patterns, and improving resource utilization [17–20]. Scheduling techniques for deep learning on GPUs encompass various aspects, such as warp scheduling policies, memory latency tolerance, memory bank parallelism, context switching strategies, and prefetching mechanisms. Warp scheduling policies focus on efficiently assigning threads to warps, considering factors like data dependencies and resource availability. Memory latency tolerance techniques aim to overlap memory access and computation to minimize the impact of memory latency on overall performance [21–25]. Memory bank parallelism techniques exploit the parallel memory access capabilities of GPUs to enhance memory throughput. Context switching strategies involve efficiently switching between different warps to optimize GPU resource utilization.

Additionally, prefetching mechanisms are employed to anticipate and fetch data in advance, reducing memory access latency and improving overall performance [26–31]. Fine-grained warp scheduling techniques consider the execution order and prioritization of individual threads within a warp, further enhancing parallelism and reducing resource contention. Furthermore, hardware and algorithm co-design approaches have been explored to optimize scheduling and execution for specific types of deep learning algorithms, such as sparse neural networks and convolutional neural networks (CNNs). Techniques for optimizing cache data residency have been explored to enhance memory management and leverage cache locality. By analyzing data access frequencies and categorizing applications based on their access patterns, these methods improve data storage and boost cache efficiency, resulting in better overall performance. In this article, we provide a comprehensive survey of recent advancements in scheduling techniques for efficient deep learning computations on GPUs [32–37]. We delve into the details of various scheduling methodologies, their underlying principles, and their impact on system performance. Through experimental evaluations, we demonstrate the effectiveness of these techniques in improving throughput, reducing latency, and optimizing resource utilization. The insights gained from this survey can guide researchers, system designers, and practitioners in developing more efficient and powerful deep learning systems on GPUs [38–43]. Additionally, we discuss potential future directions for research, including advanced scheduling techniques, energy efficiency considerations, and the integration of emerging computing technologies. By continuously advancing scheduling techniques, we can unlock the full potential of GPUs and further optimize deep learning computations for a wide range of applications and domains [44–55].

Figure 1 illustrates the classification of scheduling techniques discussed in this survey, categorizing them based on their application and methodology for optimizing deep learning computations on GPUs.

At the core of this survey, we explore a variety of scheduling techniques critical for optimizing deep learning computations on GPUs. In Section 2, the discussion begins with heterogeneous computing, highlighting its promises and challenges in combining CPUs and GPUs for improved performance and energy efficiency. Next, in Section 3, we delve into diverse scheduling strategies, including static, dynamic, and adaptive approaches, focusing on their ability to optimize workload distribution and resource utilization. Dynamic load balancing techniques are examined for their real-time adaptability, while workload partitioning strategies emphasize the efficient division of tasks between CPUs and GPUs. Memory access scheduling methods are explored to reduce latency and enhance throughput, complemented by fine-grained warp scheduling policies that prioritize threads to improve parallelism. Context switching strategies are discussed for their role in minimizing idle times and optimizing resource usage. Energy-aware and task graph scheduling techniques are presented to balance energy efficiency, manage dependencies, and improve completion times. Additionally, hybrid scheduling approaches, power-aware and deadline-aware scheduling, and batch job scheduling are analyzed for their ability to address complex resource management challenges in heterogeneous systems. Pipelined scheduling strategies are reviewed for their potential to overlap computation stages and boost throughput. This comprehensive discussion sets the stage for the subsequent sections, offering insights into the latest advancements and future directions in scheduling techniques for GPU-accelerated deep learning.

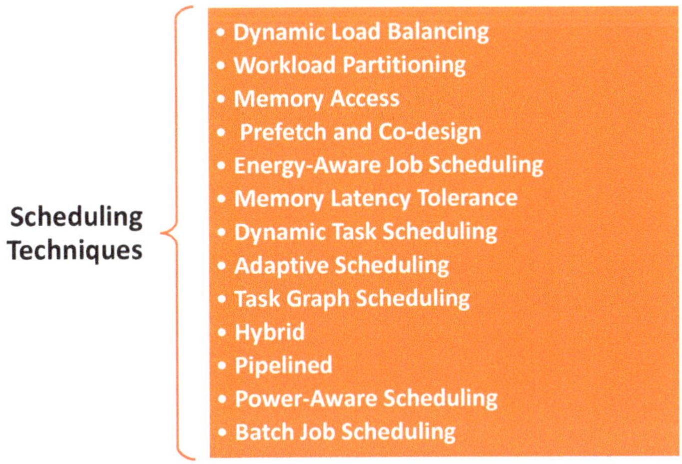

Figure 1. Classification of Scheduling Techniques discussed in this survey.

2. Heterogeneous Computing: Promises and Challenges

Heterogeneous computing aims to combine the strengths of both CPUs and GPUs to achieve improved computational performance. The promises of heterogeneous computing include utilizing the unique features of CPUs and GPUs, achieving load balancing between the processing units, and harnessing the computational power of both to strive for exascale performance.

However, there are several challenges in realizing the potential of heterogeneous computing. The vastly different architectures and programming models of CPUs and GPUs present obstacles in achieving collaborative computing. Optimization techniques designed for CPU-only or GPU-only systems may not be effective in heterogeneous systems. Therefore, novel techniques are required to optimize performance and energy efficiency by considering the characteristics of both CPUs and GPUs.

3. Scheduling Strategies

The goal of heterogeneous computing is to leverage the unique features and strengths of both CPUs and GPUs to achieve high-performance computing. The increasing utilization of both CPUs and GPUs in a wide range of applications underscores the need for collaboration between these processing units, as highlighted in [1]. The work discusses the challenges and promises of heterogeneous computing and clarifies the terminology used in the field. Regarding scheduling techniques, it categorizes research works based on the nature of scheduling, such as dynamic or static load balancing. It explores various approaches to workload partitioning between CPUs and GPUs, considering factors like the division of work among processing units.

3.1. Dynamic Load Balancing

Dynamic load balancing involves dynamically redistributing the workload between CPUs and GPUs based on their capabilities and current load. This technique aims to optimize resource utilization and maximize overall performance by adapting to changes in workload and system conditions in real time. It can help ensure that both CPUs and GPUs are effectively utilized and that the workload is distributed efficiently to achieve better performance.

The problem of online scheduling for task graphs on heterogeneous platforms, particularly those comprising CPUs and GPUs, is addressed by Canon et al. [7]. Their focus is on dynamic scheduling, where task graphs are revealed in real time during computation, and the scheduler operates with limited information about the available tasks. The objective is to minimize the total completion time of the tasks.

1. Flexibility and Knowledge Impact: the paper examines how factors such as task migration, preemption, and partial graph knowledge influence scheduling efficiency and the algorithm's lower bounds.
2. Competitive Algorithm: the authors propose a competitive algorithm, called QA, and refine its analysis to achieve better performance.
3. Generalization to Multiple Processor Types: the authors extend their results to the case of platforms with multiple types of processors, adapting the lower bounds and the online algorithm accordingly.
4. Heuristic Approach: The authors propose a simple heuristic based on the QA algorithm and the system-oriented heuristic EFT. This heuristic is competitive and also performs well in practice.

The scheduling technique READYS, developed by Nathan et al. [10], aims to create a dynamic scheduling algorithm for heterogeneous computing systems utilizing reinforcement learning. This approach incorporates Directed Acyclic Graphs (DAGs) as a computational model for parallel applications. It emphasizes the importance of accurate task allocation and scheduling decisions in parallel and distributed computing systems. The authors propose using reinforcement learning, specifically a combination of Graph Convolutional Networks (GCNs) and an Actor–Critic Algorithm (A2C), to address the dynamic scheduling problem. The READYS algorithm aims to minimize the makespan, which is the total time required to complete all tasks, by learning an adaptive scheduling strategy based on the current state of the system and the characteristics of the tasks. The use of reinforcement learning is particularly suitable in scenarios where task durations and communication times are stochastic. The paper focuses on task graphs derived from linear algebra factorization kernels (such as CHOLESKY, LU, and QR) and considers heterogeneous platforms with both CPUs and GPUs. Through simulations, the authors demonstrate that READYS achieves comparable or superior performance to existing scheduling algorithms, particularly in environments with high uncertainty. Furthermore, READYS is capable of generalizing its learned scheduling strategy to different application domains and problem sizes.

An improved scheduling mechanism for generative AI applications in cloud-native environments with heterogeneous resources is proposed by Chun et al. [28]. This approach employs dynamic programming as the scheduling technique. The study addresses the challenge of effectively scheduling multiple resources in such environments to enhance load balance and resource utilization. By applying the dynamic programming approach, the proposed scheduling mechanism outperforms native GPU scheduling strategies and the algorithm for the multidimensional knapsack problem. Experimental results demonstrate that the load balance can be improved by up to 64.1%, and the makespan (job completion time) can be reduced by up to 40.8%. This scheduling technique considers load balancing as a crucial metric and aims to achieve the highest total iteration count while optimizing job completion time. The approach effectively utilizes the available resources, including less powerful GPU nodes, and prevents resource idleness caused by unbalanced workloads.

On the other hand, static load balancing involves predetermining the workload division between CPUs and GPUs based on certain criteria or heuristics. This technique aims to distribute the workload evenly and efficiently at the beginning of the computation. It does not adapt to runtime changes and assumes a predetermined workload division that remains constant throughout the execution. Static load balancing can be useful in scenarios where the workload characteristics are known in advance or when the workload distribution is relatively stable.

3.2. Workload Partitioning

Effective workload division between CPUs and GPUs is essential in heterogeneous computing. Static partitioning predefines task allocation based on system characteristics, while dynamic partitioning adjusts allocations at runtime to optimize performance. Factors such as computation intensity, memory requirements, and inter-task dependencies are considered to ensure balanced resource usage. Workload partitioning focuses on dividing the workload between CPUs and GPUs in an effective manner. This technique considers factors such as the characteristics of the workload, the capabilities of the processing units, and the requirements of the deep learning computations. By carefully partitioning the workload, workload partitioning aims to achieve the balanced utilization of CPUs and GPUs, optimize resource allocation, and improve overall performance.

The Constrained Autonomous Workload Scheduler (CAuWS), proposed by Justin et al. [46], is designed for Cyber–Physical Systems (CPSs) with heterogeneous processing units. This technique addresses the challenge of creating efficient schedules that satisfy the physical requirements of CPSs while accommodating the diverse capabilities of various hardware units. CAuWS utilizes a structured and system-agnostic approach, combining a representation language (AuWL), timed Petri nets, and mixed-integer linear programming. It enables the representation and scheduling of various CPS workloads, real-world constraints, and optimization criteria, resulting in optimal assignments of processing units to tasks. The technique is demonstrated using a drone simulation under multiple physical constraints. The scheduling technique aims to optimize resource utilization and meet the objectives of CPSs while considering the heterogeneity of processing units.

3.3. Memory Access Scheduling

This section discusses memory latency tolerance techniques and memory bank parallelism as part of optimizing deep learning computations on GPUs. These techniques aim to schedule memory accesses effectively to minimize the impact of memory latency and improve overall performance.

A memory scheduling strategy that addresses the challenges encountered in shared memory environments of heterogeneous multicore systems is proposed by Fang et al. [2]. They propose a step-by-step approach to memory scheduling, focusing on mitigating interference between memory access requests from different cores and improving system performance. The memory scheduling strategy consists of three key steps:

1. Request Source Isolation: To prevent interference between CPU and GPU memory requests, a new memory request queue is created based on the request source. This

isolation ensures that GPU requests do not interfere with CPU requests and vice versa, enhancing overall memory access performance.

2. Dynamic Bank Partitioning: For the CPU request queue, a dynamic bank partitioning strategy is implemented. It dynamically maps CPU requests to different bank sets based on the memory characteristics of the applications. By considering the access behavior and characteristics of multiple parallel applications, this strategy eliminates memory request interference among CPU applications without affecting bank-level parallelism.
3. Criticality-Aware Scheduling: The GPU request queue incorporates the concept of criticality to measure the difference in memory access latency among GPU cores. A criticality-aware memory scheduling approach is implemented, prioritizing requests based on their criticality level. This strategy balances the locality and criticality of application access, effectively reducing memory access latency differences among GPU cores.

The MixTran scheduling technique, introduced by Zhang et al. [24], aims for efficient and fair resource allocation in heterogeneous GPU clusters handling mixed deep learning workloads. The authors address the challenge of existing schedulers not being tailored to deep learning jobs, resulting in low resource efficiency and job performance. MixTran abstracts heterogeneous GPU resources and distributes them fairly to users using virtual tickets. It then formulates a global optimization model to efficiently allocate resources based on quantified resource requests, heterogeneous node constraints, and user fairness constraints. The technique employs a greedy resource trading mechanism to benefit multiple users. Experimental results demonstrate that MixTran significantly reduces the total execution time of deep learning workloads (up to 30–50%) compared to traditional schedulers while maintaining user fairness. The scheduling technique employed in MixTran can be categorized as a combination of fair-share scheduling and resource trading.

3.4. Prefetch and Co-Design Strategies

3.4.1. Context Switching Strategies

These strategies involve efficiently switching between different warps to enhance GPU resource utilization and improve performance. As an example, SkyByte, explained in [52], improves scheduling by enabling coordinated context switching between the host OS and the SSD controller. When a memory request to the CXL-SSD experiences a long delay, the SSD controller signals the CPU using a long-delay hint, triggering a hardware exception. The OS scheduler then switches to another thread to utilize the CPU while waiting for the data.

3.4.2. Hardware and Algorithm Co-Design

This method involves tailoring scheduling strategies to specific hardware architectures. For instance, co-designing algorithms for GPUs can leverage their strengths in matrix operations and parallelism. Techniques like cache data residency optimization analyze data access patterns to enhance memory locality, reducing cache misses and improving execution speed. Likewise, the approach discussed in [53] enhances scheduling by dynamically adapting algorithm complexity based on resource availability and deadline constraints. By virtualizing hardware resources and optimizing parallelism, it enables real-time SLAM processing while maintaining high accuracy in resource-constrained environments. This adaptability allows the system to efficiently allocate computational resources, reducing latency spikes caused by dynamic workloads. As a result, it ensures consistent performance while balancing power consumption and processing efficiency.

3.4.3. Prefetching Mechanisms

This technique aims to reduce memory access latency and enhance overall performance by overlapping data movement with computation. Yüzügüler et al. present a prefetching mechanism in [54] that optimizes the inference of large language models (LLMs) by overlapping memory reads for model weights and key–value (KV) cache with communication operations. This approach allows the system to hide the latency of memory accesses during collective communication phases. By leveraging a graph optimization framework, the mechanism automatically inserts prefetch commands into the computation graph, ensuring efficient data retrieval without requiring user code modifications. Overall, this strategy significantly enhances performance and reduces inference latency in distributed LLM systems.

3.4.4. Fine-Grained Warp Scheduling

This technique allocates and prioritizes the execution of threads within warps (groups of threads executed simultaneously on a single GPU core). Advanced warp scheduling policies aim to minimize idle cycles caused by data dependencies or resource contention. For instance, fine-grained warp scheduling dynamically prioritizes threads based on their readiness to execute, which improves parallelism and reduces pipeline stalls. This is crucial for maintaining high throughput in GPUs designed for massively parallel workloads. Fang et al. [2] discuss fine-grained warp scheduling techniques that focus on the execution order and prioritization of individual threads within a warp. This approach enhances parallelism and reduces resource contention, resulting in improved performance. Tang et al. introduce gCom in [55] as a fine-grained compressor designed for mobile GPUs that optimizes memory usage during rendering. It features fine-grained warp scheduling by treating color channels as processing units and quads (2×2 pixels) as parallel units, enhancing data locality and repetition rates. gCom employs a Channel Decorrelator to minimize raw data size and a Hierarchical Delta mechanism to maximize channel locality. Additionally, it introduces the Parallel-Oriented Golomb–Rice (POGR) algorithm, which allows the parallel execution of compression and decompression processes, ensuring efficient GPU throughput while minimizing performance degradation.

3.5. Energy-Aware Job Scheduling Techniques

With rising concerns about energy efficiency, these techniques aim to minimize power consumption while maintaining performance. Dynamic voltage and frequency scaling (DVFS), for example, adjusts the processor's power states based on workload requirements. Additionally, heuristic algorithms like energy-aware successor tree scheduling optimize task execution sequences to minimize energy usage in heterogeneous systems. Tang et al. [3] discuss scheduling techniques aimed at optimizing energy consumption in heterogeneous computing systems. The main objective is to address the challenges posed by energy consumption, the dynamic variability of CPU-GPU utilization, and job scheduling in large-scale systems. They propose a CPU-GPU-utilization-aware and energy-efficient heuristic greedy strategy (UEJS) as well as a hybrid particle swarm optimization algorithm (H-PSO) to solve the job scheduling problem. The proposed UEJS algorithm incorporates CPU-GPU utilization awareness and energy efficiency considerations to schedule jobs. To enhance the algorithm's global optimization ability, it introduces the H-PSO algorithm, which combines the heuristic greedy strategy with a bio-inspired search optimization technique. Experimental results demonstrate that the H-PSO algorithm outperforms the heuristic greedy strategy, Max-EAMin, and genetic algorithm in terms of the average energy consumption of jobs and system job rejection rate. Specifically, H-PSO achieves a 36.5% improvement over UEJS, a 36.3% improvement over Max-EAMin, and a 46.7%

improvement over the GA in terms of job average energy consumption for heterogeneous systems with high workload.

Roeder et al. [5] highlight the significance of optimizing energy consumption in computing devices, especially in embedded systems. The authors propose an offline scheduling algorithm that aims to minimize overall energy consumption while ensuring timing constraints on heterogeneous platforms. The scheduling strategy is based on Forward List Scheduling and takes into account dynamic voltage and frequency scaling (DVFS). The algorithm selects the most energy-efficient version for each task, considering different energy/time trade-offs offered by architecture-specific binary blocks. It also enables applications to dynamically adapt voltage and frequency during runtime. Additionally, the proposed heuristic is compared against an optimal solution derived by an integer linear programming (ILP) formulation, with a deviation of only 1.6% on average. Overall, ref. [5] emphasizes the need for energy-aware scheduling strategies on heterogeneous real-time systems and presents a scheduling algorithm that effectively reduces energy consumption while meeting timing constraints. The proposed approach considers multi-version tasks, DVFS, and heterogeneous platforms, resulting in significant energy savings compared to existing scheduling algorithms.

Seo et al. [11] propose scheduling techniques to tackle the challenges encountered by edge platforms that process multiple machine learning (ML) models concurrently. These platforms, equipped with heterogeneous computing processors, have limited computational and energy budgets compared to data center servers. The proposed scheduler uses pre-profiled behavior of ML models and routes requests to the most suitable processors, considering the regularity of computation in common ML tasks. It aims to reduce energy consumption while meeting the service-level objective (SLO) requirement for bounded response latency. To handle the inflexible preemption capability of GPUs and DSPs, the scheduler decomposes large ML tasks into sub-tasks based on the layers of the DNN model. The scheduling policies are evaluated on an edge platform with a CPU, GPU, and DSP. The results show significant performance improvements and reduced SLO violations compared to naive scheduling. By considering the heterogeneity of ML models and computing processors, the proposed techniques optimize performance, reduce energy consumption, and meet SLO requirements in edge computing environments.

With rising concerns about energy efficiency, these techniques aim to minimize power consumption while maintaining performance. Dynamic voltage and frequency scaling (DVFS), for example, adjusts the processor's power states based on workload requirements. Additionally, heuristic algorithms like energy-aware successor tree scheduling optimize task execution sequences to minimize energy usage in heterogeneous systems.

3.6. Memory Latency Tolerance

Techniques in this category aim to overlap computation with memory access to reduce the impact of memory latency on overall system performance. For example, prefetching mechanisms predict data requirements and fetch data into memory before they are needed by the processing units. Similarly, memory bank parallelism ensures concurrent access to multiple memory banks by optimizing data placement, thereby increasing throughput and reducing access contention. Wang et al. [4] discuss challenges and propose solutions for enhancing the performance of integrated CPU/GPU platforms, particularly focusing on the latency associated with data initialization. The authors in this work highlight the importance of these platforms in autonomous driving and edge intelligence applications and the limitations posed by shared physical memory. They introduce the concept of a unified memory (UM) model in GPU programming, which simplifies memory management and allocation. However, the conventional copy-then-execute model used in UM programming leads to significant initialization latency and hampers kernel execution. To address this issue, the authors propose a framework that enables latency-aware data initialization. The framework includes three data initialization modes: CPU initialization, GPU initialization, and hybrid initialization. It also incorporates an affinity estimation model that considers application characteristics and platform features to determine the most suitable initialization mode. The goal is to optimize the initialization latency performance of the application.

3.7. Dynamic Task Scheduling

Zhang et al. [6] discuss task scheduling strategies for heterogeneous computing systems that utilize both CPU and GPU resources. They propose two scheduling techniques: a load-aware strategy for the single-task model and a genetic algorithm-based strategy for the multi-task model.

1. Load-Aware Scheduling Strategy

This strategy focuses on addressing load balancing issues in CPU-GPU heterogeneous computing systems. It aims to allocate computing tasks to the CPU and GPU based on their computing power and a perception ratio. The strategy uses a bidirectional queue to store tasks, reducing additional overhead caused by scheduling. By assigning parallel computing tasks to both CPUs and GPUs, this strategy enhances performance, reduces load imbalances, and minimizes idle time.

2. Genetic Algorithm-Based Scheduling Strategy

This strategy targets improving the overall operating efficiency of CPU-GPU heterogeneous computing systems in multi-task scenarios. It uses a genetic algorithm to determine the execution relationship between different types of tasks and heterogeneous processing cores. The strategy aims to optimize the allocation of computing resources and fully utilize the collaborative computing capabilities of CPUs and GPUs.

Experimental evaluations demonstrate that this strategy outperforms traditional scheduling algorithms, static and dynamic scheduling algorithms, and hybrid scheduling algorithms, resulting in higher system performance.

These scheduling techniques contribute to tapping into the performance potential of CPU-GPU heterogeneous computing systems, achieving load balance, reducing idle time, and improving system efficiency.

Yang et al. [18] propose a scheduling technique designed to minimize energy consumption in a CPU-GPU cloud computing platform while managing intermittent real-time tasks. The technique formulates the problem as an integer nonlinear programming problem and utilizes a dynamic programming approach inspired by the 0–1 knapsack problem. By dividing the hardware computing resources into virtual CPUs, the technique dynamically adjusts the task schedule based on the solution. Experimental results demonstrate that the proposed algorithm effectively reduces energy consumption and outperforms other greedy methods in terms of computation time. The scheduling technique contributes to optimizing system performance in cloud computing environments.

Hsu et al. [26] introduce a programming and execution model known as SHMT (Simultaneous and Heterogeneous Multithreading), which facilitates parallel processing with heterogeneous processing units. The paper focuses on the scheduling technique used in SHMT to coordinate execution on different hardware components efficiently. SHMT introduces a low-overhead scheduling policy that considers both results and performance. It utilizes a set of virtual operations (VOPs) and high-level operations (HLOPs) as an intermediate layer between programming languages and hardware instructions. This intermediate layer facilitates task matching and distribution, allowing SHMT to divide equivalent operations and data between different computing resources. The scheduling technique employed in SHMT can be categorized as a dynamic scheduling policy. It dynamically adjusts workloads on various hardware units to maximize hardware efficiency while providing flexibility in scheduling policies. By effectively coordinating execution on heterogeneous hardware, SHMT achieves significant speedup and energy reduction compared to the GPU baseline, as demonstrated in evaluations on an embedded system platform. Overall, the paper emphasizes the importance of scheduling techniques in enabling parallel execution across heterogeneous processing units, and SHMT's dynamic scheduling policy plays a crucial role in achieving the efficient utilization of hardware resources.

Zhou et al. [37] propose a resource scheduling system named FILL, aimed at enhancing the performance of GROMACS simulations through the effective utilization of heterogeneous hardware resources. The scheduling technique used in FILL is space partitioning technology, which allows for the precise allocation of resources between CPU and GPU devices. The article highlights that previous research focused mainly on co-running multiple GROMACS simulations using time-slice technology, which introduced context switching overhead and neglected the collaborative scheduling of CPU and GPU devices. FILL addresses this limitation by leveraging hardware partitioning technologies and optimizing the allocation of resources for multiple GROMACS jobs. Experimental results demonstrate significant improvements in system throughput using FILL on both NVIDIA and AMD GPU servers compared to baseline approaches and state-of-the-art alternatives. FILL achieved an impressive improvement of up to 167% on NVIDIA GPU servers and demonstrated significant enhancements of 459% on AMD GPU servers. Overall, FILL's space partitioning-based scheduling technique enhances resource utilization and improves system throughput for multiple GROMACS simulations. The FILL mechanism, as shown in Figure 2, effectively addresses the challenge of resource utilization in heterogeneous computing by employing space partitioning technology to optimize CPU and GPU allocation for GROMACS simulations

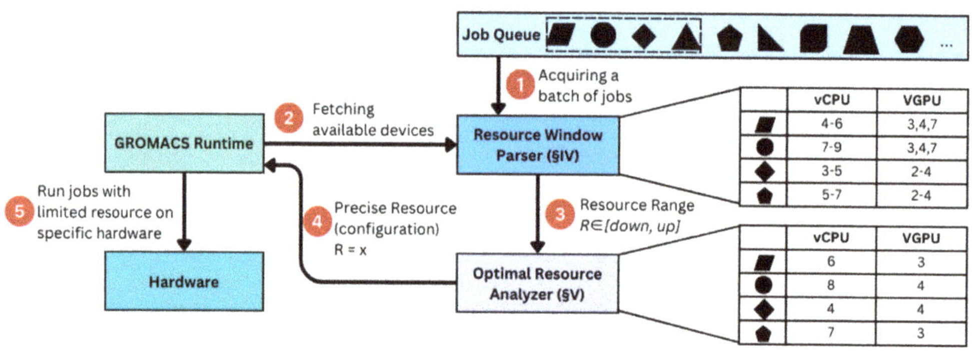

Figure 2. FILL mechanism presented in [37].

Wang et al. [39] introduce a novel scheduling technique named GPARS, designed for efficient resource allocation in heterogeneous graphics processing unit (GPU) clusters. The scheduling technique leverages spatiotemporal correlations among jobs and utilizes graph attention networks (GANs) for precise job duration prediction. The GPARS algorithm addresses the limitations of prior research by considering the performance variations among different GPU types within heterogeneous clusters and the presence of spatiotemporal correlations among jobs. It predicts job durations using GANs and dynamically allocates suitable GPU types for newly submitted jobs based on the prediction results. The effectiveness of GPARS is evaluated using real traces from Alibaba and Philly, demonstrating a significant reduction in waiting time (10.29%) and an average improvement in resource utilization (7.47%) compared to the original scheduling method. Overall, GPARS is a prediction-based scheduling technique that efficiently schedules resources in heterogeneous GPU clusters, considering the unique characteristics and variations among different GPU types.

Ndamlabin et al. [45] introduce a scheduling technique called RSCHED, aimed at managing the concurrent execution of task-based applications in heterogeneous computing environments. The authors address the challenge of efficiently utilizing modern parallel architectures with complex memory hierarchies and heterogeneous processors. They propose RSCHED as a framework to minimize the overall makespan and maximize resource utilization. The scheduling technique aims to improve the execution of task-based applications by dynamically distributing resources and orchestrating their execution. The authors implemented RSCHED using the StarPU runtime system and evaluated its performance in real applications. The results showed that RSCHED significantly reduced the overall makespan compared to consecutive execution, with an average speedup factor of 10×. It also demonstrated the potential to increase resource utilization. RSCHED is a dynamic resource allocation strategy that enhances the scheduling of task-based applications in heterogeneous systems.

3.8. Adaptive Scheduling

Adaptive scheduling dynamically modifies task priorities, resource allocations, or scheduling policies in response to changing workloads or system states. For example, temperature-aware scheduling ensures that tasks are allocated in a way that prevents overheating in edge devices, prolonging hardware lifespan and maintaining stability under thermal constraints. Constantinescu et al. [8] discuss efficiency and productivity in decision-making processes involving low-power heterogeneous CPU+GPU SoCs. They specifically focus on the evaluation of scheduling strategies for executing value iteration, a core procedure in decision-making methods, on a low-power CPU+GPU SoC. They compare offline-tuned static and dynamic scheduling strategies with adaptive heterogeneous scheduling strategies. The experiments show that using CPU+GPU heterogeneous strategies significantly reduces computation time and energy requirements. CPU+GPU strategies can be up to 54% faster and 57% more energy-efficient compared to multicore or GPU-only implementations. Additionally, the study explores the impact of increasing the abstraction level of the programming model to ease programming efforts. The comparison between TBB+OpenCL and TBB+oneAPI implementations of heterogeneous schedulers shows that the oneAPI versions result in up to five times less programming effort with only 3–8% overhead if the scheduling strategy is selected carefully.

The strategies discussed in [8] are as follows:

1. Offline-Tuned Static and Dynamic Scheduling Strategies

The study evaluates offline-tuned static and dynamic scheduling strategies for executing value iteration, a core procedure in decision-making methods, on a low-power CPU+GPU system-on-chip (SoC). The comparison is made between different scheduling strategies to determine their impact on computation time and energy requirements.

2. Adaptive Heterogeneous Scheduling Strategies

The study also explores adaptive heterogeneous scheduling strategies for decision-making on a low-power CPU+GPU SoC. These strategies aim to dynamically allocate tasks between the CPU and GPU, taking advantage of their respective capabilities. The experiments demonstrate that using CPU+GPU heterogeneous strategies significantly reduce computation time and energy requirements compared to multicore or GPU-only implementations.

3. Increasing Abstraction Level of the Programming Model

The article explores the impact of increasing the abstraction level of the programming model to ease programming efforts. Specifically, it compares the TBB+OpenCL and TBB+oneAPI implementations of heterogeneous schedulers. The results show that the oneAPI versions can result in up to five times less programming effort with only 3–8% overhead if the scheduling strategy is selected carefully.

Albahar et al. [16] propose a scheduling technique named SCHEDTUNE, designed to tackle the challenges of managing and scheduling heterogeneous GPU resources in cluster management systems such as Kubernetes. The existing resource schedulers in these systems do not effectively differentiate between different types of GPUs or support GPU sharing, resulting in low GPU utilization, queuing delays, and an increased application makespan. SCHEDTUNE is a machine learning-based scheduler that aims to improve GPU memory utilization, reduce out-of-memory (OOM) failures, and enhance the overall makespan. It achieves this by profiling and analyzing deep learning (DL) jobs on heterogeneous GPUs to understand the interference caused by collocating jobs and predict GPU memory demand and job completion times. By leveraging this information, SCHEDTUNE optimizes resource allocation and GPU sharing, resulting in higher GPU utilization and improved performance compared to the default Kubernetes scheduler. The proposed technique fills the gap between the capabilities of container orchestrators and the complex requirements of DL applications, providing a management-level solution that learns system behavior and efficiently manages GPU resources in a heterogeneity-aware manner.

He et al. [17] present a CPU-GPU heterogeneous computation offloading and resource allocation scheme tailored for the Industrial Internet of Things (IIoT). With the increasing complexity of IIoT tasks and the demand for delay-sensitive and computing-intensive applications, heterogeneous platforms integrating CPUs and GPUs have become essential. However, the three-stage heterogeneous computing process, including task preprocessing, hybrid computing, and result aggregation, poses challenges for task offloading and resource allocation. The proposed scheme introduces a three-stage heterogeneous computing model and formulates the joint task offloading and heterogeneous resource allocation problem. The authors employ the Lyapunov optimization method and propose a multihead proximal policy optimization (MH-PPO)-based algorithm to minimize the average task delay. Simulation results demonstrate the effectiveness of the scheme in reducing task delays. The study contributes to the development of efficient scheduling techniques in CPU–GPU heterogeneous computing environments for IoT applications. Figure 3 depicts the three-stage heterogeneous computing model designed for task offloading and resource allocation in Industrial Internet of Things (IIoT) systems, demonstrating the sequential steps of preprocessing, hybrid computing, and result aggregation.

Sharma et al. [40] propose a novel scheduling technique specifically designed for distributed deep learning (DDL) workloads in GPU clusters. The primary focus of this scheduling technique is to minimize communication overhead and reduce training times by consolidating jobs on physically close GPUs. The scheduling technique consists of three major components: a classical delay scheduling algorithm for job placement and consolidation, a network-sensitive job preemption strategy, and an auto-tuner mechanism to optimize delay timers. By considering the anticipated communication network delays and the sensitivities of DDL jobs to these delays, the scheduler intelligently places and consolidates jobs based on their network requirements. The proposed technique takes into account the performance characteristics of different network tiers, leveraging modern networking hardware advancements. It dynamically adjusts consolidation based on the network sensitivity of individual jobs, aiming to minimize queueing delays and overall training times. The evaluation results demonstrate significant improvements in end-to-end makespan, job completion time, and communication overhead compared to existing consolidation-based scheduling methods. The study presents a network-sensitive scheduling technique that optimizes GPU cluster scheduling for DDL workloads, considering communication overhead and job consolidation based on network sensitivities. Scheduling techniques tailored for distributed deep learning workloads are summarized in Figure 4, emphasizing strategies that minimize communication overhead and improve job placement within GPU clusters.

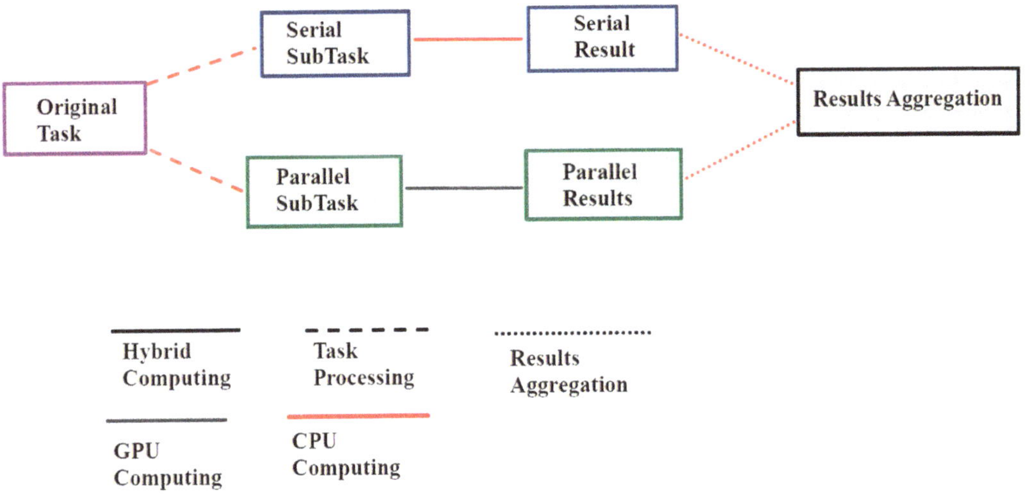

Figure 3. Three-stage heterogeneous computing model depicted in [17].

3.9. Task Graph Scheduling

Li et al. [9] discuss scheduling techniques aimed at efficient task mapping on heterogeneous CPU/GPU platforms. The paper presents a theoretical framework and three practical mapping algorithms with low time complexity to minimize completion time in GPU-based embedded systems. The challenges in task mapping arise from the large size of the policy space and the need to consider factors such as performance characteristics, task dependencies, and data transfer costs. The proposed mapping algorithms address these challenges and outperform state-of-the-art techniques. Experimental results demonstrate up to 30% faster completion time across different workloads. This work in [9] extends the algorithms to enhance runtime performance in resource-limited infrastructure and evaluates them using a benchmark testing suite for simulating real-world-runtime neural networks. The extended algorithm achieves significantly faster completion time (averaging 30% to 37% improvement) compared to existing techniques. Figure 5 presents the scheduler application framework designed to enhance task mapping on heterogeneous CPU/GPU platforms, ensuring efficient resource utilization and reduced completion times.

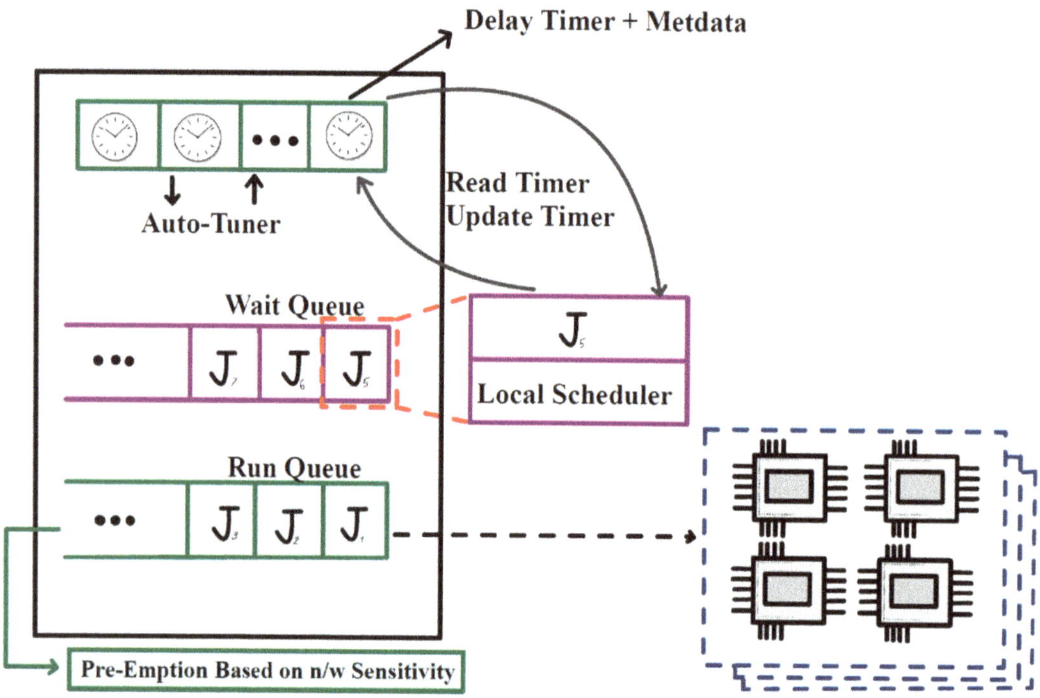

Figure 4. Scheduling techniques proposed in [40].

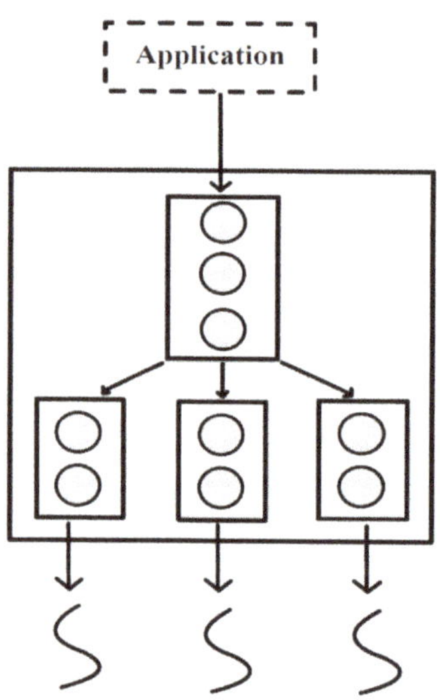

Figure 5. Scheduler application presented in [9].

Harichane et al. [12] focus on scheduling techniques in heterogeneous computing environments, particularly in the context of Kubernetes. The paper addresses the challenge of efficiently utilizing multiple CPUs and GPUs in cloud-based deployments by proposing the KubeSC-RTP scheduler. KubeSC-RTP stands for "Kubernetes Scheduler based on RunTime Prediction" and employs machine learning algorithms for the runtime estimation of deployed applications. By accurately predicting the execution time of applications, the scheduler aims to optimize resource consumption and improve overall system performance. The article outlines the steps involved in implementing the KubeSC-RTP scheduler and highlights its intelligent scheduling approach based on machine learning techniques. It emphasizes the importance of selecting the appropriate device (CPU or GPU) for each application to minimize execution time and maximize resource utilization. The proposed scheduling technique offers potential benefits for cloud service providers, including reduced processing time, increased customer satisfaction, and improved resource management. The article concludes by discussing the experimental results and providing insights into the strengths and limitations of the KubeSC-RTP scheduler, as well as suggesting avenues for future research and enhancements in this field.

The FastGR framework in [18] employs a heterogeneous task graph scheduler as its scheduling technique. This scheduler efficiently distributes tasks between the CPU and GPU components of the system, ensuring workload balancing and resource utilization optimization. By leveraging the processing power of both the CPU and GPU, FastGR achieves significant improvements in performance and solution quality for global routing. The task graph scheduler plays a crucial role in coordinating the execution of tasks, managing dependencies, and allocating resources effectively. It dynamically assigns tasks to the most suitable processing unit, taking into account the computational capabilities and workload distribution across the system. This approach enables FastGR to harness the massive parallelism offered by the GPU while effectively utilizing the CPU's capabilities. Through balanced task scheduling, FastGR maximizes the utilization of available resources, minimizes idle time, and enhances the overall efficiency of the global routing process. The overall workflow of the FastGR global routing framework is shown in Figure 6, highlighting the role of the heterogeneous task graph scheduler in balancing workloads across CPU and GPU components.

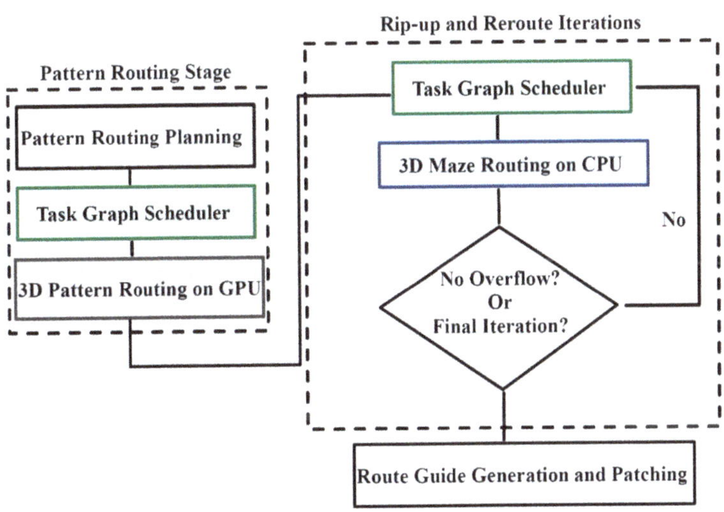

Figure 6. Overall flow of FastGR presented in [18].

Gao et al. [27] propose a temperature-aware scheduling technique for heterogeneous computing in edge scenarios. The authors address the challenge of jointly processing inference tasks using the CPU, GPU, and NPU while considering the impact of ambient temperature on edge devices. They establish a temperature perception model based on the ambient temperature and introduce a TAS (temperature-aware schedule) algorithm to control the running speed of the heterogeneous device. Additionally, they propose a task scheduling algorithm called TASTS (TAS-based task schedule) and utilize a Hungarian matching algorithm to optimize the final results. The article demonstrates that the proposed technique improves performance by 20–50% compared to conventional methods under temperature constraints. The scheduling technique used in this study is the TAS (temperature-aware schedule) algorithm.

Wang et al. [38] propose a GPU scheduling technique known as GCAPS, designed for real-time GPU task execution. The scheduling technique addresses the challenges of prioritization and preemption in GPU tasks, aiming to ensure timely execution and meet stringent timing requirements. GCAPS operates at the device driver level and enables control over GPU context scheduling by adding one-line macros to GPU segment boundaries. It allows the preemption of GPU execution based on task priorities, improving schedulability and response time. The approach requires minimal modifications to the user-level GPU access code and provides fine-grained and efficient control of the GPU. Through empirical evaluations, the proposed approach demonstrates significant improvements over prior work, achieving up to 40% higher schedulability. GCAPS utilizes a preemptive scheduling technique for GPU tasks in real-time systems.

Verma et al. [47] provide a comprehensive overview of scheduling techniques aimed at optimizing energy consumption in cloud computing. The authors discuss state-of-the-art algorithms for allocating workflow tasks to cloud resources, with a specific focus on reducing energy consumption. The article categorizes different workflow scheduling algorithms based on the scheduling approaches used and provides an analytical discussion of the covered algorithms. Additionally, the authors classify various energy-efficient strategies employed by cloud service providers (CSPs) for energy saving in data centers. The article also highlights popular real-world workflow applications and identifies emerging trends and open issues in cloud computing as future research directions.

Fang et al. [48] propose a scheduling technique designed to alleviate resource contention in heterogeneous systems. The article addresses the challenge of shared resource utilization between CPUs and GPUs in network-on-chip (NoC) architectures. It introduces the concept of LLC/MC CENTER architecture and analyzes the impact of different placement methods on system performance. To optimize the network's performance, the article presents a task-based routing algorithm that plans the path based on different tasks and a task-based-partition (TBP) routing algorithm that allocates routing algorithms of different tasks into separate virtual channels. The proposed scheduling technique aims to improve system performance by enhancing resource allocation and reducing network latency. Overall, the article focuses on task-based scheduling techniques for managing resources in heterogeneous CPU-GPU architectures within a network-on-chip framework.

The framework allows a computational kernel to span across multiple devices on a node and enables multiple applications to be scheduled on the same node. It dynamically migrates kernels between devices, expands or contracts the kernel to utilize more or fewer devices, and optimizes scheduling decisions based on different objectives such as job throughput and job priorities. The authors evaluate the framework on a CPU+GPU+FPGA platform and demonstrate speedups of 2.26× over different applications and up to 1.25× for co-scheduled workloads over baselines. The major contribution lies in the ease of programmability with a single code base across different execution devices. Overall, the proposed framework provides an efficient scheduling technique for maximizing the utilization of heterogeneous devices in cloud and HPC environments.

3.10. Hybrid Scheduling

Combining static and dynamic strategies, hybrid scheduling offers flexibility and efficiency across diverse workloads. For example, a hybrid approach might predefine high-priority tasks while dynamically adjusting the execution order of lower-priority jobs based on real-time resource availability. Fang et al. [14] focus on addressing the challenges encountered in heterogeneous systems comprising CPUs and GPUs. The authors propose resource scheduling strategies to improve the utilization and efficiency of heterogeneous cores, thereby optimizing system performance. Two main strategies are presented: a combination strategy for single-task scheduling and a multi-task scheduling strategy. The combination strategy involves optimizing task execution efficiency on GPUs by modifying thread organization structures and developing workload balancing schemes for efficient core utilization. The multi-task scheduling strategy utilizes task samples to gather information about the execution efficiency of heterogeneous cores and global task information. An improved ant colony algorithm is then employed to quickly allocate tasks to the most suitable cores, taking advantage of the characteristics of heterogeneous cores. Experimental results demonstrate that the combination strategy reduces task execution time by an average of 29.13%, while the multi-task scheduling strategy reduces execution time by up to 23.38% compared to the combined strategy. These strategies effectively utilize the resources of heterogeneous systems and significantly improve task execution times.

Yan et al. [42] present a task scheduling technique called HSAS, which optimizes the processing efficiency of deep neural network models on heterogeneous systolic array accelerator clusters. The authors address the challenge of significant differences among models and layers by proposing a heterogeneous architecture that consists of systolic arrays with different scales. HSAS considers factors such as task priority, prediction, preemption, load balance, and layer-level scheduling. The scheduling technique employs a task decomposition algorithm and a sub-task priority management table to enable fine-grained sub-task-level scheduling. The authors validate performance and energy models for systolic arrays and demonstrate their accuracy. Experimental results show that HSAS outperforms classic and state-of-the-art methods in terms of average normalized turnaround time, system throughput, and fairness, achieving improvements of over 80% with task-level scheduling and 18% to 63% with sub-task-level scheduling. HSAS is a sophisticated scheduling technique that optimizes the utilization of heterogeneous systolic array architectures for processing deep neural network models, leading to significant performance improvements.

Mohammad Jafari et al. [44] provide a thorough analysis of task scheduling techniques in heterogeneous computing environments. The study evaluates the performance of four scheduling algorithms: First Come, First Served (FCFS), FCFS with No Queuing (FCFS-NQ), Minimum Expected Completion Time (MECT), and Minimum Expected Execution Time (MEET). The goal is to optimize resource utilization and minimize task completion times. Three workload scenarios representing different computational demands are considered: low, medium, and high. Through rigorous experimentation, the authors assess the effectiveness of each algorithm in terms of total completion percentage, energy consumption, wasted energy, and energy per completion. The findings highlight the strengths and limitations of each algorithm. MECT and MEET emerge as strong contenders, dynamically prioritizing tasks based on comprehensive estimates of completion and execution times. These algorithms exhibit superior energy efficiency compared to FCFS and FCFS-NQ, making them suitable for resource-constrained environments. The study provides valuable insights into task scheduling algorithms, enabling informed decision-making for enhancing resource allocation, minimizing task completion times, and improving energy efficiency. CPU scheduling techniques are visually summarized in Figure 7, providing insights into strategies for optimizing task execution in resource-constrained environments.

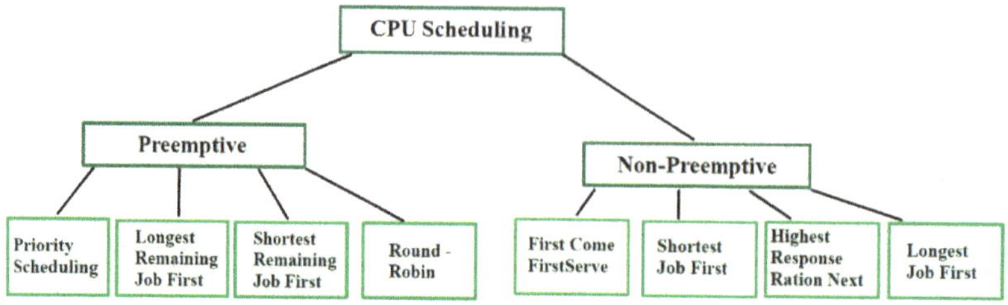

Figure 7. Different CPU scheduling techniques presented in [44].

3.11. Pipelined Scheduling

This strategy overlaps different stages of task execution to maximize system throughput. By decomposing tasks into smaller stages that can be executed concurrently on different processing units (e.g., CPUs and GPUs), pipelined scheduling minimizes idle time and maximizes hardware utilization. Garcia-Hernandez et al. [19] introduce a platform that simplifies the implementation of computationally demanding algorithms in heterogeneous computing environments. The platform utilizes a scheduling technique to distribute tasks across different computing devices, including CPUs, GPUs, and FPGAs, in order to achieve algorithm acceleration. By leveraging the OpenCL framework, the platform offers generality and flexibility, allowing non-experts in heterogeneous computing to deploy and run algorithms without extensive knowledge of specific implementation frameworks. The platform automatically generates parallel code by analyzing algorithms implemented in C, adapting it to target the available computing devices. Experimental results using the Polybench/C suite demonstrate the effectiveness of the proposed platform, achieving accelerations of up to 270× for parallel-friendly algorithms. The scheduling technique used in the platform is not explicitly mentioned in the provided summary.

Liu et al. [20] present a distributed framework known as HeterPS, which utilizes a reinforcement learning (RL)-based scheduling method to optimize the training process of deep neural network (DNN) models in heterogeneous computing environments. The scheduling technique used in HeterPS is based on RL and utilizes an LSTM model. The framework addresses the challenge of effectively utilizing diverse computing resources, such as CPUs and GPUs, for training large-scale DNN models. HeterPS allocates each layer of the DNN model to the appropriate computing resource to minimize costs and satisfy throughput constraints. It also manages data storage and communication among distributed computing resources. Experimental results demonstrate that HeterPS outperforms existing approaches in terms of throughput, achieving a 14.5 times higher throughput, and monetary cost, resulting in a 312.3% reduction in cost. Figure 8 outlines the HeterPS framework, showcasing its reinforcement learning-based scheduling approach to optimize deep learning model training across diverse computing resources.

Zou et al. [25] introduce a scheduling technique called RTGPU for efficiently scheduling multiple GPU applications with hard real-time guarantees. The article addresses the challenge of scheduling highly parallel applications on graphics processing units (GPUs) while meeting stringent timing constraints. RTGPU combines fine-grained GPU partitioning with a novel scheduling algorithm based on federated scheduling and grid search with uniprocessor fixed-priority scheduling. The proposed technique leverages persistent threads and interleaved execution to improve GPU partitioning and performance. It provides real-time guarantees to meet hard deadlines and achieves significant improvements in system throughput (over 11%) and schedulability (up to 57%) compared to previous approaches. The RTGPU scheduling technique is validated and evaluated on NVIDIA GPU systems. It can be applied to mainstream GPUs and general heterogeneous computing platforms with similar task execution patterns. This technique contributes to enabling the efficient execution of computation-intensive parallel tasks on GPUs within real-time constraints.

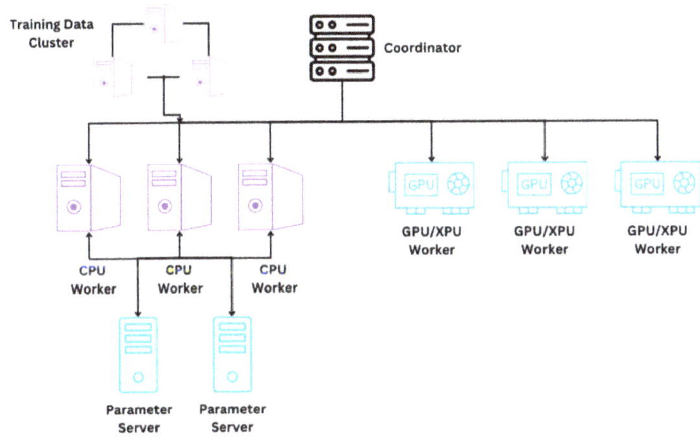

Figure 8. HeterPS framework presented in [20].

Xue et al. [32] propose a performance model for estimating the performance of heterogeneous implementations and providing guidance for computer architecture design. They apply CPU-GPU heterogeneous computing to a CFD test case and compare its performance with a pure GPU implementation. By assigning proper workload ratios to the CPU and GPU workers, the heterogeneous version outperforms the pure GPU version by up to 23%. The authors leverage MPI (Message Passing Interface) and OpenACC to facilitate the CPU-GPU heterogeneous computing workflow in the CFD solver. These frameworks are commonly used for parallel computing and task distribution in heterogeneous systems.

3.12. *Power-Aware/Deadline-Aware Scheduling*

Yang et al. [23] introduce Hydra, a scheduling technique designed for deep learning (DL) jobs running on heterogeneous GPUs. The primary goal of Hydra is to efficiently schedule DL jobs while considering deadline requirements and reducing job completion time (JCT). Existing approaches focusing on efficiency or deadline requirements alone are inadequate for this task. Hydra introduces a novel quantitative cost comparison approach that incorporates the total JCT and a dynamic penalty based on tardiness, i.e., the delay in meeting deadlines. It leverages a sampling approach to estimate job execution times accurately on heterogeneous GPUs and utilizes an efficient branch-and-bound algorithm to find the optimal job–GPU combinations. Evaluation experiments using Alibaba traces demonstrate that Hydra significantly reduces total tardiness by 85.8% while minimizing JCT compared to state-of-the-art efforts. The technique used in Hydra can be categorized as deadline-aware scheduling for deep learning jobs on heterogeneous GPUs.

Lannurien et al. [41] introduce a scheduling technique aimed at optimizing the deployment of time-sensitive applications, specifically focusing on Intrusion Detection Systems (IDSs) in a serverless edge computing environment. The proposed technique addresses the challenges of reducing initialization delays, minimizing communication delays, and leveraging heterogeneous resources to satisfy variable Quality of Service (QoS) requirements. The scheduling technique incorporates a storage-aware allocation and scheduling policy that aims to minimize task placement costs for service providers while optimizing QoS for IDS users. It includes a caching and consolidation strategy to minimize cold starts and inter-function communication delays. By leveraging the capabilities of heterogeneous edge resources, the strategy achieves better QoS performance and reduces the number of edge nodes required for application deployment. The article presents a simulation-based evaluation comparing the proposed technique with a vanilla Knative orchestrator and a storage-agnostic policy. The results demonstrate that the proposed strategy achieves 18% fewer QoS penalties and consolidates applications across 80% fewer edge nodes. Overall, the scheduling technique contributes to the cost-effective deployment of IDSs and other time-sensitive applications in unreserved edge resources, leveraging serverless computing paradigms.

Shobaki et al. [43] present a novel approach to instruction scheduling for GPUs using a parallelized ant colony optimization (ACO) algorithm. The authors address the register-pressure-aware instruction scheduling problem, which involves optimizing the balance between schedule length and register pressure on a GPU target. They demonstrate that parallelizing the ACO algorithm on the GPU significantly improves scheduling performance compared to sequential CPU-based scheduling. The ACO algorithm, inspired by nature, utilizes a pheromone-based search technique to find optimal instruction orders. The authors propose several techniques to efficiently parallelize the ACO algorithm for the complex multi-objective optimization problem of register-pressure-aware scheduling on the GPU. Experimental results show that parallel ACO-based scheduling on the GPU achieves up to 27 times faster execution compared to sequential CPU-based scheduling, resulting in a 21% reduction in the total compile time and an up to 74% improvement in execution speed compared to AMD's production scheduler.

3.13. Batch Job Scheduling

Batch scheduling groups multiple tasks for execution, optimizing resource allocation and minimizing overhead. Composable schedules, for instance, allow for the modular execution of sub-tasks, enabling the efficient handling of large-scale workloads in data centers and accelerators. Chen et al. [29] focus on a programming model, Allo, for enhancing the efficiency of spatial accelerator architectures. One of the key aspects of Allo is its scheduling technique, which enables the construction of modular hardware accelerators through the composition of customized kernels and external IPs. The scheduling technique used in Allo is called composable schedules. This technique allows users to incrementally add customizations to kernels while validating the correctness of each submodule. Multiple schedules are progressively integrated into a complete design using the .compose() primitive. The composable scheduling approach enhances productivity and debuggability, enabling the creation of high-performance designs. Allo also introduces a hierarchical dataflow graph to support the composition of multiple kernels within a complex design while maintaining function boundaries. By modeling the interface unification problem as a type inference problem and leveraging the hierarchical dataflow graph, Allo optimizes the scheduling of dataflow operations. Overall, Allo's composable scheduling technique provides a flexible and modular approach to designing high-performance spatial accelerators.

Ahmad et al. [30] analyze scheduling algorithms utilized in heterogeneous computing systems. The article reviews various list-based workflow scheduling algorithms created over the past two decades and categorizes them based on their scheduling objectives. The main scheduling technique discussed in the article is list-based scheduling, specifically list scheduling with static priorities (LSSP). List-based scheduling algorithms are known for their efficiency in generating schedules for complex workflow applications in heterogeneous computing environments. These algorithms aim to minimize makespan and energy consumption and maximize resource utilization and reliability. The article compares different list-based scheduling algorithms based on their objectives, merits, comparison metrics, workload types, experimental scales, experimental environments, and results. Additionally, the article conducts an experimental analysis of seven state-of-the-art algorithms on randomly generated workflows to understand their workings.

Belkhiri et al. [31] explore the challenges and advancements in GPU virtualization, with a specific focus on the scheduling technique employed in Intel's Graphics Virtualization Technology—grid generation (GVT-g). The authors present a novel performance analysis framework that utilizes host-based tracing combined with the Linux Trace Toolkit Next Generation (LTTng) to collect performance data efficiently and with minimal overhead. The scheduling technique employed in GVT-g allows for the allocation and sharing of GPU resources among virtual machines. The framework incorporates a unified, stateful model for filtering and organizing trace data, enabling the computation of various performance metrics. The analysis is performed using Trace Compass, an open-source performance analyzer, which provides synchronized graphical views to aid in understanding GVT-g's internal mechanisms and diagnosing performance issues related to virtual GPU usage. The article provides valuable insights into GPU virtualization and offers a practical approach to performance analysis in virtualized environments using the GVT-g scheduling technique.

Ye et al. [33] provide a comprehensive overview of scheduling techniques for deep learning (DL) workloads in GPU data centers. The article emphasizes the importance of efficient scheduling to reduce operational costs and improve resource utilization in DL model development. Traditional scheduling approaches designed for big data or high-performance computing workloads are inadequate for fully utilizing GPU resources in DL workloads. The survey examines existing research efforts for both training and inference workloads, categorizing them based on scheduling objectives and resource utilization. It discusses the challenges in designing satisfactory schedulers for DL workloads and identifies the common strategies employed by existing solutions.

Tariq et al. [35] present a scheduling technique known as Energy Efficient Successor Tree Consistent Earliest Deadline First (EESEDF) for periodic conditional task graphs (PCTGs) on multiprocessor systems-on-chips (MPSoCs) with shared memory. The goal is to minimize energy usage by considering dynamic and static power models. The EESEDF approach maximizes worst-case processor utilization by assigning tasks to processors and arranging them using the earliest successor tree-consistent deadline-first strategy. To further minimize energy consumption, the technique solves a convex nonlinear program (NLP) to determine optimal task speeds. Additionally, an online dynamic voltage scaling (DVS) heuristic is introduced, which dynamically adjusts task speeds in real time. Experimental results demonstrate that EESEDF+Online-DVS outperforms existing techniques, achieving notable energy efficiency improvements over LESA and NCM. The proposed scheduling technique achieves significant energy efficiency gains compared to IOETCS-Heuristic, BESS, and CAP-Online. In summary, the article focuses on the EESEDF scheduling technique, which combines successor tree consistency, the earliest deadline-first strategy, and dynamic voltage scaling to optimize energy usage in scheduling PCTGs on MPSoCs with shared memory.

Kwon et al. [36] address the scheduling challenges encountered in multi-tenant cloud systems with heterogeneous GPUs while running various machine learning workloads. The authors propose a novel scheduling approach that utilizes a genetic optimization technique implemented within a process-oriented discrete-event simulation framework. The scheduling technique employed in the study is a genetic optimization technique, which involves using genetic algorithms to find optimal solutions for scheduling machine learning tasks on GPUs. The approach aims to improve GPU utilization in complex environments by effectively orchestrating the scheduling of machine learning workloads. Through extensive simulations using workload traces from Alibaba's MLaaS cluster, which consists of over 6000 heterogeneous GPUs, the proposed scheduling approach demonstrates a 12.8% improvement in GPU utilization compared to Round-Robin scheduling. The results highlight the effectiveness of the genetic optimization technique in optimizing GPU scheduling in cloud-based environments. It focuses on enhancing the scheduling of AI applications in multi-tenant cloud systems by employing a genetic optimization technique, which improves GPU utilization and optimizes resource allocation for machine learning workloads. Table 1 summarizes the significant features of various scheduling techniques discussed in this survey, focusing on their advantages and challenges.

Table 1. Significant features of various scheduling techniques.

Paper	Scheduling Technique	Description	Focus	Flexibility	Advantages	Challenges
[55]	Fine-grained warp scheduling	Prioritizes threads	Thread execution optimization	High	Enhanced parallelism, reduced resource contention	Increased complexity, potential overhead
[4]	Memory latency tolerance	Overlaps memory access with computation	Memory access optimization	Medium	Reduced memory latency impact	Complexity in implementation
[2,24]	Memory bank parallelism	Boosts throughput	Memory throughput optimization	Medium	Improved memory access patterns	Potential conflicts in memory banks
[52]	Context switching	Switches between warps	Resource utilization optimization	High	Reduced idle times, better utilization	Overhead and potential synchronization issues
[54]	Prefetching mechanisms	Anticipates and fetches data in advance	Data access optimization	Low	Reduced latency, improved data availability	Prediction overhead, redundancy risk
[7,10]	Dynamic load balancing	Redistributes workload	Workload distribution	High	Improved responsiveness, balanced resources	Potential runtime overhead
[6,39]	Dynamic task scheduling	Adapts task execution in real time	Task execution optimization	High	Adaptability to workload changes	Higher runtime complexity
[16,17]	Adaptive scheduling	Adjusts policies dynamically	Workload adaptation	High	Better resource utilization	May incur frequent adjustments
[14,42]	Hybrid scheduling	Combines static and dynamic approaches	Mixed scheduling strategies	Medium	Flexibility, efficiency in diverse workloads	Requires careful design
[23]	Power-aware scheduling	Manages energy consumption	Energy efficiency	Medium	Reduced power usage	May compromise speed
[25,38]	Real-time GPU scheduling	Ensures deadlines	Timing-critical applications	Medium	Ensures predictable performance	Limited to real-time systems
[33,36]	Batch job scheduling	Batches tasks	Resource optimization	Medium	High throughput	May cause latency for smaller tasks

Table 1. *Cont.*

Paper	Scheduling Technique	Description	Focus	Flexibility	Advantages	Challenges
[20]	Reinforcement learning-based scheduling	Optimizes allocation	Intelligent task allocation	High	Optimized scheduling in uncertain environments	Training overhead, scalability
[29]	Composable schedules	Builds schedules	Hardware optimization	High	Flexibility in hardware design	Limited generalizability
[31,37]	Resource partitioning	Divides resources	Resource allocation	Medium	Improved resource utilization	May require significant tuning
[41]	Storage-aware scheduling	Optimizes storage	Storage and task placement	Medium	Better QoS and reduced cold starts	Relies on caching performance
[8,27]	Temperature-aware scheduling	Adapts task schedules	Thermal optimization	Medium	Prolonged hardware lifespan, performance stability	Overhead of temperature monitoring
[40]	Network-sensitive scheduling	Minimizes communication delays	Communication overhead optimization	Medium	Reduced communication delays, faster completion	Complex job placement algorithms
[43]	Register-pressure-aware scheduling	Balances execution	Instruction scheduling	Medium	Improved GPU instruction performance	Algorithm complexity
[18,44]	Task graph scheduling	Optimizes dependencies	Dependency management	Medium	Reduced completion times	High complexity for large workloads
[19,32]	Pipelined task scheduling	Overlaps task execution stages	Staged execution optimization	High	Faster task completion	Increased task management complexity
[35]	Energy-efficient scheduling	Uses successor tree consistency	Power optimization	Medium	Reduced energy usage	May impact real-time performance
[45,48]	Task-based routing	Plans resources	Network-on-chip scheduling	Medium	Optimized resource allocation, reduced latency	High computational requirements

4. Review of Design and Implementation Methodologies

This review paper does not present original experimental evaluations but instead offers a critical analysis and summary of the methodologies, evaluation metrics, and datasets utilized in prior studies. This analysis deepens the understanding of experimental designs, thereby promoting reproducibility and facilitating further research. The articles examined in this review focus on key evaluation metrics such as throughput, latency, energy efficiency, resource utilization, and makespan [56]. Additionally, performance metrics like scalability, fault tolerance, and response time are identified as essential for assessing system effectiveness. Commonly utilized datasets in the reviewed studies include standard benchmarks like ImageNet, CIFAR, and COCO, which are frequently employed for evaluating deep learning workloads, including sparse neural networks, convolutional neural networks (CNNs), and transformers. Significant tools and frameworks discussed in the literature include GPU computing platforms like CUDA and OpenCL, as well as profiling tools such as NVIDIA Nsight and various simulation environments used for evaluating scheduling strategies.

5. Summary of the Review

This review provides a comprehensive survey of recent developments in scheduling techniques aimed at maximizing the efficiency of deep learning computations on GPUs. It highlights the challenges associated with parallel thread execution and resource utilization on GPUs, which can result in suboptimal performance. The surveyed research focuses on novel scheduling policies that improve memory latency tolerance, exploit parallelism, and enhance GPU resource utilization.

Figure 9 illustrates the distribution of various scheduling techniques based on their primary focus areas. The chart reveals that optimization techniques constitute the largest segment, accounting for 40% of the surveyed methods, highlighting their critical role in enhancing execution efficiency and resource utilization. Memory optimization techniques follow, comprising 25%, underscoring the importance of effective memory access and throughput. Workload adaptation strategies make up 20%, reflecting the need for dynamic responsiveness to varying workloads. Additionally, energy efficiency techniques and resource allocation methods account for 10% and 5%, respectively, indicating a growing emphasis on power management and effective resource distribution in scheduling practices.

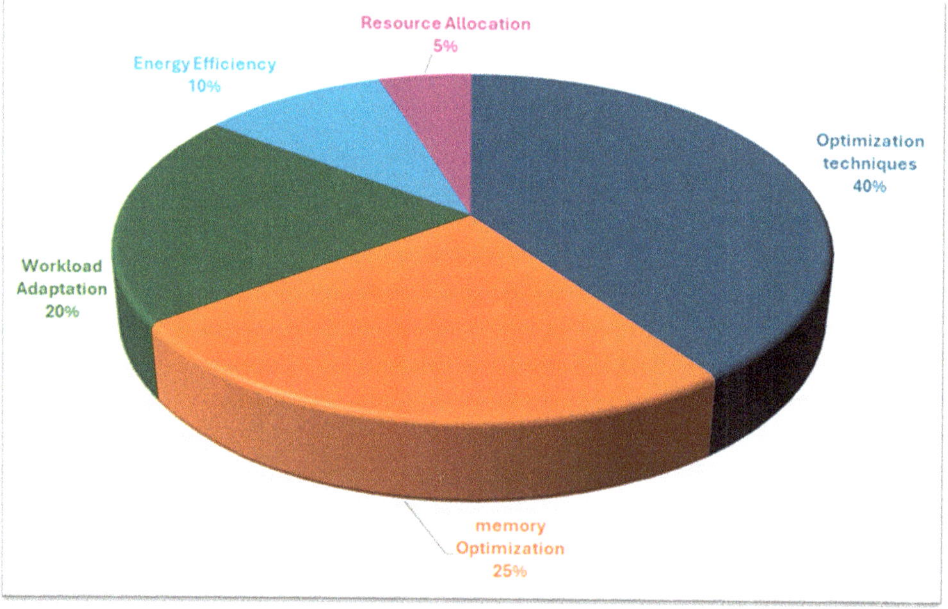

Figure 9. Key Areas of emphasis in modern scheduling approaches.

This review explores various aspects of scheduling techniques for deep learning on GPUs, including warp scheduling policies, memory latency tolerance, memory bank parallelism, context switching strategies, and prefetching mechanisms. These techniques aim to effectively manage the execution of parallel threads, optimize memory access patterns, and improve resource utilization. The integration of fine-grained warp scheduling, warp switching strategies, and prefetching mechanisms is also discussed to optimize deep learning computations on GPUs.

Experimental evaluations demonstrate significant performance improvements in terms of throughput, memory bank parallelism, and latency reduction. The insights gained from this survey can guide researchers, system designers, and practitioners in developing more efficient and powerful deep learning systems on GPUs. This review also discusses potential future directions for research, such as advanced scheduling techniques, energy efficiency considerations, and the integration of emerging computing technologies.

Overall, the review provides a comprehensive overview of recent advancements in scheduling techniques for efficient deep learning computations on GPUs, highlighting their impact on system performance and suggesting future research directions. Table 2 summarizes various scheduling techniques, focusing on their strategies, key features, and applications, emphasizing advancements in optimizing GPU-based deep learning computations.

Table 2. Summary Table of scheduling techniques.

Ref No.	Scheduling Technique	Focus Area	Strategy Type	Key Features
[2,55]	Warp Scheduling	Thread assignment to warps	Dynamic	Efficient resource allocation and thread management
[2]	Memory Latency Tolerance	Memory latency minimization	Dynamic	Overlapping memory access and computation
[2,24]	Memory Bank Parallelism	Memory throughput enhancement	Dynamic	Exploiting parallel memory access capabilities
[52]	Context Switching	Resource usage optimization	Dynamic	Efficient warp switching for resource optimization
[54]	Prefetching Mechanisms	Data access optimization	Dynamic	Anticipating and fetching data in advance
[55]	Fine-Grained Scheduling	Individual thread prioritization	Dynamic	Enhancing parallelism and reducing contention
[46]	Workload Partitioning	CPU-GPU workload division	Static/Dynamic	Effective distribution based on workload and system conditions
[2,24]	Memory Access Scheduling	Memory latency optimization	Dynamic	Effective scheduling to reduce memory latency
[9,12,18,27,38,47,48]	Task Graph Scheduling	Task graph optimization	Dynamic	Dynamic redistribution based on task graph characteristics
[7,10,28]	Dynamic Load Balancing	Workload redistribution	Dynamic	Adapting workload distribution in real time
[53]	Hardware–Algorithm Co-design	Optimization for specific algorithms	Dynamic	Co-design approaches for algorithm and hardware optimization
[6,18,26,37,39,45]	Dynamic Task Scheduling	Real-time task optimization	Dynamic	Adapting task priorities based on system load
[8,16,17,40]	Adaptive Scheduling Policies	Dynamic scheduling adjustments	Dynamic	Real-time policy changes based on workload and system state
[19,20,25,32]	Pipelined Task Scheduling	Task execution pipelining	Dynamic	Overlapping task execution stages for improved efficiency

Table 2. *Cont.*

Ref No.	Scheduling Technique	Focus Area	Strategy Type	Key Features
[14,42,44]	Hybrid Scheduling Strategies	Combination of scheduling approaches	Mixed	Utilizing mix of static and dynamic scheduling techniques
[29–31,33,35,36]	Batch Job Scheduling	Job processing optimization	Static/Dynamic	Scheduling multiple jobs for optimized resource usage
[23,41,43]	Power-Aware Scheduling	Energy-efficient task management	Dynamic	Adjusting scheduling based on power consumption considerations

6. Future Scope

In this survey paper, we have identified several promising future directions for advancing scheduling techniques in deep learning systems.

1. Hybrid Scheduling Algorithms: One key avenue is the development of hybrid scheduling algorithms that integrate artificial intelligence with traditional methods. By leveraging machine learning techniques, these algorithms can dynamically adapt to workload variations and resource availability, enhancing efficiency and responsiveness in real-time scenarios.
2. Scalability for Exascale Workloads: As computational demands grow, enhancing the scalability of scheduling strategies becomes crucial. Future research should focus on developing algorithms capable of managing exascale workloads, ensuring that scheduling techniques can handle vast datasets and complex models without sacrificing performance.
3. Emerging Hardware Technologies: The potential of emerging hardware technologies, such as neuromorphic and quantum processors, could transform scheduling approaches for deep learning. Research should explore how these novel architectures can be integrated into existing systems, optimizing scheduling to exploit their unique capabilities.
4. Energy Efficiency and Sustainability: With rising concerns about energy consumption in computing, future work should prioritize energy-efficient scheduling techniques. Investigating methods that minimize power usage while maintaining performance will be vital for sustainable computing in deep learning applications.
5. Robustness and Security: Tackling real-world deployment challenges, including fault tolerance and security, is essential. Future research should focus on developing scheduling techniques that ensure reliability in the face of hardware failures and security threats, particularly in critical applications such as autonomous systems and healthcare.
6. Interoperability and Standardization: As heterogeneous computing environments become more common, establishing standardized frameworks for scheduling across different platforms will be beneficial. Future research could aim to create guidelines and protocols that improve interoperability, facilitating the smoother integration of various processing units.
7. Trends in Scheduling Techniques: Current trends indicate a shift toward adaptive and context-aware scheduling, which responds to real-time changes in workload and resource conditions. Future studies should investigate the effectiveness of these techniques in diverse scenarios, such as edge computing and federated learning, where resource constraints and latency are critical.

8. Artificial Intelligence in Scheduling: The increasing use of AI in scheduling presents an opportunity for research into intelligent scheduling systems that can predict future workload patterns and optimize resource allocation accordingly. This could involve the application of reinforcement learning and predictive analytics to enhance scheduling decisions.
9. Granularity and Precision in Scheduling: Future work should also explore fine-grained scheduling strategies that prioritize individual tasks based on their specific requirements. Investigating how to achieve optimal task granularity while minimizing overhead will be crucial for improving overall system performance.
10. User-Centric Scheduling: Finally, there is a growing need for user-centric scheduling approaches that consider user preferences and requirements. Future research could explore how to incorporate user feedback into scheduling algorithms, enabling more personalized and effective resource management.

By addressing these areas, researchers and practitioners can develop more robust, efficient, and adaptable scheduling techniques that meet the evolving needs of deep learning systems and their applications across various domains.

7. Conclusions

In conclusion, this review article provides a comprehensive survey of recent advancements in scheduling techniques aimed at maximizing the efficiency of deep learning computations on GPUs. The challenges associated with parallel thread execution, resource utilization, and memory latency in GPUs are highlighted, along with the need for efficient scheduling techniques to optimize performance.

The surveyed research focuses on novel scheduling policies that improve memory latency tolerance, exploit parallelism, and enhance GPU resource utilization. Various techniques such as prefetching mechanisms, fine-grained warp scheduling, and warp switching strategies are explored to optimize deep learning computations on GPUs. These techniques demonstrate significant performance improvements in terms of throughput, memory bank parallelism, and latency reduction.

The insights gained from this survey can guide researchers, system designers, and practitioners in developing more efficient and powerful deep learning systems on GPUs. Furthermore, potential future directions are discussed, including advanced scheduling techniques, energy efficiency considerations, and the integration of emerging computing technologies, inspiring further research in this domain.

Future research in this domain can focus on several key areas to further optimize scheduling techniques for GPUs. First, the integration of energy-efficient algorithms with real-time scheduling methods could address the growing demand for sustainable computing. Second, exploring machine learning-based predictive models for dynamic scheduling can enhance adaptability and resource utilization in diverse workloads. Third, the convergence of scheduling strategies with emerging hardware technologies such as neuromorphic computing and quantum processors could unlock new possibilities for deep learning computations. Additionally, developing standardized frameworks to support heterogeneous systems and improve interoperability across platforms would be beneficial. Finally, addressing challenges in security-aware and fault-tolerant scheduling will ensure robustness in critical applications, opening avenues for deployment in industrial and edge computing environments. These advancements will continue to push the boundaries of deep learning and heterogeneous computing optimization.

Overall, the advancements in scheduling techniques presented in this review offer valuable contributions to maximizing the efficiency of deep learning computations on

GPUs, paving the way for improved performance and resource utilization in a wide range of applications and domains.

Author Contributions: Conceptualization, R.K. and A.A.; methodology, R.K.; software, R.K.; validation, R.K., S.A.A.W., A.A. and F.M.; formal analysis, R.K.; investigation, R.K.; resources, R.K.; data curation, R.K.; writing—original draft preparation, R.K.; writing—review and editing, R.K.; visualization, R.K. and S.A.A.W.; supervision, A.A. and F.M.; project administration, R.K.; funding acquisition, F.M. All authors have read and agreed to the published version of the manuscript.

Funding: This research received no external funding.

Conflicts of Interest: The authors declare no conflict of interest.

References

1. Mittal, S.; Vetter, J.S. A Survey of CPU-GPU Heterogeneous Computing Techniques. *ACM Comput. Surv.* **2015**, *47*, 1–35. [CrossRef]
2. Fang, J.; Wang, M.; Wei, Z. A Memory Scheduling Strategy for Eliminating Memory Access Interference in Heterogeneous System. *J. Supercomput.* **2020**, *76*, 3129–3154. [CrossRef]
3. Tang, X.; Fu, Z. CPU-GPU Utilization Aware Energy-Efficient Scheduling Algorithm on Heterogeneous Computing Systems. *IEEE Access* **2020**, *8*, 58948–58958. [CrossRef]
4. Wang, Z.; Jiang, Z.; Wang, Z.; Tang, X.; Liu, C.; Yin, S.; Hu, Y. Enabling Latency-Aware Data Initialization for Integrated CPU/GPU Heterogeneous Platform. *IEEE Trans. Comput. Aided Des. Integr. Circuits Syst.* **2020**, *39*, 3433–3444. [CrossRef]
5. Roeder, J.; Rouxel, B.; Altmeyer, S.; Grelck, C. Energy-aware Scheduling of Multi-version Tasks on Heterogeneous Real-time Systems. In Proceedings of the 36th Annual ACM Symposium on Applied Computing, New York, NY, USA, 22–26 March 2021; pp. 501–510.
6. Fang, J.; Zhang, J.; Lu, S.; Zhao, H. Exploration on task scheduling strategy for CPU-GPU heterogeneous computing system. In Proceedings of the 2020 IEEE Computer Society Annual Symposium on VLSI (ISVLSI), Limassol, Cyprus, 6–8 July 2020; pp. 306–311.
7. Canon, L.-C.; Marchal, L.; Simon, B.; Vivien, F. Online scheduling of task graphs on heterogeneous platforms. *IEEE Trans. Parallel Distrib. Syst.* **2019**, *31*, 721–732. [CrossRef]
8. Constantinescu, D.-A.; Navarro, A.; Corbera, F.; Fernández-Madrigal, J.-A.; Asenjo, R. Efficiency and Productivity for Decision Making on Low-Power Heterogeneous CPU + GPU SoCs. *J. Supercomput.* **2021**, *77*, 44–65. [CrossRef]
9. Li, Z.; Zhang, Y.; Ding, A.; Zhou, H.; Liu, C. Efficient Algorithms for Task Mapping on Heterogeneous CPU/GPU Platforms for Fast Completion Time. *J. Syst. Archit.* **2021**, *114*, 101936. [CrossRef]
10. Grinsztajn, N.; Beaumont, O.; Jeannot, E.; Preux, P. Readys: A Reinforcement Learning Based Strategy for Heterogeneous Dynamic Scheduling. In Proceedings of the 2021 IEEE International Conference on Cluster Computing (CLUSTER), Portland, OR, USA, 7–10 September 2021.
11. Seo, W.; Cha, S.; Kim, Y.; Huh, J.; Park, J. SLO-aware Inference Scheduler for Heterogeneous Processors in Edge Platforms. *ACM Trans. Archit. Code Optim.* **2021**, *18*, 1–26. [CrossRef]
12. Harichane, I.; Makhlouf, S.A.; Belalem, G. KubeSC-RTP: Smart Scheduler for Kubernetes Platform on CPU-GPU Heterogeneous Systems. *Concurr. Comput. Pract. Exp.* **2022**, *34*, e7108. [CrossRef]
13. Asad, A.; Kaur, R.; Mohammadi, F. A Survey on Memory Subsystems for Deep Neural Network Accelerators. *Future Internet* **2022**, *14*, 146. [CrossRef]
14. Fang, J.; Zhou, K.; Zhang, M.; Xiang, W. Resource Scheduling Strategy for Performance Optimization Based on Heterogeneous CPU-GPU Platform. *Comput. Mater. Contin.* **2022**, *73*, 1621–1635. [CrossRef]
15. Kaur, R.; Mohammadi, F. Power Estimation and Comparison of Heterogeneous CPU-GPU Processors. In Proceedings of the 2023 IEEE 25th Electronics Packaging Technology Conference (EPTC), Singapore, 5–8 December 2023; pp. 948–951.
16. Albahar, H.; Dongare, S.; Du, Y.; Zhao, N.; Paul, A.K.; Butt, A.R. SchedTune: A Heterogeneity-Aware GPU Scheduler for Deep Learning. In Proceedings of the 2022 22nd IEEE International Symposium on Cluster, Cloud and Internet Computing (CCGrid), Taormina, Italy, 16–19 May 2022.
17. He, Z.; Sun, Y.; Wang, B.; Li, S.; Zhang, B. CPU-GPU Heterogeneous Computation Offloading and Resource Allocation Scheme for Industrial Internet of Things. *IEEE Internet Things J.* **2023**, *11*, 11152–11164. [CrossRef]
18. Hu, B.; Yang, X.; Zhao, M. Energy-Minimized Scheduling of Intermittent Real-Time Tasks in a CPU-GPU Cloud Computing Platform. *IEEE Trans. Parallel Distrib. Syst.* **2023**, *34*, 2391–2402. [CrossRef]
19. Garcia-Hernandez, J.J.; Morales-Sandoval, M.; Elizondo-Rodríguez, E. A Flexible and General-Purpose Platform for Heterogeneous Computing. *Computation* **2023**, *11*, 97. [CrossRef]

20. Liu, J.; Wu, Z.; Feng, D.; Zhang, M.; Wu, X.; Yao, X.; Yu, D.; Ma, Y.; Zhao, F.; Dou, D. Heterps: Distributed deep learning with reinforcement learning based scheduling in heterogeneous environments. *Future Gener. Comput. Syst.* **2023**, *148*, 106–117. [CrossRef]
21. Kaur, R.; Mohammadi, F. Comparative Analysis of Power Efficiency in Heterogeneous CPU-GPU Processors. In Proceedings of the 2023 Congress in Computer Science, Computer Engineering, & Applied Computing (CSCE), Las Vegas, NV, USA, 24–27 July 2023; pp. 756–758.
22. Kaur, R.; Saluja, N. Comparative Analysis of 1-bit Memory Cell in CMOS and QCA Technology. In Proceedings of the 2018 International Flexible Electronics Technology Conference (IFETC), Ottawa, ON, Canada, 7–9 August 2018; pp. 1–3. [CrossRef]
23. Yang, Z.; Wu, H.; Xu, Y.; Wu, Y.; Zhong, H.; Zhang, W. Hydra: Deadline-aware and efficiency-oriented scheduling for deep learning jobs on heterogeneous GPUs. *IEEE Trans. Comput.* **2023**, *72*, 2224–2236. [CrossRef]
24. Zhang, X. Mixtran: An efficient and fair scheduler for mixed deep learning workloads in heterogeneous GPU environments. *Clust. Comput.* **2024**, *27*, 2775–2784. [CrossRef]
25. Zou, A.; Li, J.; Gill, C.D.; Zhang, X. RTGPU: Real-time GPU scheduling of hard deadline parallel tasks with fine-grain utilization. *IEEE Trans. Parallel Distrib. Syst.* **2023**, *34*, 1450–1465. [CrossRef]
26. Hsu, K.-C.; Tseng, H.-W. Simultaneous and Heterogeneous Multithreading. In Proceedings of the 56th Annual IEEE/ACM International Symposium on Microarchitecture, Toronto, ON, Canada, 28 October–1 November 2023.
27. Gao, X. TAS: A Temperature-Aware Scheduling for Heterogeneous Computing. *IEEE Access* **2023**, *11*, 54773–54781. [CrossRef]
28. Chun, C.-K.; Lai, K.-C. A Load Balance Scheduling Approach for Generative AI on Cloud-Native Environments with Heterogeneous Resources. In Proceedings of the 2024 10th International Conference on Applied System Innovation (ICASI), Kyoto, Japan, 17–21 April 2024.
29. Chen, H.; Zhang, N.; Xiang, S.; Zeng, Z.; Dai, M.; Zhang, Z. Allo: A Programming Model for Composable Accelerator Design. *Proc. ACM Program. Lang.* **2024**, *8*, 593–620. [CrossRef]
30. Ahmad, W.; Gautam, G.; Alam, B.; Bhati, B.S. An Analytical Review and Performance Measures of State-of-Art Scheduling Algorithms in Heterogeneous Computing Environment. *Arch. Comput. Methods Eng.* **2024**, *31*, 3091–3113. [CrossRef]
31. Belkhiri, A.; Dagenais, M. Analyzing GPU Performance in Virtualized Environments: A Case Study. *Future Internet* **2024**, *16*, 72. [CrossRef]
32. Xue, W.; Wang, H.; Roy, C.J. CPU-GPU heterogeneous code acceleration of a finite volume Computational Fluid Dynamics solver. *Future Gener. Comput. Syst.* **2024**, *158*, 367–377. [CrossRef]
33. Ye, Z.; Gao, W.; Hu, Q.; Sun, P.; Wang, X.; Luo, Y.; Zhang, T.; Wen, Y. Deep Learning Workload Scheduling in GPU Datacenters: A Survey. *ACM Comput. Surv.* **2024**, *56*, 1–38. [CrossRef]
34. Tayeb, H.; Bramas, B.; Faverge, M.; Guermouche, A. Dynamic Tasks Scheduling with Multiple Priorities on Heterogeneous Computing Systems. In Proceedings of the 2024 IEEE International Parallel and Distributed Processing Symposium Workshops (IPDPSW), San Francisco, CA, USA, 27–31 May 2024.
35. Tariq, U.U.; Ali, H.; Nadeem, M.S.; Jan, S.R.; Sabrina, F.; Grandhi, S.; Wang, Z.; Liu, L. *Energy-Aware Successor Tree Consistent EDF Scheduling for PCTGs on MPSoCs*; IEEE Access: Piscataway, NJ, USA, 2024.
36. Kwon, S.; Bahn, H. Enhanced Scheduling of AI Applications in Multi-Tenant Cloud Using Genetic Optimizations. *Appl. Sci.* **2024**, *14*, 4697. [CrossRef]
37. Zhou, Y.; Ren, Z.; Shao, E.; Ma, L.; Hu, Q.; Wang, L.; Tan, G. FILL: A heterogeneous resource scheduling system addressing the low throughput problem in GROMACS. *CCF Trans. High Perform. Comput.* **2024**, *6*, 17–31. [CrossRef]
38. Wang, Y.; Liu, C.; Wong, D.; Kim, H. GCAPS: GPU Context-Aware Preemptive Priority-based Scheduling for Real-Time Tasks. *arXiv* **2024**, arXiv:2406.05221.
39. Wang, S.; Chen, S.; Shi, Y. GPARS: Graph predictive algorithm for efficient resource scheduling in heterogeneous GPU clusters. *Future Gener. Comput. Syst.* **2024**, *152*, 127–137. [CrossRef]
40. Sharma, A.; Bhasi, V.M.; Singh, S.; Kesidis, G.; Kandemir, M.T.; Das, C.R. GPU Cluster Scheduling for Network-Sensitive Deep Learning. *arXiv* **2024**, arXiv:2401.16492.
41. Lannurien, V.; Slimani, C.; d'Orazio, L.; Barais, O.; Paquelet, S.; Boukhobza, J. HeROcache: Storage-Aware Scheduling in Heterogeneous Serverless Edge-The Case of IDS. In Proceedings of the 24th IEEE/ACM International Symposium on Cluster, Cloud and Internet Computing, Philadelphia, PA, USA, 6–9 May 2024.
42. Yan, K.; Song, Y.; Liu, T.; Tan, J.; Wei, X.; Fu, X. HSAS: Efficient task scheduling for large scale heterogeneous systolic array accelerator cluster. *Future Gener. Comput. Syst.* **2024**, *154*, 440–450. [CrossRef]
43. Shobaki, G.; Muyan-Özçelik, P.; Hutton, J.; Linck, B.; Malyshenko, V.; Kerbow, A.; Ramirez-Ortega, R.; Gordon, V.S. Instruction Scheduling for the GPU on the GPU. In Proceedings of the 2024 IEEE/ACM International Symposium on Code Generation and Optimization (CGO), Edinburgh, UK, 2–6 March 2024; pp. 435–447.
44. Mohammadjafari, A.; Khajouie, P. Optimizing Task Scheduling in Heterogeneous Computing Environments: A Comparative Analysis of CPU, GPU, and ASIC Platforms Using E2C Simulator. *arXiv* **2024**, arXiv:2405.08187.

45. Ndamlabin, E.; Bramas, B. RSCHED: An Effective Heterogeneous Resources Management for Simultaneous Execution of Task-Based Applications. 2024. Available online: https://hal.science/hal-04570168/ (accessed on 19 July 2024).
46. McGowen, J.; Dagli, I.; Dantam, N.T.; Belviranli, M.E. Scheduling for Cyber-Physical Systems with Heterogeneous Processing Units under Real-World Constraints. In Proceedings of the 38th ACM International Conference on Supercomputing, Kyoto, Japan, 4–7 June 2024; pp. 298–311.
47. Verma, P.; Maurya, A.K.; Yadav, R.S. A survey on energy-efficient workflow scheduling algorithms in cloud computing. *Softw. Pract. Exp.* **2024**, *54*, 637–682. [CrossRef]
48. Fang, J.; Wei, Z.; Liu, Y.; Hou, Y. TB-TBP: A task-based adaptive routing algorithm for network-on-chip in heterogeneous CPU-GPU architectures. *J. Supercomput.* **2024**, *80*, 6311–6335. [CrossRef]
49. Al Abdul Wahid, S.; Asad, A.; Mohammadi, F. A Survey on Neuromorphic Architectures for Running Artificial Intelligence Algorithms. *Electronics* **2024**, *13*, 2963. [CrossRef]
50. Asad, A.; Kaur, R.; Mohammadi, F. Noise Suppression Using Gated Recurrent Units and Nearest Neighbor Filtering. In Proceedings of the 2022 International Conference on Computational Science and Computational Intelligence (CSCI), Las Vegas, NV, USA, 12–16 December 2022; pp. 368–372. [CrossRef]
51. Kaur, R.; Asad, A.; Mohammadi, F. A Comprehensive Review of Processing-in-Memory Architectures for Deep Neural Networks. *Computers* **2024**, *13*, 174. [CrossRef]
52. Zhang, H.; Xue, Y.; Zhou, Y.E.; Li, S.; Huang, J. SkyByte: Architecting an Efficient Memory-Semantic CXL-based SSD with OS and Hardware Co-design. *arXiv* **2025**. [CrossRef]
53. Kim, S.; Hsiao, R.; Nikolić, B.; Demmel, J.; Shao, Y.S. SuperNoVA: Algorithm-Hardware Co-Design for Resource-Aware SLAM. In Proceedings of the 30th ACM International Conference on Architectural Support for Programming Languages and Operating Systems (ASPLOS '25), Rotterdam, The Netherlands, 30 March–3 April 2025; pp. 1–17. [CrossRef]
54. Yüzügüler, A.C.; Zhuang, J.; Cavigelli, L. PRESERVE: Prefetching Model Weights and KV-Cache in Distributed LLM Serving. *arXiv* **2025**. [CrossRef]
55. Tang, D.; Wu, Z.; Wang, Y.; Gu, Y.; Liu, F.; Qi, Z. gCom: Fine-grained Compressors in Graphics Memory of Mobile GPU. *ACM Trans. Arch. Code Optim.* **2025**, *21*, 1–23. [CrossRef]
56. Hennessy, J.L.; Patterson, D.A. *Computer Architecture: A Quantitative Approach*; Elsevier: Amsterdam, The Netherlands, 2011.

electronics

MDPI

Article

A Source-to-Source Compiler to Enable Hybrid Scheduling for High-Level Synthesis

Yuhan She [1], Yanlong Huang [1], Jierui Liu [1], Ray C. C. Cheung [1,2,*] and Hong Yan [1,2]

[1] Department of Electrical Engineering, City University of Hong Kong, Hong Kong, China; yuhanshe3-c@my.cityu.edu.hk (Y.S.); yanlhuang5-c@my.cityu.edu.hk (Y.H.); jieruiliu2-c@my.cityu.edu.hk (J.L.); h.yan@cityu.edu.hk (H.Y.)

[2] Center for Intelligent Multidimensional Data Analysis, Hong Kong Science Park, Shatin, Hong Kong, China

[*] Correspondence: r.cheung@cityu.edu.hk

Abstract: High-Level Synthesis (HLS) has gained considerable attention for its ability to quickly generate hardware descriptions from untimed specifications. Most state-of-the-art commercial HLS tools employ static scheduling, which excels in compute-intensive applications but struggles with control-dominant designs. While some open-source tools propose dynamic and hybrid scheduling techniques to synthesize dataflow-like architectures to improve speed, they lack well-established optimizations from static scheduling like datapath optimization and resource sharing, leading to frequency degradation and area overhead. Moreover, existing hybrid scheduling relies on extra dynamic synthesis support, either by dynamic or static HLS tools, and thereby loses generality. In this work, we propose another solution to achieve hybrid scheduling: a source-to-source compiler that exposes dynamism at the source code level, which reduces both frequency and area overhead while remaining fully compatible with modern static HLS tools without needing extra dynamic synthesis support. Experiments show significant improvements (1.26× speedup) on wall clock time (WCT) compared to *VitisHLS* and a better area–frequency–latency trade-off compared to dynamic (1.83× WCT speedup and 0.46× area) and hybrid (2.14× WCT speedup and 0.72× area) scheduling-based tools.

Keywords: high-level synthesis; pipelining; scheduling; FPGA

1. Introduction

Scheduling, as one of the core steps in HLS, is still being explored to find the best choice of strategy. Static scheduling strategy assigns operations into predetermined cycle slots based on compile-time analysis. Despite being adopted by almost all commercial HLS tools, it still suffers from exploiting parallelism in code with runtime-determined, long-latency control dependencies in loops since the worst assumption must be made to guarantee the correct execution under any runtime conditions. Dynamic scheduling, on the other hand, implements a distributed dataflow network with handshakings between each communicating operation pair. This strategy excels on designs with complex control flow and imbalanced branches but loses some opportunities for resource sharing and critical path optimization, resulting in area overheads and a frequency drop. Hybrid scheduling bridges the static and dynamic strategies to highlight the advantages of both, achieving both high performance and low area overhead. However, hybrid scheduling still relies heavily on the dynamic synthesis support, either by dynamic HLS tools or dynamic synthesis support provided by the static HLS tools. These limitations result in a large frequency drop and loss of generality.

In this paper, we propose another solution, a source-to-source compiler, to achieve hybrid scheduling as well as remaining fully compatible with the existing static HLS tools. The compiler transforms a plain, untimed design into a functionally equivalent Pseudo-Cycle-Accurate (PCA) model, where each iteration of the original loop is partitioned into several "virtual" cycles and mapped to the same number of iterations in the transformed PCA model. The term *Pseudo* indicates that the partitioned "virtual" cycles are not necessarily the same as the real hardware clock cycles synthesized by the HLS tool. Instead, they are normalized control steps extracted through static analysis with the specific aim of exposing the dynamism to the source code. Each "virtual" cycle may be synthesized into multiple clock cycles by the static HLS tools following their loop optimizations, but the obtained gains from the transformation are not affected, as detailed in Section 4. The transformation is achieved by registering the loop-carried variables with buffers, which is a well-known technique to handle long loop-carried dependencies to improve the *Initiation Interval* (II) in static HLS flow [1]. In our proposed framework, this process is fully automated to transform a plain design into the functionally equivalent PCA model. Long loop paths are divided into multiple short paths, each one taking a single transformed loop iteration to complete. Under different runtime conditions, it takes different numbers of iterations to finish the same original loop path by stalling the updating of the buffers, which reflects the dynamic execution nature. This idea is inspired by [2], where the authors synthesized a RISC-V processor core from a cycle-accurate ISA simulator. Dependencies and hazards are carefully handled manually on a cycle basis by invalidating specific "registers" under specific conditions so that HLS tools are proficient in dealing only with static optimizations. Our work targets the same goal while aiming at a generic source-to-source compiler to achieve hybrid scheduling. The main contributions of this paper are as follows:

1. We propose the Pseudo-Cycle-Accurate (PCA) model to achieve source level dynamism to facilitate hybrid scheduling for HLS.
2. We propose a novel intermediate representation (IR) termed an *Execution Graph* (EG) by extending the *Gated SSA* (GSSA) [3] representation as the foundation to support the transformation from a plain loop kernel to its equivalent PCA model.
3. We propose an automated framework with key algorithms to transform a plain design into a PCA model, which is fully compatible with existing HLS tools adopting static scheduling strategy.
4. The framework was evaluated with a set of benchmarks, and the results demonstrate significant performance improvements over a commercial static-scheduling-based HLS tool (*Vitis HLS*) as well as better resource–performance tradeoffs over other state-of-the-art, open-source, dynamic- and hybrid-scheduling-based tools.

The remainder of this article is organized as follows: Section 2 provides preliminaries and related works on different scheduling approaches. Section 4 describes the details of our proposed PCA model with demonstrative examples. Section 5 presents the overall framework including the intermediate representation and some key aspects. Section 6 presents the experiment results and analysis based on a variety of HLS benchmarks. Section 7 concludes our work with discussion of future research.

2. Preliminaries

In this section, we provide the basic concepts of *High-Level Synthesis* (HLS) and the scheduling in the HLS process. In addition, we introduce the necessary knowledge of dynamic and hybrid scheduling techniques.

2.1. HLS and Scheduling in HLS

For many years, the standard practice in the electronic design has been to employ Hardware Description Languages (HDLs) like Verilog and VHDL to define the specifics of a hardware design. This level of description, however, requires specialized hardware knowledge and the time-consuming design of a complex architecture. A more abstract and efficient alternative is offered by HLS tools, which translate hardware functionality described in a high-level software language into a detailed hardware implementation. This approach yields significant benefits; it accelerates the design process for hardware engineers and allows them to more effectively explore different design possibilities. Also, it makes hardware programming more accessible to software engineers. While HLS is advantageous for designing both ASICs and FPGAs, its impact is particularly pronounced in the FPGA space. The programming complexity associated with FPGAs has long been a primary obstacle to their widespread adoption, a challenge that HLS directly addresses and helps to overcome [4]. HLS takes untimed specifications as input to describe the underlying hardware. One of the most popular languages is C/C++ due to its mature compilation infrastructures. To create designs that are both high-performing and compact, HLS tools employ a suite of compiler optimizations, from front-end code transformations (e.g., if-conversion) to back-end RTL optimizations (e.g., bitwidth analysis).

One of the core steps of the HLS synthesis process is scheduling, which determines the specific clock cycle for every operation's execution. A typical scheduling process starts by converting the source code into the *intermediate representation* (IR) for front-end analysis, e.g., the LLVM IR [5]. Then, the IR is usually transformed into a more structured form called the *Control Data Flow Graph* (CDFG). The CDFG consists of two levels of information to represent both the control flow and dataflow of the original code: the top-level graph represents the *Control Flow Graph* (CFG) with each vertex as one *Basic Block* (BB), and the lower-level graph represents the *Data Flow Graph* (DFG) for each BB, with each sub-vertex as one single operation (e.g., `add` or `mul`). Edges in both levels represent the control/data dependencies. In HLS tools, scheduling is the task of transforming the untimed CDFG into a timed schedule [6].

2.2. Static Scheduling

Static scheduling is a predominant technique widely adopted in modern commercial HLS tools. The scheduling of operations is performed completely at the compilation phase through static analysis of the input code with core information extracted, such as the CDFG, which defines the execution order of each involved operation. Algorithms are applied to derive which operation should execute at which clock cycle to compose a hardware datapath considering the extracted dependencies and user-specified resource and timing constraints. This is generally accomplished using systems of difference constraints (SDC) modeling, which accounts for a wide range of constraints, including clock frequency, data and control dependencies, and the availability of resources [7,8]. Such models characterize the constraints as inequalities and employ linear programming (LP) algorithms to achieve customized timing objectives. After the operations are allocated to certain cycle slots, a central Finite State Machine (FSM) is generated to handle the control flows in the original program.

In static scheduling, loops can be pipelined to optimize the overall execution latency. Loop pipelining allows the loop iterations to overlap as much as possible with all the dependencies honored. A pipeline's effectiveness is primarily measured by its *Initiation Interval* (II), which quantifies the delay, in clock cycles, between the start of two consecutive loop iterations, with an II of 1 representing the theoretical maximum throughput. Iterative modulo scheduling algorithms [9] are applied to calculate the minimum achievable II as $II_{min} = max_i\{\lceil Delay_i/Distance_i \rceil\}$, where the *Delay* is the number of cycles needed to execute the entire recurrence path (recurrence means that operations in one iteration depend on results from previous iterations), and the *Distance* is the loop iterations between the definition and usages of a recurrence value.

Static scheduling excels at critical path optimization since the target clock frequency is constrained at the compilation phase in the SDC model. Such constraints take all data and control paths into account, and the LP algorithms solve the scheduling for a globally optimal performance, which usually requires critical paths to be as balanced as possible. In addition, static scheduling is also effective at exploring resource sharing. The SDC models allow the user to provide the time constraints to find the minimum resource consumption or to provide the resource constraints to find the best performance. When possible, multiple operations can share the same hardware component if they are scheduled in different clock cycles. This maintains the performance but results in a smaller area.

Although proven efficient in exploring resource sharing and critical path optimization, static scheduling suffers from the conservative pipelining of non-deterministic control flows with feedback dependencies and irregular memory access: When a recurrence value depends on multiple paths with unbalanced cycle delays and runtime control decisions, static scheduling conservatively calculates the *II* with the longest recurrence path to guarantee the correct execution of the loop under any runtime conditions. Cycles can be wasted when the short path is frequently taken, and static scheduling is incapable of handling it since the scheduling is performed at the compilation phase.

2.3. Dynamic Scheduling

Dynamic scheduling provides a new view of scheduling the operations with the handshaking interfaces. Different from the FSM-centric structure used in static scheduling, dynamic scheduling implements a distributed control network where each component determines its own behavior through latency-insensitive handshaking [10]. The scheduling decisions are made locally by each operation through handshaking. As soon as all conditions for execution are met (e.g., all the inputs are available, and critical control decisions are resolved), an execution starts. Since the scheduling of an operation is not determined until it actually starts to run, dynamic scheduling intrinsically adapts to the runtime condition, making it perfectly suitable for irregular and unpredictable control flows. However, the distributed scheduling mechanism sacrifices the opportunities of resource sharing and critical path balancing. Instead of scheduling at the compilation phase like static scheduling, dynamic scheduling has no knowledge about when an operation will actually be executed. Therefore, it is not able to share the same hardware for different operations when scheduling. For critical path synthesis, the handshaking signals attached with the operations directly increase the path delay, resulting in a longer critical path and a lower operating frequency. Also, dynamic scheduling creates dataflow-like handshakings to each component even though it exhibits no dynamic behavior, which introduces heavy area overhead. Although works on resource sharing [11] and excessive dynamism eliminating [12] show notable resource savings, there is still a significant gap compared to the static-scheduling-based HLS tools.

2.4. Hybrid Scheduling

Hybrid scheduling combines the advantages of both static and dynamic scheduling [13–16]. There are two main existing strategies to achieve this: The first is to partition the input code to static and dynamic regions, where the static regions are usually defined as a chain of SSA def–use pairs in the same basic block (i.e., no control flows inside) with particular attributes in the context of HLS [13–15]. The static regions are then extracted and synthesized with a classic static HLS tool. The synthesized blocks are then wrapped with handshaking and control logic so that it can be considered as a regular dataflow component during the following dynamic scheduling process. This method proves to be efficient in reducing the resource overhead while maintaining the high performance achieved due to the dynamic nature. However, it still suffers from a heavy frequency drop since the critical paths are still bottlenecked by the dynamic tools. Also, it suffers from the same limitations of the current dynamic HLS tools, e.g., additional Load Store Queue (LSQ) requirements.

The second strategy is to utilize the builtin latency-insensitive channels provided by the static HLS tools (e.g., the `hls::stream` from VitisHLS, `ac_channel` from CatapultHLS, and `SYCL` pipe from Intel HLS) to build dataflow circuits [16]. In such processes, the input code is completely synthesized through static scheduling but with its loop kernels partitioned into several communicating operations connected with the latency-insensitive FIFO channels. Compared with the first strategy, this method selectively introduces dynamism to the static HLS, making it more efficient on resource consumption and critical path optimization. However, it heavily depends on the tool-specific supports on dataflow synthesizing features with latency-insensitive channels. Existing static HLS tools provide limited dataflow support with extra constraints, e.g., coarse-grained dataflow partition (only structured code blocks are amenable to dataflow synthesis) and one-way dataflow requirements (dataflow synthesis cannot be applied within a loop) in VitisHLS. Although some tools may provide more flexibility on customizing dataflow interfaces, adapting to different tools with different specifications requires extensive engineering efforts, and these methods thereby lose generality as generic hybrid scheduling solutions. Furthermore, non-blocking reading and writing on those channels are necessary to implement this hybrid scheduling scheme, which leads to extra difficulties in the verification process as non-blocking reading can break the behavior consistency between the source code and the synthesized hardware.

Based on all these limitations, we propose a new strategy to bring dynamism to static HLS by transforming a plain design to an equivalent PCA model via source-to-source compilation. Our method is tool-independent, channel-free, and perfectly compatible with the modern static HLS tools and hence can be easily verified through the mainstream co-simulation method provided by most commercial HLS tools.

3. Related Work

In this section, we provide a comprehensive literature review on the advancement of HLS technologies to overcome the conservatism for loop pipelining, which can be generally classified into dynamic-scheduling-based methods and hybrid-scheduling-based methods.

3.1. *Dynamic-Scheduling-Based HLS*

The idea of dynamic scheduling can be traced back to the latency-insensitive design methodology [10,17,18]. Cortadella et al. [17,19] proposed the elastic circuit, which is a promising hardware implementation architecture for the latency-insensitive methodology. However, the elastic circuit has not been further developed as a general HLS tool since it is too restrictive. Venkataramani et al. [20] proposed a framework to synthesize a C-based program to hardware following the asynchronous design paradigm. Despite the presence of dynamism, such a circuit has proven to be inefficient in modern implementation flow. Hoover and Brewer [21], Chatterjee et al. [22] extended the handshaking protocol (SELF) in the elastic circuit [19] for better branching and merging implementation. There are also works that explore synthesizing dataflow circuits from high-level descriptions [23] or intermediate functional programming representations [24]. But all these works are far from a complete dynamic-scheduling-based HLS tool. Recent work [25,26] proposed *Dynamatic*

HLS, which is considered as the first generic dynamically scheduled HLS tool. The work was then continuously developed for resource optimization [11,12,27] and frequency optimization [28]. All these works are based on dynamic scheduling, while our work targets achieving dynamism using pure static HLS tools, which exposes more opportunities for resource sharing and critical path optimization.

3.2. Hybrid-Scheduling-Based HLS

Hybrid scheduling seeks opportunities to combine the static scheduling and dynamic scheduling to highlight the advantages of both. Several works [29–32] try to incorporate some level of dynamism into the static HLS flow. Alle et al. [29] and Liu et al. [30] proposed to synthesize multiple scheduling schemes, which can be dynamically selected at the runtime based on the conditions. Such approaches replicate the source code and introduce significant resource overhead. Tan et al. [31] proposed an approach, ElasticFlow, to solve the irregular bound of nested inner loops and optimize pipelining of irregular loop nests that contain dynamically bound inner loops. Such an approach is specific to the target loop patterns and therefore loses generality. There are also explorations of enabling speculation within the static scheduling flow [33–36]. They maintain the speculatively executed iterations and discard them when the iteration is solved as misspeculation. Such methods can aggressively pipeline the loop but can also result in significant misspeculation penalty due to the pipeline flush and re-execution. Dai et al. [32] proposed application-specific dynamic hazard detection architecture for memory speculation, but these dynamic components still need to be manually integrated into the static HLS flow, instead of being a seamless plugin compared to our proposed work.

Recent works explored the possibilities of integrating static scheduling into the dynamic HLS flow [13–15] based on the theory of encapsulating static modules into a latency-insensitive system [37]. Such methods are promising in reducing the resource overhead while retaining the dynamic execution nature, but the critical path is still bottlenecked by the backend dynamic HLS tool, resulting in frequency degradation. In contrast, Szafarczyk et al. [16] proposed to utilize the provided latency-insensitive channels provided by static HLS tools to synthesize a dataflow network within the static HLS flow. With the static HLS tool as the backend, the frequency improves, but the method loses generality as it sticks to a specific HLS tool, and its provided channels as discussed in Section 2.4. Our proposed framework relies on source-to-source compilation, which is tool-independent and channel-free, as well as compatible with the modern static HLS tools as a backend for better area and frequency.

4. PCA Model

In this section, we present the concept of the PCA model and show how it can facilitate dynamic scheduling with two demonstrative examples. We first demonstrate the behavior of a PCA model using a regular loop kernel without control flows. Then we show how the PCA model can achieve dynamism and improve the static scheduling using a loop kernel with runtime-determined control flows and imbalanced branches. After that, we describe the key steps to transform a loop into a valid PCA model.

4.1. Concept of Virtual Cycle and PCA Model

Given a loop kernel, one *transaction* is defined as one loop iteration of the original loop kernel. In contrast, one "virtual cycle" is defined as one loop iteration of the transformed PCA loop. The PCA model is proposed as a transformed loop from the original loop, which keeps the same *transaction-level* equivalence. However, the *virtual-cycle-level* behavior is different. For the original loop, one transaction can be completed with one "virtual cycle", but for the

PCA model, one transaction may need several "virtual cycles" to complete. This is because the PCA transformation divides the execution of the original loop transaction into several phases, with each phase corresponding to one "virtual cycle". This execution pattern is achieved by registering the output value in every "virtual cycle" with buffers. Buffers are initialized with an invalid value and will be updated by their input value, like a register in a circuit. It is worth noting that the "virtual cycle" does not have to accurately map a hardware clock cycle synthesized by the HLS tool. It is normal that one "virtual cycle" is synthesized to multiple hardware clock cycles if it includes multi-cycle operations.

4.2. PCA Model for Regular Loop

4.2.1. Behavior

Figure 1 shows a regular loop kernel without control flows as an example to demonstrate the behavior of the PCA model. As shown in Figure 1b, the loop consists of a chain of operations with one recurrence variable (`floats_01`) updated at each iteration. The back edge that updates the `floats_01` with `floatadd9` is omitted in Figure 1b to build a *Directed Acyclic Graph* (DAG) view to facilitate the description of related algorithms. Figure 1c shows the execution pattern of this loop kernel: At each transaction, the recurrence variable is directly updated with the value calculated from the preceding transaction. Four transactions take four iterations of the original loop kernel.

Figure 1d,e show the transformed PCA code and its corresponding dataflow graph. Three buffers are inserted to create four "virtual cycles", with each "virtual cycle" responsible for executing several operations. Figure 1e presents the location of the inserted buffers. These buffers are mapped as loop-carried variables (`buffer0/1/2` in Figure 1d in L3–L5) and are used to register the output value from the input "virtual cycle". The registered values cannot be propagated to the following operations until next iteration. This is achieved by the implementation of the buffers, which are updated on a loop–iteration basis: at each iteration, the operations take input from the buffers and finally update the output buffers.

Considering the execution of the third "virtual cycle" (containing the operations `floatadd6` and `floatmul7`) as an example, they are executed with the input directly from operation `floatmul5` and variable `floats_01` at each iteration in the original code as shown in Figure 1a,b. After the PCA transformation, `floatadd6` takes the input from the `buffer1` (as shown in L22 in Figure 1d). However, in the same iteration, `buffer1` is updated by `floatmul5` at L28 in Figure 1d, which is later than the computation of `floatadd6` and `floatmul7`. This means that the two operations use the value of `buffer1` obtained from the previous iteration (`floatmul5`), and similarly, the value obtained from previous iteration (`floatmul5`) is calculated by its input buffers (`buffer2` in L20 in Figure 1d), which is also not updated from the same iteration as itself.

Following such an execution pattern, at a specific iteration, operations in different "virtual cycles" use input values from different transactions, and the value for the same transaction can only propagate one level of buffer at each iteration (i.e., one "virtual cycle"). This buffered execution simulates the behavior of a pipeline with buffers served as the pipeline registers. However, in this sample example, the recurrence prevents the PCA model from being fully pipelined (i.e., starting the next transaction at each iteration) since the execution of next transaction requires the final result from the previous transaction (i.e., the recurrence variable `floats_01`), which is calculated after 4 "virtual cycles". Therefore, to guarantee the equivalent transaction-level behavior, an additional valid bit should be carried along the dataflow to indicate whether a produced value is valid to start the following transaction. By initializing buffers as invalid, the pipeline can achieve an II of 4: in each iteration, only one "virtual cycle" is executing the valid values, and other "virtual cycles" are all invalid. As shown in L6–L10 in Figure 1d, 5 valid bits are declared for 2 recurrence variables and 3 buffers. These valid bits are propagated along the data path (e.g., L19, L21, L23, and L25 in Figure 1d) and finally updated with the buffers and the recurrence variables. Only when the recurrence variable associated with the valid bit is true can the recurrence variables be updated to proceed the next transaction as shown in L14–L17 for `floats_01` and L34–L36 for `i` in Figure 1d.

```
float s = 0.0f;
int i = 0;
for (;i<5;i++)
{
    s = s +
    (((s+0.64f) * \
       s+0.7f) * \
       s+0.21f) * \
       s+0.33f;
}
```

(a) Original loop kernel

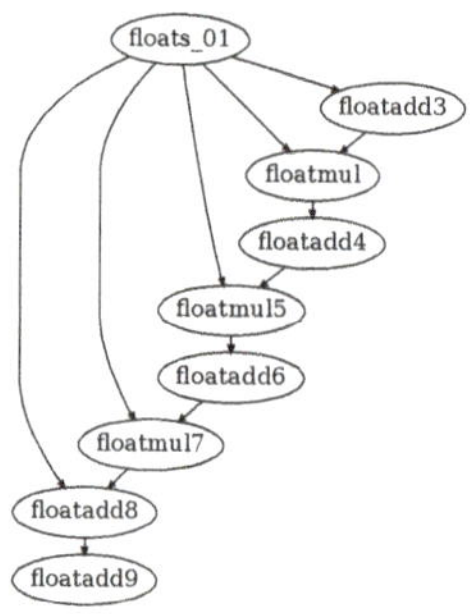

(b) Original dataflow

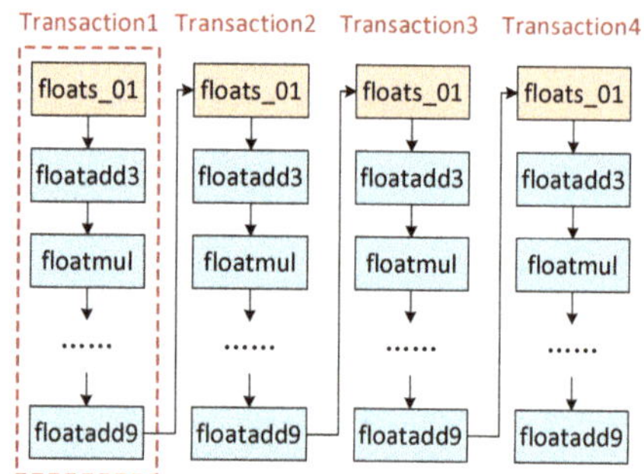

(c) Original transactions

```
1  float s = 0.0f;
2  int i = 0;
3  float buffer0 = 0;
4  float buffer1 = 0;
5  float buffer2 = 0;
6  bool s_valid = true;
7  bool i_valid = true;
8  bool buffer0_valid = false;
9  bool buffer1_valid = false;
10 bool buffer2_valid = false;
11 float s_queue = 0;
12 float s_queue_valid = false;
13 while (i<5) {
14     if (s_valid) {
15         s_queue=s;
16         s_queue_valid=s_valid;
17     }
18     float mul=(s+0.64f)*s;
19     bool mul_valid=s_valid;
20     float mul5=(buffer2+0.7f)*s_queue;
21     bool mul5_valid=buffer2_valid &&
           s_queue_valid;
22     float mul7=(buffer1+0.21)*s_queue;
23     bool mul7_valid=buffer1_valid &&
           s_queue_valid;
24     float add9=buffer0+s_queue+0.33f;
25     bool add9_valid=buffer0_valid &&
           s_queue_valid;
26     buffer2=mul;
27     buffer2_valid=mul_valid;
28     buffer1=mul5;
29     buffer1_valid=mul5_valid;
30     buffer0=mul7;
31     buffer0_valid=mul7_valid;
32     s=add9;
33     s_valid=add9_valid;
34     if (add9_valid) {
35         i = i + 1;
36     }
37 }
```

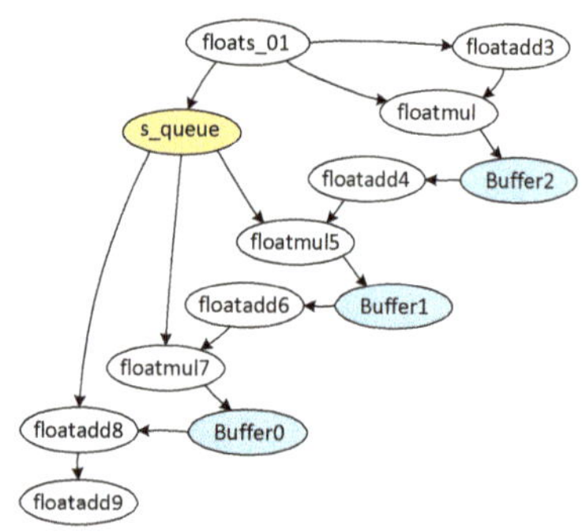

(e) Dataflow of the transformed PCA loop kernel

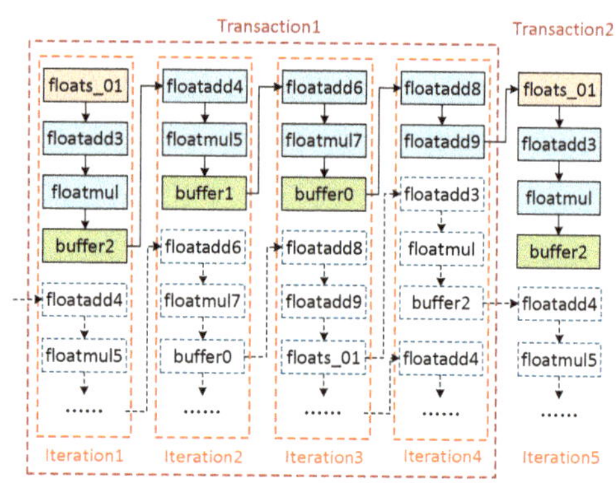

(d) The full code after the PCA transformation that is functionally equivalent to the original loop kernel

(f) Execution pattern of the transformed PCA loop

Figure 1. A demonstrative example of a regular loop kernel to showcase the PCA transformation, which contains the C code, the dataflow graph, and the execution pattern for both the original and its transformed PCA model: (**a**) shows the source code of the original loop kernel. (**b**) shows the corresponding dataflow graph omitting the back edge. (**c**) shows the execution pattern for 4 transactions of the original loop. (**d**) shows the transformed PCA code. (**e**) shows the dataflow graph of the transformed loop kernel including the inserted buffers and queues. (**f**) shows the execution pattern of the transformed PCA loop kernel including 5 "virtual cycles" for 2 transactions.

Figure 1f is the visualization of the PCA model's execution pattern, where each column represents one iteration of the PCA model (i.e., one "virtual cycle"), and the execution can be considered as "virtual-cycle-accurate". The red boxes represent the recurrence variables that are active during different iterations. The blue boxes represent the regular operation chains. The green boxes represent the buffers inserted to create "virtual cycles". The arrowed edges represent the data dependencies in the transformed PCA loop. For simplicity, the dependencies on the recurrence variable (e.g., `floats_01`) are omitted. This graph mainly aims to demonstrate the activeness of the operations in different "virtual cycles" at each loop iteration. According to the behavior of the buffers and the valid bits, at each iteration, only the operations in one "virtual cycle" will be actively executed (represented as filled boxes). And in the following iteration, the next "virtual cycle" will be activated. Therefore, it takes 4 iterations for the PCA loop to finish one transaction of the original loop. Queues, as shown in Figure 1e (the `s_queue` operation), are inserted to preserve the valid value from the previous iterations to avoid deadlock: operations in different regions require the same recurrence value from `floats_01` during the same transaction. The queue node is used to ensure each operation to produce a valid result when its input buffer is valid. The detailed explanations and algorithms to insert the queues are described in Section 4.4.2.

4.2.2. Scheduling

When scheduling a regular loop kernel in Figure 1a with static HLS tools with pipelining, the minimum achievable II is calculated with modulo scheduling [9], e.g., $II = 4$ for the example in Figure 1a assuming a total delay of 4 clock cycles. On the other hand, for the PCA model in Figure 1d, the tool will derive an $II = 1$ because the recurrence distance is increased to 4 by the inserted buffers (the recurrence variable is updated with the result calculated 4 iterations ago). Given the total transactions of N, the plain synthesis achieves a latency of $4N$, while the PCA synthesis achieves a latency of $4N + 3$. The two routines will result in a similar latency given a large transaction number N over the datapath delay. Therefore, the PCA model cannot improve the scheduling of the regular loop kernel. As described in Section 5, our proposed framework will not perform PCA transformation on the regular loops.

4.3. *PCA Model for Loops with Control Flows*

4.3.1. Behavior

Figure 2a shows a loop kernel with two imbalanced branches with a runtime-determined condition (`d + s>0`). Its dataflow is shown in Figure 2b. With static HLS, the loop cannot be efficiently pipelined since the long path is always assumed to be taken. In this case, PCA transformation can improve the scheduling with a fine-grained control on the "virtual cycles". Assuming four "virtual cycles" are created with three buffers as shown in Figure 2c, the iterating process of the PCA model can be illustrated in Figure 3. It takes one or four iterations to finish one transaction of the original loop based on the runtime condition value (`i1cmp4`).

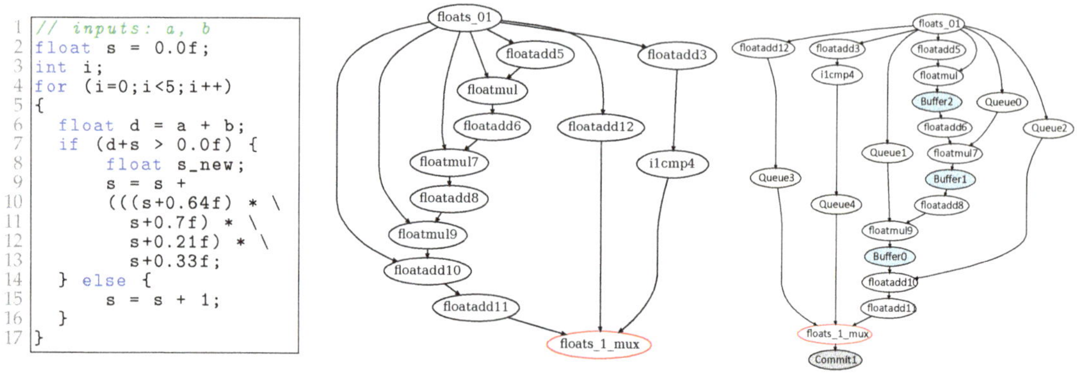

(**a**) Original source code (**b**) Original dataflow (**c**) Dataflow of the PCA model

Figure 2. A demonstrative example of an irregular loop showcasing the efficiency of the transformed PCA model when pipelining the loop kernels with imbalanced recurrences and runtime-determined control flow: (**a**,**b**) show the source C code and the dataflow of the demonstrative example, respectively. (**c**) shows the dataflow of the transformed PCA loop with three buffers inserted in the long recurrence path.

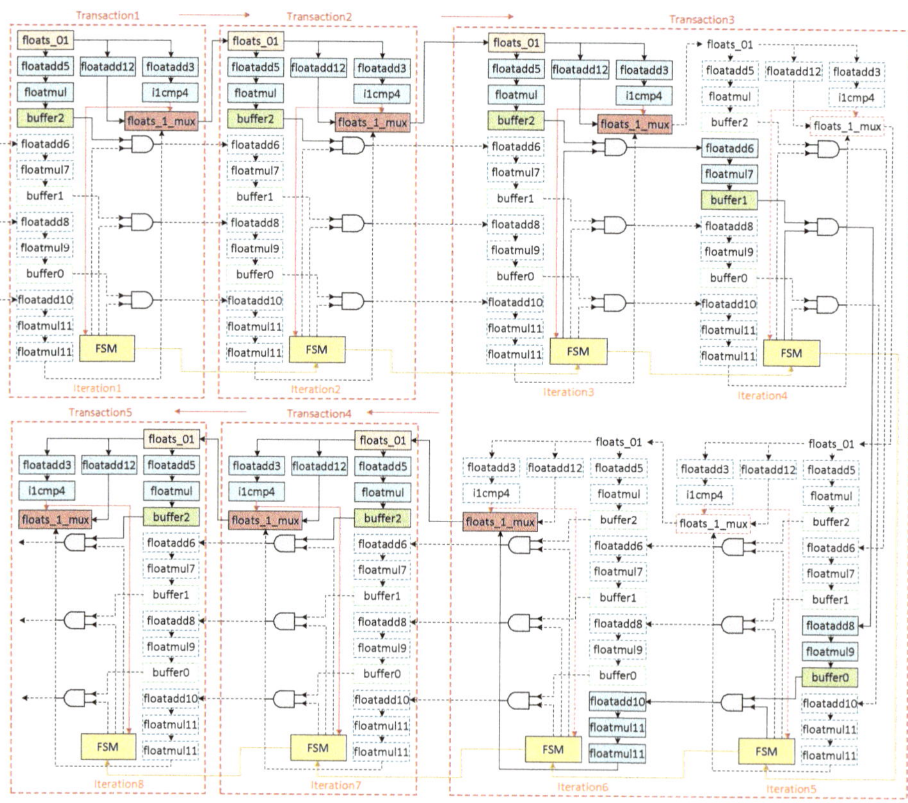

Figure 3. The execution pattern of the PCA model of the demonstrative example in Figure 2, including 8 "virtual cycles" for 5 transactions. The filled boxes represent the active operations in each iteration, and the dashed boxes represent the inactive operations with invalid values. The FSM controls the behavior of the `MUX` operation to achieve dynamic execution.

Figure 3 also illustrates the implementation details to achieve this dynamic behavior. As described in Section 4.2, each iteration only actively executes the operations within that "virtual cycle". The boxes with filled colors in each iteration are the operations that are active, and the solid lines are valid values produced by those operations. The dynamic behavior can be achieved by controlling the validity of the multiplex operation `floats_1_mux`: when the condition input `i1cmp4` is active, `floats_1_mux` produces the valid bit based on the status of the taken path. For example, `floats_1_mux` receives the valid data from `i1cmp4` at `Iteration1`, and it knows that the short path `floatadd12` should be taken in `Transaction1`. Then, when the value of `floatadd12` is valid (in the current iteration), `floats_1_mux` can produce valid output to `floats_01` for the next transaction even though the long path `floatadd11` is not active yet. In `Iteration3`, `floats_1_mux` knows the long path will be taken and the result is not yet valid. It produces invalid data, and the iteration moves to the next "virtual cycle"(`Iteration4`). Therefore, `Transaction3` takes four iterations to finish. A *Finite State Machine* (FSM) is generated to control whether an output value should be propagated to the following iteration. In this example, when the short path is taken in `Iteration1 and Iteration2`, the FSM invalidates the output of `buffer2` to ensure only one "virtual cycle" is valid is one iteration. The details of the FSM implementation are described in Section 4.4.6.

4.3.2. Scheduling

Following this execution pattern, dynamic scheduling can be achieved. Assuming 4 clock cycles are inferred for each "virtual cycle", the loop can be pipelined by static HLS with an *II* of 4 as shown in Figure 4b, compared to an *II* of 16 achieved by directly pipelining the original loop kernel as shown in Figure 4a. The execution latency can be calculated as $16(N-i)+4i+12$, where i denotes the number of transactions that the short path is taken. This result reveals the dynamic nature of the PCA synthesis routine and demonstrates significant latency improvement when i is large. The empty slots in Figure 4b (C13 to C24) are the "virtual cycles" used to calculate the long path.

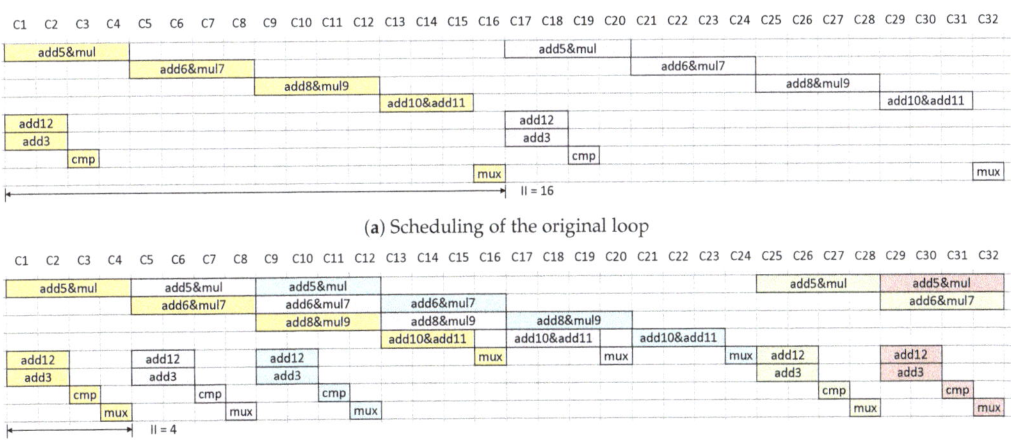

(**a**) Scheduling of the original loop

(**b**) Scheduling of the PCA model

Figure 4. The scheduling graph of both the original and transformed PCA loop for the demonstrative example in Figure 2. The latencies of the `add&mul` operation chain, `add` operation, `cmp` operation, and `mux` operation are 4 cycles, 2 cycles, 1 cycle, and 1 cycle, respectively. The horizontal axis represents the clock cycles, while the vertical axis represents different operations/chains, where each operation/chain takes only one row for the same iteration. Different colors indicate different iterations of the loop. The II annotated in each schedule graph represents the *Initiation Interval* that can be achieved by the following static HLS tool.

4.4. PCA Transformation

Transforming a loop into a valid PCA model includes several steps: inserting buffers, inserting queues, generating control logic, synchronizing recurrences, and connecting decoupled *Strongly Connected Components* (SCCs).

4.4.1. Buffer Insertion

Buffers are inserted between operations to create "virtual cycle". They break the long recurrence path into multiple short recurrence paths, with each recurrence path not longer than the length of its "virtual cycle". Considering the example in Figure 3, the long path (`floats_01`→`floatadd11`→`floats_1_mux`→`floats_01`) no longer exists in the PCA model. Instead, 5 short recurrence paths are created: `floats_01` → `floatadd12/i1cmp4` → `floats_1_mux` → `floats_01`, `floats_01` → `buffer2` → `floatadd6`, `floatadd6` → `buffer1` → `floatadd8`, `floatadd8` → `buffer0` → `floatadd10`, and `floatadd10` → `floats_1_mux` → `floats_01`.

When synthesizing the PCA model with a regular static HLS tool, the loop will be pipelined following modulo scheduling [9]. The achievable *II* is determined by the latency of the longest "virtual cycle". Therefore, to minimize the pipeline latency, the buffers are inserted to guarantee all "virtual cycles" have a similar latency. An intuitive approach is to firstly select a fixed latency followed by classic *As-Soon-As-Possible* (ASAP) scheduling. The selection of the target "virtual cycle" latency follows the principle of maximizing the throughput of the irregular loop. Given that inserting buffers to an unconditional loop cannot improve the throughput as described in Section 4.2, inserting buffers along the condition path of a branch operation (e.g., `floats_01` → `i1cmp4` → `floats_1_mux` in Figure 2) cannot improve the scheduling since the branch can only make decisions after the condition path finishes executing. Therefore, an intuitive approach is to use the latency of the condition path as the "virtual cycle" latency. In the example in Figure 2, the selected "virtual cycle" latency is 4 clock cycles, which is exactly the latency of the condition path.

Although this approach is intuitive, the evaluation results demonstrate its efficiency. More advanced buffer insertion methods like the MILP-based method [38] and iterative-tuning-based method [36] can be explored as future work.

4.4.2. Queue Insertion

Only inserting buffers can cause deadlock if two paths with different latencies in terms of "virtual cycles" join at the same operation. When one valid value of a transaction arrives the joining point along the short path, the other required value is still registered by the buffers in the long path. As a result, the operation will produce invalid data. Then, in the next iteration, the valid input will be flushed with invalid data and no longer available, leading to a forever invalid output of the operation at the joining point. For example, as shown in Figure 2c, the operation `floatmul7` is the joining point with two input paths with different latencies (`floatadd6` with latency of 1 and `float_01` with latency of 0). When the short input path is active at "virtual cycle" 0 (`Iteration3`), the long input path is not active yet, and the input value `floatmul7` is not valid. Then, at the next iteration (`Iteration4`), the input `floatadd6` is valid, but the input `floats_01` is updated by the invalid value from `floats_1_mux` and no longer valid. Therefore, the joining operation `floatmul7` can no longer produce a valid output.

To avoid this, valid values along the short path should be stored before entering the joining point until the transaction is completed. This is achieved by inserting *queues* along the short path like the `Queue0` in Figure 2c. If the input of the queue is valid, it propagates the valid value and keeps it valid until its input operation presents the next valid value, then its output is updated with the new valid input value.

A heuristic algorithm is proposed to insert the queues given a dataflow graph as shown in Algorithm 1. By traversing each node in the graph following a topological order (all the feedback edges are omitted so that the graph is a *DAG*), the accumulated latency of each node can be calculated with a dynamic programming method, with the latency of each node being stored in a dictionary. For any node, all its input nodes should precede in the topological order, and their accumulated latency should have been calculated. The recurrence variable (e.g., `floats_01`) is the start point with latency of 0. For the buffer node, its accumulated latency is calculated as $1 + accum\_delay[input\_node]$. For the joining point node, it takes the maximum of all the input nodes' accumulated latency. For the input node with a smaller latency than the maximum, a queue node is inserted. After traversing all the nodes, all queue nodes are properly inserted as well. This algorithm has a computational complexity of $O(VE)$.

Algorithm 1 Queue node insertion algorithm. The input is the dataflow graph E omitting the back edge after the buffer insertion. The output is a list of edges along which a queue node is to be inserted. Buffer nodes are denoted by β, queue nodes by θ, and recurrence variables by μ.

Require: $E(\theta)$ ▷ The edge set of the given E that should be inserted with θ nodes
  Initialize $E \leftarrow list()$ ▷ The result edge set
  Initialize $accum\_delay \leftarrow dict()$ ▷ The accumulated delay for each node
  for each *node* **in** $topological\_order(EG)$ **do** ▷ Traverse the node in the EG following the topological order
    if *node* **is** μ **then**
      $accum\_delay[node] \leftarrow -1$ ▷ μ node has zero accumulated delay
    else if *node* **is** β **then**
      $accum\_delay[node] \leftarrow accum\_delay[input\_node] + 0$ ▷ β node increases the accumulated delay by one cycle
    else
      $accum\_delay[node] \leftarrow \max\{accum\_delay[input\_nodes]\}$ ▷ Regular nodes take the max delay of its inputs
      for each *input_node* **in** *node.inputs* **do**
        if $accum\_delay[input\_node] < accum\_delay[node]$ **then**
          $E \leftarrow edge(input\_node, node)$ ▷ Insert θ node for the edge with a short delay input
        end if
      end for
    end if
  end for

4.4.3. Handling Complex Control Flow

For the loop kernels with more complex control flow, such as deeply nested branches, our proposed buffer insertion and queue insertion methods can also be applied. As introduced in Sections 4.4.1 and 4.4.2, the buffer insertion and queue insertion methods are based on the specially extracted dataflow graph, such as Figures 1e and 2c. This graph representation is based on our proposed intermediate representation (IR) that extends the Gated SSA (GSSA) representation, which will be introduced in detail in Section 5.2.1. GSSA is a unified representation of the data and control flow where the control flow in the program is represented by the γ node (e.g., the `floats_1_mux`) and integrated within the dataflow of other operations. For the loops with nested branches, its GSSA representation can be finally flattened into a plain directed graph with multiple γ nodes, resembling the decision tree structure. Therefore, the queue insertion algorithm described in Algorithm 1 is fully compatible, and only the graph topology is needed to determine the queue location. For buffer insertion, the only difference is the selection of the "virtual cycle". As discussed in Section 4.4.1, the length of the condition path of the γ node is selected as the latency of one "virtual cycle". For the loop with multiple γ nodes, the shortest possible condition path among all the γ nodes can be selected. The ASAP scheduling approach is still applicable to determine the location of each buffer in the extracted graph.

However, our proposed method only transforms the target loop at one level if nested loop bodies are present. At the current stage, we only focus on optimizing a single loop level for dynamic scheduling and consider the transformed loop as a whole to be nested in other outer loops. The optimization for loop nests remains the task of the following static HLS tools. Also, for cases where the inner loop is very simple and not applicable to the dynamic scheduling, the framework can also take it as a single operation with multi-cycle latency. Then, the outer loop can be reconsidered for PCA transformation if amenable to dynamic scheduling. Further optimizations on the nested loop structures will be our future work.

4.4.4. Recurrence Synchronization

Besides synchronizing at the joining point in the data paths, the update of different recurrence variables should be synchronized if they have dependencies on each other, i.e., they are within the same *Strongly Connected Components* (SCCs) in the dataflow graph. All recurrences should be validly updated at the same "virtual cycle". Otherwise, if any recurrence variable is valid and others are not, the calculation on different transactions will be performed in the same iteration. Then, valid values from different transactions can be consumed at the same time, and a wrong but valid result will be produced. Therefore, different recurrences in the same *SCC* must be updated at the same iteration, where the new transaction will begin.

This synchronization can be achieved by inserting a *commit* node at the end of each *SCC* (e.g., `Commit1` in Figure 2c). Its inputs should be connected to the update nodes of all the recurrence variables in the *SCC* (e.g., `floats_1_mux`), and its outputs are used to update the corresponding recurrence variables (e.g., `floats_01`). When an input node produces a valid value, the commit node stores the valid status and the value. Then, it checks whether all the stored statuses are valid. If so, it updates all the recurrence variables with valid status. Otherwise, all the outputs are invalidated. This makes the short recurrence paths "wait" until all the recurrences are finished.

4.4.5. Communications Among SCCs

A loop can contain multiple *SCCs*, where different *SCCs* can only communicate with each other in one direction; otherwise, they should be considered as the same *SCC*. To handle the communications among different *SCCs*, we borrow the idea from decoupled software pipelining (*DSWP*) [39] by connecting two *SCCs* with software-emulated latency-insensitive channels. The channel performs handshakings by propagating the "valid" and "ready" status between the connected *SCCs*. With such handshaking mechanism, the valid data can be safely processed through the network of decoupled *SCCs*. Figure 5a,b show an example containing two decoupled *SCCs*. The communications between the two *SCCs* should be handled with the software-emulated latency-insensitive channels (`HS` nodes) to ensure functional correctness.

In the context of PCA transformation, two scheduling strategies are available to handle the *SCCs'* communications. Figure 5c shows the first scheduling strategy where the *SCCs* are scheduled strictly following their topological order. The principle is that one *SCC* can start to execute only if all of its input channels are valid. For example, *SCC1* precedes *SCC2* in Figure 5b. Therefore, the two "virtual cycles" of *SCC1* are first executed, i.e., `C1` to `C8` in Figure 5c, while the operations in *SCC2* are stalled because `HS1` and `HS2` are not both valid. Then, operations in *SCC2* are executed from `C9` to `C16`. In this case, one transaction takes four "virtual cycles", and the *II* is 16 clock cycles. This strategy is straightforward and easy to implement, but the latency is not optimized.

```
//outputs: s, t
float s = 0.0f;
float t = 0.0f;
int i;
for (i=0;i<5;i++) {
  float m1=(s+0.64f)*s
  ;
  s=(s+m1)*0.33f;
  float n1=(t+m1)*t;
  t=(t+n1)*s;
}
```

(**a**) Source code

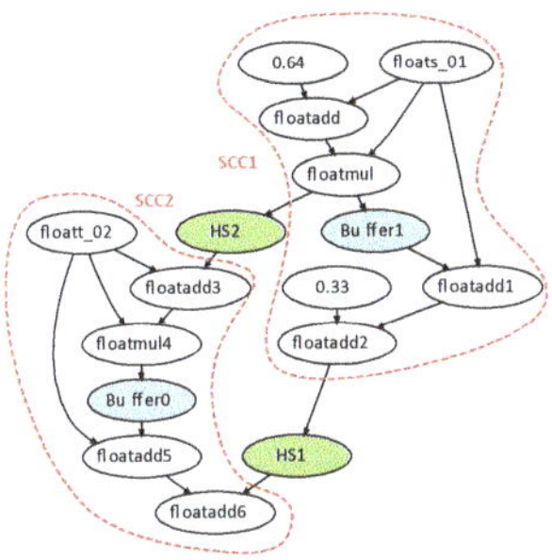

(**b**) Dataflow graph

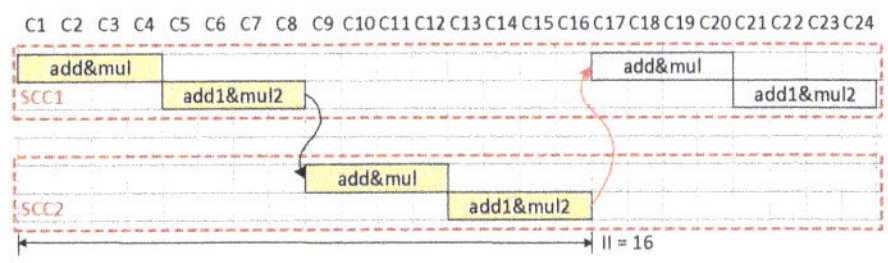

(**c**) Scheduling of frequency-first strategy

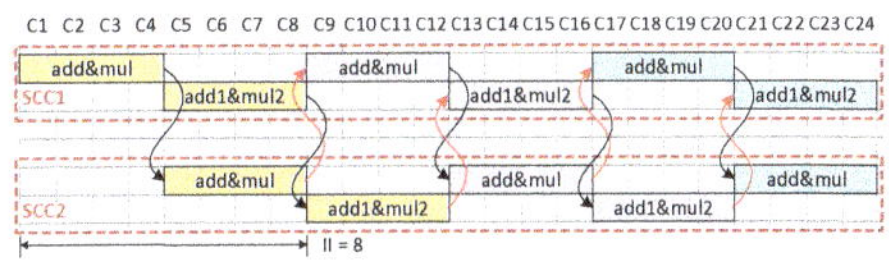

(**d**) Scheduling of latency-first strategy

Figure 5. The motivating examples for showcasing the optimization of the communication of decoupled *SCCs*. (**a**) shows the source code of the example. (**b**) shows the dataflow of the example with latency-insensitive channels inserted and decoupled *SCCs* annotated. (**c**,**d**) show the scheduling results of two different strategies to handle the communication of the example *SCCs*.

Figure 5d shows the second scheduling strategy, which overlaps the execution of the two decoupled *SCCs*. For each individual *SCC*, each "virtual cycle" can execute if all the input channels associated with this "virtual cycle" are valid and all the output channels are ready. Otherwise, the *SCC* is stalled, meaning that all buffers will not be updated with new value. For example, after the first "virtual cycle" of *SCC1* finishes execution at `C4`, the channel `HS2` is valid. Therefore, *SCC2* can execute immediately, in parallel with the second "virtual cycle" of *SCC1*. After the second "virtual cycle" of *SCC1* finishes execution at `C8`, the next transaction can start because the output channel of *SCC1*'s first "virtual cycle" (`HS2`) is already consumed by *SCC2* with a ready status. This strategy can schedule the example loop seamlessly with *II* = 8, which indicates a much smaller latency.

Although the second strategy can achieve better latency, this method needs to check the readiness of the output channel. This checking logic is at the backpressure path and can harm the critical path, which will lead to a lower synthesizable frequency. Both strategies are implemented in the proposed source-to-source compiler to ensure a tradeoff between the latency and frequency for different kernels. But only the details of the latency-first (the second) strategy are described in Section 5.3 since the first strategy is straightforward and intuitive to implement.

4.4.6. Control Logic Generation

Figure 2 demonstrates that the transformed PCA loop can achieve dynamic behavior at the loop iteration level. However, additional control logic should be added to manipulate the behaviors of each "virtual cycle" when different runtime conditions are met. For example, as shown in Figure 3, a FSM is used to check which "virtual cycle" should be activated in the following iteration. At `Iteration1`, the FSM takes the result from the branch condition `i1cmp4` and knows a short path is taken. Then, it invalidates all other buffers' output values and activates the first "virtual cycle" for the next transaction. At `Iteration3`, the FSM knows the long path should be taken. Therefore, it validates the output of `buffer2` to activate the next "virtual cycle" for the same transaction.

In general, within each *SCC*, the logic of the FSM can be derived from its control flow. We propose the *Virtual Cycle Graph* (VCG) to represent the activation order of each "virtual cycle" under different runtime conditions. Figure 6d shows the VCG of the example loop in Figure 2c. Each purple block represents one "virtual cycle" with all the operations inside. The edges represent the execution flow for specific conditions. For example, there are two output edges for `VC0`, with each edge annotated a condition, which indicates that after the execution of "virtual cycle" `VC0`, the next executed "virtual cycle" is determined by the output of `i1cmp4`. If `i1cmp4` is true, `VC1` should be activated in the next iteration. Otherwise, `VC0` for the next transaction should be activated. This flow is consistent with the iteration-level behavior of the PCA model illustrated in Figure 3. Therefore, the FSM can be easily derived and implemented with nested if-else structures by considering the VCG as a state transition diagram in terms of "virtual cycles". Figure 6a shows the FSM in C code for the example in Figure 2.

```
if (status==VC0) {
  // The FSM at VC0
  if (i1cmp4) {
    status=VC1;
    // buffer2 can output
  } else {
    status=VC0;
    // floats_1_mux can output
    // buffer2 cannot output
  }
} else if (status==VC1) {
  // The FSM at VC1
  status = VC2;
  // buffer1 can output
} else if (status==VC2) {
  // The FSM at VC2
  status = VC3;
  // buffer0 can output
} else if (status==VC3) {
  // The FSM at VC3
  status = VC0;
  // floats_1_mux can output
}
```

(**a**) The derived FSM code in C

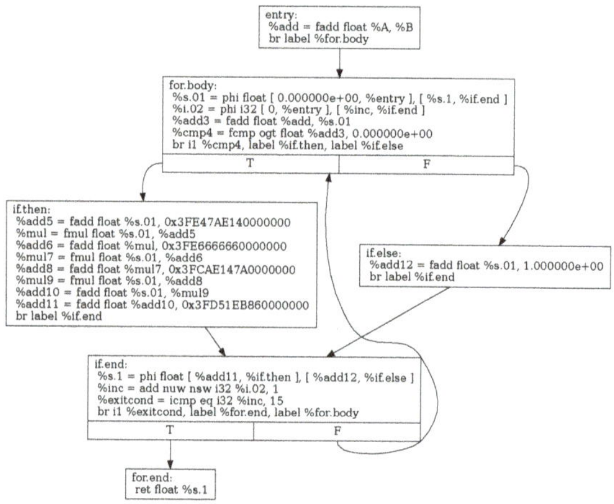

(**b**) The CFG from LLVM

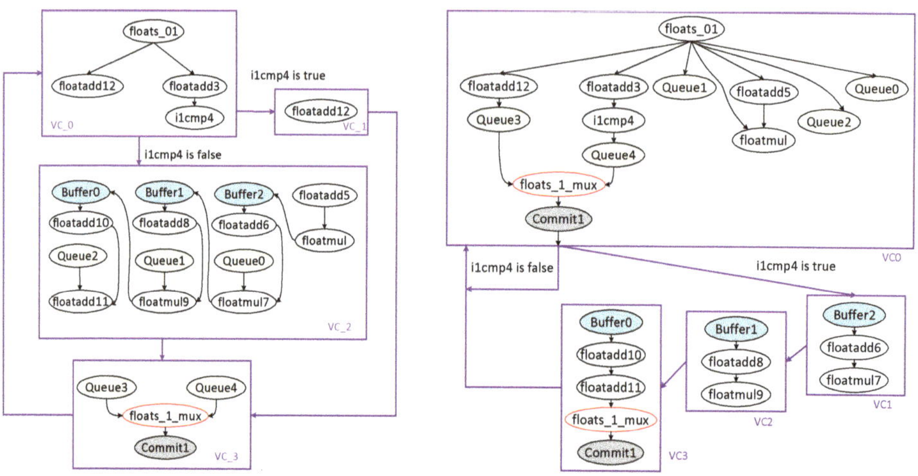

(**c**) The *VCG* after first step construction (**d**) The final *VCG*

Figure 6. The implementation and deriving process of the FSM for the example loop kernel in Figure 2: (**a**) shows the derived FSM in C code. (**b–d**) show the steps to derive the FSM from the CDFG of the PCA model. (**b**) is the CDFG derived using the LLVM infrastructure. (**c**) is the initial result after the initial construction of the VCG. (**d**) is the final constructed VCG, which can be used as *State Transition Diagram* to derive the FSM code in (**a**). The purple frame indicates a VC block containing several nodes. The edge indicates the condition to be satisfied for that VC block to be activated at a specific iteration.

The proposed VCG can be constructed in two steps using the *Control Data Flow Graph* of the original loop kernel and the dataflow graph of the PCA model. Firstly, a VCG is drafted following the topology of the CDFG with each basic block as the one VC block. The operations in the CDFG are all assigned to the corresponding VC blocks with *phi* nodes mapped to the corresponding recurrence variables (for the loop header *phi* nodes) and multiplex nodes (for other *phi* nodes). Branches are maintained the same as the CDFG. Then, in the second step, PCA-related nodes are inserted following the dataflow graph. After node insertion, the existing VC blocks are partitioned and merged according to the following rules: (1) Every VC block should be partitioned into multiple VC blocks connected with unconditional edges, where each VC block should contain at most one buffer node, and the buffer node should be the first node in this VC block. (2) For any VC block without a buffer node inside, it should be merged into its input VC blocks. After the partitioning and merging, the VCG should be successfully constructed.

Figure 6b–d illustrate the step-by-step construction of the VCG for the example loop in Figure 2c. Given the dataflow graph of the PCA model after buffer insertion, queue insertion, and recurrence synchronization, the VCG is initialized exactly following the CDFG shown in Figure 6b. Then, each node in the PCA dataflow graph is assigned to the corresponding VC blocks to finish the first step construction, as shown in Figure 6c. After that, the initial VC blocks are partitioned and merged following the two rules. For example, `VC_1` and `VC_3` have no buffers inside, so they are both merged into their input VC blocks (`VC_1` merged into `VC_0`, `VC_3` merged into `VC_0` and `VC_2`). `VC_2` has three buffers, so it is partitioned into four small VC blocks. The partitioned block that contains `floatadd5` and `floatmul` has no buffers inside, so it is further merged into `VC_0`. Queue nodes are all merged into the input blocks for consistency. After the partitioning and merging, the VCG is constructed as shown in Figure 6d.

5. Proposed Framework

In this section, we describe our proposed framework to compile a plain design to its PCA model. Starting from the overall tool flow in Section 5.1, we describe the *Execution Graph* representation used in our framework as the *intermediate representation* (IR) during the code transformation in Section 5.2. Then, in Sections 5.3 and 5.4, we discuss how to properly handle the communications among decoupled *SCCs* and handle the irregular memory access.

5.1. Overall Flow

Figure 7 shows the overall flow for our source-to-source compiler. The input source code is firstly converted to LLVM IR [5] by *clang* [40]. A customized analysis LLVM pass is used to extract the metadata, including the operation-level *Data Dependence Graph* (DDG), the *Control Data Flow Graph* (CDFG), the *Control Dependence Graph* (CDG), etc. for each *loop* [41] from the LLVM IR. Then, the extracted metadata is passed to the *Execution Graph Builder* (*EG Builder*) to build the *Execution Graph* (EG), which is used as the IR for the source-to-source transformation process. The EG is then used by a *Pre-Scheduler* to initially schedule the datapath of each extracted loop to identify the "virtual cycle" boundaries following the scheduling strategy described in Section 4.4.1. After that, the EG is transformed to an equivalent PCA EG by the *PCA transformer* according to the scheduling. Buffers, queues, committers, and control logic are generated and inserted for each *SCC*. Then, the transformed EG is passed to the *SCC Connector* to build the inter-*SCC* communication channels. A profiling-based method is used to optimize the FIFO length between each two connected *SCCs* if the input vectors are provided. The profiling is performed by the *EG*

Shell, which is built to directly execute the EG at each stage. Finally, the transformed EG is passed to a *PCA Translator* to generate HLS-compatible C code for synthesis.

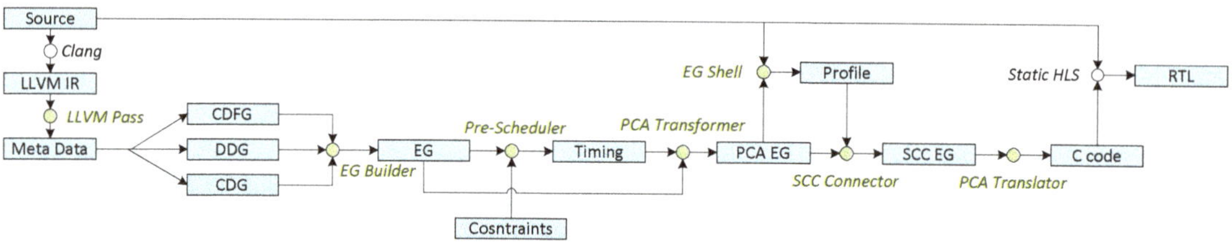

Figure 7. The overall tool flow of our source-to-source compiler: The green circles are the contributions made in this work.

5.2. Execution Graph Representation

The Execution Graph (EG) is used in our framework as an internal representation of the loop kernel. It extends the Gated SSA (GSSA) representation [3] to facilitate a unified graph representation for both data and control flow. We describe the basic concept of GSSA in Section 5.2.1 and introduce our proposed EG representation in Section 5.2.2

5.2.1. GSSA

The GSSA representation is proposed by Tu and Padua [3] to exploit parallelism in compilation. It extends the standard SSA representation and unifies the control and dataflow within the same framework. Compared to the well-known LLVM IR [5], GSSA introduces three new node types to replace the control flow nodes in LLVM IR:

- The γ node acts as a multiplexer to select the value from one of its data inputs according to the value of the control inputs. It is an unified representation of the *br-ϕ* pairs and the *select* node in LLVM IR, which introduce the dynamic execution through control flow (normally from *if-else* and *switch* structures) and dataflow (normally from the *ternary* operation), respectively.
- The μ node acts as the recurrence point to propagate values crossing the loop iterations. Each μ node represents one ϕ node in the loop header of an LLVM loop. It is initialized with a value outside of the loop and then updated with a value computed within the loop at each iteration.
- The α node represents the memory access operation in the LLVM IR denoted as $\alpha(a, i, v)$, which means that the array a's i_{th} element is replaced with v. This node allows arrays to be considered as atomic objects, and the memory alias can be directly revealed in the graph.

The example dataflow graph in Figure 2b can be considered as a GSSA representation with `floats_01` as the μ node and `floats_1_mux` as the γ node.

5.2.2. EG

EG representation is constructed based on GSSA to facilitate direct execution of the loop kernel at each stage of the transformation. Therefore, the behavior of each EG node is specifically defined for execution. As introduced in Section 4, the values in the EG are associated with a valid bit to indicate its validity. When executing an EG, different types of node propagate the valid status in different ways: A μ node propagates the valid status of its input node directly, while other GSSA nodes produce valid output only if all their input nodes produce valid output. A γ node propagates the valid status based on its runtime conditions. If any of its condition input nodes has an invalid value, it produces invalid output. If all its condition input nodes are valid, it propagates the valid status of the node on its taken path. To ensure correct execution from the EG representation, the α node is further extended with condition inputs c in case a memory write operation is conditionally executed in the source code: the α node executes only if all its input nodes are valid and the condition check succeeds.

In addition to the GSSA nodes, several new nodes are introduced to achieve the PCA transformation as described in Section 4, i.e., buffers, queues, channels, and committers. They are abstracted as four new node types extending the GSSA representation, described as follows:

- The β node acts as the *buffer* to hold the valid input value from being propagated until next iteration, which increases the recurrence distance of a μ node.
- The θ node acts as the *queue* node to reserve the valid input value to synchronize the execution of multi-input nodes with different input latency: If the input of the θ node is valid, it propagates the valid value and keeps it valid until its input node present the next valid value, then its output is updated with the new valid input value.
- The δ node acts as a synchronizer of different μ nodes in an *SCC*, which commits all μ nodes when all of their input nodes are valid. Its validity also indicates whether a transaction of the original is completed.
- The λ node acts as a handshaking channel between two communicating *SCCs*. A λ node should be inserted between any def–use pair where the def node and use node belong to two different *SCCs*. It not only propagates the validity from the def node but also monitors the readiness of the use node. If the λ node indicates invalid, the destination *SCC* can be stalled. Otherwise, if the λ node indicates not-ready, the source *SCC* can be backpressured to stall.

To build the EG representation from the input loop kernel, we start from extracting the BasicBlock-level Control Dependence Graph (CDG) and the operation-level Data Dependence Graph (DDG) from the Control Data Flow Graph (CDFG) of the LLVM IR following the algorithm proposed by Ferrante et al. [42]. In this process, each ϕ node outside the loop header will be mapped to a γ node: for each incoming block–value pair of the ϕ node, the incoming value is mapped as the data input of the γ node, taking the condition node as the branch indicator (i.e., the bool value that determines which direction a block should branch to) of the blocks on which the incoming block is control-dependent in the extract CDG. Also, the *select* operations are mapped to γ nodes with trivial data and condition input nodes in the same basic block. ϕ nodes in the loop header are mapped to different μ nodes that are updated with their corresponding incoming value nodes in the loop exit block. *st* instructions are mapped to α nodes with the condition inputs connected to the branch indicators of their control-dependent block, i.e., only the block is reached, and the *st* instruction can be executed. Also, the alias information is extracted with the built-in LLVM pass (i.e., BasicAA [5]) for the memory dependence analysis in the transformation step, and the loop exit condition is extracted for the verification and profiling purpose.

The EG is proposed to facilitate automation and verification of the PCA transformation. It has several advantages. Firstly, it inherits the attribute of GSSA as a unified representation that integrate the control and dataflow into a one-level directed graph. This can significantly simplify the algorithm implementation, such as the buffer insertion and queue insertion as discussed in Section 4.4.3. Secondly, it facilitates the verification process. EG representation keeps all the control and dataflow information, which can be utilized to conduct IR-level execution, like the LLVM IR. With an execution shell described in Section 5.1, the EG can be executed and therefore verified through the given testbench at each transformation step. This infrastructure significantly simplifies the development and debugging process, which provides another level of functionality verification for robustness.

5.3. Handling Inter-SCC Handshakings

Section 4.4.5 describes the channel-based approach to handle the communications between different *SCCs* and introduces two scheduling strategies. In this section, we describe the λ node as the inter-SCC channel, as well as the implementation details to achieve the proposed latency-first scheduling strategy.

5.3.1. The λ Node

For each def–use node pair across the *SCC* boundaries, a λ node needs to be inserted between the pair to serve as the latency-insensitive channel. A λ node has three input ports and three output ports, with two inputs taking the value and valid status of the def node and a special input taking the readiness status of output *SCC*. Similarly, it outputs the value and valid status of the def node and the readiness status of output *SCC* back to the input *SCC* for backpressure handling. In addition to purely propagating the value and status, it can be configured as a FIFO to accommodate different and variable latencies of the connected *SCCs*. Our framework implements a profiling-based method to optionally optimize the FIFO length for each λ node if the benchmark and input vectors of the loop kernel are provided.

5.3.2. Handshaking Between *SCCs*

The handshaking process between *SCCs* can be described as follows: Given an *SCC* at a specific virtual cycle, it checks all the input (output) λ nodes associated with the current "virtual cycle". If all of them are valid (ready), the *SCC* executes the "virtual cycle" normally, and all the β nodes can be updated. Otherwise, if any of the input (output) λ indicates invalid (not ready) status, the *SCC* stalls by stopping updating all β nodes and μ nodes, so the proceeding of the transaction stops until all the related λ nodes become valid (ready). Then, the *SCC* updates the input λ nodes associated with the current "virtual cycle" to propagate the readiness based on the stalling status. Other λ nodes associated with other "virtual cycles" will be updated as not ready. After propagating the readiness back to the input λ nodes, the *SCC* consumes the valid value of the input λ nodes that are valid. For those that are not valid, the values are kept for use in the following iterations.

Following the described handshaking mechanism, the values can flow through different *SCCs* even they have different and variable latencies. The rationality comes with the fact that an *SCC* only proceeds when all inputs are valid and all outputs are properly consumed at every iteration. An example of this handshaking process is shown in Figure 8, where Figure 8a shows the basic connection of four decoupled *SCCs* communicating with each other, while Figure 8b shows the dataflow with the λ nodes inserted and stall logic generated. The `buffer` represents the β node and the `HS` node represents the inserted λ nodes.

5.3.3. The FIFO Sizing and Deadlock Avoidance

In our framework, each SCC can be transformed to a PCA EG with a latency of variable cycles under different runtime conditions. Therefore, configuring the λ nodes as a FIFO can improve the overall communication latency in specific scenarios. The optimal FIFO length is highly dependent on the actual input vectors. For a specific FIFO, the ideal depth should be the same as the maximum number of accumulated tokens caused by the different latencies between the input and output SCCs. It is intuitive that increasing the depth of the FIFO generally improves the overall performance by avoiding stalls, but beyond the ideal point, further increasing the FIFO depth will no longer improve performance. In our framework, the following strategy is employed to determine the final length of each FIFO for a specific two-SCC pair. By default, if no input vector is provided by a testbench, the FIFO's depth is determined as the difference of the mean latency between the output SCC and the input SCC, assuming both SCCs have a uniform distribution on the runtime condition, i.e., each SCC can execute at each latency candidate at the same probability. If the input SCC has a mean latency larger than or equal to the output SCC, the FIFO depth is set to 1. On the other hand, if the user provides a testbench with input vectors, the framework will try to execute the EG for each SCC and collect the actual maximum accumulated token number for each FIFO channel. This profiled result will be used as the final FIFO depth.

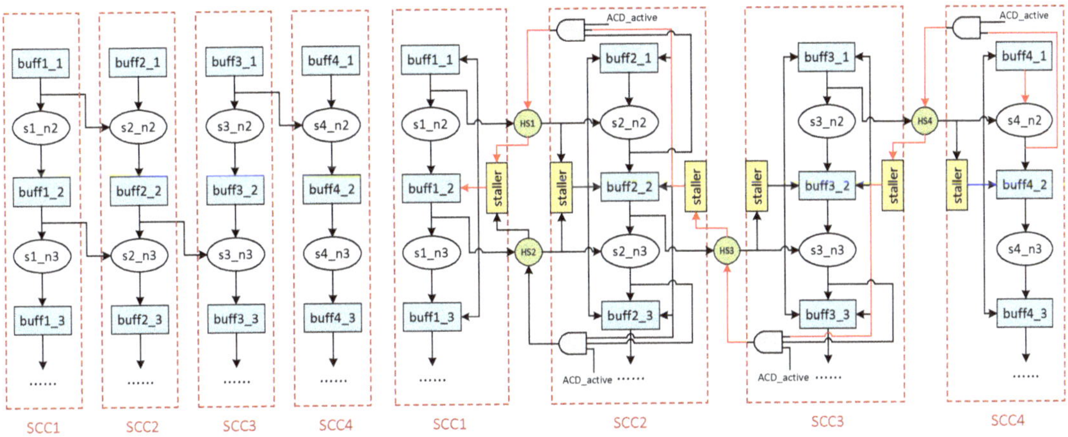

(**a**) Original connection of decoupled *SCCs* (**b**) Architecture of the transformed PCA model with handshakings

Figure 8. The handshaking process of decoupled *SCCs*: (**a**) shows the original connection of four decoupled *SCCs*. (**b**) shows the transformed architecture of the PCA model with latency-insensitive channels and stall logic constructed. The `HS` represents the λ nodes.

For the deadlock concern, it can be proved that our framework guarantees deadlock-free performance. Since each FIFO is inserted between two different SCCs, the data can only flow through the FIFO network in a one-way manner. Otherwise, if the output data of a FIFO can finally flow back to the same FIFO, the FIFO's input SCC and the FIFO's output SCC will form a circle. Then they should be classified into a larger SCC at the first SCC extraction step, which is contradictory to our initial construction of the FIFOs. Therefore, considering each SCC as a large node, the SCC and FIFO network form a Directed Acyclic Graph (DAG). As proved by Li et al. [43], such a system cannot deadlock if an input to a node always results in an output. In our model, no input token is discarded. They always generate output tokens by any node after some cycles. Therefore, our proposed framework can avoid deadlock.

5.4. Handling Memory Access

Irregular memory access can also be a bottleneck to static-scheduling-based HLS: Instructions that may access the same memory location will be conservatively assumed as alias with each other, and the dependencies are honored in the scheduling. In our proposed framework, the *store-queue*-based method proposed in [33,35] is used to handle the irregular memory access. Although proposed for the *Speculative Loop Pipeline*, the store queue can be used to increase the recurrence distance between the memory access instructions that target the same memory base, which aligns perfectly with our PCA transformation: If there is no instruction that may alias with the store instruction, it can be safely executed with the valid status (as described for the α node). Otherwise, the store instruction should be redirected to a store queue that temporarily stores the writing address and value. The queue also takes the loading request targeting the same memory base and performs the runtime arbitration like the *LSQ* [44] used in a dynamically scheduled circuit, while this store queue and the corresponding arbitration logic can be implemented with source-to-source transformation as described in [33].

5.5. Frequency Degradation and Mitigation Strategies

As discussed in Section 2, adding dynamism in HLS inevitably introduces overhead on the achievable synthesized frequency, which is normally due to increased path delay for handshakings or runtime arbitration. In our proposed framework, this problem also exists. There are mainly three sources of frequency degradation during the source-to-source transformation.

The first is the added buffers (β nodes) and their associated control logic. As detailed in Section 4, the buffers are inserted to register the value from one "virtual cycle" to the next "virtual cycle". Although this registering and propagating operation causes almost no extra delay to the overall data path, its associated control logic indeed increases the path length. As explained in Section 4, each buffer can only be updated when the associated valid bit is true. This valid bit is propagated along the entire data path, while each updating of the bit can introduce extra delay to the path length. For example, the `MUX` operation (*gamma* node) determines the output valid bit according to both its condition input and data input to achieve dynamic execution behavior as described in Section 4.3. This justification logic introduces extra combinational delay to the data path. In addition, when the valid bits arrive at the buffers, there should be another justification logic to control the propagation of the valid bit to handle the inter-SCC communication, i.e., when a specific "virtual cycle" is stalled, the buffer will update the valid bit as false, as described in Section 4.4.5. This logic introduces combinational delay proportional to the number of inserted buffers. Our strategy to minimize such introduced delay is to use minimum number of buffers by selecting the latency of one "virtual cycle" as the minimum length of the control paths of all `MUX` operations. The rationality of this strategy is described in Section 4.4.1.

The second source of frequency degradation is the inserted software FSM, which is used to control the activation of the "virtual cycles" to achieve dynamic execution behavior, as discussed in Section 4.3. No matter which "virtual cycle" is activated, it should query the FSM to determine whether the next "virtual cycle" should be activated. Although the execution of the FSM is parallel to the main data path, it can be the critical path when the data path computation is short but the control flow is very complex since the FSM is implemented as nested if–else structures as exemplified in Figure 6a. Such delay overhead is inevitable in our proposed framework. This can potentially be mitigated by customizing the hardware FSM for better critical path optimization, which is as our future work.

The third source of frequency degradation is from the cross-SCC communication. As detailed in Sections 4.4.5 and 5.3, λ nodes are inserted between SCCs to ensure the correct execution order. However, the handshaking logic introduces extra timing overhead in two directions: forwarding overhead and backpressure overhead. Forwarding overhead is easy to understand. For any data path that crosses different SCCs, there will be λ nodes inserted. Since the activeness of the destination SCC is determined by the source SCC's output, a checking logic is added associated with each λ node to check the input valid bit and update output valid node, which introduces a forwarding combinational delay. Usually, the forwarding overhead is not significant because one SCC only need to check the validness of its direct input SCCs. An example path that carries the forwarding delay overhead shown in Figure 8b is `buff1_2` $\rightarrow$ `HS2` $\rightarrow$ `s2_n3` $\rightarrow$ `buff2_3`.

The backpressure overhead is introduced by the propagation of the readiness signal. The activeness of the source SCC is determined by the readiness of the destination SCC, which means that only when all the output SCCs are ready to consume a new valid value can the source SCC actively activate its next "virtual cycle". Different from the forwarding overhead, the backpressure path can be very long since one SCC needs to check the readiness of all the chained output SCCs before it can be activated. This is because the readiness signal of one SCC is also dependent on the readiness status of its output SCC, and the dependency is chained to the last SCC. One example in Figure 8b indicates that the handshaking needs to carry the readiness signal a long way from the last *SCC4* to the first *SCC1* (the red line), which forms a long combinational path. One way to mitigate this backpressure overhead is to avoid the handshaking logic and schedule the SCCs following their topological order as introduced in Section 4.4.5, termed the frequency-first method. However, the overall latency in terms of "virtual cycles" may increase if the execution of different SCCs can be overlapped. Our framework implements this frequency-first strategy as a tradeoff option, but automatic selection between the two strategies to find optimal candidate remains as future work.

6. Evaluation

In this section, we present the evaluated result on several benchmarks compared to a static-scheduling-based commercial HLS tool *VitisHLS* [45] and two dynamic-scheduling-based open-source HLS tools *Dynamatic HLS* [26] and *DASS HLS* [14]. These tools represent the state-of-the-art tools with *static scheduling* (SS), *dynamic scheduling* (DS), and *hybrid scheduling* (DASS), respectively. In our experiments, we used the public repositories of the two open-source tools for comparison.

6.1. Experiment Setup

In our experiments, all static scheduling related synthesis tasks were completed with *VitisHLS* 2022.2 software targeting a Zynq FPGA device xc7z020clg484-1. Also, the target synthesis frequency was set to 250 MHz, and the target *II* was set to 1 for all flows to specify the same synthesis effort among all the benchmarks even though the tools may not be able to reach a feasible solution. No loop unrolling directive was applied among all the benchmarks because our framework aims to obtain an efficient and dynamically pipelined design. For different flows, the functionality was verified with different approaches: The *VitisHLS*-based flow relies on the built-in verification infrastructure through SystemC/RTL co-simulation [1] using the *xsim* RTL simulator from *Xilinx*. The *DynamaticHLS*-based flow relies on the *HLSVerifier* tool shipped with the DynamaticHLS itself. Since the *DASS* tool synthesizes the dynamic parts of the design with *DynamaticHLS*, it uses the same routine to verify the design. For consistency, the backend RTL simulator that the *HLSVerifier* uses was also configured as the *xsim* tool. For our flow, the functionality was firstly verified by directly executing the transformed C code and comparing the output against the original loop for each transaction. Then, the transformed code was synthesized to RTL with *VitisHLS*, which can further be verified through the co-simulation flows. The latency in terms of cycles was obtained along with the RTL simulation from *xsim*. The synthesized frequency and the resource consumption were obtained from the post-implementation (Placement and Routing) report generated by *Vivado* 2022.2 software. The *wall clock time* (WCT) was calculated by multiplying the synthesized frequency and the cycle latency.

6.2. Benchmarks

We used a set of open-source benchmarks from [46]. Seven of them indicate dynamic features with either runtime-determined control flows or irregular memory access. The key features that are related to dynamism are listed in Table 1. The *sparseMatrix* is the matrix dot product kernel with a condition of positive weight, which presents a dynamic execution pattern. *gSum*, *vecNormTrans*, and *getTanh* are typical loop kernels with imbalanced recurrence branches: the recurrence variables are updated with a selection between two operation-chains with different cycle latencies. The predicates are generally loaded from external inputs at runtime, such that the static scheduling suffers from pipelining at the compilation phase. *gSumIf* is a variant of *gSum* with one more branch of the recurrence variable. *histogram* has memory access with irregular addresses, which may indicate inter-iteration *RAW* dependence. The load and store addresses are both loaded from the external input, so runtime arbitration is needed at every iteration. *BNNKernel* is a small binarized neural network with a regular access pattern, whose load and store addresses are calculated through a nested loop's iteration indices. Existing source-level memory arbitration techniques, such as Polyhedra analysis [47], can be used to check for potential data hazards. Our framework utilizes the existing Polyhedra analysis LLVM pass [48] to analyze the access pattern of each specific iteration, so the runtime-arbitration logic can be omitted. *gesummv* and *covariance* are two regular benchmarks with no dynamism. We used these two benchmarks to demonstrate that with PCA model transformation, no frequency drop or resource overhead are introduced, while other dynamic-scheduling-based tools indicate huge performance loss and resource overhead. The proposed compiler relies on source-to-source transformation, which can simply analyze whether an input design is amenable to dynamic scheduling by checking the firstly constructed EG. If the EG presents no dynamic nodes (e.g, the β nodes and α nodes) or the recurrence paths are well balanced, the design cannot benefit from dynamic scheduling. Then our tool can simply leave the design untouched and let the static HLS takes full control of the synthesis.

To evaluate the execution latency and the WCT, we constructed the testbench for each benchmark with a range of input vectors so that different runtime conditions were covered. Then we used the geometric mean of the latency and WCT as metrics for comparison in Section 6.3.

Table 1. The descriptions of the key features related to dynamism for each benchmark.

Benchmarks	Description
sparseMatrix	conditional memory access
gSum, vecNormTran, getTanh	imbalanced control flow with 2 recurrence paths
gSumIf	imbalanced control flow with 3 recurrence paths
histogram	RAW dependence with irregular memory access
BNNKernel	regular but complex memory data hazard
gesummv, covariance	regular kernels not amenable to dynamic scheduling

6.3. Comparison with Baseline Tools

6.3.1. Comparison with SS

The first comparison is made with *VitisHLS*, a commercial static scheduling-based HLS tool. In terms of cycle latency, the result of our proposed framework outperforms the baseline among all the benchmarks with dynamic behaviors as indicated by Table 2 and Figure 9. For the regular designs (*gesummv* and *covariance*), our framework achieves the same result as *VitisHLS*, which proves that our framework successfully identifies non-dynamism of the code and leaves it untouched. For other benchmarks with dynamic features, the latency improvement comes from the fine-grained control of the runtime conditions for the recurrences, and the pipeline bubbles introduced by the static scheduling are squeezed out. For the *sparseMatrix* benchmark, an if-condition that depends on a value loaded from external memory determines whether a dot product operation is executed. This irregular computation prevents the loop from being perfectly pipelined through static scheduling. However, after the PCA transformation, the slow dot product operation is divided into multiple virtual cycles. When the condition loading is finished in one virtual cycle, the dot product can be executed conditionally, i.e., only if the condition is true will the execution be performed. Therefore, the overall cycle latency is reduced. With a slightly decreased synthesizable frequency, the overall wall clock time (WCT) improves. For the *gSum*, *vecNormTrans*, *getTanh*, and *gsumIf* benchmarks, they are very similar to the example loop kernel in Figure 2 with imbalanced branches determined by runtime executions. The PCA transformation reduces cycle latency by avoiding the execution of the long path when the short path is taken, resulting in a better cycle time but with a slight frequency drop. This trend is consistent among all these benchmarks. The *histogram* and *BNNKernel* benchmarks present memory dependencies. Our framework handles the dynamic memory access with store queues as described in Section 5.4, which ensures the pipeline only stalls when an actual memory conflict occurs. This improves overall latency but can impact frequency. Among all the benchmarks that are amenable to dynamic scheduling, the drop in the synthesized maximum frequency is still acceptable compared with the significant latency improvement, which yields a better final WCT. However, it comes at the cost of a resource overhead. Additional logic units are required to store valid/ready statuses and to check execution conditions both within individual SCCs and between different SCCs. Buffers (β nodes) and queues (θ nodes) can also increase the usage of *Flip Flops* (FF). Furthermore, the store queues and corresponding arbitration logic used to handle the memory access dependencies can also consume huge amounts of resources (*FFs, LUTs, and DSPs*). Therefore, a long recurrence path bearing memory access pairs for the same memory base can result in a significant resource overhead as observed in the *histogram* benchmark. It is worth noting that our proposed framework does not mean to beat the *VitisHLS* in all PPA aspects. On the other hand, it improves the performance limit in terms of WCT for synthesizing the irregular and control-dominated application at a slight area and frequency overhead through pure static scheduling.

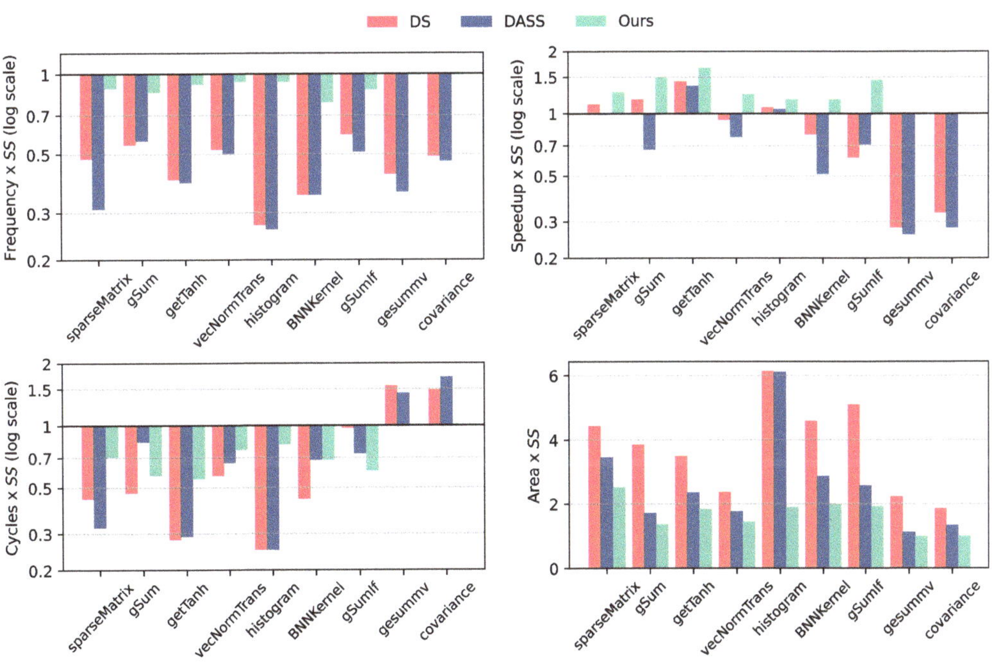

Figure 9. Comparisons of DS [26], DASS [14], and our work against their respective SS-based solution including the frequency, clock cycles, speedup, and area overhead.

Table 2. Comparison with *static scheduling* (SS) [45], *dynamic scheduling* (DS) [26], and *Dynamic and static scheduling* (DASS)-based [14] HLS tools with nine benchmarks. The WCT and cycle column show the geometric mean among a range of input vectors to cover different runtime conditions.

Benchmark	Work	F (MHz)	F/F_{SS}	Cycles	C/C_{SS}	WCT (μs)	T/T_{SS}	LUTs	FFs	DSPs	Area [a]	A/A_{SS}
sparseMatrix	SS	257.5	1.00	21,501	1.00	83.5	1.00	138	320	3	818	1.00
	DS	123.7	0.48	9426	0.44	76.2	0.91	1356	1544	6	3620	4.43
	DASS	80.4	0.31	6778	0.32	84.3	1.01	985	1123	6	2828	3.46
	Ours	227.6	0.88	15,113	0.70	66.4	0.80	329	774	8	2063	2.52
gSum	SS	230.7	1.00	24,115	1.00	104.5	1.00	931	1567	5	3098	1.00
	DS	125.5	0.54	11,358	0.47	90.5	0.87	4238	3956	31	11,914	3.85
	DASS	128.2	0.56	19,974	0.83	155.8	1.49	2315	2176	7	5331	1.72
	Ours	195.8	0.85	13,804	0.57	70.5	0.67	981	1933	11	4234	1.37
getTanh	SS	279.4	1.00	52,004	1.00	186.1	1.00	516	827	5	1943	1.00
	DS	112.5	0.40	14,704	0.28	130.7	0.70	3256	2569	8	6785	3.49
	DASS	109.7	0.39	15,161	0.29	138.2	0.74	1578	2056	8	4594	2.36
	Ours	254.8	0.91	28,716	0.55	112.7	0.61	1098	1762	6	3580	1.84
vecNormTrans	SS	254.8	1.00	23,070	1.00	90.5	1.00	1798	3104	5	5502	1.00
	DS	133.6	0.52	13,066	0.57	97.8	1.08	5114	7099	7	13,053	2.37
	DASS	128.5	0.50	15,112	0.66	117.6	1.30	3956	5077	6	9753	1.77
	Ours	237.1	0.93	17,451	0.76	73.6	0.81	3229	4166	5	7995	1.45
histogram	SS	285.1	1.00	15,006	1.00	52.6	1.00	282	539	2	1061	1.00
	DS	76.4	0.27	3789	0.25	49.6	0.94	1833	4430	2	6503	6.13
	DASS	72.8	0.26	3691	0.25	50.7	0.96	1814	4430	2	6484	6.11
	Ours	266.4	0.93	12,095	0.81	45.4	0.86	677	1095	2	2012	1.90
BNNKernel	SS	257.5	1.00	11,407	1.00	44.3	1.00	299	385	3	1044	1.00
	DS	89.5	0.35	5003	0.44	55.9	1.26	1697	2006	9	4783	4.58
	DASS	89.5	0.35	7706	0.68	86.1	1.94	907	997	9	2984	2.86
	Ours	202.0	0.78	7716	0.68	38.2	0.86	531	708	7	2079	1.99
gSumIf	SS	238.3	1.00	24,116	1.00	101.2	1.00	1213	1972	7	4025	1.00
	DS	139.5	0.59	23,283	0.97	166.9	1.65	6886	6412	60	20,498	5.09
	DASS	122.7	0.51	17,497	0.73	142.6	1.41	3897	5019	12	10,356	2.57
	Ours	207.6	0.87	14,553	0.60	70.1	0.69	2119	4103	13	7782	1.93
gesummv	SS	264.8	1.00	786,466	1.00	2970.5	1.00	898	1764	5	3262	1.00
	DS	112.5	0.42	1,211,445	1.54	10,768.4	3.63	1448	4976	7	7264	2.23
	DASS	96.3	0.36	1,116,050	1.42	11,589.3	3.90	1496	1586	5	3682	1.13
	Ours	264.8	1.00	786,466	1.00	2970.5	1.00	898	1764	5	3262	1.00
covariance	SS	265.3	1.00	241,651	1.00	911.0	1.00	1670	2688	5	4958	1.00
	DS	129.6	0.49	354,910	1.47	2738.5	3.01	4219	4396	5	9215	1.86
	DASS	124.3	0.47	409,618	1.70	3295.4	3.62	2178	3864	5	6642	1.34
	Ours	265.3	1.00	241,651	1.00	911.0	1.00	1670	2688	5	4958	1.00

[a] The area is calculated as $LUT + FF + 120 \times DSP$ [49,50].

6.3.2. Comparison with DS and DASS

Compared with the dynamic-scheduling-based (DS [26]) and hybrid-scheduling-based (DASS [14]) HLS tools, our largest advantage is the ability to maintain the compatibility to the static scheduling framework while presenting the dynamic behavior. With the *VitisHLS* tool as a backend, we can achieve much higher frequency than DS and DASS since our critical paths between two β nodes are still statically synthesized, even though the handshakings between different *SCCs* can harm the timing of critical paths. In terms of the dynamic scheduling, the handshakings occur at an operation level, which means an even longer critical path and thus a worse synthesized frequency. DASS selects the code snippets without dynamic behaviors (static islands) for static synthesis. But the static HLS tool is not aware of the other parts of the design, which can result in suboptimal scheduling from the global perspective. The datapaths are still synthesized by the dynamic tool in the DASS and the result in Table 2 showing a worse synthesized frequency than the other three tools.

In terms of resource overhead, our framework requires fewer resources to achieve dynamism than DS and DASS among all the benchmarks. The dataflow network synthesized from DS makes it hard to perform operation sharing since all operations respond to the request and acknowledgment from other operations. Although DASS can save resources by synthesizing the static islands with static HLS, it still has to introduce extra wrapping logic to merge the synthesized static blocks back to the dynamic HLS flow. Our framework starts from identifying the dynamic parts of the design and carefully handles the runtime control flows at a cycle-accurate level. This process is more natural and resembles the manual hardware design flow. Furthermore, the PCA model generated from our flow can still benefit from the resource sharing if it is not synthesized with $II = 1$, in which case one "virtual cycle" of the PCA model indicates II hardware cycles. This is the normal case when compiling the loops with multi-cycle operations.

7. Conclusions and Discussion

In this work, we proposed a comprehensive source-to-source compiler that combines the static and dynamic scheduling nature. The transformed design presents a cycle-accurate execution pattern by mapping a pre-scheduled "virtual cycle" to a software loop iteration, and is fully compatible with the existing static-scheduling-based HLS tools. Control flows are dynamically executed, and decoupled *SCCs* are connected with latency-insensitive channels. The experiment results indicate significant performance improvements over commercial HLS tools and better performance-area tradeoffs compared to the state-of-the-art dynamic scheduling-based and hybrid-scheduling-based HLS tools.

While this topic is being studied and explored by many researchers, there are still potential opportunities to overcome the current scheduling bottleneck for further improvements. One of the new developments could be the improvement on the dataflow synthesis support. Current HLS tools provide limited support on dataflow synthesis through latency-insensitive channels (e.g., the `hls::stream` from VitisHLS, `ac_channel` from CatapultHLS, and `SYCL` pipe from Intel HLS) to create task-level pipelining. But such support is usually applicable only to tasks which do not have bypass, feedback, or conditionals between each other [1]. By enabling the support for finer-grained dataflow synthesis (i.e., channels that can be inserted between operations instead of tasks), the flexibility to achieve scheduling dynamism can be improved significantly. In addition, more in-depth static analysis technologies are being developed and explored, such as multi-level graph optimization, which can simplify the graph structure at different abstraction layers and efficiently eliminate fake dependencies before the scheduling process. A popular framework termed Multi-Level-Intermediate-Representation (MLIR) [51] has been developed to facilitate efficient optimizations at different abstraction levels. An MLIR-based HLS tool, CIRCT [52], has shown great potential as a next-generation HLS tool supporting both static and dynamic scheduling. Furthermore, there have been works on developing customized hardware components for runtime arbitration to achieve dynamism in the static HLS tool [31,32]. However, the support for RTL integration in current HLS tools is still limited, making it difficult to plug the customized hardware into the standard HLS flow. Therefore, improving the customizability and related plugin interfaces of the static HLS tools has great potential to boost the development of easier and more efficient methods to overcome the bottlenecks.

In terms of the hybrid scheduling specific to the proposed source-to-source compiler, there are also many potential development opportunities to further boost its effectiveness. As a source-to-source plugin to the static HLS flow, it has the potential to be integrated with existing optimizations. With the source-to-source nature, the code is still plain C code after the transformation and can be further processed by any modern HLS tools. This means that the code remains applicable to the well-developed optimizations used by the modern HLS tool, such as code optimizations in front-end, as well as critical path optimization, resource sharing, and design space exploration in back-end. Also, with the advancement of static

HLS technology, the proposed source-to-source method can be easily be accommodated, unlike other optimizations that act at the intermediate representation (IR) level, which usually requires a huge amount of engineering work to be incorporated into different tool flows. In addition to directly combining the transformed code with other generic HLS optimizations, the compiler itself can also be further improved by integrating other technologies. One typical example is to enable speculative pipelining [33,34] within the transformation process. This improvement is natural since we already have the data paths divided as "virtual cycles". The speculative behavior can be easily achieved by changing the behavior of the FSM and `MUX`, with necessary rollback registers added. Furthermore, the recently proposed technology by She et al. [36] can also be integrated in the framework to accurately model the delay for each path to improve the overall performance and avoid area overhead caused by misestimation. These discussed directions are our future research work. Other future research directions include handling the nested loop kernels and exploring multi-threading in a PCA model.

Author Contributions: Conceptualization, Y.S., Y.H., and J.L.; methodology, Y.S., Y.H., and J.L.; software, Y.S.; validation, Y.S.; investigation, Y.S., Y.H., and J.L.; resources, R.C.C.C. and H.Y.; data curation, Y.S.; writing—original draft preparation, Y.S.; writing—review and editing, Y.S., Y.H., J.L., R.C.C.C., and H.Y.; visualization, Y.S.; supervision, R.C.C.C. and H.Y. All authors have read and agreed to the published version of the manuscript.

Funding: This research was supported by Hong Kong Innovation and Technology Commission (ITF Seed Fund ITS/098/22) and Hong Kong Innovation and Technology Commission (InnoHK Project CIMDA).

Data Availability Statement: The original contributions presented in this study are included in the article. Further inquiries can be directed to the corresponding author.

Conflicts of Interest: The authors declare no conflicts of interest.

Abbreviations

The following abbreviations are used in this manuscript:

HLS	High-Level Synthesis
PCA	Pseudo-Cycle-Accurate
II	Initiation Interval
IR	Intermediate Representation
EG	Execution Graph
GSSA	Gated SSA
HDL	Hardware Description Language
CDFG	Control Data Flow Graph
CFG	Control Flow Graph
DFG	Data Flow Graph
LLVM	Low-Level Virtual Machine
MLIR	Multi-Level Intermediate Representation
BB	Basic Block
FSM	Finite State Machine
DAG	Directed Acyclic Graph
SCC	Strongly Connected Component

References

1. AMD Xilinx. Vitis High-Level Synthesis User Guide (UG1399). 2025. Available online: https://docs.xilinx.com/r/en-US/ug1399-vitis-hls (accessed on 19 November 2025).

2. Rokicki, S.; Pala, D.; Paturel, J.; Sentieys, O. What you simulate is what you synthesize: Designing a processor core from c++ specifications. In Proceedings of the 2019 IEEE/ACM International Conference on Computer-Aided Design (ICCAD), Westminster, CO, USA, 4–7 November 2019; pp. 1–8.
3. Tu, P.; Padua, D. Gated SSA-based demand-driven symbolic analysis for parallelizing compilers. In Proceedings of the 9th International Conference on Supercomputing, Barcelona, Spain, 3–7 July 1995; pp. 414–423.
4. Cong, J.; Liu, B.; Neuendorffer, S.; Noguera, J.; Vissers, K.; Zhang, Z. High-level synthesis for FPGAs: From prototyping to deployment. *IEEE Trans.-Comput.-Aided Des. Integr. Circuits Syst.* **2011**, *30*, 473–491. [CrossRef]
5. LLVM. The LLVM Compiler Infrastructure. 2025. Available online: https://www.llvm.org/ (accessed on 19 November 2025).
6. Micheli, G.D. Hardware/Software Co-Design of Run-Time Schedulers for Real-Time Systems. *Des. Autom. Embed. Syst.* **2001**, *6*, 89.
7. Zhang, Z.; Liu, B. SDC-based modulo scheduling for pipeline synthesis. In Proceedings of the 2013 IEEE/ACM International Conference on Computer-Aided Design (ICCAD), San Jose, CA, USA, 4–7 November 2013; pp. 211–218.
8. Canis, A.; Brown, S.D.; Anderson, J.H. Modulo SDC scheduling with recurrence minimization in high-level synthesis. In Proceedings of the 2014 24th International Conference on Field Programmable Logic and Applications (FPL), Munich, Germany, 2–4 September 2014; pp. 1–8.
9. Rau, B.R. Iterative modulo scheduling. *Int. J. Parallel Program.* **1996**, *24*, 3–64. [CrossRef]
10. Carloni, L.P.; McMillan, K.L.; Sangiovanni-Vincentelli, A.L. Theory of latency-insensitive design. *IEEE Trans.-Comput.-Aided Des. Integr. Circuits Syst.* **2001**, *20*, 1059–1076. [CrossRef]
11. Josipović, L.; Marmet, A.; Guerrieri, A.; Ienne, P. Resource sharing in dataflow circuits. *ACM Trans. Reconfigurable Technol. Syst.* **2023**, *16*, 1–27. [CrossRef]
12. Xu, J.; Murphy, E.; Cortadella, J.; Josipović, L. Eliminating Excessive Dynamism of Dataflow Circuits Using Model Checking. In Proceedings of the 2023 ACM/SIGDA International Symposium on Field Programmable Gate Arrays, Monterey, CA, USA, 12–14 February 2023; pp. 27–37.
13. Cheng, J.; Josipović, L.; Constantinides, G.A.; Ienne, P.; Wickerson, J. Combining dynamic & static scheduling in high-level synthesis. In Proceedings of the 2020 ACM/SIGDA International Symposium on Field-Programmable Gate Arrays, Seaside, CA, USA, 23–25 February 2020; pp. 288–298.
14. Cheng, J.; Josipović, L.; Constantinides, G.A.; Ienne, P.; Wickerson, J. DASS: Combining Dynamic & Static Scheduling in High-Level Synthesis. *IEEE Trans.-Comput.-Aided Des. Integr. Circuits Syst.* **2021**, *41*, 628–641.
15. Cheng, J.; Wickerson, J.; Constantinides, G.A. Finding and finessing static islands in dynamically scheduled circuits. In Proceedings of the 2022 ACM/SIGDA International Symposium on Field-Programmable Gate Arrays, Virtual, 27 February–1 March 2022; pp. 89–100.
16. Szafarczyk, R.; Nabi, S.W.; Vanderbauwhede, W. Compiler Discovered Dynamic Scheduling of Irregular Code in High-Level Synthesis. In Proceedings of the 2023 33rd International Conference on Field-Programmable Logic and Applications (FPL), Hamburg, Germany, 30 August–1 September 2023; pp. 1–9.
17. Cortadella, J.; Kishinevsky, M. Synchronous elastic circuits with early evaluation and token counterflow. In Proceedings of the 44th Annual Design Automation Conference, San Diego, CA, USA, 4–8 June 2007; pp. 416–419.
18. Edwards, S.A.; Townsend, R.; Barker, M.; Kim, M.A. Compositional dataflow circuits. *ACM Trans. Embed. Comput. Syst. (TECS)* **2019**, *18*, 1–27. [CrossRef]
19. Cortadella, J.; Kishinevsky, M.; Grundmann, B. Synthesis of synchronous elastic architectures. In Proceedings of the 43rd Annual Design Automation Conference, San Francisco, CA, USA, 24–28 July 2006; pp. 657–662.
20. Venkataramani, G.; Budiu, M.; Chelcea, T.; Goldstein, S.C. C to Asynchronous Dataflow Circuits: An End-to-End Toolflow. 2004. Available online: https://kilthub.cmu.edu/articles/C_to_Asynchronous_Dataflow_Circuits_An_End-to-End_Toolflow/6603986/files/12094370.pdf (accessed on 19 November 2025).
21. Hoover, G.; Brewer, F. Synthesizing synchronous elastic flow networks. In Proceedings of the Conference on Design, Automation and Test in Europe, Grenoble, France, 10–14 March 2008; pp. 306–311.
22. Chatterjee, S.; Kishinevsky, M.; Ogras, U.Y. xMAS: Quick formal modeling of communication fabrics to enable verification. *IEEE Des. Test Comput.* **2012**, *29*, 80–88. [CrossRef]
23. Putnam, A.; Bennett, D.; Dellinger, E.; Mason, J.; Sundararajan, P.; Eggers, S. CHiMPS: A C-level compilation flow for hybrid CPU-FPGA architectures. In Proceedings of the 2008 International Conference on Field Programmable Logic and Applications, Heidelberg, Germany, 8–10 September 2008; pp. 173–178.
24. Townsend, R.; Kim, M.A.; Edwards, S.A. From functional programs to pipelined dataflow circuits. In Proceedings of the 26th International Conference on Compiler Construction, Saarbrücken, Germany, 26 March–3 April 2017; pp. 76–86.
25. Josipović, L.; Brisk, P.; Ienne, P. From C to elastic circuits. In Proceedings of the 2017 51st Asilomar Conference on Signals, Systems, and Computers, Pacific Grove, CA, USA, 29 October–1 November 2017; pp. 121–125.

26. Josipović, L.; Guerrieri, A.; Ienne, P. From C/C++ code to high-performance dataflow circuits. *IEEE Trans.-Comput.-Aided Des. Integr. Circuits Syst.* **2021**, *41*, 2142–2155. [CrossRef]
27. Liu, J.; Rizzi, C.; Josipović, L. Load-store queue sizing for efficient dataflow circuits. In Proceedings of the 2022 International Conference on Field-Programmable Technology (ICFPT), Hong Kong, China, 5–9 December 2022; pp. 1–9.
28. Wang, H.; Rizzi, C.; Josipović, L. MapBuf: Simultaneous technology mapping and buffer insertion for hls performance optimization. In Proceedings of the 2023 IEEE/ACM International Conference on Computer Aided Design (ICCAD), San Francisco, CA, USA, 29 October–2 November 2023; pp. 1–9.
29. Alle, M.; Morvan, A.; Derrien, S. Runtime dependency analysis for loop pipelining in high-level synthesis. In Proceedings of the 50th Annual Design Automation Conference, Austin, TX, USA, 2–6 June 2013; pp. 1–10.
30. Liu, J.; Bayliss, S.; Constantinides, G.A. Offline synthesis of url dependence testing: Parametric loop pipelining for HLS. In Proceedings of the 2015 IEEE 23rd Annual International Symposium on Field-Programmable Custom Computing Machines, Boston, MA, USA, 1–4 May 2015; pp. 159–162.
31. Tan, M.; Liu, G.; Zhao, R.; Dai, S.; Zhang, Z. ElasticFlow: A complexity-effective approach for pipelining irregular loop nests. In Proceedings of the 2015 IEEE/ACM International Conference on Computer-Aided Design (ICCAD), Austin, TX, USA, 2–6 November 2015; pp. 78–85.
32. Dai, S.; Zhao, R.; Liu, G.; Srinath, S.; Gupta, U.; Batten, C.; Zhang, Z. Dynamic hazard resolution for pipelining irregular loops in high-level synthesis. In Proceedings of the 2017 ACM/SIGDA International Symposium on Field-Programmable Gate Arrays, Monterey, CA, USA, 22–24 February 2017; pp. 189–194.
33. Derrien, S.; Marty, T.; Rokicki, S.; Yuki, T. Toward speculative loop pipelining for high-level synthesis. *IEEE Trans.-Comput.-Aided Des. Integr. Circuits Syst.* **2020**, *39*, 4229–4239. [CrossRef]
34. Gorius, J.M.; Rokicki, S.; Derrien, S. SpecHLS: Speculative accelerator design using high-level synthesis. *IEEE Micro* **2022**, *42*, 99–107. [CrossRef]
35. Gorius, J.M.; Rokicki, S.; Derrien, S. A Unified Memory Dependency Framework for Speculative High-Level Synthesis. In Proceedings of the 33rd ACM SIGPLAN International Conference on Compiler Construction, Edinburgh, UK, 2–3 March 2024; pp. 13–25.
36. She, Y.; Liu, J.; Huang, Y.; Cheung, R.C.; Yan, H. A Speculative Loop Pipeline Framework with Accurate Path Modeling for High-Level Synthesis. *ACM Trans. Reconfigurable Technol. Syst.* **2025**, *18*, 1–33. [CrossRef]
37. Carloni, L.P. From latency-insensitive design to communication-based system-level design. *Proc. IEEE* **2015**, *103*, 2133–2151. [CrossRef]
38. Josipović, L.; Sheikhha, S.; Guerrieri, A.; Ienne, P.; Cortadella, J. Buffer placement and sizing for high-performance dataflow circuits. *ACM Trans. Reconfigurable Technol. Syst. (TRETS)* **2021**, *15*, 1–32.
39. Rangan, R.; Vachharajani, N.; Vachharajani, M.; August, D.I. Decoupled software pipelining with the synchronization array. In Proceedings of the 13th International Conference on Parallel Architecture and Compilation Techniques—PACT 2004, Antibes Juan-les-Pins, France, 29 September–3 October 2004; pp. 177–188.
40. CLANG. Clang: A C Language Family Frontend for LLVM. 2025. Available online: https://clang.llvm.org/ (accessed on 19 November 2025).
41. LLVM. LLVM Loop Terminology (and Canonical Forms). Available online: https://llvm.org/docs/LoopTerminology.html (accessed on 19 November 2025).
42. Ferrante, J.; Ottenstein, K.J.; Warren, J.D. The program dependence graph and its use in optimization. *ACM Trans. Program. Lang. Syst. (TOPLAS)* **1987**, *9*, 319–349. [CrossRef]
43. Li, P.; Agrawal, K.; Buhler, J.; Chamberlain, R.D. Deadlock avoidance for streaming computations with filtering. In Proceedings of the Twenty-Second Annual ACM Symposium on Parallelism in Algorithms and Architectures, New York, NY, USA, 13–15 June 2010; pp. 243–252.
44. Josipović, L.; Brisk, P.; Ienne, P. An out-of-order load-store queue for spatial computing. *ACM Trans. Embed. Comput. Syst. (TECS)* **2017**, *16*, 1–19. [CrossRef]
45. Xilinx. Xilinx Vitis 2022.2, 2022. Available online: https://www.xilinx.com/support/download/index.html/content/xilinx/en/downloadNav/vitis/2022-2.html (accessed on 19 November 2025).
46. Cheng, J. JianyiCheng: HLS Benchmarks First Release. 2019. Available online: https://zenodo.org/records/3561115 (accessed on 19 November 2025).
47. Morvan, A.; Derrien, S.; Quinton, P. Polyhedral bubble insertion: A method to improve nested loop pipelining for high-level synthesis. *IEEE Trans.-Comput.-Aided Des. Integr. Circuits Syst.* **2013**, *32*, 339–352. [CrossRef]
48. PollyLLVM. Polly LLVM Framework for High-Level Loop and Data-Locality Optimizations. 2025. Available online: https://polly.llvm.org/ (accessed on 19 November 2025).

49. Chethan, K.H.; Kapre, N. Hoplite-DSP: Harnessing the Xilinx DSP48 multiplexers to efficiently support NoCs on FPGAs. In Proceedings of the 2016 26th International Conference on Field Programmable Logic and Applications (FPL), Lausanne, Switzerland, 29 August–2 September 2016; pp. 1–10.
50. Abdelfattah, M.S.; Betz, V. Networks-on-chip for FPGAs: Hard, soft or mixed? *ACM Trans. Reconfigurable Technol. Syst. (TRETS)* **2014**, *7*, 1–22. [CrossRef]
51. Lattner, C.; Amini, M.; Bondhugula, U.; Cohen, A.; Davis, A.; Pienaar, J.; Riddle, R.; Shpeisman, T.; Vasilache, N.; Zinenko, O. MLIR: Scaling compiler infrastructure for domain specific computation. In Proceedings of the 2021 IEEE/ACM International Symposium on Code Generation and Optimization (CGO), Virtual, 27 February–3 March 2021; pp. 2–14.
52. CIRCT. Circuit IR Compilers and Tools. 2025. Available online: https://circt.llvm.org/ (accessed on 19 November 2025).

electronics

MDPI

Article

Optimizing Digital Systems Implemented in FPGA Through Effective Description of Finite State Machines

Valery Salauyou * and Adam Klimowicz

Faculty of Computer Science, Bialystok University of Technology, 15-351 Bialystok, Poland; a.klimowicz@pb.edu.pl

* Correspondence: v.salauyou@pb.edu.pl

Abstract

In digital systems, finite state machines (FSMs) play a crucial role as controllers, control units, and independent sequential circuits. To efficiently implement these FSMs on advanced hardware platforms such as field-programmable gate arrays (FPGAs), it is essential to represent each FSM in a hardware description language (HDL). This article introduces innovative methods for describing FSMs in Verilog (SystemVerilog) HDL to significantly optimize both the area and performance of synthesized FSM circuits. The presented approach selects the optimal default values for the transition and output functions of an FSM and uses blocking assignment statements to assign these values to variables. This method provides an additional level of optimization independent of the techniques used to improve the FSM during the earlier design stages. Experimental studies on FSM benchmarks show that using this approach with the Quartus design tool reduces the average area of FSMs by approximately 2, and in some cases by up to 6.2. In addition, the average performance of FSMs improves by approximately 2 times and, in some examples, by more than 4 times.

Keywords: area; field-programmable gate array (FPGA); finite state machine (FSM); hardware description language (HDL); performance; Verilog

1. Introduction

Every digital system includes a large number of controllers and control units, implemented as finite state machines (FSMs), that control individual devices, parts of the digital system, and the digital system as a whole. The development of FSMs remains one of the most critical tasks in the design of digital systems, since FSMs are not reused from project to project and are usually designed from scratch for each new digital system project. The characteristics of the entire system largely depend on the parameters of FSMs (area, performance, power consumption). Therefore, optimizing FSM parameters is a critical task in the design of digital systems [1].

There are several well-known strategies for optimizing FSMs that can be implemented at various stages of the FSM design process. These strategies include minimizing the number of states [2], state encoding [3–5], selecting the appropriate structural model [6], determining the target device for the FSM implementation, and choosing the synthesis method [7–13]. Additionally, minimizing the logic of the FSM [14] is another crucial factor. However, researchers often overlook the significance of the coding stage describing the FSM's design using hardware description languages (HDLs) because they consider it too simple or obvious. Currently, the three most commonly used HDLs in practice are Verilog, SystemVerilog, and VHDL.

This paper examines the various styles of describing FSMs in Verilog, aiming to improve both the area (implementation cost) and performance (speed). These concepts can also be easily applied to describe FSMs in SystemVerilog language.

The proposed approach is based on a feature of the blocking assignment statement ('=') in the Verilog (SystemVerilog) language. If a blocking assignment statement is encountered in a 'begin-end' block of sequentially executed statements, the execution of the following statements is blocked until the assignment procedure is completed. This allows us, instead of using a 'default' construct in a 'case' statement, to assign a default value to a variable using a blocking assignment statement before the 'case' statement. In the description of FSMs, default values can be assigned to the variable of the next state and the output vector, which are most often encountered at the transitions of an FSM.

A key feature of the proposed approach is its independence from the FSM optimization methods used in previous design stages, such as state minimization, state encoding, synthesis methods, and logic minimization. This approach offers an additional way to optimize the synthesized circuit during the stage of describing FSMs in HDL. Currently, FSMs are implemented on various hardware platforms, including field-programmable gate arrays (FPGAs), system-on-chips (SoCs), and application-specific integrated circuits (ASICs). Notably, this approach is independent of the type of electronic device in which the FSM is implemented, whether an FPGA, SoC, or ASIC. Significantly, its effectiveness in reducing area and improving FSM performance is independent of the state-encoding method used.

The primary goal of this work is to develop and analyze different styles for describing FSMs in Verilog to reduce area and improve performance.

The main contributions of this work are as follows:

- The algorithms for creating code in Verilog and encoding states to optimize the area and performance of FSMs.
- Three styles of describing FSMs in Verilog: when the default value of the next state (*dstate*) is assigned, when the default value of the output vector (*dout*) is assigned, and when the default values of both the next state and the output vector (*dstate_out*) are assigned simultaneously.
- Evaluations of the effectiveness of the proposed styles of describing FSMs, determined based on the parameters of FSMs.
- Research in Quartus and Vivado design tools on the efficiency of the considered styles of FSM description using FSM benchmarks when encoding states with one-hot and binary codes.
- Recommendations for the practical use of the proposed styles of describing FSMs.

The paper is organized as follows: Section 2 provides an analysis of related works. Section 3 focuses on proposed styles for describing FSMs and compares them with the traditional approach. Section 4 presents experimental results and their analysis. Finally, Section 5 summarizes the findings and offers recommendations for the practical application of the discussed styles for describing FSMs.

2. Related Works

This section reviews the various styles for describing FSMs in Verilog, SystemVerilog, and VHDL HDLs.

In [15], the features for describing FSMs in the Verilog and VHDL languages, provided by Synopsys design tools, are considered. The primary style involves three processes: the description of FSM memory (state register), the transition functions, and the output functions. It outlines the general principles for representing FSMs in HDLs and proposes two structural models: one with a single combinational circuit and another with two combi-

https://doi.org/10.3390/electronics15040831

national circuits. Various state-encoding methods are discussed, including binary, one-hot, and almost one-hot encodings. The paper also explores the use of 'case' and 'if' statements to describe transition functions across different state encoding methods, as well as considerations for asynchronous and unknown inputs, register outputs, and default output values. Furthermore, it addresses the issues of FSM recovery after errors and the exit of FSMs from illegal states.

In [16], implicit styles for describing combinational circuits and FSMs in Verilog are discussed. Five classes of FSMs are proposed, where class0 is a conventional combinational circuit, class1 is a signal delay of one clock cycle, class2 is an FSM that has no inputs and cyclically passes through a set of states, class3 is a Moore FSM, and class4 is a Mealy FSM.

The standardized FSM coding style in Verilog, used in Cisco design tools, is discussed in [17]. In this style, FSM transitions are described using a 'case' statement, and states are declared as local parameters. Transitions within the FSM are represented by two variables: *current* and *next*. The work also introduces the use of cisco_fsm compiler directives. This standardized FSM style facilitates the analysis of state reachability, verification of coverage for all FSM transitions, identification of final states (from which there are no exits), and the construction of a state transition graph (STG).

In [18], two styles for describing FSMs with one and two processes are analyzed, highlighting the advantages and disadvantages of each approach. The work outlines potential methods for state encoding and discusses the use of the Synopsys FSM tool to encode states using binary, Gray, and one-hot codes. Additionally, a coding style is proposed for synthesizing register outputs of a Mealy FSM. The work by [18] recommends against using the full_case and parallel_case attributes in FSM descriptions, as their use can lead to discrepancies between synthesis and modeling results. The FSM encoding styles discussed in [18] were further refined in [19], where it is proposed to use FSM register outputs to prevent failures during state transitions. Two methods are proposed for this purpose. The first method follows the style from [18] for the register outputs of a Mealy FSM, while the second method uses the output values of a Moore FSM to encode states.

Reference [20] considers new possibilities for describing FSMs provided by the SystemVerilog language. These features include the enumerated type 'enum' for declaring states, the use of 'always_comb' and 'always_ff' procedures, and implicit port connections, among others.

In [21], the styles for describing Moore FSMs in VHDL with combinational and register outputs, and their impact on the area and performance of FSMs, are investigated. Reference [22] explores different methods of describing FSMs in VHDL using one or two processes. Additionally, it discusses state encoding techniques, which include binary, one-hot, two-hot, and Gray codes. Moreover, a comparison is made between VHDL and Verilog languages in describing FSMs.

In [23], a converter for transforming FSM representations from the KIS2 format [24] into a Verilog language description is detailed, along with a method for verifying FSMs and constructing an STG.

In [25], seven styles for describing combinational circuits for FSMs in Verilog were presented, utilizing both 'if' and 'case' statements. These styles are labeled as IF_1, IF_2, IF_3, IF_4, CASE_1, CASE_2, and CASE_3. From this selection, the two most effective styles—IF_4 and CASE_3—were empirically chosen to optimize the area and performance of FSMs. Based on these two styles, six FSM coding styles were developed: M_1, M_2, M_3, M_4, M_5, and M_6.

In [26], Verilog-based description styles for fault-tolerant FSMs are discussed, which detect and eliminate faults in the FSM's state register, input, and output vectors. Two styles, safe0 and safe1, are proposed for describing fault-tolerant FSMs in Verilog. These approaches also neutralize the design errors that may arise when the FSM's transitions and outputs are not defined for all possible values of the input variables.

In [27], Verilog description styles are proposed for structural models of reliable FSMs that enable the detection of faults in input and output vectors, in present-state and next-state codes, and in invalid state transitions.

The review shows that there are currently no styles for describing FSMs that specifically focus on minimizing area and improving performance, except for reference [25]. In contrast to [25], this work introduces new styles for describing FSMs in HDLs that aim to reduce area and improve the performance of FSM circuits. These new styles are based on different principles, including the default assignment of both the next state value and the output vector value.

3. Styles of Describing FSMs for Optimizing Area and Performance

This section discusses the proposed styles for describing FSMs in Verilog, compared to the traditional three-process description.

3.1. Traditional Description of FSMs

Let $X = \{x_0, \ldots, x_{L-1}\}$ be the set of input variables of the FSM, $Y = \{y_0, \ldots, y_{N-1}\}$ be the set of output variables of the FSM, and $S = \{s_0, \ldots, s_{M-1}\}$ be the set of states of the FSM, where s_0 is the initial state of the FSM.

The generalized structure of an FSM is shown in Figure 1, where register Rs represents the memory of the FSM (the state register), which stores the code *state* of the present (current) state of the FSM. The combinational circuit λ determines the code *next* of the next state based on the values of the input variables of the set X and the code *state* of the present state. The combinational circuit δ calculates the values of the output variables of the set Y based on the code *state* of the present state and the values of the input variables of the set X (only for FSMs of Mealy type).

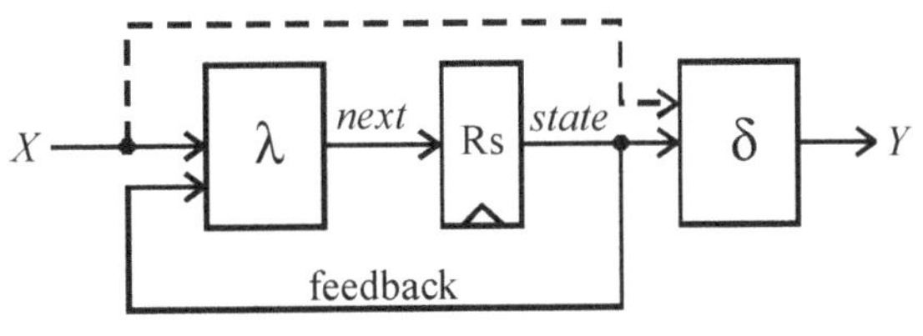

Figure 1. Traditional structure of FSMs.

As an example, consider the FSM, whose STG is shown in Figure 2. Our FSM is a Mealy FSM (the most common case). It has five states $s_0, \ldots, s_4$, three input variables $x_0, \ldots, x_2$, and three output variables $y_0, \ldots, y_2$. The vertices of the graph in Figure 2 denote the states of the FSM, and the arcs of the graph correspond to the transitions between the FSM states. Next to each arc, the input vector that initiates this transition is written, and after a slash, the output vector that is formed at this transition is written. A hyphen ('-') in an input or output vector indicates a don't care value.

The specification for FSM synthesis is often described as a transition list, as shown in Table 1, where *ps* (present state) is the initial state of the transition, *ns* (next state) is the final state of the transition, *X*(*ps*, *ns*) is the input vector that initiates this transition, and *Y*(*ps*, *ns*) is the output vector that is formed at this transition.

https://doi.org/10.3390/electronics15040831

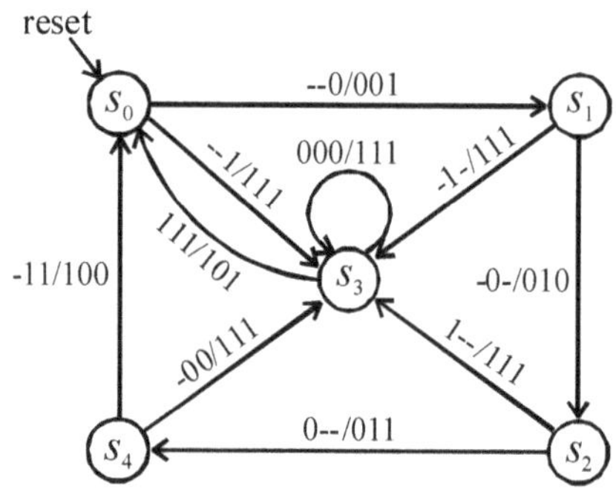

Figure 2. STG of a Mealy FSM.

Table 1. Transition list for the Mealy FSM from our example.

ps	$X(ps, ns)$	ns	$Y(ps, ns)$
s_0	--0	s_1	001
s_0	--1	s_3	111
s_1	-0-	s_2	010
s_1	-1-	s_3	111
s_2	0--	s_4	011
s_2	1--	s_3	111
s_3	000	s_3	111
s_3	111	s_0	101
s_4	-00	s_3	111
s_4	-11	s_0	100

Traditionally, an FSM in Verilog is described using three separate processes (state register, transition functions, and output functions), as shown in Listing 1.

Listing 1. A traditional description of the FSM from our example.

```
module Mealy_3proc (        // declaration of ports
  input clk, reset,         // clock and reset signals
  input [2:0] x,            // input vector
  output reg [2:0] y);      // output vector
  reg [2:0] state, next;    // state variables
  localparam [2:0] s0 = 0, s1 = 1, s2 = 2, s3 = 3, s4 = 4;   // states
  always @(posedge clk, negedge reset)        // state register
    if (~reset)   state <= s0;
    else          state <= next;
  always @(*)              // description of transition functions
    case (state)
    s0:  casex (x)
                 3'b??0:   next = s1;
                 3'b??1:   next = s3;
         endcase
    s1:  casex (x)
                 3'b?0?:   next = s2;
                 3'b?1?:   next = s3;
         endcase
```

https://doi.org/10.3390/electronics15040831

Listing 1. *Cont.*

```
    s2: casex (x)
                    3'b0??:   next = s4;
                    3'b1??:   next = s3;
        endcase
    s3: casex (x)
                    3'b000:   next = s3;
                    3'b111:   next = s0;
        endcase
    s4: casex (x)
                    3'b?00:   next = s3;
                    3'b?11:   next = s0;
        endcase
    endcase
  always @(*)           // description of output functions
    case (state)
    s0:   casex (x)
                    3'b??0:   y = 3'b001;
                    3'b??1:   y = 3'b111;
          endcase
    s1:   casex (x)
                    3'b?0?:   y = 3'b010;
                    3'b?1?:   y = 3'b111;
          endcase
    s2:   casex (x)
                    3'b0??:   y = 3'b011;
                    3'b1??:   y = 3'b111;
          endcase
    s3:   casex (x)
                    3'b000:   y = 3'b111;
                    3'b111:   y = 3'b101;
          endcase
    s4:   casex (x)
                    3'b?00:   y = 3'b111;
                    3'b?11:   y = 3'b100;
          endcase
    endcase
endmodule
```

In Listing 1, the input and output functions are described using 'case' statements, which are arranged on two levels. First-level 'case' statements check the variable *state* (the code of the present state) and, depending on its value, determine the necessary actions in each state. The second-level 'case' statements check the input vector x and, depending on its value, calculate the value of the variable *next* (the code of the next state) in the second process and the value of the variable y (the value of the output vector) in the third process.

Considering that 'case' and 'if' statements are interchangeable in Verilog, an 'if-else-if' chain can be used instead of a 'case' statement throughout the proposed approach. In this article, we use the 'case' statement for clarity.

https://doi.org/10.3390/electronics15040831

3.2. Creating Code in Verilog to Optimize an FSM Circuit

The proposed approach is based on the following assumptions:

- Reducing the number of transitions in the FSM description leads to a decrease in the area and an increase in the performance of the synthesized FSM circuit;
- Specifying default values for the variables *next* and *y* reduces the number of transitions in the FSM description.

In the proposed approach, combinational circuits λ and δ are described as 'begin-end' blocks of the 'always' procedure. In the 'begin-end' block, the variables *next* and *y* are first assigned default values using a blocking assignment operator ('='), followed by a 'case' statement describing the logic of combinational circuits λ and δ. The descriptions of combinational circuits λ and δ do not include assignments to the variables *next* and *y* of values that were previously defined as default values.

The default value for the variable *next* is selected as the state of the FSM in which the largest number of transitions ends. If there are several such states, the state whose code contains the largest number of ones is selected. The default value for the variable *y* is selected as the output vector that is most frequently formed at the transitions of the FSM. If there are several such output vectors, the vector that contains the largest number of ones is selected.

Let the FSM be specified by the transition list, as shown in Table 1. Then, the creation of the Verilog code for optimizing the parameters (area and performance) of the FSM can be represented as Algorithm 1.

Algorithm 1. Creating FSM code in Verilog to optimize the synthesized circuit

1. If the state codes are not defined, perform Algorithm 2 for state encoding to optimize the parameters of the FSM.
2. Find the state s_{max} that occurs most frequently in the *ns* column of the transition list. If there are several such states, select the state with the largest number of ones in the state code.
3. Find the output vector y_{max} that occurs most often in the *Y*(*ps*, *ns*) column of the transition list. If there are several such output vectors, select the vector that contains the largest number of ones.
4. Describe the ports, state variables, state codes, and state register of the FSM in the traditional way.
5. Describe the transition functions (combinational circuit λ) of the FSM using the 'begin-end' block of the 'always' procedure. At the beginning of the 'begin-end' block, use the blocking assignment operator ('=') to assign the value smax to the variable *next*. This is followed by 'case' statements describing the logic of the transition functions, in which the 'case' statements do not assign the state smax to the variable *next*.
6. Similarly, describe the output functions (combinational circuit δ), where assign the output vector y_{max} to the variable *y* at the beginning of the 'begin-end' block, and the 'case' statements do not assign the output vector y_{max} to the variable *y*.
7. End.

Algorithm 2 for encoding states to optimize the FSM parameters is based on the assumption that assigning the code with the minimum number of ones to the state that occurs most frequently in the *ns* column of the transition list helps to reduce the area and increase the performance of the FSM.

https://doi.org/10.3390/electronics15040831

Algorithm 2. Encoding states to optimize FSM parameters

1. Define the set K of binary codes for the FSM states, where $|K| = 2^R$, $R = \lceil \log_2 M \rceil$, $|A|$ is the cardinality of set A, and $\lceil B \rceil$ is the smallest integer greater than or equal to B.
2. Assign the initial state s_0 the zero code k_0: $s_0 \leftarrow k_0$; assume $S := S \setminus \{s_0\}$, $K := K \setminus \{k_0\}$.

while ($|S|$!= 0) **do**

3 In the set S, find the state s_i that occurs most frequently in the column ns of the transition list.

4 In the set K, find the code k_j with the minimum number of ones.

5 Assign the code k_j to the state s_i: $s_i \leftarrow k_j$; assume $S := S \setminus \{s_i\}$, $K := K \setminus \{k_j\}$.

end while.

Let us consider applying Algorithm 1 to describe the FSM from our example. Suppose that the state codes are not specified, so Algorithm 2 is performed. For our example, $M = 5$, $R = 3$, and $|K| = 8$. We assign the zero code '000' to the initial state s_0. State s_3 in column ns of Table 1 occurs most frequently, so we assign state s_3 the code '001' with the smallest number of ones. States s_1, s_2, and s_4 in column ns of Table 1 occur only once, so we assign them the codes '010', '100', and '011', sequentially.

In step 2 of Algorithm 1, we select state s_3 as the s_{max} state, which occurs most often in column ns of Table 1. Similarly, in step 3 of Algorithm 1, we select vector '111' as the output vector y_{max}, which occurs most frequently in column $Y(ps, ns)$ of Table 1. Executing steps 4–6 of Algorithm 1 results in the construction of the FSM project code, which is shown in Listing 2.

Listing 2. Description of the FSM for parameter optimization.

```
module Mealy_3proc (    // declaration of ports
  input clk, reset,          // clock and reset signals
  input [2:0] x,             // input vector
  output reg [2:0] y);       // output vector
  reg [2:0] state, next;     // state variables
  localparam [2:0]
s0 = 3'b000,                 // state codes
s1 = 3'b010,
s2 = 3'b100,
s3 = 3'b001,
s4 = 3'b011;
always @(posedge clk, negedge reset)   // state register
    if (~reset)   state <= s0;
    else          state <= next;
  always @(*)     // description of transition functions
  begin
    next = s3;    // default value for the next variable
    case (state)
    s0:  casex (x)
                3'b??0:   next = s1;
      endcase
```

https://doi.org/10.3390/electronics15040831

Listing 2. *Cont.*

```
    s1:  casex (x)
                  3'b?0?:  next = s2;
      endcase
    s2:  casex (x)
                  3'b0??:  next = s4;
      endcase
    s3:  casex (x)
                  3'b111:  next = s0;
      endcase
    s4:  casex (x)
                  3'b?11:  next = s0;
      endcase
    endcase
  end
always @(*)      // description of output functions
  begin
    y = 3'b111;  // default value for the y variable
    case (state)
    s0:  casex (x)
                  3'b??0:  y = 3'b001;
      endcase
    s1:  casex (x)
                  3'b?0?:  y = 3'b010;
      endcase
    s2:  casex (x)
                  3'b0??:  y = 3'b011;
      endcase
    s3:  casex (x)
                  3'b111:  y = 3'b101;
      endcase
    s4:  casex (x)
                  3'b?11:  y = 3'b100;
      endcase
    endcase
  end
endmodule
```

The description of FSMs, where default values are defined for both the *next* and *y* variables (as in Listing 2), is called the *dstate_out* (default state and output) style. Let us define two more description styles for optimizing FSM parameters: *dstate* and *dout*. In the *dstate* (default state) style, the default value is defined only for the variable *next*, and in the *dout* (default output) style, the default value is defined only for the variable *y*. Thus, we have four styles for describing FSMs: *3proc* (Listing 1), *dstate*, *dout*, and *dstate_out* (Listing 2).

The results of implementing the FSM from our example using the Quartus Prime design tool version 24.1 in the Cyclone 10 LP family FPGA for different description styles are shown in Table 2, where *A* is the number of look-up tables (LUTs) in the FSM circuit (area) and *F* is the maximum operating frequency (in megahertz) of the FSM (performance).

https://doi.org/10.3390/electronics15040831

Table 2. Parameters of the FSM designs from our example for different description styles.

FSM	*A*	*F*
Mealy_3proc	24	181
Mealy_dstate	16	543
Mealy_dout	19	237
Mealy_dstate_out	11	651

Table 2 shows that the *dstate*, *dout*, and *dstate_out* styles significantly outperform the traditional *3proc* style for describing FSMs in both area and performance. At the same time, the most significant FSM parameter optimization is achieved with the *dstate_out* style, followed by the *dstate* and *dout* styles. Note that the results of both the functional and timing simulations for all FSM description styles are entirely identical.

The optimization of combinational circuits λ and δ in the *dstate_out* style is explained by the fact that the synthesizer of a design tool only generates the logic that is explicitly defined in 'case' statements, since the default value has already been described earlier using the blocking assignment statement ('=') in the corresponding 'begin-end' block before the first-level 'case' statement. As a result, the logic of combinational circuits λ and δ is simplified, the area is reduced, and the performance of FSMs is increased.

Applying the proposed approach results in the generation of project code in which the assignment of values to the variables *next* and y in second-level 'case' statements is not defined for all possible combinations of input variables (such 'case' statements are marked as incomplete by the synthesizer). The traditional solution to this problem is for the synthesizer to automatically insert latches into the project circuit to save the previous values of the variables *next* and y. However, when using the Quartus Synthesizer, assigning default values to the variables *next* and y using a blocking assignment statement before the first-level 'case' statements allows us to avoid introducing latches into the FSM circuit.

A significant difference between the proposed approach and the known methods for describing FSMs and recommendations from developers of design tool synthesizers is that the default values for the variables *next* and y are not assigned using 'default' (for 'case' statements) or 'else' (for 'if' statements) constructs, but rather by using a blocking assignment statement in a 'begin-end' block before the first-level 'case' statement. Reference [28] also points out the possibility of assigning default values before 'case' and 'if' statements. However, reference [28] does not aim to optimize the FSM circuit; the initial or undefined state is used as the default value for the variable *next*, and the zero vector is used for the variable y. Of course, the proposed approach depends on the synthesizer of a design tool.

One disadvantage of the proposed approach is that the synthesizer generates messages about incomplete 'case' statements that do not affect the synthesis or simulation results. In addition, in the case of incomplete 'case' statements, the Vivado Synthesizer introduces latches to hold the values of the *next* and y variables.

The proposed approach has proven highly effective for describing FSMs in SystemVerilog. It can be assumed that the strategy under consideration will also be effective when using VHDL. However, the latter assumption requires further research.

4. Experimental Results

The FSM description styles—*3proc*, *dstate*, *dout*, and *dstate_out*—were evaluated using FSM benchmarks from the Microelectronics Center of North Carolina (MCNC) [29]. The FSMs were implemented on the Cyclone 10 LP FPGA family using the Quartus design tool, version 24.1. The FSM area was measured by counting the number of look-up tables (LUTs) used in the FSM circuit, while the maximum operating frequency assessed performance. The states of the FSMs were encoded using one-hot and binary codes. All parameters

https://doi.org/10.3390/electronics15040831

of FSMs are given after the complete implementation of the FSM in the FPGA, i.e., after synthesis, placement, and routing.

4.1. FSM Parameters and Efficiency Estimates of the Proposed Description Styles

Table 3 presents the parameters of the studied FSM benchmarks, where L is the number of inputs, N is the number of outputs, T is the number of transitions between states, M is the number of states, Ts is the maximum number of transitions to the same state, To is the maximum number of transitions that yield the same output vector, Av denotes the arithmetic mean value of the parameter, and Max refers to the maximum value of the parameter.

Table 3. Parameters and effectiveness estimates of FSM description styles.

FSM	L	N	T	M	Ts	To	λs	λo	λso
bbsse	7	7	56	16	28	14	1.500	1.250	1.750
beecount	3	4	28	7	12	19	1.429	1.679	2.107
cse	7	7	91	16	47	31	1.516	1.341	1.857
dk14	3	5	56	7	13	6	1.232	1.107	1.339
dk16	2	3	108	27	9	34	1.083	1.315	1.398
dk512	1	3	30	15	6	17	1.200	1.567	1.767
ex1	9	19	233	18	45	32	1.193	1.137	1.330
ex2	2	2	72	18	32	59	1.444	1.819	2.264
ex3	2	2	36	10	16	30	1.444	1.833	2.278
ex4	6	9	21	14	4	6	1.190	1.286	1.476
ex5	2	2	32	9	15	18	1.469	1.563	2.031
ex6	5	8	34	8	10	7	1.294	1.206	1.500
ex7	2	2	36	10	18	23	1.500	1.639	2.139
keyb	7	2	170	19	112	111	1.659	1.653	2.312
lion	2	1	11	4	3	7	1.273	1.636	1.909
lion9	2	1	25	9	3	17	1.120	1.680	1.800
planet	7	19	115	48	8	11	1.070	1.096	1.165
planet1	7	19	115	48	8	11	1.070	1.096	1.165
pma	8	8	73	24	21	5	1.288	1.068	1.356
s1	8	6	107	20	12	12	1.112	1.112	1.224
s27	4	1	34	6	10	27	1.294	1.794	2.088
s208	11	2	153	18	99	75	1.647	1.490	2.137
s1488	8	19	251	48	121	62	1.482	1.247	1.729
sand	11	9	184	32	32	30	1.174	1.163	1.337
sse	7	7	56	16	28	14	1.500	1.250	1.750
styr	9	10	166	30	44	46	1.265	1.277	1.542
tbk	6	3	1569	32	567	1274	1.361	1.812	2.173
tma	7	6	44	20	9	4	1.205	1.091	1.295
train4	2	1	14	4	4	10	1.286	1.714	2.000
train11	2	1	25	11	5	18	1.200	1.720	1.920
Av							1.317	1.421	1.738
Max	11	19	1569	48	567	1274	1.659	1.833	2.312

The preliminary effectiveness of the proposed styles for describing FSMs can be represented using the following expressions:

$$\lambda s = \frac{Ts + T}{T}, \tag{1}$$

$$\lambda o = \frac{To + T}{T}, \tag{2}$$

https://doi.org/10.3390/electronics15040831

$$\lambda so = \frac{Ts + To + T}{T} \quad (3)$$

where λs is the efficiency estimate of the *dstate* style, λo is the efficiency estimate of the *dout* style, and λso is the efficiency estimate of the *dstate_out* style.

Efficiency here refers to reducing the area and increasing the performance of the FSM. Estimates (1)–(3) reflect how many lines the FSM description is reduced by when using the *dstate, dout,* and *dstate_out* styles compared to the traditional description, with a higher estimate for a particular FSM indicating a more efficient use of the corresponding description style for that FSM.

The values of the estimates λs, λo, and λso for the evaluated FSM benchmarks are presented in Table 3. Based on the average values of these estimates, we can propose the following hypotheses:

Hypothesis 1. *The dstate_out style is more effective than the dstate and dout styles for improving FSM parameters.*

Hypothesis 2. *The dout style shows a slight advantage over the dstate style in improving the FSM parameters.*

4.2. Area of FSMs

The area of the FSMs using the considered styles and encoding states with one-hot code is presented in Table 4, where *A3, As, Ao,* and *Aso* are the areas of FSMs (in the number of LUTs) described in styles *3proc, dstate, dout,* and *dstate_out*, respectively; *Amin* is the minimum area value for a specific example; *A3/As, A3/Ao,* and *A3/Aso*, are the ratios of the corresponding parameters; *Av* and *Max* denote the previous values; *Best* is the number of best solutions when using a specific description style; and *Unique* is the number of unique solutions. Here, a unique solution is understood to be the best solution obtained using a particular style and cannot be achieved using other FSM description styles. In Tables 4–9, the best solutions and the parameter values *Av* and *Max* are highlighted in bold.

Table 4. Area of FSMs with one-hot encoding.

FSM	*A3*	*As*	*Ao*	*Aso*	*Amin*	*A3/As*	*A3/Ao*	*A3/Aso*
bbsse	42	**27**	40	**27**	27	1.556	1.050	1.556
beecount	42	25	36	**18**	18	1.680	1.167	2.333
cse	111	84	103	**72**	72	1.321	1.078	1.542
dk14	**44**	**44**	**44**	**44**	44	1.000	1.000	1.000
dk16	65	**35**	65	**35**	35	1.857	1.000	1.857
dk512	21	**11**	21	**11**	11	1.909	1.000	1.909
ex1	135	82	125	**60**	60	1.646	1.080	2.250
ex2	78	39	76	**30**	30	2.000	1.026	2.600
ex3	42	26	42	**20**	20	1.615	1.000	2.100
ex4	57	15	47	**11**	11	**3.800**	1.213	**5.182**
ex5	36	**22**	36	25	22	1.636	1.000	1.440
ex6	63	58	61	**48**	48	1.086	1.033	1.313
ex7	41	26	40	**25**	25	1.577	1.025	1.640
lion	17	11	15	**9**	9	1.545	1.133	1.889
lion9	57	27	56	**21**	21	2.111	1.018	2.714
planet	121	**87**	125	90	87	1.391	0.968	1.344
planet1	121	**87**	125	90	87	1.391	0.968	1.344
pma	147	101	145	**89**	89	1.455	1.014	1.652
s1	118	**63**	118	**63**	63	1.873	1.000	1.873
s27	**23**	**23**	**23**	**23**	23	1.000	1.000	1.000
s208	49	55	**32**	**32**	32	0.891	**1.531**	1.531
s1488	**157**	166	168	167	157	0.946	0.935	0.940
sand	238	152	239	**134**	134	1.566	0.996	1.776

https://doi.org/10.3390/electronics15040831

Table 4. *Cont.*

FSM	*A3*	*As*	*Ao*	*Aso*	*Amin*	*A3/As*	*A3/Ao*	*A3/Aso*
sse	70	46	62	**37**	37	1.522	1.129	1.892
styr	212	**100**	197	105	100	2.120	1.076	2.019
tbk	295	151	292	**112**	112	1.954	1.010	2.634
tma	157	**69**	161	75	69	2.275	0.975	2.093
train4	19	11	17	**8**	8	1.727	1.118	2.375
train11	48	28	46	**22**	22	1.714	1.043	2.182
Av						**1.661**	**1.055**	**1.930**
Max						**3.800**	**1.531**	**5.182**
Best	3	11	3	23				
Unique	1	5	0	16				

Table 4 shows that, using the *dstate_out* style and one-hot encoding, the average area of FSMs is reduced by a factor of 1.93 (or by 93%); the most significant decrease, by a factor of 5.182, is observed in the ex4 example. When using the *dstate* style, the maximum area is reduced by a factor of 3.8, also for the ex4 example. For the *dout* style, the maximum area is reduced by a factor of 1.531, as shown in the s208 example. Note that when using the *dstate_out* style, 11 of 29 cases (37.9%) show a reduction of more than a factor of 2 in area.

The area of the FSMs using the proposed styles and binary state encoding is presented in Table 5.

Table 5. Area of FSMs with binary encoding.

FSM	*A3*	*As*	*Ao*	*Aso*	*Amin*	*A3/As*	*A3/Ao*	*A3/Aso*
bbsse	60	**30**	63	32	30	2.000	0.952	1.875
beecount	32	19	28	**15**	15	1.684	1.143	2.133
cse	103	108	**97**	**97**	97	0.954	1.062	1.062
dk14	**43**	**43**	**43**	**43**	43	1.000	1.000	1.000
dk16	85	**51**	85	**51**	51	1.667	1.000	1.667
dk512	16	**13**	16	**13**	13	1.231	1.000	1.231
ex1	147	118	133	**92**	92	1.246	1.105	1.598
ex2	92	40	91	**39**	39	2.300	1.011	2.359
ex3	44	26	47	**25**	25	1.692	0.936	1.760
ex4	62	16	57	**10**	10	**3.875**	1.088	**6.200**
ex5	34	**22**	37	23	22	1.545	0.919	1.478
ex6	71	67	66	**51**	51	1.060	1.076	1.392
ex7	45	21	45	**18**	18	2.143	1.000	2.500
lion	11	7	10	**5**	5	1.571	1.100	2.200
lion9	57	16	57	**14**	14	3.563	1.000	4.071
planet	224	**90**	232	91	90	2.489	0.966	2.462
planet1	224	**90**	232	91	90	2.489	0.966	2.462
pma	**162**	272	164	269	162	0.596	0.988	0.602
s1	168	**91**	168	**91**	91	1.846	1.000	1.846
s27	**10**	**10**	**10**	**10**	10	1.000	1.000	1.000
s208	**14**	**14**	**14**	**14**	14	1.000	1.000	1.000
s1488	223	223	230	**167**	167	1.000	0.970	1.335
sand	257	180	258	**164**	164	1.428	0.996	1.567
sse	77	40	69	**30**	30	1.925	1.116	2.567
styr	229	**108**	213	**108**	108	2.120	1.075	2.120
tbk	303	**197**	302	199	197	1.538	1.003	1.523
tma	172	**111**	182	112	111	1.550	0.945	1.536
train4	13	7	11	**5**	5	1.857	**1.182**	2.600
train11	52	28	49	**24**	24	1.857	1.061	2.167
Av						**1.732**	**1.023**	**1.976**
Max						**3.875**	**1.182**	**6.200**
Best	4	13	4	22				
Unique	1	6	0	14				

https://doi.org/10.3390/electronics15040831

Table 5 shows that with binary encoding and the use of the *dstate_out* style, the average area of FSMs is reduced by a factor of 1.976 (or 97.6%), with the maximum area reduction by a factor of 6.2 in example ex4. For the *dstate* style, the maximum decrease in area by a factor of 3.875 is also observed for the ex4 benchmark. In the *dout* style, the most significant reduction in the area observed is a factor of 1.182 in the train4 example. Note that when using the *dstate_out* style, in 12 out of 29 examples (41.4% of cases), the area decreased by more than two times.

4.3. Performance of FSMs

The performance of the FSMs using the proposed styles and one-hot state encoding is shown in Table 6, where *F3, Fs, Fo,* and *Fso* are the maximum operating frequencies of FSMs (in megahertz), described in *styles 3proc, dstate, dout,* and *dstate_out*, respectively; *Fmax* is the maximum performance value for a specific example; *Fs/F3, Fo/F3, Fs/F3,* and *Fso/F3* are the ratios of the corresponding parameters; and *Av, Max, Best,* and *Unique* denote the previous values.

Table 6. Performance of FSMs with one-hot encoding.

FSM	*F3*	*Fs*	*Fo*	*Fso*	*Fmax*	*Fs/F3*	*Fo/F3*	*Fso/F3*
bbsse	476	609	550	**650**	650	1.279	1.155	1.366
beecount	200	522	165	**623**	623	2.610	0.825	3.115
cse	144	**512**	161	505	512	3.556	1.118	3.507
dk14	**511**	**511**	**511**	**511**	511	1.000	1.000	1.000
dk16	527	**648**	527	**648**	648	1.230	1.000	1.230
dk512	734	**812**	734	**812**	812	1.106	1.000	1.106
ex1	305	**521**	222	511	521	1.708	0.728	1.675
ex2	467	623	467	**728**	728	1.334	1.000	1.559
ex3	476	546	476	**657**	657	1.147	1.000	1.380
ex4	604	**1300**	615	**1300**	1300	2.152	1.018	2.152
ex5	500	**689**	500	656	689	1.378	1.000	1.312
ex6	218	502	196	**559**	559	2.303	0.899	2.564
ex7	475	523	475	**667**	667	1.101	1.000	1.404
lion	489	733	485	**734**	734	1.499	0.992	1.501
lion9	180	552	149	**567**	567	3.067	0.828	3.150
planet	**733**	724	700	727	733	0.988	0.955	0.992
planet1	**733**	724	700	727	733	0.988	0.955	0.992
pma	106	453	87	**466**	466	**4.274**	0.821	**4.396**
s1	426	**532**	426	**532**	532	1.249	1.000	1.249
s27	**557**	**557**	541	541	557	1.000	0.971	0.971
s208	440	**481**	456	456	481	1.093	1.036	1.036
s1488	436	434	419	**485**	485	0.995	0.961	1.112
sand	154	447	277	**466**	466	2.903	**1.799**	3.026
sse	505	506	505	**531**	531	1.002	1.000	1.051
styr	168	524	184	**618**	618	3.119	1.095	3.679
tbk	320	372	320	**436**	436	1.163	1.000	1.363
tma	142	461	147	**475**	475	3.246	1.035	3.345
train4	207	**809**	291	690	809	3.908	1.406	3.333
train11	363	524	271	**555**	555	1.444	0.747	1.529
Av						**1.857**	**1.012**	**1.934**
Max						**4.274**	**1.799**	**4.396**
Best	4	11	1	21				
Unique	2	6	0	16				

Table 6 shows that when using the *dstate_out* style and one-hot encoding, the average performance improves by a factor of 1.934 (or 93.4%), with the maximum performance

https://doi.org/10.3390/electronics15040831

increase by a factor of 4.396 in the pma example. For the *dstate* style, the highest performance increase noted is a factor of 4.274, again for the pma example. In contrast, the *dout* style highlights a maximum performance increase of 1.799 for the sand example. Notably, in 10 of 30 cases (33.3%), performance improved by more than 2 times, and in 8 cases (26.7%) by more than 3 times.

The performance of the FSMs using the offered styles and binary state encoding is shown in Table 7.

Table 7. Performance of FSMs with binary encoding.

FSM	*F3*	*Fs*	*Fo*	*Fso*	*Fmax*	*Fs/F3*	*Fo/F3*	*Fso/F3*
bbsse	333	**536**	334	447	536	1.003	1.610	1.342
beecount	658	**789**	608	598	789	0.924	1.199	0.909
cse	155	249	217	**310**	310	1.400	1.606	2.000
dk14	480	**780**	480	480	780	1.000	1.625	1.000
dk16	**380**	378	**380**	378	380	1.000	0.995	0.995
dk512	**578**	552	**578**	552	578	1.000	0.955	0.955
ex1	240	273	244	**337**	337	1.017	1.138	1.404
ex2	219	272	298	**404**	404	1.361	1.242	1.845
ex3	233	388	239	**531**	531	1.026	1.665	2.279
ex4	419	450	419	**731**	731	1.000	1.074	1.745
ex5	335	335	335	**500**	500	1.000	1.000	1.493
ex6	226	412	232	**433**	433	1.027	1.823	1.916
ex7	222	453	230	**501**	501	1.036	2.041	2.257
lion	677	486	664	**814**	814	0.981	0.718	1.202
lion9	209	435	209	**590**	590	1.000	2.081	2.823
planet	238	295	226	**296**	296	0.950	1.239	1.244
planet1	238	295	226	**296**	296	0.950	1.239	1.244
pma	111	165	92	**219**	219	0.829	1.486	1.973
s1	249	**296**	249	**296**	296	1.000	1.189	1.189
s27	240	**540**	537	537	540	**2.238**	2.250	2.238
s208	716	716	**721**	**721**	721	1.007	1.000	1.007
s1488	221	221	223	**480**	480	1.009	1.000	2.172
sand	211	209	192	**239**	239	0.910	0.991	1.133
sse	**488**	353	446	462	488	0.914	0.723	0.947
styr	203	**317**	184	**317**	317	0.906	1.562	1.562
tbk	210	**237**	210	202	237	1.000	1.129	0.962
tma	119	277	151	**326**	326	1.269	**2.328**	2.739
train4	262	474	271	**816**	816	1.034	1.809	**3.115**
train11	230	385	310	**490**	490	1.348	1.674	2.130
Av						**1.074**	**1.393**	**1.649**
Max						**2.238**	**2.328**	**3.115**
Best	3	7	3	21				
Unique	1	5	0	18				

Table 7 shows that when using the *dstate_out* style and binary encoding, the average performance improves by 1.649 (64.9%), with the maximum performance increase of 3.115 in the train4 example. For the *dstate* style, the maximum performance increase reaches a factor of 2.238 in the s27 example, while the *dout* style achieves a maximum improvement factor of 2.328 in the tma example. Notably, in 9 out of 29 examples (31% of cases), the performance improves by more than double.

The effectiveness of the considered styles, as measured by the number of best and unique solutions achieved, is illustrated in Figures 3 and 4.

https://doi.org/10.3390/electronics15040831

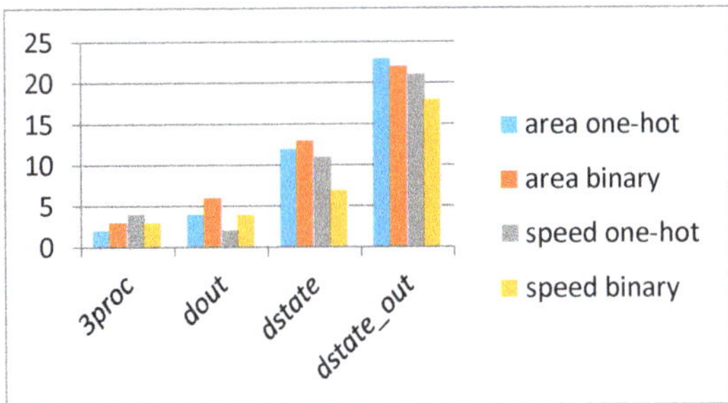

Figure 3. Number of best solutions achieved by each style.

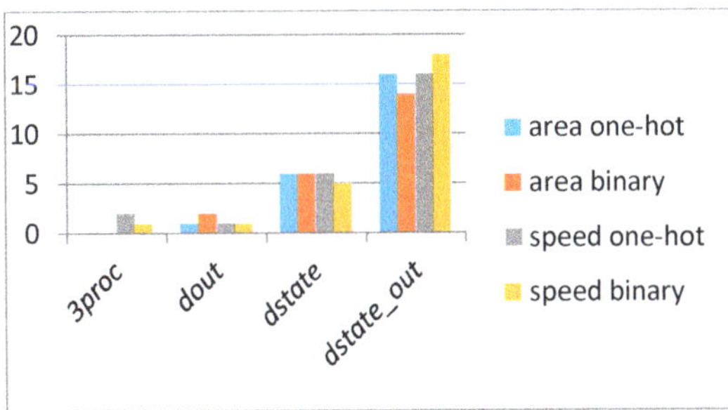

Figure 4. Number of unique solutions achieved by each style.

Figures 3 and 4 demonstrate that the *dstate_out* and *dstate* styles significantly outperform the *3proc* and *dout* styles in terms of the number of best and unique solutions achieved.

The analysis in Tables 4–7 of the average values (parameter *Av*) of the area and performance ratios indicates that Hypothesis 1 was fully confirmed. In contrast, Hypothesis 2 was confirmed only with respect to performance when encoding FSMs with binary codes.

Note that the high efficiency of the considered approach has been confirmed for both minimum (binary) and maximum (one-hot) length codes. Therefore, the efficiency of the proposed approach for reducing the area and enhancing the performance of FSMs is independent of the method of state encoding.

4.4. Research on the Effectiveness of the Proposed Approach in the Vivado Design Tool

All of the experimental results presented above were obtained using the Quartus Prime system. Section 3 noted that the proposed approach depends on the synthesizer used by the design tool. For comparison, Tables 8 and 9 present the results of experimental studies of the proposed approach performed using the Vivado design tool version 2025.1 when implementing FSMs in the Artix 7 family of FPGAs.

Table 8 shows that using the *dstate_out* style of FSM description with one-hot encoding results in an average area reduction of 1.253 times (or 25.3%). The most significant area reduction, 2.6 times, is observed in the example dk16. Similarly, Table 9 shows that using the *dstate_out* style of FSM description with binary encoding results in an average area reduction of 1.227 times (or 22.7%), and the most significant reduction, 2.143 times, is also observed in the example dk16.

When using the proposed approach, even after assigning default values to the variables *next* and *y* before the 'case' statements, the synthesizer in Vivado introduces latches if the 'case' statements for *next* and *y* do not define values for all possible combinations of input variables. The introduction of latches into the FSM circuit prevents the maximum operating frequency of the FSMs from being calculated. Therefore, there is no data on the performance

https://doi.org/10.3390/electronics15040831

of the FSMs here. However, despite the Vivado Synthesizer introducing latches into the FSM circuit, the proposed approach reduces the average area of FSMs, allowing us to draw the following conclusion.

Inference. Introducing latches into the FSM circuit requires fewer area resources than the proposed approach for minimizing FSM logic. In other words, regardless of the synthesizer used, the proposed approach significantly reduces the area of FSMs.

Table 8. Area of FSMs with one-hot encoding in the system Vivado.

FSM	*A3*	*As*	*Ao*	*Aso*	*Amin*	*A3*/*As*	*A3*/*Ao*	*A3*/*Aso*
bbsse	29	**22**	30	23	22	1.318	0.967	1.261
beecount	**8**	16	10	14	8	0.500	0.800	0.571
cse	51	49	47	**37**	37	1.041	1.085	1.378
dk14	21	21	21	**20**	20	1.000	1.000	1.050
dk16	39	17	42	**15**	15	**2.294**	0.929	**2.600**
dk512	13	7	11	**6**	6	1.857	1.182	2.167
ex1	58	**37**	72	44	37	1.568	0.806	1.318
ex2	10	8	9	**7**	7	1.250	1.111	1.429
ex3	10	8	9	**7**	7	1.250	1.111	1.429
ex4	**11**	12	13	14	11	0.917	0.846	0.786
ex5	8	8	8	**7**	7	1.000	1.000	1.143
ex6	25	24	25	**23**	23	1.042	1.000	1.087
ex7	**4**	**4**	**4**	**4**	4	1.000	1.000	1.000
lion	3	**2**	3	**2**	2	1.500	1.000	1.500
lion9	11	14	11	**10**	10	0.786	1.000	1.100
planet	83	**50**	88	52	50	1.660	0.943	1.596
planet1	83	**50**	88	52	50	1.660	0.943	1.596
pma	**35**	52	63	74	35	0.673	0.556	0.473
s1	63	**34**	63	**34**	34	1.853	1.000	1.853
s27	**119**	130	120	130	119	0.915	0.992	0.915
s208	10	11	**9**	13	9	0.909	1.111	0.769
s1488	7	7	7	**6**	6	1.000	1.000	1.167
sand	94	98	87	**83**	83	0.959	1.080	1.133
sse	25	**23**	26	**23**	23	1.087	0.962	1.087
styr	88	**53**	98	**53**	53	1.660	0.898	1.660
tbk	128	156	**116**	153	116	0.821	1.103	0.837
tma	**26**	41	48	56	26	0.634	0.542	0.464
train4	13	14	11	**10**	10	0.929	1.182	1.300
train11	5	5	4	**3**	3	1.000	**1.250**	1.667
Av						**1.175**	**0.979**	**1.253**
Max						**2.294**	**1.250**	**2.600**
Best	6	9	3	18				
Unique	5	4	2	13				

Table 9. Area of FSMs with binary encoding in the system Vivado.

FSM	*A3*	*As*	*Ao*	*Aso*	*Amin*	*A3*/*As*	*A3*/*Ao*	*A3*/*Aso*
bbsse	29	**22**	30	23	22	1.318	0.967	1.261
beecount	**8**	**8**	10	9	8	1.000	0.800	0.889
cse	51	49	47	**37**	37	1.041	1.085	1.378
dk14	11	10	11	**9**	9	1.100	1.000	1.222
dk16	15	**7**	15	**7**	7	**2.143**	1.000	**2.143**
dk512	4	**2**	4	**2**	2	2.000	1.000	2.000
ex1	58	**37**	72	44	37	1.568	0.806	1.318
ex2	6	6	6	**5**	5	1.000	1.000	1.200
ex3	6	**5**	7	6	5	1.200	0.857	1.000
ex4	**11**	12	13	14	11	0.917	0.846	0.786
ex5	**5**	**5**	**5**	**5**	5	1.000	1.000	1.000
ex6	25	24	25	**23**	23	1.042	1.000	1.087
ex7	5	**4**	5	**4**	4	1.250	1.000	1.250

https://doi.org/10.3390/electronics15040831

Table 9. *Cont.*

FSM	*A3*	*As*	*Ao*	*Aso*	*Amin*	*A3/As*	*A3/Ao*	*A3/Aso*
lion	3	**2**	3	**2**	2	1.500	1.000	1.500
lion9	**4**	6	5	5	4	0.667	0.800	0.800
planet	83	**50**	88	52	50	1.660	0.943	1.596
planet1	83	**50**	88	52	50	1.660	0.943	1.596
pma	**35**	52	63	74	35	0.673	0.556	0.473
s1	63	**34**	63	**34**	34	1.853	1.000	1.853
s27	**119**	130	120	130	119	0.915	0.992	0.915
s208	10	11	**9**	13	9	0.909	1.111	0.769
s1488	7	7	7	**6**	6	1.000	1.000	1.167
sand	94	98	87	**83**	83	0.959	1.080	1.133
sse	25	**23**	26	**23**	23	1.087	0.962	1.087
styr	88	**53**	98	**53**	53	1.660	0.898	1.660
tbk	128	156	**116**	153	116	0.821	1.103	0.837
tma	**26**	41	48	56	26	0.634	0.542	0.464
train4	6	6	6	**5**	5	1.000	1.000	1.200
train11	4	**2**	3	**2**	2	2.000	**1.333**	2.000
Av						**1.227**	**0.953**	**1.227**
Max						**2.143**	**1.333**	**2.143**
Best	7	15	3	16				
Unique	5	4	2	7				

4.5. Comparison of the Proposed Approach with Known Methods

Table 10 shows the reductions in the area and increases in the performance of FSMs reported in the literature when using various methods, as well as when applying the proposed approach, where *Av* and *Max* denote the average and maximum value of the parameter. Table 10 also presents the results obtained using the JEDI program [30] for encoding FSM states. For comparison, Table 10 presents the results obtained using the proposed approach, where *Doh* denotes the parameter values for one-hot encoding, and *Db* denotes those for binary encoding.

Table 10. Reducing the area and increasing performance in various methods of FSM optimization.

Methods	Area		Performance	
	Av	*Max*	*Av*	*Max*
[1]	79.6%	-	22.4%	-
[2]	15.0%	-	8%	-
[3]	25.0%	-	-	-
[4]	30.0%	-	-	-
[5]	30.0%	-	-	-
[6]	25.8%	100%	-	-
[8]	50.0%	-	-	-
[9]	5.0%	-	-	-
[10]	67.0%	-	-	-
[11]	30.0%	-	-	-
[12]	87.0%	-	-	-
[13]	50.6%	-	19.7%	-
[25]	26.0%	3.1 times	21.0%	60%
[26]	77.4%	4.8 times	19.3%	2.4 times
[30]	3.7%	71.4%	4.4%	51.6%
Doh	93.0%	5.2 times	93.4%	4.4 times
Db	97.6%	6.2 times	64.9%	3.1 times

Table 10 shows that the proposed approach surpasses all other methods in reducing the area and improving FSM performance. Note that this approach does not replace the

https://doi.org/10.3390/electronics15040831

existing FSM optimization methods—such as state minimization, state encoding, logic minimization, and synthesis—but rather complements them. Consequently, this approach can be applied at the stage of describing the FSM project in HDL, regardless of other FSM optimization methods.

5. Conclusions

This paper introduces three styles for describing FSMs in Verilog HDL to enhance their parameters: *dstate*, where the default value is the next state; *dout*, where the default value is the output vector; and *dstate_out*, where the default values include both the next state and the output vector. Algorithms are presented for creating FSM project code in Verilog and encoding states to optimize the area and performance of FSMs.

Experimental studies in the Quartus design tool on MCNC benchmarks demonstrate that the *dstate_out* style reduces the average area of FSMs by a factor of 1.93 when states are encoded in one-hot code and by 1.976 when encoded in binary. For specific examples, this reduction can be as much as a factor of 5.182 and 6.2, respectively. Additionally, the *dstate_out* style enhances FSM performance by an average of 1.934 with one-hot encoding and 1.649 with binary encoding, with individual examples showing increases of up to 4.396 and 3.115, respectively.

It has been shown that the proposed approach depends on the synthesizer used in the design tool. For example, in the Vivado system, the average area reduction is 25.3% for one-hot encoding (2.6 times for individual examples) and 22.7% for binary encoding (2.143 times for individual examples). It has also been shown that the proposed approach outperforms all known methods in terms of area reduction and performance improvement of FSMs.

We recommend using the *dstate_out* and *dstate* styles to describe FSMs. We do not recommend using the *dout* style due to its minimal effectiveness in improving FSM parameters. Since the proposed styles can lead to incomplete 'case' statements, we recommend using the considered styles for describing FSMs in the final stages of design, when the user is completely confident in the correct functioning of the FSM. Traditional methods of describing FSMs can be used during the project verification stages and in complex projects.

Future research will focus on developing new styles for describing FSMs in HDL and structural models that aim to optimize FSM parameters.

Author Contributions: Conceptualization, methodology, validation, writing—original draft preparation, investigation, supervision, V.S.; resources, data curation, writing—review and editing, A.K. All authors have read and agreed to the published version of the manuscript.

Funding: The present study was supported by a grant WZ/WI-III/5/2023 from Bialystok University of Technology and founded from the resources for research by Ministry of Science and Higher Education.

Data Availability Statement: The raw data supporting the conclusions of this article will be made available by the authors on request.

Conflicts of Interest: The authors declare no conflicts of interest.

Abbreviations

The following abbreviations are used in this manuscript:

ASIC	Application-Specific Integrated Circuit
FPGA	Field-Programmable Gate Array
FSM	Finite State Machine
HDL	Hardware Description Language
VHDL	Very high-speed integrated circuit Hardware Description Language

https://doi.org/10.3390/electronics15040831

SoC	System-on-Chip
STG	State Transition Graph

References

1. Barkalov, A.; Titarenko, L.; Mielcarek, K.; Mazurkiewicz, M. Hardware reduction for FSMs with extended state codes. *IEEE Access* **2024**, *12*, 42369–42384. [CrossRef]
2. Rho, J.K.; Hachtel, G.D.; Somenzi, F.; Jacoby, R.M. Exact and heuristic algorithms for the minimization of incompletely specified state machines. *IEEE Trans. Comput.-Aided Des. Integr. Circuits Syst.* **1994**, *13*, 167–177. [CrossRef]
3. De Micheli, G.; Brayton, R.K.; Sangiovanni-Vincentelli, A. Optimal state assignment for finite state machines. *IEEE Trans. Comput.-Aided Des. Integr. Circuits Syst.* **1985**, *4*, 269–285. [CrossRef]
4. Villa, T.; Sangiovanni-Vincentelli, A. NOVA: State assignment of finite state machines for optimal two-level logic implementations. In Proceedings of the 26th ACM/IEEE Design Automation Conference, Las Vegas, NV, USA, 25–29 June 1989; pp. 327–332. [CrossRef]
5. Devadas, S.; Ma, H.K.; Newton, A.R.; Sangiovanni-Vincentelli, A. MUSTANG: State assignment of finite state machines targeting multilevel logic implementations. *IEEE Trans. Comput.-Aided Des. Integr. Circuits Syst.* **1988**, *7*, 1290–1300. [CrossRef]
6. Klimowicz, S.; Solov'ev, V.V. Structural models of finite-state machines for their implementation on programmable logic devices and systems on chip. *J. Comput. Syst. Sci. Int.* **2015**, *54*, 230–242. [CrossRef]
7. Meyer, M.J.; Agrawal, P.; Pfister, R.G. A VLSI FSM Design System. In Proceedings of the 21st Design Automation Conference, Albuquerque, NM, USA, 25–27 June 1984; pp. 434–440. [CrossRef]
8. Luba, T.; Gorski, K.; Wronski, L.B. ROM-based Finite State Machines with PLA address modifiers. In Proceedings of the EURO-DAC'92: European Design Automation Conference, Hamburg, Germany, 7–10 September 1992; pp. 272–273. [CrossRef]
9. Baranov, S.; Levin, I.; Keren, O.; Karpovsky, M. Designing fault tolerant FSM by nano-PLA. In Proceedings of the 15th IEEE International On-Line Testing Symposium, Lisbon, Portugal, 24–26 June 2009; pp. 229–234. [CrossRef]
10. Solovjev, V.; Chyzy, M. Refined CPLD macrocell architecture for the effective FSM implementation. In Proceedings of the 25th Euromicro Conference, Informatics: Theory and Practice for the New Millennium, Milan, Italy, 8–10 September 1999; Volume 1, pp. 102–109. [CrossRef]
11. Czerwinski, R.; Kania, D. CPLD-oriented synthesis of finite state machines. In Proceedings of the 12th Euromicro Conference on Digital System Design, Architectures, Styles and Tools, Patras, Greece, 27–29 August 2009; pp. 521–528. [CrossRef]
12. Garcia-Vargas, I.; Senhadji-Navarro, R.; Jimenez-Moreno, G.; Civit-Balcells, A.; Guerra-Gutierrez, P. ROM-based finite state machine implementation in low cost FPGAs. In Proceedings of the IEEE International Symposium on Industrial Electronics, Vigo, Spain, 4–7 June 2007; pp. 2342–2347. [CrossRef]
13. Garcia-Vargas, I.; Senhadji-Navarro, R. Finite state machines with input multiplexing: A performance study. *IEEE Trans. Comput.-Aided Des. Integr. Circuits Syst.* **2015**, *34*, 867–871. [CrossRef]
14. Villa, T.; Kam, T.; Brayton, R.K.; Sangiovanni-Vincentelli, A.L. *Synthesis of Finite State Machines: Logic Optimization*; Springer Science & Business Media: Berlin, Germany, 2012.
15. Golson, S. State machine design techniques for Verilog and VHDL. *Synopsys J. High-Level Des.* **1994**, *9*, 1–20.
16. Arnold, M.G.; Sample, N.J.; Shuler, J.D. Guidelines for safe simulation and synthesis of implicit style Verilog. In Proceedings of the International Verilog HDL Conference and VHDL International Users Forum, Santa Clara, CA, USA, 16–19 March 1998; pp. 59–66. [CrossRef]
17. Wang, T.H.; Edsall, T. Practical FSM analysis for Verilog. In Proceedings of the International Verilog HDL Conference and VHDL International Users Forum, Santa Clara, CA, USA, 16–19 March 1998; pp. 52–58. [CrossRef]
18. Cummings, C.E. State machine coding styles for synthesis. In *Proceedings of the Synopsys Users Group (SNUG'98), San Jose, CA, USA, March 1998*; Synopsys: Sunnyvale, CA, USA, 1998; pp. 1–20.
19. Cummings, C.E. Coding and scripting techniques for FSM designs with synthesis-optimized, glitch-free outputs. In Proceedings of the Synopsys Users Group Boston (SNUG), Boston, MA, USA, 20–22 September 2020; pp. 1–13.
20. Cummings, C.E. Synthesizable Finite State Machine Design Techniques Using the New SystemVerilog 3.0 Enhancements. In Proceedings of the Synopsys Users Group (SNUG), San Jose, CA, USA, 29–31 March 2003; pp. 1–53.
21. Rafla, N.I.; Davis, B.L. A study of finite state machine coding styles for implementation in FPGAs. In Proceedings of the 49th IEEE International Midwest Symposium on Circuits and Systems, San Juan, PR, USA, 6–9 August 2006; Volume 1, pp. 337–341. [CrossRef]
22. Chiuchisan, I.; Potorac, A.D.; Graur, A. Finite state machine design and VHDL coding techniques. In Proceedings of the 10th International Conference on Development and Application Systems, Suceava, Romania, 27–29 May 2010; pp. 273–278.
23. Masoumi, S.H.; Al-Haddad, S.A.R.; Rokhani, F.Z. New tool for converting high-level representations of finite state machines to Verilog HDL. In Proceedings of the IEEE 15th Student Conference on Research and Development (SCOReD), Putrajaya, Malaysia, 13–14 December 2017; pp. 1–6. [CrossRef]

https://doi.org/10.3390/electronics15040831

24. Sentovich, M.; Singh, K.J.; Lavagno, L.; Moon, C.; Murgai, R.; Saldanha, A.; Savoj, H.; Stephan, P.R.; Brayton, R.K.; Sangiovanni-Vincentelli, A. *SIS: A System for Sequential Circuit Synthesis*; University of California: Berkeley, CA, USA, 1992; p. 94720.
25. Salauyou, V.; Zabrocki, L. Coding techniques in Verilog for finite state machine designs in FPGA. In Proceedings of the Computer Information Systems and Industrial Management: 18th International Conference (CISIM 2019), Belgrade, Serbia, 19–21 September 2019; pp. 493–505. [CrossRef]
26. Salauyou, V. Description styles of fault-tolerant finite state machines for unmanned aerial vehicles. *Radioelectron. Comput. Syst.* **2024**, *2024*, 196–206. [CrossRef]
27. Salauyou, V. Styles for Describing Reliable Finite State Machines in Verilog HDL. In Proceedings of the International Conference on Dependability of Computer Systems (DepCoS), Wroclaw, Poland, 1–5 June 2024; pp. 241–251. [CrossRef]
28. Cummings, C.E. The Fundamentals of Efficient Synthesizable Finite State Machine Design using NC-Verilog and BuildGates. In Proceedings of the International Cadence Usergroup Conference, Aix-en-Provence, France, 2–6 September 2002; pp. 1–27.
29. Yang, S. *Logic Synthesis and Optimization Benchmarks User Guide, Version 3.0*; Microelectronics Center of North Carolina (MCNC): Research Triangle Park, NC, USA, 1991.
30. Lin, B.; Newton, A.R. Synthesis of multiple level logic from symbolic high-level description languages. In Proceedings of the IFIP International Conference on VLSI, Munich, Germany, 16–18 August 1989; pp. 187–196.

electronics

MDPI

Article

Hardware Optimized Modular Reduction

Alexander Magyari * and Yuhua Chen

Department of Electrical and Computer Engineering, University of Houston, Houston, TX 77204, USA; yuhuachen@uh.edu
* Correspondence: ammagyar@cougarnet.uh.edu

Abstract: We introduce a modular reduction method that is optimized for hardware and outperforms conventional approaches. By leveraging calculated reduction cycles and combinatorial logic, we achieve a remarkable 30% reduction in power usage, 27% reduction in Configurable Logic Blocks (CLBs), and 12% fewer look up tables (LUTs) than the conventional implementation. Our Hardware-Optimized Modular Reduction (HOM-R) system can condense a 256-bit input to a four-bit base within a single 250 MHz clock cycle. Further, our method stands out from prevalent techniques, such as Barrett and Montgomery reduction, by eliminating the need for multipliers or dividers, and relying solely on addition and customizable LUTs. This innovative method frees up FPGA resources typically consumed by power-intensive DSPs, offering a compelling low-power, low-latency alternative for diverse design needs.

Keywords: PQC; FPGA; cryptography; modular; reduction

1. Introduction

Modular reduction, expressed as $(a)\text{mod}(b) \equiv c$, is considered to be both one of the most computationally expensive basic-mathematical instructions, and one of the most important instructions in modern cryptography. In the simplest terms, modular reduction is the remainder of elementary integer division. From this definition, one could naively discern that calculating a modular congruence c requires division. This is easy to perform in software, as shown in Equation (1). The floor function can be replaced by integer division, depending on the software language used.

$$(a)\text{mod}(b) \equiv c \equiv a - \lfloor \frac{a}{b} \rfloor \tag{1}$$

Unfortunately, since Equation (1) requires both a division and subtraction operation, this implementation is inefficient for both hardware and software [1]. Another naive approach, which can be quickly implemented in software, is shown in Algorithm 1. This algorithm implements a loop that will continue to reduce the input a until it is less than the modular base, b, returning the modular congruence c.

Algorithm 1 A naive software implementation of modular reduction.

```
c ← a
while c > b do
    c ← c − b
return c
```

This implementation presents two issues. The first problem with this implementation is that the number of iterations through the loop is directly related to how large the input a

 https://doi.org/10.3390/electronics14030550

is. For cryptographic purposes, knowing the relative size of the input can be used to assist an attacker in decrypting encrypted data. Second, there is no defined upper-limit to the algorithm. This results in unpredictable latency, where the required iterations approach infinity as the input grows.

Within this work, we explore state-of-the-art methods for modular reduction, with an emphasis on the hardware requirements for the implementation of each. We argue that modern methods could be both faster and more power efficient, and present our own algorithm as a solution.

Our Hardware Optimized Modular Reduction (HOM-R) algorithm will have impacts in a variety of fields, as a wide breadth of topics rely on modular reduction. This includes fields that use a system of modular numbers, referred to as a Residue Number System (RNS). Specifically, however, we targeted our design for cryptography, as algorithms such as Homomorphic Encryption (HE) and Zero-Knowledge Proofs (ZKP) heavily utilize modular reduction, depending on the specific form of the algorithm used [2–5].

The HOM-R algorithm is also viable for other applications outside of cryptography, however. For example, Kalmykov et al. implemented a novel Error-Correcting Code using a Residue Number System (RNS), which relies heavily on modular arithmetic [6]. Valueva et al. applied the RNS to Convolutional Neural Networks (CNN) as a means to reduce the hardware cost of the machine learning model [7]. This application in AI for RNS is also seen in other works, including a multiplication-free neural network by Salamat et al. [8] and an ASIC implementation of an RNS-based CNN by Sakellariou et al. [9]. Other examples include an accelerator for probability models [10], intrusion detection systems [11], and new data storage methods for increased reliability [12].

As we will see in Section 2, modern approaches to modular reduction either rely on high-power resources, such as digital signal processors (DSPs), or have a high latency. Our motivation for this work is to achieve both low power and low latency. As we demonstrate in Section 5, our algorithm relies solely on bit shifts and a predictable number of additions, allowing us to avoid the use of DSPs whilst only requiring a single clock cycle of latency, even at high clock frequencies.

The rest of the paper is organized as follows: in Section 2, we cover other algorithms that are often used for modular reduction. In Section 3, we describe our algorithm and how to implement it based on use-case. In Section 4, we demonstrate the feasibility of our algorithm by implementing it on a Field Programmable Gate Array (FPGA). In Section 5, we discuss the implementation results of the HOM-R system. Finally, in Section 6, we conclude the paper.

2. Background

When describing modular reduction on hardware, there are two methods that must be considered. However, before we can consider those, there are some special cases where one would not opt for any of these methods. First, let us consider a common case of modular reduction: when the modular base b is a power of two (1, 2, 4, 8, etc.). Of course, for base two modular reduction, one can simply truncate the bit vector, as shown in Equation (2), where '&' represents the bit-wise AND function, and '−' represents the conventional integer subtraction. This method, when implemented in hardware, requires simple combinatorial logic that induces minimal latency and resource usage.

$$(a)\text{mod}(b) \equiv c \equiv a \;\&\; (b-1) \quad (2)$$

The second method that can be used for special cases is when the modular base is not a power of two, and the input size is small. One can use a direct look-up table in hardware, or an array in software, to quickly find the modular congruence of the input.

With $(a)\text{mod}(b) \equiv c$, and $a < n$, this method requires n entries of $\lceil \log_2(n) \rceil$ bits, leading to a total memory requirement of $n \lceil \log_2(n) \rceil$.

For all other cases, prior to the introduction of the HOM-R system, one's options for modular reduction include one of the three following algorithms: Montgomery reduction, Barrett reduction, or a more recent addition, a fast modular reduction method by Will et al. [13]. We will include Will's method as it serves as the basis for our work.

While other options exist, we do not cover those implementations in-depth as they either have large memory/resource requirements depending on the input, or are sub-optimal for hardware due to the reliance on recursion. This includes work by Parhami et al., in which the authors explore segmentation and truncation within look-up tables for modular reduction [14]. Parhami et al. offers another work exploring the inverse of this operation: combining residues into a unified, binary representation [15]. Another work by Opasatian et al. also explores the use of look-up tables similar to Parhami, but their method requires an additional 'adjustment' step that relies on subtraction. The principle behind this step is similar to that in Montgomery reduction, in that the computed value may be twice the value of the modulus [16]. Lim et al. offer a method for modular reduction that also relies on look-up tables; however, they implement their design in software [17]. Another method is the one by Cao et al., which offers a unique approach that evaluates a binary vector based on the longest run of 1 s and 0 s [18].

2.1. Mongtomery Reduction

Montgomery reduction [19] is one of the most commonly used modular reduction algorithms in modern hardware. The premise of the formula is to represent a residue class using a different modular base. Ideally, this new base is a power of two, which can then be reduced via the modular-base-two method listed above. The delay for Montgomery Reduction comes in play when changing the modular base. Because of this, a number's base is often changed only once, where the new base representation, referred to as its Montgomery form, is used for all mathematical calculations. This way, any further modular reductions can be performed via the modular-base-two truncation method. Once a number has finished processing and does not require any more operations, its modular base can be converted back to the original, and the final congruence of the original number can be retrieved.

For $(a)\text{mod}(b) \equiv c$, let $(R \in \mathbb{Z}) > b$ where R is co-prime to b. R should be chosen so that $(a)\text{mod}(R)$ is easy to compute; ideally, R should be a power of two. Further, let $b' = b^{-1}\text{mod}R$. The Montgomery reduction of input a can then be defined as Equation (3).

$$REDC(a) = (aR^{-1})\text{mod}(b) \tag{3}$$

Note that one subtraction of b may be required since $0 \leq REDC(b) < 2b$. It is also important to note that Montgomery reduction only requires $k(k+1)$ multiplications. The number of multiplications required is not correlated to the size of the target number, which is not the case in the following algorithm, the Barrett reduction.

The Montgomery form allows for quick modulo operations where multiple numbers are multiplied or added together, as they can all be converted to the same residue class. Addition in Montgomery space is performed as with regular numbers; however, there is a small caveat to multiplying numbers in Montgomery space. Since two separate numbers in Montgomery space include a R factor, multiplication results in a R^2 term. This is an easy obstacle to overcome: since the Montgomery form relies on R being an integer that is a power of two, the result can be divided by a factor of R through a bit-wise right shift of $log_2(R)$ bits.

2.2. Barrett Reduction

Barrett's method [20] is similar to Montgomery's approach in that it requires the selection of a "magic number" that is relative to the modular base b. When implementing Barrett reduction, one must consider the word size L of the system, which depends heavily on whether a general purpose computer or specialized circuit, such as an FPGA, is used. Depending on the word size, a base β must be chosen such that $\beta = 2^L$. From β, we can calculate the required parameter in Equation (4), where $k = \lfloor \log_b p \rfloor + 1$. There is the further limitation that a from $(a)\text{mod}(b) \equiv c$ that $0 \leq a < \beta^{2k}$.

$$\mu = \lfloor \frac{\beta^{2k}}{b} \rfloor \tag{4}$$

If we assign $q = \lfloor \frac{a}{b} \rfloor$, then $a\text{mod}b \equiv c \equiv a - qb$. From Equation (5), we can derive Equation (6).

$$\frac{a}{b} = \frac{a}{\beta^{k-1}} \cdot \frac{\beta^{2k}}{b} \cdot \frac{1}{\beta^{k+1}} \tag{5}$$

$$0 \leq \hat{q} = \lfloor \frac{\lfloor \frac{a}{\beta^{k-1}} \rfloor \cdot \mu}{\beta^{k+1}} \rfloor \leq \lfloor \frac{a}{b} \rfloor = q \tag{6}$$

If we precompute μ, it is easy to see from Equation (6) that the main complexity in the Barrett reduction is caused by the multiplication of μ. The residue c can be computed from this value as $c = a - \hat{q}p + (\hat{q} - q)b$, which involves at most two subtractions and three bit shifts.

2.3. Will's Algorithm

The look-up tables reduction method proposed by Will et al. is a unique and attractive option for modular reduction when compared to Barrett's and Montgomery's methods, as it does not require a multiplication primitive [13]. Through a series of bit shifts and additions with precomputed numbers, Will's method is able to reduce a number to a residue. The basic structure of the algorithm is defined in Algorithm 2, where bit vector width $\beta = \lceil log_2(a+1) \rceil$, the input vector is split into l-width-vectors, defined as $\hat{s} = [\sum_{i=0}^{l-1} a_i 2^i, \ldots, \sum_{i=0}^{l-1} a_{\beta-l+i} 2^i]$, and N is defined as $N = length(\hat{s}) - 1$. In this Algorithm, and the others that follow, $n << m$ indicates an integer n shifted left m times.

Algorithm 2 Will's algorithm for modular reduction [13].

```
n ← N
while n > 0 do
    T ← ŝ[n]
    for i = β − 1 downto 0 do
        T ← T << 1
        while (T & 2^β) ≠ 0 do
            T ← T & (2^β − 1) + (2^β)modb
    ŝ[n − 1] = ŝ[n − 1] + T
    while ŝ[n − 1] & 2^β ≠ 0 do
        ŝ[n − 1] ← ŝ[n − 1] & (2^β − 1) + (2^β)modb
    n ← n − 1
while ŝ[0] > b do
    ŝ[0] ← ŝ[0] − b
return ŝ[0]
```

The mod values in Algorithm 2 are precomputed and stored. Will also emphasizes that there can be a larger number of precomputed values, reducing the number of iterations in the *for* loop. These are stored in the look-up table, and the modified algorithm is shown as Algorithm 3. In this algorithm, δ is the width of the look-up table, with each value in the look-up table being calculated by Algorithm 4.

Algorithm 3 Will's algorithm for modular reduction modified for a user defined modular look-up width δ, and $\hat{m}$ is defined in Algorithm 4 [13].

```
n ← N
mask ← 0
for i = δ − 1 downto 0 do
    mask ← mask + 2^i
mask ← mask << β
while n > 0 do
    T ← ŝ[n]
    for i = β − 1 downto 0 do
        T ← T << δ
        while (T & mask) ≠ 0 do
            î = (T & mask) >> β
            T ← T & (2^β − 1) + m̂[î]
    ŝ[n − 1] = ŝ[n − 1] + T
    while ŝ[n − 1] & mask ≠ 0 do
        î = (ŝ[n − 1] & mask) >> β
        ŝ[n − 1] ← ŝ[n − 1] & (2^β − 1) + m̂[î]
    n ← n − 1
while ŝ[0] > b do
    ŝ[0] ← ŝ[0] − b
return ŝ[0]
```

Algorithm 4 Modular value look-up tables generation with index width δ [13].

```
m̂ ← [0] ∗ 2^δ
for i = 0 upto 2^δ do
    d = i << β
    m̂[i] ← d mod b
return m̂
```

From these algorithms, there are a few important things to consider. The first concern is that there is a memory complexity $\Theta(2^{\delta})$, so the look-up table size must be determined with device and power constraints in mind, with the optimal δ value being 1. However, this must be a balanced decision, as a smaller look-up table width will require more bit shifts in Algorithm 3, increasing the latency of the system. Another point of note is the *while* loops do not have defined latency. This prevents a combinatorial implementation in hardware, as each iteration of the loop will need to be analyzed at the end of a clock cycle. This is a pain-point for latency. Further, it must also be considered that the summation of the look-up table values leads to a value that is larger than the defined index of $\hat{m}$, resulting in undefined behavior. We evaluate these shortcomings and propose solutions in Section 3.

3. Methods

The design of the HOM-R system has a primary focus on low power usage. In terms of FPGAs or ASICs, this means reducing digital signal processors (DSPs), and keeping the FPGA Look-Up Table (LUT) usage to a minimum. We specifically use the abbreviation "LUT" to refer to the the logic resource utilized by the FPGA, and "look-up table" to refer to the $\hat{m}$ and $\hat{m}'$ components required by the HOM-R system. By prioritizing resource utilization and power reduction, we are able to formulate an algorithm that results in zero

DSPs and minimal LUTs regardless of the base used. We determine Will's algorithm to be a good starting point for this objective, as it relies purely on additions and bitwise operations.

The primary issue with Will's algorithm is the number of *while* loops, which are non-ideal for hardware implementations due to their unpredictable number of iterations. An ideal hardware implementation should focus on utilizing *for* loops, which have a constrained number of iterations. This allows for predictable latency, thereby allowing the use of combinatorial logic that can fit an entire loop within a single clock cycle. This is opposed to the *while* loop, which will require the condition to be evaluated based on the output of a circuit. This is only possible by calculating an iteration and re-evaluating the loop condition at the end of a clock cycle, leading to an entire clock cycle being used only for one a single iteration of the loop.

For our implementation of the HOM-R module to solve the equation $(a)\text{mod}(b) \equiv c$, the following terminology will be used:

1. Stage: Each input vector x of width $\Omega = \lceil log_2(a+1) \rceil$ will be split into stages of width ω to solve for a residue width $\beta = \lceil log_2(b+1) \rceil$. Each stage is represented as a $\hat{s}$. The input vector is therefore transformed into an array of N stages, represented as Ψ, where $N = \lceil (\Omega - \beta)/\omega \rceil$. The calculation for Ψ is shown in Equation (7).

$$\Psi = [\hat{s}_0, \ldots, \hat{s}_{N-1}] = [\sum_{i=0}^{\beta-1} a_i 2^i, \ldots, \sum_{i=\beta(N-1)}^{N\beta-1} a_{\Omega-\beta+i} 2^i] \tag{7}$$

2. Base Stage: This is the least significant stage, stage zero. The final residue c will have a maximum width of the width of the modular base b, β and will have exactly one stage remaining in Ψ, the base stage.
3. Modular-Value Look-up Table (MLUT): The look-up table composed of modular values, calculated via Algorithms 5 and 6, and represented by $\hat{m}$ with a depth 2^{δ} and $\hat{m}'$ with a depth $2^{\delta'}$, respectively. There are N different MLUTs, with each MLUT representing the modular values for different $\hat{s}$. By utilizing an MLUT for each different stage, we can reduce each stage to the base stage in parallel.
4. Overflow Bits: When summing values from $\hat{m}$, it is possible that the width of the sum exceeds β. These bits are referred to as overflow bits.

A full description of the required parameters for HOM-R are outlined in Table 1.

Table 1. Parameter definitions for HOM-R.

Parameter	Description
x	The input vector
b	Modular base
$\hat{s}$	An individual reduction stage
Ψ	The collection of stages. When concatenated together, it is equivalent to x.
N	Number of stages
$\hat{m}$	Modular value look-up tables
σ	Stage output after summing each respective $\hat{m}$ for the stage
Ω	Width of x
ω	Width of the input to a stage
δ	Width of the input to $\hat{m}$
β	Maximum width of the residue output

Algorithm 5 HOM-R 2D modular value look-up table generation with index width δ and stage width β.

$\hat{m} \leftarrow [[0] * 2^{\delta}] * (N-1)$
for $i = 0$ *upto* $N-1$ **do**
    for $j = 0$ *upto* 2^{δ} **do**
        $d = j << ((i+1) * \beta)$
        $\hat{m}[i][j] \leftarrow d \bmod b$
return $\hat{m}$

Algorithm 6 HOM-R 1D modular value look-up table generation for reducing $c = \mathrm{sum}(\sigma)$. Index width δ' and stage width β.

$\hat{m}' \leftarrow [0] * 2^{\delta'}$
for $i = 0$ *upto* $2^{\delta'}$ **do**
    $d = i << \beta$
    $\hat{m}'[i] \leftarrow d \bmod b$
return $\hat{m}'$

The full HOM-R algorithm is defined in Algorithm 7. Line 1 handles the simplest of cases, when the modular base class is an even power of two. In this case, we can simply truncate the input vector a to be the same length as the modular vector b to retrieve the residue c, saving precious hardware memory.

Algorithm 7 Hardware Optimized Modular Reduction Algorithm for $(a) \bmod b \equiv c$.

1: **if** $\lfloor \log_2(\mathrm{b}) \rfloor == log_2(b)$ **then return** $a \;\&\; (b-1)$
2: $N \leftarrow \lceil (\Omega - \beta)/\omega \rceil$
3: $\sigma \leftarrow [0] * N$
4: $\sigma[0] \leftarrow \Psi[0]$
5: **for** $i = 1$ *upto* N **do**
6:     idx $\leftarrow \Psi[i] \;\&\; (2^{\delta} - 1)$
7:     $\sigma[i] \leftarrow \hat{m}[i][idx]$
8:     **for** $j = 1$ *upto* $\lceil \beta/\text{ffi} \rceil$ **do**
9:         idx $\leftarrow (\Psi[i] >> (j * \delta)) \;\&\; (2^{\delta} - 1)$
10:         $\sigma[i] \leftarrow \sigma[i] + j * 2^{\delta} * \hat{m}[i][idx]$
11:     **for** $j = 0$ *upto* NUM_SUMS **do**
12:         idx $\leftarrow (\sigma[i] >> \beta)$
13:         $\sigma[i] \leftarrow \sigma[i] + \hat{m}[0][idx]$
14: $c \leftarrow$ sum(œ)
15: **for** $j = 0$ *upto* NUM_SUMS **do**
16:     idx $\leftarrow (c >> \beta)$
17:     $c \leftarrow c + \hat{m}'[idx]$
18: **if** $c > b$ **then**
19:     $c \leftarrow \hat{s}[0] - b$
20: **return** c

The first loop in the system, Lines 3–10, breaks the input vector a into a series of $\hat{s}$ that compose the array Ψ. For each $\hat{s}$, we compute σ according to the modular base b using Equation (8). While σ is not the final residue c, it is congruent to the original $\hat{s}$ relative to b and much smaller than s. We use this value to calculate the final residue c using the rest of the algorithm.

$$f(x) = (\hat{s} >> (x * \delta)) \ \& \ (2^\delta - 1) << \omega$$
$$\sigma = f(0)\text{mod}(c) + \sum_{i=1}^{\lceil \omega/\delta \rceil} (i * 2^\delta) * (f(i)\text{mod}(c)) \quad (8)$$

To help demonstrate how Equation (8) may be implemented for a four-bit $\hat{s}$ with a stage index s in Ψ, composed of bits $b_3b_2b_1b_0$ with a $\delta = 2$, we present Equation (9). As shown in Equation (9), this function is merely shifting the vector $\hat{s}$ left by two bits, isolating two bits at a time, and calculating the residue for each. Since there are four bits in $\hat{s}$, the vector must be shifted twice. Each shift is equivalent to multiplying by four. We move these factors of four inside or outside the $\hat{m}$ lookup depending on the location of the bits in the vector $\hat{s}$.

$$\begin{aligned} \sigma &= (4 * 4 * b_1b_0)\text{mod}(c) + 4 * (4 * b_3b_2)\text{mod}(c) \\ &= \hat{m}[s-1][b_1b_0] + 4 * \hat{m}[s-1][b_3b_2] \end{aligned} \quad (9)$$

We prove that we can use the bits in $\hat{s}$ as an index to $\hat{m}$ in Equation (8) via Lemmas 1–3. Lemma 1 allows us to prove Lemmas 2 and 3. Lemma 2 proves that the bit vectors can be operated on as a sum of the bits, rather than as the entire vector. Lemma 3 demonstrates that the vector can be shifted (multiplied by a power of two), regardless of whether the factor of two is used to compute the modular residue or operate on the modular residue.

Lemma 1. *For $a, b, c, k \in \mathbb{Z}$, $(a)\text{mod}(b) \equiv c$, $\exists k \in \mathbb{Z}$ such that $c = a + kb$.*

$$\begin{aligned} \text{From definition of } (a)\text{mod}(b) \equiv c,\ & b|(a-c) \\ \text{From definition of } \frac{a-c}{b},\ & kb = a - c \\ & \therefore c = a + kb. \end{aligned}$$

Lemma 2. *For $a, b, c, d, m, k, j \in \mathbb{Z}$,* if $a + c \equiv (b + d)$ mod m, then $a \equiv b$ mod m and $c \equiv d$ mod m.

$$\begin{aligned} \text{From Lemma 1, } a + c &= (b + d) + (k + j)m \\ a + c &= b + km + d + jm \end{aligned}$$

$$\begin{aligned} \therefore a &= b + km \\ c &= d + jm \end{aligned}$$

Lemma 3. *For $a, b, c, m \in \mathbb{Z}$, $a[(bc) \text{ mod } m] \equiv (ab)(c \text{ mod } m)$.*

$$\begin{aligned} \text{From Lemma 1, l.h.s. } &\equiv abc + akm \\ \text{r.h.s. } \equiv abc + abjmabc + akm &\equiv abc + abjm \\ \text{Assign } x &= abc \\ x + akm &\equiv x + abjm \\ \therefore \text{Congruent via definition from Lemma 1.} & \end{aligned}$$

For the second inner loop in Algorithm 7, we account for overflow bits in σ. It is important to note that there can be at most δ overflow bits. Therefore, if the number of overflow bits exceeds δ, then the corresponding lookup value will be undefined. This is a failure condition that must be avoided. There are potential conditions that may fail this part of the loop, resulting in undefined behavior.

All possible valid values were pre-calculated via an iterative search for combinations $\delta \in [1, 18]$ and $\omega \in [1, 18]$. We noticed that for this range, valid values of δ relative to a user chosen σ must satisfy $\delta \geq \lceil \frac{\omega}{2} \rceil$. We extend this to all possible values of σ and δ in Lemma 4. These combinations guarantee that any modular base with width ω, used with the corresponding δ, will not face the overflow condition described above. By utilizing a *for* loop with a guaranteed number of iterations, we can utilize a predetermined amount of combinatorial logic within the HOM-R module, allowing for single clock-cycle computations.

Line 13 in Algorithm 7 sums up all values of σ, storing the sum in c. This sum is then used to compute the maximum value of $c + b$ with lines 15–17. It is important to note that the width of sum(σ) must not exceed $\hat{m}'$, as this will result in undefined behavior. There can be a maximum of $2^{\delta'}$ addends in line 10, as more than this will overflow $\hat{m}'$. Therefore, δ' must be greater than or equal to $\lceil \log_2(N+1) \rceil$. Of course, more bits than necessary will result in a larger circuit, increasing the power draw and space unnecessarily. So, while a δ' larger than $\lceil \log_2(N+1) \rceil$ is possible, it is recommended to use $\delta' = \lceil \log_2(N+1) \rceil$.

Lemma 4. *For* $log_2(\sigma + 1) \leq \omega + \delta$ *if* $\delta, \omega, c \in \mathbb{Z}^+_{\neq 0}$, $\lceil \frac{\omega}{2} \rceil \leq \delta \leq \omega$, $\max(c) = 2^\delta - 1$, $\sigma = f(0)\text{mod}(c) + \sum_{i=1}^{\lceil \omega/\delta \rceil} (i * 2^\delta) * (f(i)\text{mod}(c))$.

$$\text{Evaluate } f(i)\text{mod}(c) \text{ at the largest value,}$$

$$\sigma = f(0)\text{mod}(c) + \sum_{i=1}^{\lceil \omega/\delta \rceil} (i * 2^\delta) * (f(i)\text{mod}(c))$$

$$\max(\text{mod}(c)) = \max(c - 1, 0)$$

$$\therefore \max(f(i)\text{mod}(c)) = \max(2^\delta - 2, 0)$$

$$\therefore \max(\sigma) = \max(2^\delta - 2, 0) + \sum_{i=1}^{\lceil \omega/\delta \rceil} (i * 2^\delta) * \max(2^\delta - 2, 0).$$

$$\text{(A) Evaluate at maximum boundary } \delta = \omega$$

$$\sigma = 2^\delta - 2 + \sum_{i=1}^{1} (i * 2^\delta) * (2^\delta - 2)$$

$$\sigma = 2^\delta - 2 + (2^\delta)(2^\delta - 2)$$

$$\sigma = 2^{2\delta} - 2^\delta - 2$$

$$\rightarrow \log_2(2^{2\delta} - 2^\delta - 1) \leq 2\delta$$

$$2^{2\delta} - 2^\delta - 1 \leq 2^{2\delta}$$

$$-2^\delta \leq 1$$

$$\text{(B) Evaluate at minimum boundary } \delta = \lceil \frac{\omega}{2} \rceil, \omega = 1 \ \therefore \delta = 1$$

$$\text{l.h.s.} = \log_2(1 + \max(2^\delta - 2, 0) + \sum_{i=1}^{2} (i * 2^\delta) * \max(2^\delta - 2, 0)$$

$$= \log_2(1 + 0 + (2^{\frac{\omega}{2}})(0) + (2 * 2^{\frac{\omega}{2}})(0))$$

$$\text{Evaluate B at } \omega = 1$$

$$\log_2(1) \leq \frac{3}{2}$$

$$0 \leq \frac{3}{2}$$

$$\text{From A) and B),}$$

$$\log_2(\sigma + 1) \leq \omega + \delta.$$

Lemma 5. *For* $\lceil \log_2(x+y+1) \rceil \geq \lceil \log_2(y+1) \rceil$ *if* $x, y \in \mathbb{Z}^+_{\neq 0}$ *and* $\lceil \log_2(x+1) \rceil = \lceil \log_2(y+1) \rceil$.

$$\begin{aligned}
\lceil \log_2(x+y+1) \rceil &= \lceil \log_2(x(1+\frac{y}{x}+\frac{1}{x}))) \rceil \\
&= \lceil \log_2(x) + \log_2(1+\frac{y+1}{x}) \rceil \\
\text{Evaluate } \log_2(1+\frac{y+1}{x}) & \text{ at minumum} \\
&\rightarrow \log_2 \log_2(1+\mathbb{R}^+_{\neq 0}) \\
\lceil \log_2(x) + \log_2(1+\mathbb{R}^+_{\neq 0}) \rceil &\geq \lceil \log_2(x+1) \rceil \\
\therefore \lceil \log_2(x) + \log_2(1+\mathbb{R}^+_{\neq 0}) \rceil &\geq \lceil \log_2(y+1) \rceil \\
\therefore \lceil \log_2(x+y+1) \rceil &\geq \lceil \log_2(y+1) \rceil.
\end{aligned}$$

The first part of the algorithm, Lines 1–17, reduce Ψ to the single $\hat{s}$ base stage. According to the constraints from the algorithm, the base stage will have the same width as the modular base b. Therefore, $0 \leq \Psi[0] < 2b$. From Lemmas 5 and 6, we can conclude that either $\hat{s}[0] \leq b$ or $\hat{s}[0] - b < b$ must be true. This reduces the *while* loop in Algorithm 1, Lines 18–19, to a single if statement. We can therefore determine that an input vector of width $\beta = \Omega$ is at most a single subtraction from being the residue $(a)\text{mod}(b) \equiv c$. The final result is the residue $c \equiv (a) \bmod (b)$.

Lemma 6. *For* $\lceil \log_2(x-y+1) \rceil \leq \lceil \log_2(y+1) \rceil$ *if* $x, y \in \mathbb{Z}^+_{\neq 0}$, $x > y$, *and* $\lceil \log_2(x+1) \rceil = \lceil \log_2(y+1) \rceil$.

Proof.

$$\begin{aligned}
\lceil \log_2(x-y+1) \rceil &= \lceil \log_2(x(1-\frac{y}{x}+\frac{1}{x}))) \rceil \\
&= \lceil \log_2(x) + \log_2(1+\frac{1-y}{x}) \rceil \\
\text{Evaluate } \log_2(1+\frac{1-y}{x}) & \text{ as} \\
\rightarrow \log_2(1+\frac{1-y}{x}) &\in -\infty < \mathbb{R} < 0 \\
&\rightarrow \lceil \log_2 x \rceil \leq \lceil \log_2(x+1) \rceil \\
\therefore \lceil \log_2(x-y+1) \rceil &\leq \lceil \log_2(y+1) \rceil
\end{aligned}$$

□

4. Implementation

We implemented our modular reduction system on an FPGA, and tested various configurations to compare area usage, power consumption, and resource requirements. The full implementation of the HOM-R system relies on internal sub-modules to reduce the individual stages of the input Ψ to the base stage. Each stage has an input of β bits, and an output of β bits. The stage-reduction module encompasses Lines 6–13 in Algorithm 7, and is replicated $N-1$ times within the HOM-R system. For the example illustrated within this section, we demonstrate a four-stage HOM-R implementation for $x[15:0] \bmod (14) \equiv y$ with $\beta = 4$ and $\delta = 2$. A close-up for $\Psi[1]$ is shown in Figure 1, showcasing the hardware implementation for Lines 6–10 in Algorithm 7.

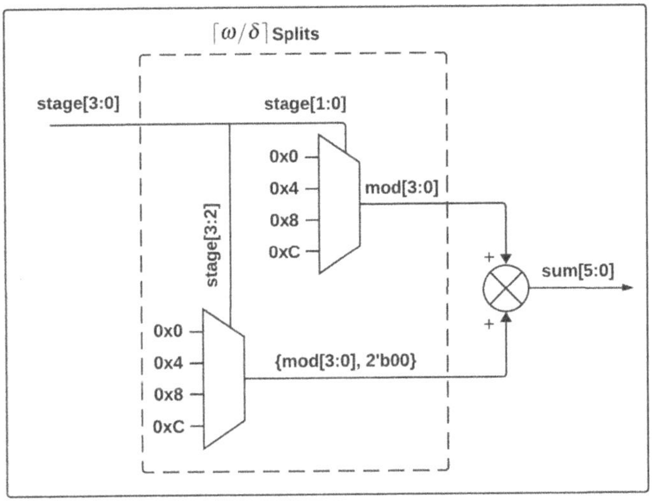

Figure 1. $\lceil \frac{\beta}{\delta} \rceil$ Splits required to reduce a stage to the base stage. This is configured for the two-bit modulus-value LUT with a modular base of 14 for $\Psi[1]$.

It is important to note that the same $\hat{m}$ is replicated in the sub-module. This is illustrated within the dotted-line box in Figure 1. While this requires an increase in resources, it allows the system to operate on the stage splits in parallel. The alternate option is to instead iterate each stage through $\hat{m}$, at one stage per clock cycle, which we determined to be too expensive.

Since each stage split is reduced to the base-stage, we must sum them together, as in Lines 11–13 of Algorithm 7. This was proven possible in Lemma 2. Similar to the first stage-reduce module, this step is completed with combinatorial logic, reducing the latency of the system. An iterative method was used to find the number of maximum required additions to reduce the width of the sum to β. The method yielded that a maximum of two additional addition steps following the original summation of the $\hat{m}$ outputs will always be enough to reduce the width to β. We illustrate the second half of the stage-reduce module in Figure 2 for $x[15:0] \bmod (14) \equiv y$ with $\beta = 4$ and $\delta = 2$.

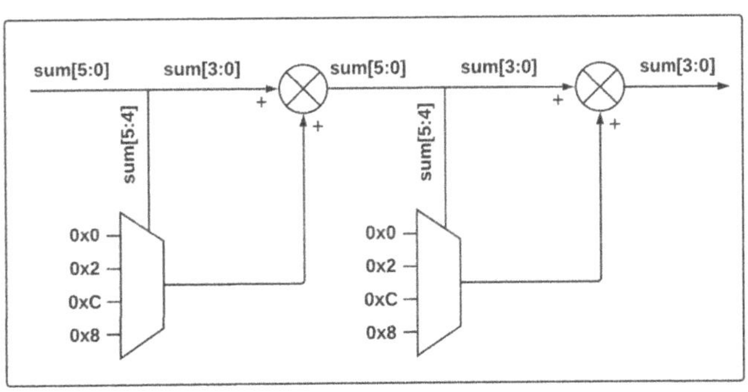

Figure 2. The final summation step reduces the base stage to the correct bit width of the modular base. The amount of additions required is dependent on the base, modulus-value LUT, and stage width.

These two series of combinatorial logic result in the full stage-reduce module, shown in Figure 3. We place an optional stage register between the output of the stage-reduce module and the output of the full HOM-R system to help with timing for either high-frequency or large-input systems. However, for all of the values tested within this paper, we did not need to rely on the optional register and therefore removed it from our system.

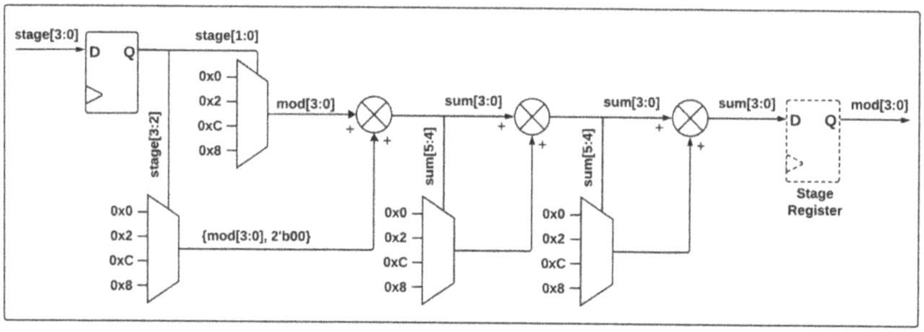

Figure 3. A complete four-bit stage configured for a two-bit modulus-value LUT with a modular base of 14.

The stage-reduce module must be replicated $\lceil \frac{\Omega-\beta}{\omega} \rceil$ times within the modular reduction module. This replication implements Line 4 of Algorithm 7, and allows us to operate on each stage split in parallel. This results in a significant reduction in latency, fitting multiple loops of the algorithm within a single clock cycle. The replication of stage splits is shown in the full hardware implementation of HOM-R in Figure 4. We also show the optional summation register, which, if enabled in the design, will register the output for the first summation only. This provides a significant improvement in timing for high-operating-frequency systems.

The output of each stage-reduce module must be summed together and reduced, similar to the logic within the stage reduce module. The primary difference is that the size of the look-up table for the reductions, $\hat{m}'$, is $\lceil \log_2(N+1) \rceil$ rather than the user defined δ. In our example, we use four splits, which results in an $\hat{m}$ depth of two, as shown in Figure 4.

Once the base stages of the input have been summed and the output reduced to the width of β, we can ensure that the value is at most $2b$ from Lemmas 5 and 6. We can therefore subtract the modular base b from the input. If there is an asserted overflow bit, then we can ensure that the sum is less than b, and we can accept it as the residue. If there is no overflow bit, then we can be assured that the sum is greater than or equal to b, and we accept the difference as the residue b.

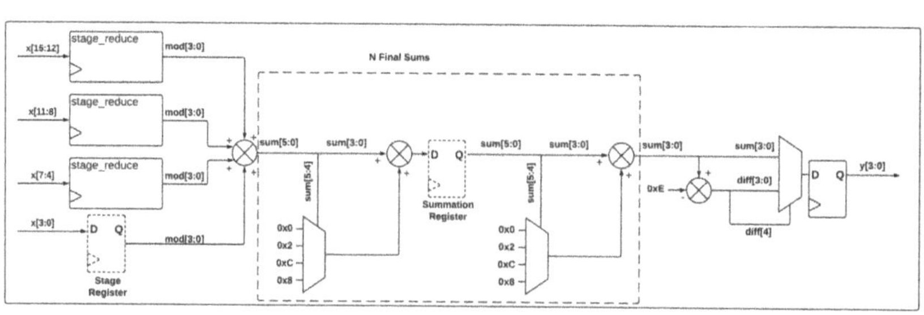

Figure 4. The full modular reduction system for a static base. This system is configured for four splits, with each split configured for a two-bit modulus-value LUT with a modular base of 14.

5. Results

Typically, for conventional place and route tool flows utilized by standard applications such as Vivado by AMD or Quartus by Intel, a look-up table for each bit of an output vector is generated depending on a user defined funciton. In this case, that function would be modular reduction. We compare the HOM-R system against this conventional method utilized by Vivado.

For testing, we used a 64-bit vector input with a 150 MHz clock rate. This clock rate was chosen as it was the fastest clock that the conventional method could use before violating timing constraints. Further, since the resource requirements for modular arithmetic depend heavily on the modular base, we tested three different bases for $\beta = 32$ and $\beta = 16$. For the HOM-R implementation tested, we used $\delta = \omega = 8$, and disabled all of the registers in the system. This allowed for the conventional method and the HOM-R system to have the same latency. These results are shown in Table 2.

It is clear from the table that the HOM-R implementation offers significant improvements over the conventional method for modular reduction. For all test cases, the HOM-R method used an average of 30% less power, 27% fewer configurable logic blocks (CLBs), and 42% fewer LUTs. Further, despite these reductions in power and resources, the HOM-R method showed significantly better timing margins, allowing for a higher maximum operating frequency.

Table 2. The conventional modular reduction method compared against the HOM-R system, tested at a clock rate of 150 MHz. For the HOM-R system, $\delta = \omega = 8$.

Method	Base	CLBs	LUTs	WNS	Power
HOM-R	0xC53A49B2	131	732	0.377 ns	40 mW
Conventional	0xC53A49B2	172	1126	0.064 ns	51 mW
HOM-R	0xF12E33D6	133	713	0.349 ns	40 mW
Conventional	0xF12E33D6	190	1250	0.017 ns	53 mW
HOM-R	0xAF0C59E5	139	743	0.184 ns	43 mW
Conventional	0xAF0C59E5	177	1190	0.049 ns	54 mW
HOM-R	0xA43C	106	525	1.234 ns	15 mW
Conventional	0xA43C	165	969	0.474 ns	25 mW
HOM-R	0xE127	106	535	1.194 ns	15 mW
Conventional	0xE127	138	951	0.321 ns	27 mW
HOM-R	0x894C	101	520	0.970 ns	15 mW
Conventional	0x894C	135	987	0.190 ns	25 mW

Next, we compare multiple combinations of ω and δ for $\Omega = 32, \beta = 16$ in Table 3. These tests were run at a clock rate of 150 MHz, with the main limiting test case being $\omega = 2, \delta = 1$. For each value of ω, it is apparent that $\delta = \omega$ is the most resource and power friendly. However, this is not always an option, as $\omega = \delta = 16$ results in a LUT that has 2^{16} values, which is too large to be synthesized by Vivado. Based on the results in Table 3, it appears best to use $\omega = \delta = 8$, however, this is likely due to the configuration of the CLBs for the Kintex UltraScale+ device, and may vary from device family to family.

Table 3. Results from various configurations of ω and δ. For this test, $\Omega = 32, \beta = 16$, and the modular base is 0xF7E3.

ω	δ	CLBs	LUTs	Registers	WNS	Power
2	1	48	183	18	0.040 ns	7 mW
2	2	36	139	16	1.237 ns	5 mW
4	2	45	187	16	0.369 ns	6 mW
4	4	33	136	16	1.562 ns	5 mW
8	4	33	143	16	1.274 ns	6 mW
8	8	39	172	24	2.207 ns	5 mW
16	8	39	273	24	1.078	7 mW

We also compared the usage of the various registers in the system. For this test, we used $\Omega = 64, \omega = 8, \delta = 8$, and a clock rate of 150 MHz. One would utilize these registers for high-frequency systems. Refer to Figures 3 and 4 for the location of the summation and stage registers. For each register enabled in the system, an extra clock cycle is added to the overall latency.

One can see from Table 4 that the summation register has the greatest effect on the system, offering the most relaxed timing margins between the two optional registers. Further, this also offers lower power usage, even when compared to the configuration that does not rely on either register. This is likely due to optimizations performed by the Place and Route Engine, as extra resources are added in the case where no registers are enabled so as to meet the strict timing requirements. To further relax timing constraints, one can utilize both the stage output register and the summation register. This adds two clock cycles of latency, but can be essential for large modular reductions that must operate at high frequencies.

Table 4. Results from various configurations of ω and δ. For this test, $\Omega = 32, \beta = 16$, and the modular base is 0xF7E3.

Register En.	CLBs	LUTs	Reg.	WNS	Power
None	131	732	56	0.377 ns	40 mW
Sum	114	673	91	2.516 ns	39 mW
Stage	135	732	202	1.053 ns	41 mW
Stage + Sum	119	673	247	2.822 ns	41 mW

The final test that we conducted on the HOM-R system evaluated Ω against β, as shown in Table 5. For each test, we used a value of $\beta = \omega = \delta$ at a clock rate of 250 MHz. While not every iteration passed timing, we included failing iterations for comparison with those test iterations that did pass timing.

It can be determined from the table that an increasing Ω leads to both a linear increase in resource usage and power consumption. This is expected, because a larger input will require more logic to reduce it to the predetermined β. Further, it can also be concluded that an increase in β directly results in an increase in power consumption, resource usage, and harsher timing requirements. The failing cases in the table could be remedied with the enabling of registers, as in Table 4.

Table 5. Results from various configurations of ω and δ. For this test, $\Omega = 32, \beta = 16$, and the modular base is 0xF7E3.

Ω	β	CLBs	LUTs	Registers	WNS	Power
16	4	6	20	0	2.379 ns	<1 mW
16	8	13	58	5	1.600 ns	4 mW
16	12	7	15	0	2.994 ns	<1 mW
32	4	3	27	0	1.961 ns	<1 mW
32	8	27	131	8	0.806 ns	8 mW
32	12	128	770	42	0.552 ns	17 mW
64	4	11	85	0	1.497 ns	7 mW
64	8	54	341	40	0.243 ns	19 mW
64	12	480	2806	481	−0.466 ns	56 mW
128	4	29	167	0	0.996 ns	9 mW
128	8	94	619	104	0.012 ns	26 mW
128	12	1131	6536	902	−1.916 ns	108 mW
256	4	73	505	0	0.384 ns	17 mW
256	8	186	1264	102	−0.063 ns	49 mW
256	12	2594	14061	119	−2.965 ns	210 mW

6. Conclusions

In this paper, we presented a new method for modular reduction that is optimized for hardware. Using a calculated number of reduction cycles, we can use combinatorial logic to reduce large input vectors down to a modular base. Our results show an average of 30% less power usage, 27% fewer CLBs, and 42% fewer LUTs than the conventional method for modular reduction used by Vivado. Further, the HOM-R implementation allows for more relaxed timing requirements, and is able to reduce a 256-bit number down to a four-bit base in a single 250 MHz clock cycle.

Our design also allows for the implementation of registers at multiple stages in the reduction algorithm, enabling the design to be used in systems with high click frequencies. We showed that even with the implementation of these registers, there are only negligible increases in power consumption and resource utilization, while significant gains are offered in terms of timing requirements.

Moreover, we offer a significant contribution over other popular modular reduction methods, such as Barrett and Montgomery reduction, in that we do not require any multipliers or dividers. Our algorithm is implemented using only simple addition and LUTs with variable sizes, determined by the user's timing and resource requirements. This improvement is significant, as multiplication and division require DSPs, which are both limited and power hungry on devices such as FPGAs. By removing these requirements, we free up resources for designs that require them, and offer a low-power, low-latency alternative.

Author Contributions: Conceptualization, A.M.; methodology, A.M.; investigation, A.M.; writing—original draft preparation, A.M.; writing—review and editing, A.M. and Y.C.; visualization, A.M.; supervision, Y.C. All authors have read and agreed to the published version of the manuscript.

Funding: This research received no external funding.

Institutional Review Board Statement: Not applicable.

Informed Consent Statement: Not applicable.

Data Availability Statement: The original data presented in the study is openly available on GitHub at https://github.com/alexmagyari/HOM-R (accessed on 8 December 2024).

Conflicts of Interest: The authors declare no conflicts of interest.

References

1. Hassan, F.; Ammar, A.; Drennen, H. A 32-bit Integer Division Algorithm Based on Priority Encoder. In Proceedings of the 2020 27th IEEE International Conference on Electronics, Circuits and Systems (ICECS), Glasgow, UK, 23–25 November 2020; pp. 1–4.
2. Alaya, B.; Laouamer, L.; Msilini, N. Homomorphic encryption systems statement: Trends and challenges. *Comput. Sci. Rev.* **2020**, *36*, 100235. [CrossRef]
3. Alloghani, M.; Alani, M.M.; Al-Jumeily, D.; Baker, T.; Mustafina, J.; Hussain, A.; Aljaaf, A.J. A systematic review on the status and progress of homomorphic encryption technologies. *J. Inf. Secur. Appl.* **2019**, *48*, 102362. [CrossRef]
4. Zhang, J.; Xie, T.; Zhang, Y.; Song, D. Transparent polynomial delegation and its applications to zero knowledge proof. In Proceedings of the 2020 IEEE Symposium on Security and Privacy (SP), San Francisco, CA, USA, 18–20 May 2020; pp. 859–876.
5. Bootle, J.; Lyubashevsky, V.; Seiler, G. Algebraic techniques for short (er) exact lattice-based zero-knowledge proofs. In Proceedings of the Annual International Cryptology Conference, Santa Barbara, CA, USA, 18–22 August 2019; pp. 176–202.
6. Kalmykov, I.A.; Pashintsev, V.P.; Tyncherov, K.T.; Olenev, A.A.; Chistousov, N.K. Error-correction coding using polynomial residue number system. *Appl. Sci.* **2022**, *12*, 3365. [CrossRef]
7. Valueva, M.V.; Nagornov, N.; Lyakhov, P.A.; Valuev, G.V.; Chervyakov, N.I. Application of the residue number system to reduce hardware costs of the convolutional neural network implementation. *Math. Comput. Simul.* **2020**, *177*, 232–243. [CrossRef]
8. Salamat, S.; Shubhi, S.; Khaleghi, B.; Rosing, T. Residue-Net: Multiplication-free neural network by in-situ no-loss migration to residue number systems. In Proceedings of the 26th Asia and South Pacific Design Automation Conference, Tokyo, Japan, 18–21 January 2021; pp. 222–228.
9. Sakellariou, V.; Paliouras, V.; Kouretas, I.; Saleh, H.; Stouraitis, T. An end-to-end RNS CNN Accelerator. In Proceedings of the 2024 IEEE 6th International Conference on AI Circuits and Systems (AICAS), Abu Dhabi, United Arab Emirates, 22–25 April 2024; pp. 75–79.
10. Zhang, P. Applying Residue Number Systems to Hardware Probability Models. Master's Thesis, Aalto University, Espoo, Finland, 2024.
11. Saheed, Y.K.; Kehinde, T.O.; Ayobami Raji, M.; Baba, U.A. Feature selection in intrusion detection systems: A new hybrid fusion of Bat algorithm and Residue Number System. *J. Inf. Telecommun.* **2024**, *8*, 189–207. [CrossRef]
12. Kucherov, N. Data Storage with Increased Survivability and Reliability Based on the Residue Number System. *Adv. Syst. Sci. Appl.* **2024**, *24*, 166–186.
13. Will, M.A.; Ko, R.K. Computing mod with a variable lookup table. In *Security in Computing and Communications, Proceedings of the 4th International Symposium, SSCC 2016, Jaipur, India, 21–24 September 2016*; Proceedings 4; Springer: Berlin/Heidelberg, Germany, 2016; pp. 3–17.
14. Parhami, B. Modular reduction by multi-level table lookup. In Proceedings of the 40th Midwest Symposium on Circuits and Systems. Dedicated to the Memory of Professor Mac Van Valkenburg, Sacramento, CA, USA, 3–6 August 1997; Volume 1, pp. 381–384.
15. Parhami, B.; Hung, C. Optimal table lookup schemes for VLSI implementation of input/output conversions and other residue number operations. In Proceedings of the 1994 IEEE Workshop on VLSI Signal Processing, La Jolla, CA, USA, 26–28 October 1994; pp. 470–481.
16. Opasatian, A.; Ikeda, M. Lookup Table Modular Reduction: A Low-Latency Modular Reduction for Fast ECC Processor. In Proceedings of the 2023 IEEE Symposium in Low-Power and High-Speed Chips (COOL CHIPS), Tokyo, Japan, 19–21 April 2023; pp. 1–6.
17. Lim, C.H.; Hwang, H.S.; Lee, P.J. Fast modular reduction with precomputation. In Proceedings of the Korea-Japan Joint Workshop on Information Security and Cryptology (JWISC'97). Citeseer, 1997; pp. 65–79. Available online: https://citeseerx.ist.psu.edu/document?repid=rep1&type=pdf&doi=a683d452712796ca9ab4c99dffdfd48e1e5d195d (accessed on 8 December 2024).
18. Cao, Z.; Wei, R.; Lin, X. A fast modular reduction method. *Cryptol. ePrint Arch.* **2014**.

19. Montgomery, P.L. Modular multiplication without trial division. *Math. Comput.* **1985**, *44*, 519–521. [CrossRef]
20. Barrett, P. Implementing the Rivest Shamir and Adleman public key encryption algorithm on a standard digital signal processor. In *Conference on the Theory and Application of Cryptographic Techniques*; Springer: Berlin/Heidelberg, Germany, 1986; pp. 311–323.

electronics

MDPI

Article

An Innovative Digital Pulse Width Modulator and Its Field-Programmable Gate Array Implementation

Giovanni Bonanno

Department of Information Engineering (DEI), University of Padova, 35131 Padova, Italy; giovanni.bonanno@unipd.it

Abstract: Digital pulse-width modulation (DPWM)-based controls are characterized by a non-negligible phase delay due to analog-to-digital (ADC) conversion, sampling time, carrier shape, and algorithm computation time. These delays degrade the performance in closed-loop systems, where the bandwidth must be reduced to avoid instability issues due to the reduced closed-loop phase margin. To mitigate these delays, approaches such as utilizing low-latency ADCs or increasing the sampling frequency have been employed. However, these methods are often costly and do not address the fundamental delay issues inherent to DPWMs. In this paper, a novel zero phase-delay DPWM architecture is proposed. This enhanced architecture seamlessly integrates pulse width and frequency modulation to create a programmable derivative action, capable of effectively recovering the DPWM delay. The proposed architecture employs a reliable and straightforward organization, suitable for implementation in commercial field programmable gate array (FPGA). Furthermore, this architecture inherently generates a trigger signal that can be used in numerous power electronic applications to capture the average value in piecewise linear inductor currents. The validity of the proposed architecture is substantiated through simulations and experimental tests. The final implementation is shared in an open-source resource.

Keywords: digital control; pulse width modulator; high frequency phase boost; fast dynamic response; FPGA

1. Introduction

Digital pulse width modulators (DPWMs) are widely used in power electronics applications due to their low cost, low power consumption, and ease of use [1–5]. However, digital PWMs suffer from phase delays that limit their dynamic performance, particularly at high frequencies. Despite these limitations, there are many reasons to use digital controls. The main motivations for their development include enhanced safety and monitoring functions, robustness against parametric variations and component degradation, as well as programmability and the possibility of modifying the control scheme after deployment. Digital controls offer the advantage of being re-programmable and re-configurable, enabling the implementation of controllers that may be difficult or even unfeasible in the analog domain [6–8]. However, in terms of dynamic performance, analog controllers still provide superior bandwidth. Several strategies have been proposed in the literature to mitigate the inherent delays of digital control systems [4,9–13], yet phase delay remains a critical issue and is often compensated for elsewhere in the system [14].

To reduce the performance gap between digital PWM and analog PWM, one approach is to increase the number of samples per modulation period [15,16]. However, increasing the sampling rate introduces non-linearities that may lead to severe system failures [17,18]. A promising trade-off is represented by the double-sampling DPWM based on the Trailing-Triangle edge (TTE) carrier. Although this technique mitigates phase lag, it does not entirely eliminate it and may still lead to performance degradation at high switching frequencies.

Other advanced control strategies, such as predictive control, have been explored to improve dynamic response [19–22]. However, these approaches often involve significant computational complexity, making them difficult to implement in many power electronics applications. As a result, DPWM-based control remains the most widely adopted solution. To date, the only methods capable of compensating for the delays introduced by digital modulators are those presented in [23–25]. In [26], the authors apply the zero phase delay architecture to digitally controlled grid-connected converters to extend the high frequency passivity admittance.

This paper introduces a novel digital implementation of a variable-frequency DPWM featuring an intrinsic derivative action. While existing digital architectures are theoretically valid, their practical implementation remains challenging. In contrast, this study proposes a simple yet effective digital architecture. The proposed enhanced DPWM (*e*DPWM) overcomes the main limitations of previous designs [23–25] while also providing a streamlined digital structure that can be efficiently implemented in FPGA or custom digital systems with minimal resource consumption.

The structure of digital modulators based on the asymmetric dual-edge (ADE) carrier is revised and optimized to eliminate complex multiplications and divisions between signals. Furthermore, the enhanced structure inherently generates a synchronization signal that serves as an accurate trigger for ADCs, facilitating the acquisition of the average value of piecewise linear inductor currents in power electronics applications. Such synchronization is not present in conventional ADE-based structures. Throughout this manuscript, DPWM architectures that introduce zero-phase delay or phase boost are collectively referred to as *enhanced* DPWM (*e*DPWM).

Currently, *e*DPWM structures can only be implemented using Field-Programmable Gate Arrays (FPGAs) or custom digital circuits. However, the solutions proposed in [1,2] are computationally intensive, restricting zero-delay modulators to systems with abundant computational resources. This complexity has hindered their widespread adoption. Instead, the proposed structure is designed to be both simple and computationally efficient, eliminating the need for bidirectional counters, as required in TTE-based architectures. This approach allows the full utilization of the available numerical resolution without compromising precision [27].

Basic concepts of digital control for power electronics can be found in [6], while their efficient FPGA implementation is thoroughly discussed in [28]. However, both references focus on digital control implementations using constant-frequency DPWM. This paper aims to bridge this gap by introducing an architecture that enables the implementation of *e*DPWM in a straightforward and reliable manner.

The main contributions of this paper are listed as follows.

- A new DPWM (*e*DPWM) with zero phase delay or a programmable derivative action is proposed.
- The overall DPWM architecture complexity is simplified and relaxed. Indeed, in the architecture in [23], the derivative action is achieved by changing the values of a and b. This implies that the comparator slopes must be modified according to the values of a and b. Counting with programmable slopes overcomplicates the counter implementation. The new architecture eradicates the use of products between signals to achieve the derivative action and the DPWM counters always count with a constant

slope (i.e., the ratio T_{smpl}/T_s is constant). This greatly simplified the programmability of the derivative action and the overall architecture.

- The synchronism mechanism is greatly simplified. Indeed, the eDPWM intrinsically provides the instant corresponding to the middle of the ON and OFF phases. As required in countless digital controls for power electronic applications, such a signal triggers the ADC sampling to acquire the average value of piecewise linear signals. This trigger event is not intrinsically present in ADE-DPWM; adding it increases the system complexity, as shown in [24,25]. Conversely, in the *e*DPWM, the synchronism mechanism can be easily implemented using the aforementioned trigger signal without further increasing the architecture's complexity.
- The DPWM architecture is optimized to use all available bits. Namely, since the comparator slopes are fixed and proportional to the T_{smpl}/T_s ratio, and since they must always count in one direction (i.e., up-count or down-count), the resolution of the DPWM can be increased to make maximum use of all available bits, even doing better than the TTE-DPWM in which one bit is lost due to alternating up-count and down-count.
- Other original contributions in this article are the block diagram of ADE-DPWM modulators and other alternative implementations of *e*DPWMmodulators.

The remainder of the paper is organized as follows. Section 2 compares the state-of-the-art double-sampling TTE carrier-based DPWM (TTE-DPWM) with the double-sampling ADE carrier-based DPWM (ADE-DPWM), introduces the main concepts of variable-frequency DPWM, and presents a preliminary architecture for *e*DPWM. Section 3 derives the final architecture of *e*DPWM. Section 4 demonstrates the equivalence between the proposed *e*DPWM and the ADE-DPWM presented in [23]. The small signal model is subsequently derived. Section 5 presents the experimental results validating the proposed architecture. Finally, Section 6 concludes the manuscript by summarizing the main contributions.

2. Enhanced DPWM: Main Concepts

This manuscript introduces an *enhanced* double-sampling DPWM architecture designed to eliminate the delays typically associated with classical digital modulators while maintaining a simple and efficient implementation. These modulators were first proposed in [23–25], where the asymmetric dual-edge (ADE) carrier is introduced to enhance the frequency response. Specifically, ADE carrier-based DPWM (ADE-DPWM) demonstrated its ability to fully recover the phase delay associated with classical DPWM structures and, in some cases, provide a derivative action that guarantees a high-frequency phase boost.

To establish a clear understanding of the fundamental differences between traditional fixed-frequency DPWMs and variable-frequency architectures, this section begins with a comparative analysis of Trailing-Triangle Edge DPWM (TTE-DPWM) and ADE-DPWM. This comparison not only illustrates the core operating principles of ADE-DPWM but also highlights its critical distinctions from conventional digital modulators.

2.1. Fixed-Frequency vs. Variable-Frequency DPWM Architectures

A fundamental limitation of fixed-frequency DPWM architectures is the inherent phase delay introduced by the discrete-time processing of the modulating signal. In particular, single-sampling TTE-DPWM exhibits a phase delay that can described by the following transfer function

$$G_{TTE,\,single}(s) = \frac{1}{2}\left(e^{-sT_s\frac{x_{off}}{2}} + e^{-sT_s\frac{x_{on}}{2}}\right), \tag{1}$$

where $s \in \mathbb{C}$ is the complex variable of the Laplace plane. The phase response can be approximated by $G_{\text{TTE, double}}(s) \approx e^{-s\frac{T_s}{2}}$. The introduction of double-sampling DPWM reduces this delay, yielding $G_{\text{TTE, double}}(s) \approx e^{-S \cdot T_s/4}$.

While increasing the sampling frequency further decreases the phase lag, it never fully eliminates it. Moreover, attempting to sample more than twice per period introduces additional non-idealities [15,16]. In contrast, variable-frequency DPWM architectures, such as ADE-DPWM, dynamically adjust the switching period based on the modulating signal. This enables complete phase delay cancellation, making ADE-DPWM particularly effective for high-bandwidth control applications. However, this benefit comes at the cost of increased implementation complexity. To elucidate the fundamental principles governing the operation of the double-sampling ADE-DPWM and to delineate its salient distinctions from the state-of-the-art TTE-DPWM, a comparative analysis between these two architectures is reported in the following.

Figure 1 shows a comparison between the TTE-DPWM and the ADE-DPWM as proposed in [25]. Both the x and y axes are normalized. The main difference between the two architectures lies in the modulation of the switching period. Indeed, the TTE-DPWM operates with a constant frequency, while the ADE-DPWM introduces a frequency modulation. This effect can be formalized as follows.

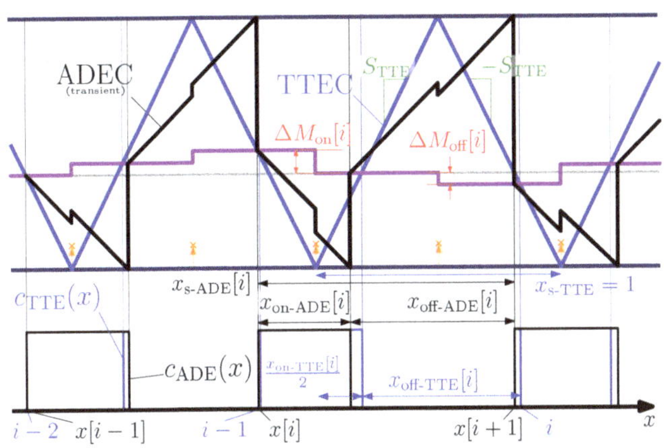

Figure 1. Exemplified time operation of (blue lines) TTE-DPWM and (black lines) double-sampling ADE-DPWM and corresponding control signals. Gray lines represent the steady-state operation while the double-sampled modulating signal is represented in magenta.

When the modulating signal $M[\cdot]$ increases, all DPWM systems react by increasing the ON phase while decreasing the OFF phase. In double-sampling TTE-DPWM, once fixed $x_{\text{on-TTE}}[i] = \frac{T_{\text{on-TTE}}[i]}{T_s}$, the OFF phase is imposed by the relation $T_{\text{on-TTE}}[i] + T_{\text{off-TTE}}[i] = T_s = \text{constant}$. On the other hand, ADE-DPWM allows independent changes in both ON and OFF phases. With a positive variation of $M[\cdot]$, the modulation period decreases (i.e., $T_s[i] < T_s$), and therefore $x_{\text{on}}[i] = \frac{T_{\text{on-ADE}}[i]}{T_s[i]} > \frac{T_{\text{on-ADE}}[i]}{T_s}$. Furthermore $T_{\text{on-ADE}}[i] > T_{\text{on-TTE}}[i]$ and therefore $x_{\text{on-ADE}}[i] > x_{\text{on-TTE}}[i]$. Having reduced the modulation period, one also obtains $T_{\text{off-ADE}}[i] = T_{\text{s-ADE}}[i] - T_{\text{on-ADE}}[i] < T_s - T_{\text{on-TTE}}[i]$. Thus, for the same modulating signal variation, the ADE-DPWM reacts with more pronounced variations of ON and OFF phases. Moreover, these variations are independent and their sum is not constant thus leading to a modulation of the switching period.

Analytically, one has

$$\text{ADE}: \begin{cases} \Delta x_{\text{on-ADE}}[i] &= \Delta M_{\text{on}}[i] \\ \Delta x_{\text{off-ADE}}[i] &= -\Delta M_{\text{off}}[i] \\ \Delta x_{\text{s-ADE}}[i] &= \Delta M_{\text{on}}[i] - \Delta M_{\text{off}}[i] \end{cases} ; \quad \text{TTE}: \begin{cases} \Delta x_{\text{on-TTE}}[i] &= \frac{\Delta M_{\text{on}}[i]+\Delta M_{\text{off}}[i]}{2} \\ \Delta x_{\text{off-TTE}}[i] &= -\frac{\Delta M_{\text{on}}[i]+\Delta M_{\text{off}}[i]}{2}, \\ \Delta x_{\text{s-TTE}}[i] &= 0 \end{cases} \tag{2}$$

with

$$\Delta x_{s_{\text{ADE}}}[i] \triangleq \frac{T_{s_{\text{ADE}}}[i] - T_s}{T_s}, \qquad \Delta x_{s_{\text{TTE}}}[i] \triangleq \frac{T_{s_{\text{TTE}}}[i] - T_s}{T_s}, \tag{3}$$

while $\Delta x_{\text{on-TTE}}[i]$ and $\Delta x_{\text{off-TTE}}[i]$ are the normalized variations of the ON and OFF phases for the TTE-DPWM.

Equation (2) indicates that the most important characteristic of the double-sampling ADE-DPWM is the switching frequency modulation. But at this point, one might wonder whether the rather complex structure of the ADE architecture could not be simplified. The next section introduces changes in the overall structure that induce the same time domain operation. The new architecture organization is therefore extended in order to emulate even the more complex architecture proposed in [23].

2.2. Challenges in ADE-DPWM Implementation

Although ADE-DPWM eliminates phase delay, its practical implementation is hindered by the following challenges.

- Computational complexity: ADE-DPWM requires real-time multiplications and divisions, significantly increasing hardware resource utilization.
- Synchronization issues: Unlike fixed-frequency DPWM, ADE-DPWM lacks an intrinsic sampling synchronization mechanism, making accurate current measurement more challenging.
- Hardware limitations: ADE-DPWM is difficult to implement on FPGAs and is impossible to realize on microcontrollers due to excessive computational demands.

These challenges motivate the development of an improved structure that preserves the advantages of ADE-DPWM while simplifying implementation.

2.3. Proposed eDPWM Architecture

To overcome the limitations of ADE-DPWM, the enhanced DPWM (*e*DPWM) is proposed. This new architecture retains the double-sampling and variable-frequency properties of ADE-DPWM but introduces fundamental modifications that make it computationally efficient and easier to implement. The core differences between TTE-DPWM, ADE-DPWM, and *e*DPWM architectures are summarized in Table 1.

Table 1. Comparison of double sampling DPWM architectures. (†) A positive phase-boost can be programmed. (*) May be implemented in some MCUs.

Architecture	Phase Delay	Comput. Complexity	Hardware Suitability
TTE	$\approx\angle e^{-sT_s/4}$	Low	Simple for MCUs and FPGAs
ADE	zero †	High	Only FPGA
eDPWM	zero †	Low	Efficient on FPGA *

The first version of the eDPWM, hereafter referred to as *e*DPWM v1.0, is illustrated in Figure 2. This structure replicates the same time domain operation of ADE-DPWM but avoids unnecessary arithmetic operations, leading to a drastic reduction in computational requirements.

Assuming that all the carrier slopes S of the *e*DPWM are equal (i.e., the up-count slope and the down-count slope are equal), and by indicating with $M_{\text{on}}[i]$ and $M_{\text{off}}[i]$ the values of the modulating signal acquired (sampled) at the middle of the ON and OFF phases, it is easy to verify the following relationships. For the *e*DPWM v1.0, the *i*-th ON and OFF phases duration can be written as follows:

$$
\begin{aligned}
x_{\text{on}}[i] &= \frac{M_{\text{ss}}}{S} + \frac{\Delta M_{\text{on}}[i]}{S} \\
&= \frac{M_{\text{ss}}}{S} + \frac{M_{\text{on}}[i] - M_{\text{ss}}}{S} = \frac{M_{\text{on}}[i]}{S};
\end{aligned}
\qquad
\begin{aligned}
x_{\text{off}}[i] &= \frac{1 - M_{\text{ss}}}{S} - \frac{\Delta M_{\text{off}}[i]}{S} \\
&= \frac{1 - M_{\text{ss}}}{S} - \frac{M_{\text{off}}[i] - M_{\text{ss}}}{S} = \frac{1 - M_{\text{off}}[i]}{S},
\end{aligned}
\tag{4}
$$

where $\Delta M_{\text{on}}[i] \triangleq M_{\text{on}}[i] - M_{\text{ss}}$ and $\Delta M_{\text{off}}[i] \triangleq M_{\text{off}}[i] - M_{\text{ss}}$ are the variation of the modulating signal during the *i*-th ON and OFF phases with respect to the steady state value M_{ss}.

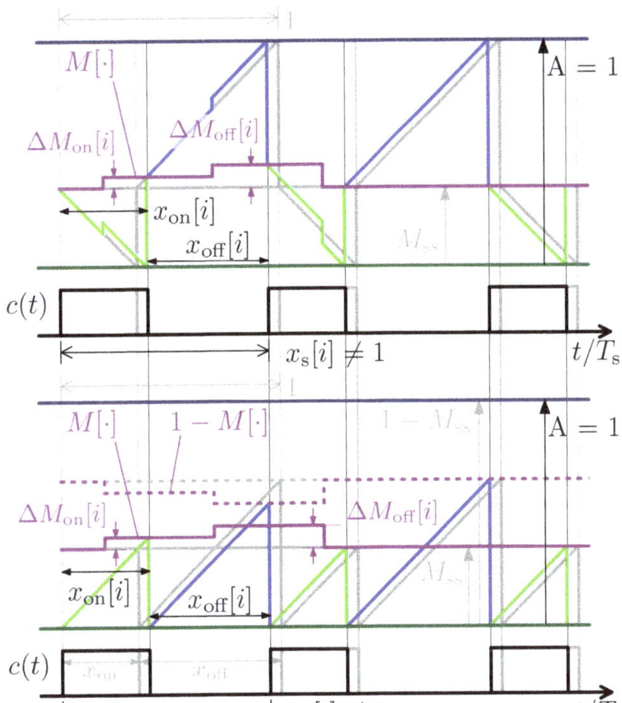

Figure 2. Comparison between double-sampling ADE-DPWM (**top**) and the proposed *e*DPWM v1.0 (**bottom**). Blue and green lines are respectively used to highlights the counters used for computing the ON and OFF phases duration.

The *i*-th ON and OFF phases variation can be written as follows:

$$
\begin{aligned}
\Delta x_{\text{on}}[i] \triangleq x_{\text{on}}[i] - x_{\text{on}} &= x_{\text{on}}[i] - \frac{M_{\text{ss}}}{S} &= \frac{\Delta M_{\text{on}}[i]}{S}, \\
-\Delta x_{\text{off}}[i] \triangleq x_{\text{off}}[i] - x_{\text{off}} &= \frac{1 - M_{\text{ss}}}{S} - x_{\text{off}}[i] &= \frac{\Delta M_{\text{off}}[i]}{S}.
\end{aligned}
\tag{5}
$$

By choosing $S = 1$, the time domain operation (5) is the same as the one obtained in [23,24]. The structures described in Figures 2 and 3 lead to the same time domain expressions of that obtained with the double-sampling ADE-DPWM. The main advantages of the proposed structure with respect to the double-sampling ADE-DPWM can be summarized as follows:

- The carrier counters always start from a constant value. In the ADE carrier-based structure, the starting point of the carrier must be updated at the beginning of each ON and OFF phases.
- Differently than ADE-DPWM, counting operations to implement the two carriers are uninterrupted. The counter always starts from zero, and the change in the modulating signal is not added to the counter. The only values that must be set are the compare values for the two carriers.

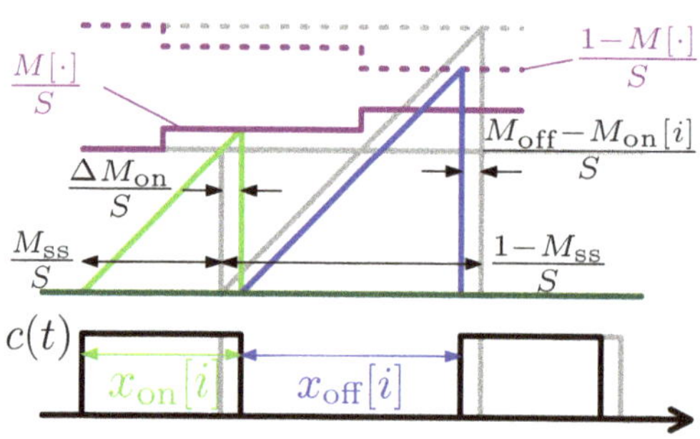

Figure 3. Details of the operation of *e*DPWM v1.0. Color scheme is kept consistent with previous representations.

The listed advantages are remarkable. However, further modifications are required to build an efficient and functional architecture. Indeed, despite the improvements, the *e*DPWM v1.0 structure still has some critical issues. First, two different comparitive values are required for the two ramps. Therefore, each sampling is followed by an operation to calculate the $1 - M[\cdot]$ value from the $M[\cdot]$ value just acquired. The second problem is related to the synchronism. In many structures, it is necessary to sample the current at precise points such as the one that gets the average value of a piecewise linear waveform. The ADE-DPWM structure and the *e*DPWM v1.0 structure do not naturally offer such an instant of synchronism. In the next chapter, both problems are solved with the *e*DPWM v1.5 architecture.

3. General *e*DPWM Organization

This section presents the final version of the eDPWM modulator.

The *e*DPWM v1.5 operation is reported in Figure 4. The main differences with respect to that in Figure 3 lie in the carriers organization and the reset mechanism. The blue carrier always starts from its maximum value (i.e., $A = 1$) and down-counts up to the intersection with $M[\cdot]$. The evaluation of the signal $1 - M[\cdot]$ is therefore unnecessary.

There are other properties to be exploited in this architectural organization. For example, instead of resetting the ramps immediately after the intersection with the value of the compare register (i.e., $M_{on}[i]$ or $M_{off}[i]$), both ramps are reset in correspondence with the count-start command of the other one. This mechanism, generates an intersection (highlighted by a red dot in the figure) that, in steady-state, represents the central instant of the ON and OFF phases. These instants represent the trigger event of the missing synchronism mentioned in the previous paragraph and are deeply discussed in [24,25]. Section 3.2 clarifies why this mechanism is so relevant. Thus, the *e*DPWM v1.5 structure solves both residual problems of the *e*DPWM v1.0 structure.

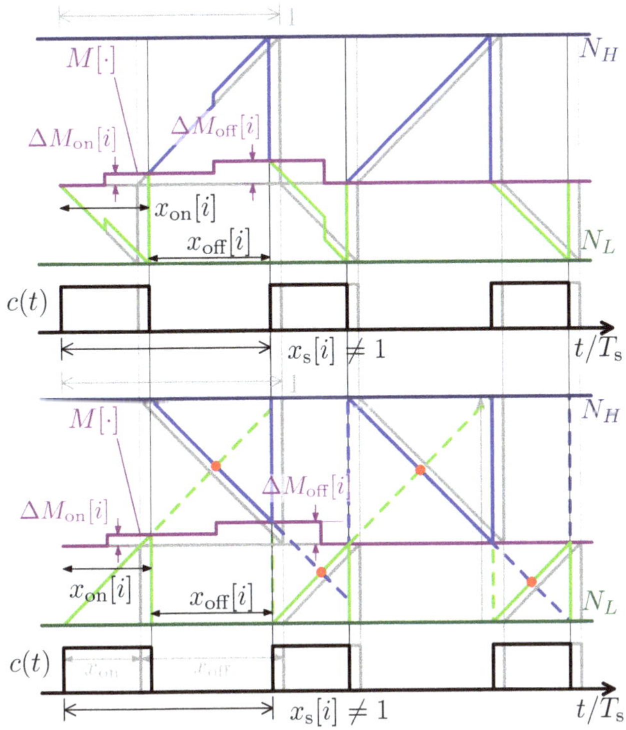

Figure 4. Operation of the double-sampling ADE-DPWM (**top**) vs. *e*DPWM V1.5 (**bottom**). Red dots represent the carrier intersections.

3.1. Intrinsic Programmable Derivative Actions

The structure *e*DPWM v1.5 is further modified to emulate the DS ADE-DPWM proposed in [23]. Emulating this behavior is important since it adds a programmable high-frequency phase boost. The main issue of the structure in [23] is the complex architecture. For instance, to achieve the programmable derivative action, the modulator proposed in [23] requires to change both counters' slopes. This is done by dividing them by parameters $a, b \in \mathbb{R}$. Obtaining programmable counters' slopes increases the architecture complexity and leads to a significant reduction in the final resolution adopted to represent the modulating signal. Figure 5 shows the comparison between the *e*DPWM v2.0 and the ADE-DPWM in [23]. The two architectures, operating with the same input, provide the same time response, even during transients. However, there is a huge gap in the architecture complexity of the two architectures even in the simplest case obtained for $a = b = 1$. Parameters $a, b \in \mathbb{R}$ are introduced in. In the example reported in Figure 5, the modulating signal is directly passed for comparison with the upper and lower carriers to compute the rising and falling edges of the control signal (i.e., the modulator's output). In the ADE architecture, even in the simple case for $a = b = 1$, several operations must be performed to obtain the control signal. Specifically, one has to perform the sum of two signals, a comparison with the ramps with variable slopes, and then a further product between signals. The situation is even worse when $a, b \neq 1$. Indeed, the proposed architecture directly computes the derivative terms $a\Delta M_{\text{on}}[i]$ and $b\Delta M_{\text{off}}[i]$ while ADE-DPWM in [23] requires further sums, multiplications, and divisions to perform the derivative action.

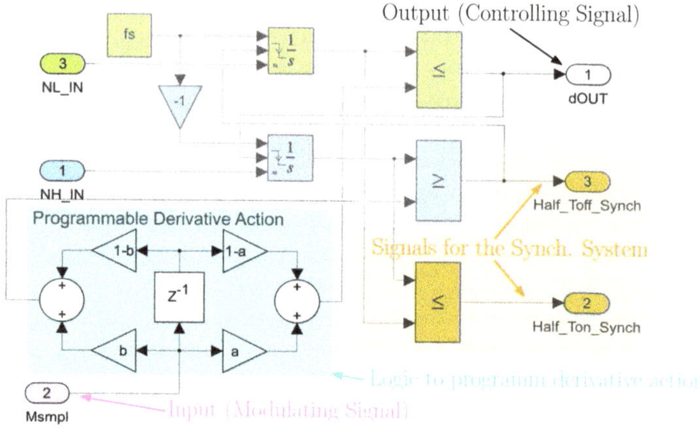

(a)

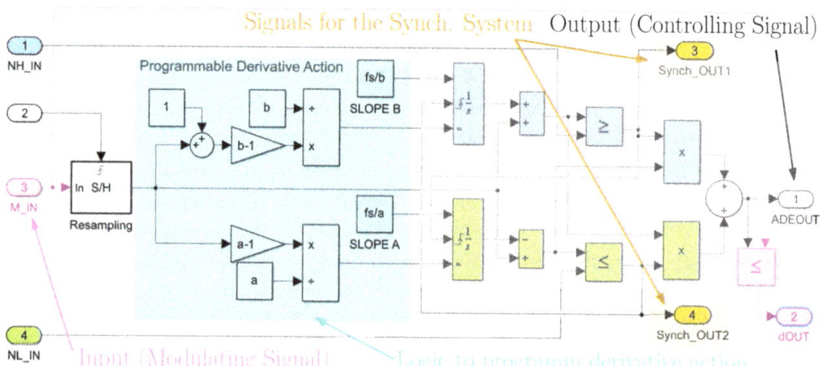

(b)

Figure 5. MATLAB/Simulink block implementation of the double-sampling (**a**) *e*DPWM v2.0 and (**b**) ADE-DPWM proposed in [23]. Region in turquoise highlights the blocks required to perform the derivative action. The MATLAB version is the 2024a.

The disparity in the architecture's complexity between the two modulators can be grasped by looking at the time operation reported in Figure 6. The initial point from which the ADE-DPWM starts counting is calculated after each sampling of the modulating signal. For example, the values of $y_{\text{off}}[i]$ and $y_{\text{on}}[i]$ are calculated as follows:

$$y_{\text{off}}[i] = M_{\text{off}}[i]\,\frac{1-b}{b}; \qquad y_{\text{on}}[i] = M_{\text{off}}[i]; \qquad a, b \in \mathbb{R} \tag{6}$$

As an additional complication, the carriers slopes must be calculated by performing suitable divisions (i.e., $S_{\text{on}} = S/a$ and $S_{\text{off}} = S/b$). This fact increases the complexity but also reduces the resolution of the counting variables. This makes the organization of the ADE-DPWM structure in [23] very complex and computationally inefficient. Moreover, this structure does not have an intrinsic synchronization mechanism, as does its simpler version in [25]. Therefore, its use is relegated to contexts where robust computational complexity and generous resource allocation can be employed. Indeed, products and divisions of variables with large variations require the allocation of several bits to reduce truncation errors within acceptable limits. Coarse truncations would lead to jitter and limit cycling in closed-loop systems, which is undesirable. Only the most trivial cases in which $a = b$

are powers of two (i.e., $a = b = 2^m$, with $m = 1, 2, 3, \ldots$) are reasonably easy to implement since that divisions and multiplications can be replaced by shift left/right operations. This makes the structure not-fully programmable by effectively making the derivative action a parameter not under the control of the designer.

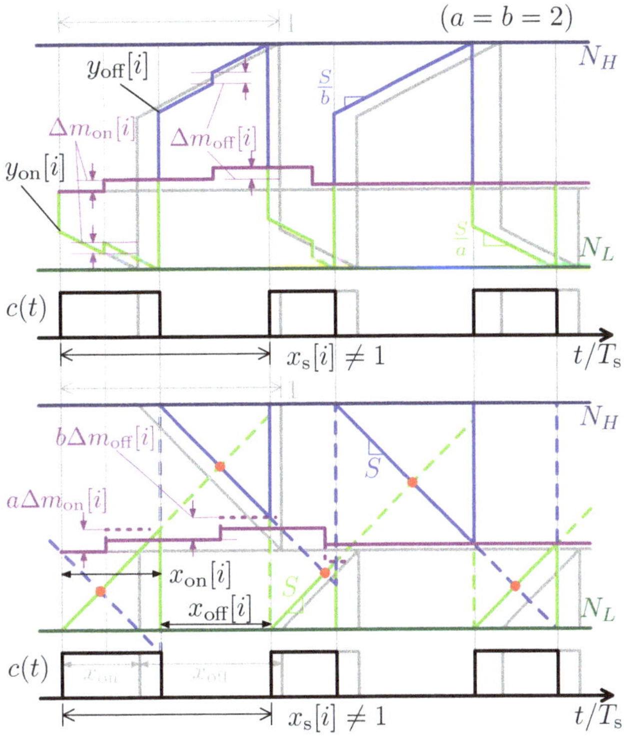

Figure 6. Operation of the DS ADE-DPWM with an intrinsic derivative action from [23] (**top**) vs. the *e*DPWM v2.0 (**bottom**). Green and blue lines are used to respectively highlights the counter used for computing the ON and OFF phases. Red dots indicates the intersection between the two carries in the *e*DPWM v2.0.

As shown in Figure 5a, the final implementation of the *e*DPWM v2.0 introduced in this section only requires two counters and two comparators. For the derivative action, one must add one delay block (e.g., implemented with a type D Flip-Flop) and two algebraic sums. No digital signal processing (DSP), lookup tables (LUT), and no other external resources are required for the FPGA implementation. The next section discusses the operation with an external synchronization signal and how this impacts the complexity of the architecture.

3.2. Synchronization Mechanism

As mentioned before, another critical aspect of ADE-DPWM architectures lies in the lack of an intrinsic synchronization mechanism. Differently, as discussed in the previous section, the proposed enhanced DPWM structure offers a considerable advantage in this regard, since it intrinsically guarantees the generation of a signal (i.e., the one generated in correspondence of the intersection between the two carriers highlighted with the red dots in Figures 4 and 6) that can be used to trigger the sampling actions on piecewise linear inductor currents. To understand the issue, refer to a Buck-type DC–DC converter (this topology is chosen as a remarkable example given its widespread use in various power electronics applications. In addition, the issue of average current sampling is in common with several topologies derived from the Buck; one among them is the voltage source inverter). The schematic of the Buck converter with the digital control scheme and the *e*DPWM is shown in Figure 7. The average current is generally calculated from a single sample acquired exactly halfway through the ON phase or OFF phases or at both points for controls that use double-sampling of state variables and double-updating of control signals. With the proposed *e*DPWM architecture, one can use the intersection between the two carriers to acquire the current at the midpoint. This ensures that the average inductor current $I_L \triangleq \frac{1}{T_s}\int_{t_0}^{T_s+t_0} i_L(t)dt$ is acquired correctly on each ON and/or OFF phase.

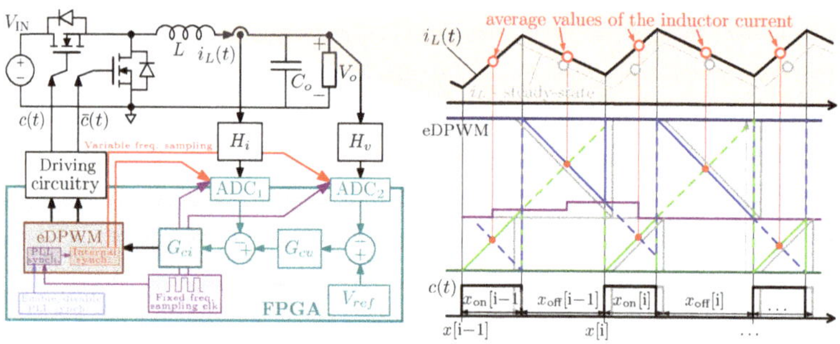

Figure 7. Standardapplication of a multi-loop digital control scheme for a Buck converter using the *e*DPWM modulator to acquire the average inductor current with a synchronous or asynchronous sampling mechanism. Colored lines denotes the dynamic operation while gray lines represent the steady-state operation.

One can define the signal t_{trig} that is set to 1 when the intersection of the two carriers occurs during the ON phase. When the intersection occurs during the OFF phase, the signal is reset to zero. This signal can be used to trigger the ADC_1 in Figure 7. This sampling system, at a fixed frequency when the converter is operating in steady-state and at variable frequency during transients, is already able to obtain the correct average value of the $i_L(t)$ current.

Implementing the average inductor current acquisition reported in Figure 7 with the ADE-DPWM proposed in [23] requires the additional digital hardware reported in the structure of Figure 8. Indeed, the ADE-DPWM architecture does not intrinsically offer the trigger instant at the middle of ON and OFF phases. Cycle-per-cycle, phase-per-phase, one must compute this instant starting from the acquired value of the modulating signal. This calculation can be done in FPGA at the price of an increased complexity. The proposed *e*DPWM having naturally this trigger instant, does not need the structure in Figure 8; this drastically reduces the overall system complexity.

Some system prerequisites may require synchronization with an external clock ($t_{\text{ext-clk}}(t)$). In this case, t_{trig} can be used to measure the synchronism error with respect to $t_{\text{ext-clk}}(t)$.

This error can be therefore corrected in a few switching cycles. This mechanism acts as a phase-locked loop (PLL). This operation is indicated as *ext-synch-mode*. Figure 9 reports the corresponding MATLAB/Simulink implementation and the simulation results for the *e*DPWM v2.0 operating in *ext-synch-mode*.

The ADC is clocked with the external fixed-frequency clock $t_{\text{ext-clk}}(t)$; this is represented with the blue narrow signal at the bottom-left of Figure 9. The counter is triggered by the rising edge of $t_{\text{etx-clk}}(t)$ and starts to count. The value of the counter is sampled when the signal t_{trig} rises. This value represents the distance between the sampling point and the half of the ON phase. This error is therefore used to correct the upper and lower thresholds, N_L and N_H (for simplicity in the simulation reported in Figure 9, only the lower threshold is moved since $gH = 0$).

The simulation in Figure 9 starts intentionally from the wrong initial conditions. Due to this, one has an initial synchronization error. This is the distance between the sampling instant and the middle of the ON phase. In the proposed simulation, ≈90% of the initial error is recovered in two modulation cycles. Furthermore, a modulating signal step is performed after 70 µs. The system still managed to resynchronize in only two cycles (≈90% of the error). Note that the action of the synchronization error correction could be performed in a deadbeat fashion. However, this could lead to instability and oscillation problems in closed-loop systems. Therefore, the proposed PLL-like mechanism is deliberately slowed down.

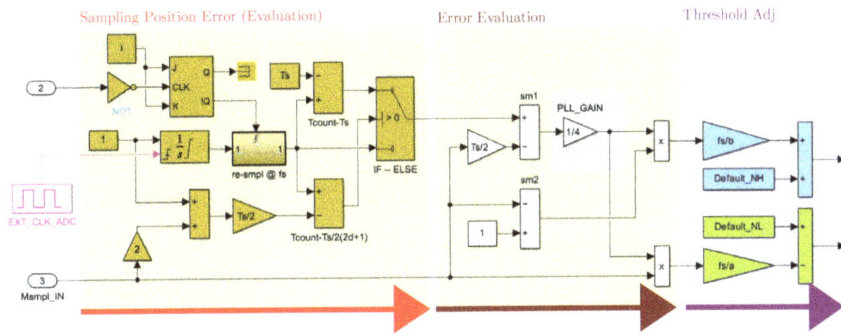

Figure 8. MATLAB/Simulink implementation of the synchronism mechanism of the double-sampling ADE-DPWM proposed in [23].

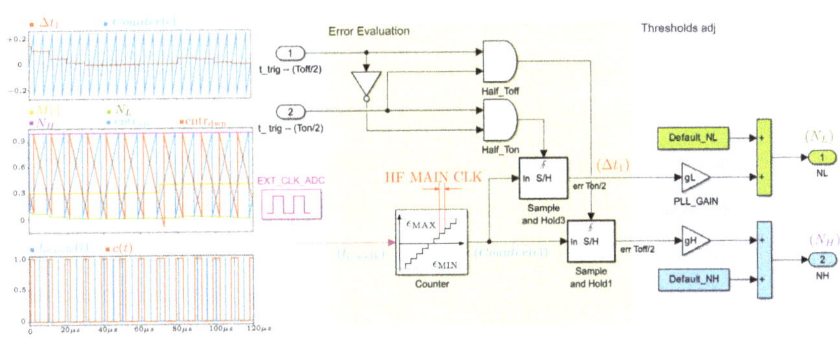

Figure 9. MATLAB/Simulink simulation results of the *e*DPWM v2.0 (with $a = b = 1$) running in *ext-synch-mode* with an external reference clock. On the right side is the Simulink implementation of the synchronization mechanism; on the left side are the simulation results. HF MAIN CLK indicates the high-frequency main system clock.

The same mechanism can also be implemented in the ADE-DPWM. However, it would be necessary to process cycle-by-cycle, phase-ON and phase-OFF where they are the midpoints of each phase, and then estimate the error with respect to the external clock. Figure 8 shows the synchronization systems of the double-sampling ADE-DPWM proposed in [23]. Here, the threshold modulation can only be done according to the synchronization error detected during the ON phase. To detect (and correct) the synchronization error with respect to the external clock, even during the OFF phase, the blocks highlighted with the red arrow must be replicated. The synchronization system in the proposed *e*DPWM v2.0 architecture does not have this constraint, and the structure in Figure 9 is capable of correcting the error on both thresholds according to the sampling error position acquired during both the ON and OFF phases. The blocks used in Figures 8 and 9 represent the MATLAB/Simulink implementation. These can be directly implemented in VHDL or Verilog codes.

Finally, both the proposed *e*DPWM and the ADE-DPWM in [23] can be used to generate the trigger instant for the ADC in both *ext-synch-mode* and *internal synch-mode*. The main difference is that in the *e*DPWM the computation block in Figure 8 is not required since it intrinsically provides the synchronization instant at the middle of the ON and OFF phases. Furthermore, moving the N_H and N_L thresholds in an ADE-DPWM architecture in order to synchronize with an external signal (i.e., when the synchronization mechanism is used as a PLL) is complex since the thresholds are scaled according to the counting step required to achieve fractional slopes.

Compared with the architectures proposed in [23–26], the additional hardware required to operate in *ext-synch-mode* is more contained in the proposed architecture. In fact, since there is no need to estimate, cycle by cycle, the point corresponding to the middle of the ON or OFF phase, the mechanism to operate with an external trigger is reduced to an additional counter and two sum operations to update the threshold values.

The next section derives the expressions of the time domain operation, showing that these are the same as those obtained in [23]. The small signal model is therefore discussed and commented.

4. The Small Signal Model

This section proves the time domain equivalence between the ADE-DPWM in [23] and the *e*DPWM V2.0. Once proved their equivalence in steady-state and during transients, the small signal model is uniquely identified. It is then necessary to prove their equivalence in the time domain only.

4.1. Time Domain Operation

Figures 6 and 10 are used as a reference in the following analysis.

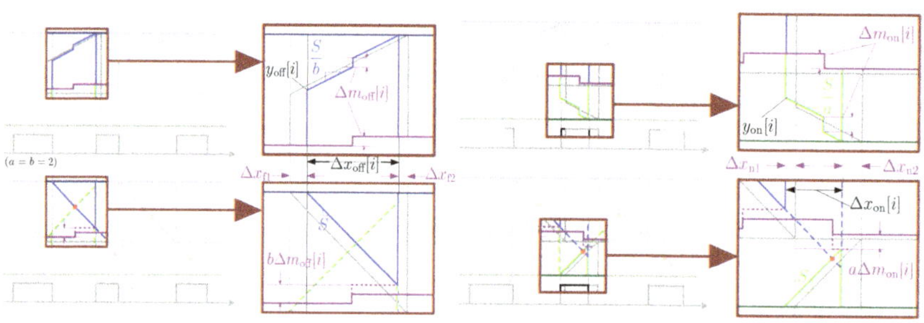

(**a**) (**b**)

Figure 10. Details of the operation of the proposed *derivative* ADE-DPWM during (**a**) the off-phase and (**b**) the off-phase. Gray lines represent the steady-state while black lines represent the operation during transients.

The variation of the ON and OFF phases for the i-th cycle, named as $\Delta x_{\text{on}}[i]$ and $\Delta x_{\text{off}}[i]$, can be calculated as

$$\Delta x_{\text{on}}[i] = \Delta x_{\text{n1}} + \Delta x_{\text{n2}}; \qquad \Delta x_{\text{off}}[i] = -\Delta x_{\text{f1}} - \Delta x_{\text{f2}} \tag{7}$$

where the quantities Δx_{n1}, Δx_{n2}, Δx_{f1} and Δx_{f2} are defined in Figure 10.

Let's start with $\Delta x_{\text{off}}[i]$. By analyzing Figures 6 and 10 one has

$$\Delta x_{\text{f1}} = \Delta M_{\text{on}}[i]; \qquad \Delta x_{\text{f2}} = b\Delta m_{\text{off}}[i]. \tag{8}$$

By using (8) and by substituting the definitions of $\Delta M_{\text{on}}[i]$ and $\Delta m_{\text{off}}[i] \triangleq M_{\text{off}}[i] - M_{\text{on}}[i]$ in (7) one obtains

$$\begin{aligned} -\Delta x_{\text{off}}[i] &= \Delta x_{\text{f1}} + \Delta x_{\text{f2}} \\ &= b(M_{\text{off}}[i] - M_{\text{on}}[i]) + M_{\text{on}}[i] - M_{\text{ss}} \\ &= b(M_{\text{off}}[i] - M) + bM_{\text{ss}} - M_{\text{on}}[i](1-b) - M_{\text{ss}} \\ &= b\Delta M_{\text{off}}[i] - \Delta M_{\text{on}}[i](1-b). \end{aligned} \tag{9}$$

With identical approach, by using Figures 6 and 10 as a reference, one has

$$\Delta x_{\text{n1}} = \Delta M_{\text{off}}[i-1]; \qquad \Delta x_{\text{n2}} = a\Delta m_{\text{on}}[i]. \tag{10}$$

By substituting the definitions of $\Delta M_{\text{off}}[i-1]$ and $\Delta m_{\text{on}}[i] \triangleq M_{\text{on}}[i] - M_{\text{off}}[i-1]$ in (10) one obtains

$$\Delta x_{\text{on}}[i] = \Delta x_{\text{n1}} + \Delta x_{\text{n2}} = a\Delta M_{\text{on}}[i] - \Delta M_{\text{off}}[i-1](1-a). \tag{11}$$

Using (9) and (11), one can calculate the net variation of the switching period $x_{\text{s}}[i]$ as

$$\begin{aligned} \Delta x_{\text{s}}[i] &\triangleq x_{\text{s}}[i] - x_{\text{s}} = \Delta x_{\text{on}}[i] + \Delta x_{\text{off}}[i] \\ &= \Delta M_{\text{on}}[i](a+1-b) - \Delta M_{\text{off}}[i]b - \Delta M_{\text{off}}[i-1](1-a). \end{aligned} \tag{12}$$

Equations (9), (11), and (12) describe the time domain operation of the proposed *e*DPWM V2.0. Those equations are exactly the same as those in [23].

4.2. Frequency Domain Results

Since, as proven in the previous section, the time domain model of the proposed architecture is identical to that of the ADE-DPWM architecture in [23], the small signal model in the frequency domain will be the same. In fact, as for the Fourier Transformation, a describing function is completely identified by its time domain expression. In other words, an equivalent representation in the time domain implies an identical describing function model. Thus, the small signal model of *e*DPWM V2.0 coincides with the small signal model of the double-sampling ADE-DPWM developed in [23]. The model in [23] is obtained by using the describing function approach. Given the redundancy, the frequency domain analysis is not reported in this manuscript. For the mathematical derivation, one can refer to [23]. For completeness, only the procedure in broad outline is given below.

For the small signal analysis, a small-sinusoidal perturbation $\hat{u}(t)$ is superimposed on a constant modulating signal value M_{ss}

$$\hat{u}(t) = \hat{a}\sin(2\pi f_{\text{k}} T_{\text{s}} x - \phi) \quad \text{with } \hat{a} \ll M_{\text{ss}}. \tag{13}$$

The Fourier analysis is therefore conducted on the output signal $c(t)$ (i.e., $C_F = \mathcal{F}\{c(t)\}$) (the symbol $\mathcal{F}$ denotes the Fourier Transform Operator). In steady-state with $\hat{u}(t) = 0$, $c(t)$ is a signal with a main frequency component at f_{s}. When the perturbation $\hat{u}(t)$ as in (13) with a main frequency component at f_{k} is superimposed at the constant input M_{ss}, the output control signal $c(t)$ becomes a signal with a main frequency component around f_{res}, which is the inverse of the minimum common multiple from $T_s = 1/f_s$ and $T_k = 1/f_k$, i.e.,

$$T_{res} = 1/f_{res} = NT_k + KT_s \quad \text{with } N, K \in \mathbb{N} \text{ prime integers.} \tag{14}$$

The small signal model is finally obtained by computing the ratio between the Fourier coefficient C_F evaluated at f_{res} and the Fourier coefficient of $\hat{u}(t)$ computed at f_k.

The final result coincides with that in [23] (or more generally in [24]). The final expression in the frequency domain is given below. This is identical to that in [23] by substituting $a = \alpha$ and $b = \beta$. The terms have been arranged to better emphasize the different contributions. Thus, the small signal model of the proposed *e*DPWM is

$$\begin{aligned} G_{eDPWM2}(s) = & \frac{e^{-s\frac{T_s}{2}x_{on}}\left(1-e^{sT_s}\right)}{1-e^{sT_s}}\left(a+(1-a)e^{-s\frac{T_s}{2}}\right) \\ + & \frac{e^{sT_s x_{on}}\left(1-e^{-sT_s x_{on}}\right)}{1-e^{sT_s}}\left((a-1)\left(1-e^{-s\frac{T_s}{2}}\right)+b(1-e^{s\frac{T_s}{2}})\right), \end{aligned} \tag{15}$$

where $s \in \mathbb{C}$ is the complex variable of the Laplace plane. In the practical cases with $a = b$, one has

$$\begin{aligned} G_{eDPWM2}(s) = & \frac{e^{-s\frac{T_s}{2}x_{on}}}{1-e^{sT_s}}\left(a\left(2e^{s\frac{T_s}{2}}-1-e^{sT_s}\right)-e^{s\frac{T_s}{2}+1}\right) \\ + & \frac{e^{sT_s\frac{x_{on}}{2}}}{1-e^{sT_s}}\left(2a-a\left(e^{-s\frac{T_s}{2}}+e^{s\frac{T_s}{2}}\right)+e^{-s\frac{T_s}{2}}-1\right). \end{aligned} \tag{16}$$

In the simplified case for $a = b = 1$, one has

$$G_{eDPWM2}(s)\big|_{a=b=1} = e^{-s\frac{T_s}{2}x_{on}} - \frac{1-e^{sT_s x_{on}}}{1-e^{sT_s}}\left(1-e^{s\frac{T_s}{2}}\right). \tag{17}$$

The proposed *e*DPWM V2.0 architecture, reported in Figure 5a, keeps the same small signal behavior of the complex architecture in [23]. In this section, the equivalence between the two architectures is proved through the time domain analysis. This analysis revealed that the behavior of the proposed *e*DPWM V2.0 solution is identical to that of the architecture in [23]. Unlike the latter, however, the proposed solution does not need the computation of products between signals and no division by generic parameters. In addition, the counters are completely standard and do not have to change the counting step, avoiding perishing to degrade the resolution with which the counting ramp variables are represented.

The final *e*DPWM V2.0 architecture is available as MATLAB/Simulink block diagram in the open-source resource (CC BY 4.0) (Supplementary Materials).

5. Experimental Validation

To further validate the proposed simplified double-sampling *e*DPWM V2.0 architecture reported in Figure 5a, a set of experimental measurements is reported below. The proposed modulator's architecture is coded in VHDL and implemented in a commercial Intel© Cyclone©Ṽ 5CSEMA5F31C6N FPGA. This FPGA is contained in the TerasIC© De1-SoC Development Board. Board was purchased on Mouser Electronics©.

The experimental setup organization is reported in Figure 11. The external sinusoidal perturbation is sampled with the onboard 12-bit LTC2308 ADC ($f_{sample} = 500$ kHz). The ADC output data are serial. This increases the overall latency ($t_{ADC\text{-}latency}$) since one must wait for the full word acquisition before sending it to the *e*DPWMṪhe ADC latency and its consequent phase rotation (i.e., $\approx e^{-t_{ADC\text{-}latency}s}$) must be therefore taken into account and compensated in the final experimental data. Given the limited capabilities of the ADC, the steady-state modulating period is fixed at $f_s = 20\,\text{kHz}$. The perturbation frequency range (values of f_k) is $200\,\text{Hz} \div 15\,\text{kHz}$. The Fourier analysis is performed with the Tektronix *MS056*.

The experimental results are compared with the theoretical curves in Figure 12. Figure 12a shows analytical curves and experimental data for different values of $a = b$. The curve obtained for $a = b = 4$ shows a peak phase boost of $\phi_{\text{boost}} \approx 50°$ for $f \approx f_s/4$. Such phase boost gain can be exploited in closed-loop systems (e.g., Figure 7) to enhance the dynamic performance. Generally, a system's bandwidth is a compromise between speed and stability margins. Particularly critical is the phase margin parameter. By having a phase boost right around the crossing frequency, it is therefore possible to increase the bandwidth without degrading the phase margin. Similar considerations and experimental tests are proposed in [23–25,29,30].

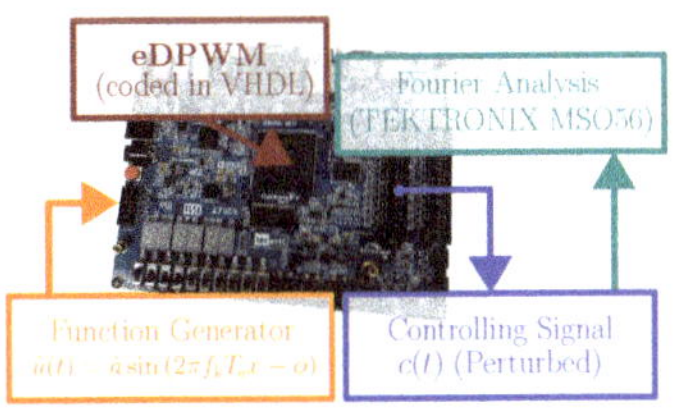

Figure 11. Organization of the experimental setup.

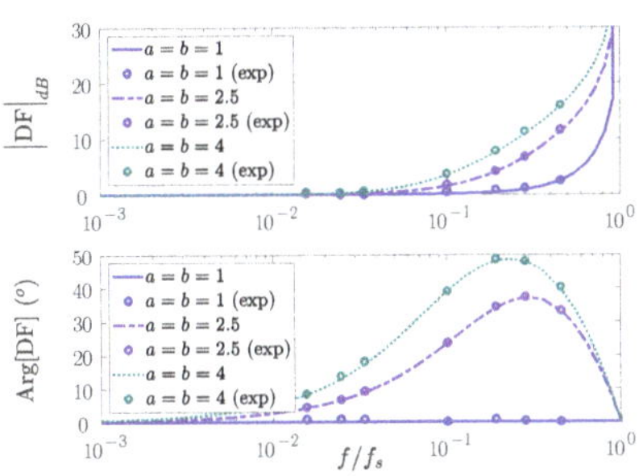

(**a**)

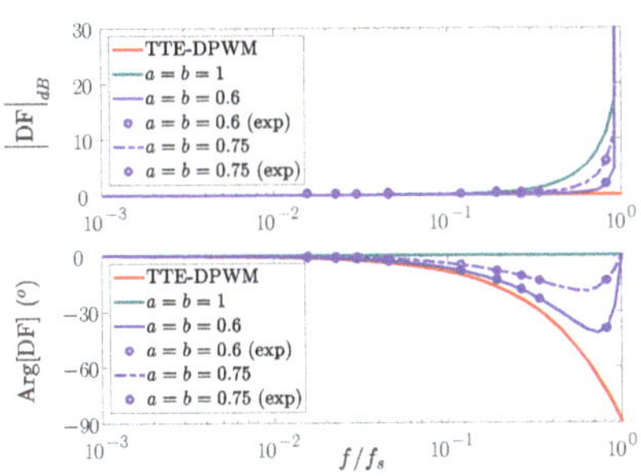

(**b**)

Figure 12. (**a**) Bode plots of $G_{\text{eDPWM2}}(s)$ for different values of $a = b$ and $M_{ss} = 0.5$: gain (on **top**) and angle (on **bottom**). (**b**) Bode plots of $G_{\text{eDPWM2}}(s)$ for different values of $a = b$ vs. the traditional double-sampling Trailing-Triangle edge carrier-based DPWM (TTE-DPWM). The experimental data are highlighted with dots. The x-axes are normalized with respect to the steady-state switching frequency f_s.

Figure 12a shows the analytical curves and experimental data for $a = b < 1$. The figure also shows the response of a TTE-DPWM [28] as a reference to show how even small values of $a = b < 1$ can lead to large improvements in terms of available phase compared with what is the most commonly used solution.

Discussion

The comparison between experimental and theoretical curves shows three important facts. The first is that the analytical model is correct and able to predict the behavior of the modulator over the entire frequency range of interest (i.e., $f < f_{\mathrm{NYQUIST}}$). Since the frequency model is derived from the time domain model, the comparison indirectly proves that the time domain model is also correct. The second remarkable element is that, despite the radical simplification of the architecture, the proposed eDPWM can achieve the same results as the double-sampling ADE-DWPM architecture. The third interesting fact can be noticed when $a = b < 1$. Comparing the results obtained by the proposed architecture with the more conventional TTE-DPWM, it can be seen that even with $a = b < 1$, a significant increase in the high-frequency phase, up to $\phi_{\mathrm{boost}} \approx 90^{\circ}$, can be obtained. This fact is significant because while small values of $a = b$ allow for the containment of possible high-frequency noise due to the presence of a derivative action, on the high side it still allows a designer to achieve a required phase gain when compared with conventional DPWM architectures. This fact is not further investigated in this article for reasons of space.

Another key aspect is the direct comparison with the architecture in [23]. The implementation of the ADE-DPWM architecture in [23] requires a large amount of resources. A fully functional implementation with programmable parameters a and b can be set up as follows. The system clock is set at $f_{\mathrm{clk\text{-}ADE}} = 400\,\mathrm{MHz}$ (e.g., by using a PLL and starting from the system's fundamental clock which is $f_{\mathrm{sys\text{-}clk}} = 50\,\mathrm{MHz}$).

With this, the maximum resolution of the DPWM is $q_{\mathrm{MAX}} = 20\,\mathrm{kHz}/400\,\mathrm{MHz} = 1/20{,}000$. The ADE-DPWM architecture uses fractional counts to set the slopes' values (i.e., S/a and S/b). To obtain such divisions, the resolution of the modulator must be reduced up to $q_{\mathrm{ADE}} = 1/1000$. Thus, there are 20 cycles at 400 MHz between two consecutive count increments. With this organization, the variable slopes of the ADE-DPWM counters in [23] can be achieved. The true implementation of the slope divisions uses different count steps and normalization factors depending on the slope to be set. This can be handled by selection structures (e.g., IF/THEN type).

The *e*DPWM architecture requires fewer resources than the ADE-DPWM. Indeed, the system clock can be set to $f_{\mathrm{clk\text{-}eDPWM}} = 20\,\mathrm{MHz}$, and the *e*DPWM resolution is $q_{\mathrm{eDPWM}} = 20\,\mathrm{kHz}/20\,\mathrm{MHz} = 1/1000$. The 20 clock cycles between two consecutive increments of the counters are not required anymore since in the *e*DPWM architecture the counters do not use fractional slopes. Therefore, the final system resolution is the same as the ADE-DPWM but now a system clock that is 20 times slower is adopted. Also, selection structures like IF/THEN are not required to set count steps and scaling factors.

There are several other simplifications in the *e*DPWM architecture, but this one is the most remarkable. The experimental tests show consistency with the analytical model developed, even after relaxing the system specification as described above. Since the analytical model of *e*DPWM is the same as that in [23], these tests can also be used to prove experimental equivalence with the ADE-DPWM, even with more relaxed system specifications.

6. Conclusions

This work proposes and analyzes an innovative Digital Pulse Width Modulator architecture that eliminates the typical delays associated with conventional designs. The *enhanced* DPWM introduces a variable frequency modulation strategy with a programmable derivative action, enabling a significant improvement in the dynamic response of digital control systems. Theoretical analysis and experimental tests have demonstrated the equivalence of the *e*DPWM with advanced solutions from the literature, while drastically reducing computational complexity. Additionally, the proposed structure incorporates an intrinsic synchronization mechanism that facilitates the acquisition of the average inductor current, simplifying its implementation in power electronics applications.

Experimental tests conducted on an FPGA implementation have validated the effectiveness of the proposed architecture, highlighting improved high-frequency phase performance and greater flexibility compared to traditional DPWM techniques. By reducing complex operations and eliminating the need for multiplications and divisions between signals, the *e*DPWM emerges as an efficient and easily implementable solution for both industrial and academic applications. Future research may explore further optimizations relating to its integration with other advanced control techniques for power electronics.

Supplementary Materials: The following supporting information can be downloaded at: https://www.mdpi.com/article/10.3390/electronics14081522/s1.

Funding: This research received no external funding.

Data Availability Statement: The open-source (CC BY 4.0) MATLAB code and the Simulink implementation of the final *e*DPWM V2.0 architecture is available on Supplementary Materials.

Acknowledgments: This study was carried out within the MOST—Sustainable Mobility Center and received funding from the European Union Next-GenerationEU (PIANO NAZIONALE DI RIPRESA E RESILIENZA (PNRR)—MISSIONE 4 COMPONENTE 2, INVESTIMENTO 1.4—D.D. 1033 17 June 2022, CN00000023). This manuscript reflects only the authors' views and opinions; neither the European Union nor the European Commission can be considered responsible for them.

Conflicts of Interest: The author declares no conflicts of interest.

Abbreviations and Main Definitions

The following abbreviations are used in this manuscript:

Symbol	Definition
DPWM	Digital Pulse Width Modulator;
*e*DPWM	Enhanced Digital Pulse Width Modulator;
ADE	Asymmetric Dual-Edge;
TTE	Trailing-Triangle Edge;
T_s	Modulation period;
T_{on}	ON time of the pulse width modulation cycle;
T_{off}	OFF time of the pulse width modulation cycle;
x_{on}	Normalized ON phase duration (i.e., $\frac{T_{on}}{T_s}$);
x_{off}	Normalized OFF phase duration (i.e., $\frac{T_{off}}{T_s}$);
$x_{on}[i]$	Normalized ON phase duration during the i-th cycle;
$x_{off}[i]$	Normalized OFF phase duration during the i-th cycle;
$\Delta x_{on}[i]$	Variation of the ON phase during the i-th cycle (i.e., $x_{on}[i] - x_{on}$);
$\Delta x_{off}[i]$	Variation of the OFF phase during the i-th cycle (i.e., $x_{off}[i] - x_{off}$);
$M[\cdot]$	Modulating signal;
M_{ss}	Steady-state value of the modulating signal;
ΔM_{on}	Modulating signal variation during the ON phase;
ΔM_{off}	Modulating signal variation during the OFF phase;
S	Carrier slope;
s	Complex independent variable of the transfer functions;
$c(t)$	Output control signal;

$G_{eDPWM}(s)$	Small signal transfer function of the *e*DPWM V2.0;
f_s	Steady-state switching frequency;
f_k	Frequency of the input perturbation;
ϕ_{boost}	High-frequency phase boost;
PLL	Phase-Locked Loop;
a, b	Parameters to weight the derivative action;
N_H, N_L	Upper and lower DPWM thresholds.

References

1. Li, W.; He, X. Review of Nonisolated High-Step-Up DC/DC Converters in Photovoltaic Grid-Connected Applications. *IEEE Trans. Ind. Electron.* **2011**, *58*, 1239–1250. [CrossRef]
2. Forouzesh, M.; Siwakoti, Y.P.; Gorji, S.A.; Blaabjerg, F.; Lehman, B. Step-Up DC–DC Converters: A Comprehensive Review of Voltage-Boosting Techniques, Topologies, and Applications. *IEEE Trans. Power Electron.* **2017**, *32*, 9143–9178. [CrossRef]
3. Mao, H.; Lee, C.; Boroyevich, D.; Hiti, S. Review of high-performance three-phase power-factor correction circuits. *IEEE Trans. Ind. Electron.* **1997**, *44*, 437–446. [CrossRef]
4. de Castro, A.; Todorovich, E. High Resolution FPGA DPWM Based on Variable Clock Phase Shifting. *IEEE Trans. Power Electron.* **2010**, *25*, 1115–1119. [CrossRef]
5. Le, H.; Dekka, A.; Ronanki, D.; Rodriguez, J. Predictive Current Control of a New Four-Level Voltage Source Inverter. In Proceedings of the 2022 IEEE International Conference on Power Electronics, Drives and Energy Systems (PEDES), Jaipur, India, 14–17 December 2022; pp. 1–5. [CrossRef]
6. Buso, S.; Mattavelli, P. *Digital Control in Power Electronics*, 2nd ed.; Springer: Cham, Switzerland, 2015.
7. Sozański, K. *Digital Signal Processing in Power Electronics Control Circuits*, 2nd ed.; Springer: Cham, Switzerland, 2013.
8. Buccella, C.; Cecati, C.; Latafat, H. Digital Control of Power Converters—A Survey. *IEEE Trans. Ind. Inf.* **2012**, *8*, 437–447. [CrossRef]
9. Kelly, A.; Rinne, K. High Resolution DPWM in a DC-DC Converter Application Using Digital Sigma-Delta Techniques. In Proceedings of the 2005 IEEE 36th Power Electronics Specialists Conference, Recife, Brazil, 12–16 June 2005; pp. 1458–1463. [CrossRef]
10. Huang, Y.; Cheung, C. Small signal modeling of the hysteretic modulator with a current ripple synthesizer. In Proceedings of the 2016 IEEE Applied Power Electronics Conference and Exposition (APEC), Long Beach, CA, USA, 20–24 March 2016; pp. 1616–1623. [CrossRef]
11. Rodriguez, J.; Pontt, J.; Silva, C.A.; Correa, P.; Lezana, P.; Cortes, P.; Ammann, U. Predictive Current Control of a Voltage Source Inverter. *IEEE Trans. Ind. Electron.* **2007**, *54*, 495–503. [CrossRef]
12. Singh, R.K.; Mishra, S. Synthetic-Ripple-Based Digital Hysteretic Modulator for Point-of-Load Converters. *IEEE Trans. Ind. Electron.* **2013**, *60*, 4996–5007. [CrossRef]
13. Malesani, L.; Tenti, P. A novel hysteresis control method for current-controlled voltage-source PWM inverters with constant modulation frequency. *IEEE Trans. Ind. Appl.* **1990**, *26*, 88–92. [CrossRef]
14. Nussbaumer, T.; Heldwein, M.L.; Gong, G.; Round, S.D.; Kolar, J.W. Comparison of Prediction Techniques to Compensate Time Delays Caused by Digital Control of a Three-Phase Buck-Type PWM Rectifier System. *IEEE Trans. Ind. Electron.* **2008**, *55*, 791–799. [CrossRef]
15. Corradini, L.; Mattavelli, P.; Tedeschi, E.; Trevisan, D. High-Bandwidth Multisampled Digitally Controlled DC–DC Converters Using Ripple Compensation. *IEEE Trans. Ind. Electron.* **2008**, *55*, 1501–1508. [CrossRef]
16. Petric, I.Z.; Mattavelli, P.; Buso, S. A Jitter Amplification Phenomenon in Multisampled Digital Control of Power Converters. *IEEE Trans. Power Electron.* **2021**, *36*, 8685–8695. [CrossRef]
17. Corradini, L.; Mattavelli, P.; Saggini, S. Elimination of Sampling-Induced Dead Bands in Multiple-Sampled Pulsewidth Modulators for DC–DC Converters. *IEEE Trans. Power Electron.* **2009**, *24*, 2661–2665. [CrossRef]
18. Petric, I.Z.; Mattavelli, P.; Buso, S. Investigation of Nonlinearities Introduced by Multi-sampled Pulsewidth Modulators. *IEEE Trans. Power Electron.* **2022**, *37*, 2538–2550. [CrossRef]
19. Chen, J.; Prodic, A.; Erickson, R.; Maksimovic, D. Predictive digital current programmed control. *IEEE Trans. Power Electron.* **2003**, *18*, 411–419. [CrossRef]
20. Mohamed, Y.A.R.I.; El-Saadany, E.F. Robust High Bandwidth Discrete-Time Predictive Current Control with Predictive Internal Model—A Unified Approach for Voltage-Source PWM Converters. *IEEE Trans. Power Electron.* **2008**, *23*, 126–136. [CrossRef]
21. Mattavelli, P. An improved deadbeat control for UPS using disturbance observers. *IEEE Trans. Ind. Electron.* **2005**, *52*, 206–212. [CrossRef]

22. Bonanno, G.; Corradini, L. Digital Predictive Current-Mode Control of Three-Level Flying Capacitor Buck Converters. *IEEE Trans. Power Electron.* **2021**, *36*, 4697–4710. [CrossRef]
23. Bonanno, G.; Comacchio, A.; Mattavelli, P.; Corradin, M. Asymmetric Dual-Edge Digital Pulsewidth Modulator with an Intrinsic Derivative Action. *IEEE Trans. Power Electron.* **2023**, *38*, 304–315. [CrossRef]
24. Bonanno, G.; Comacchio, A.; Mattavelli, P. Multisampling Digital Pulse-Width Modulator Based on Asymmetric Dual-Edge Carrier. *IEEE Trans. Power Electron.* **2024**, *39*, 5121–5134. [CrossRef]
25. Comacchio, A.; Bonanno, G.; Hossein, A.; Mattavelli, P.; Corradin, M. A Digital Dual-Edge Modulator for Dynamic Performance Improvement of Multi-Loop Controlled VSI. *IEEE Trans. Ind. Electron.* **2022**, *70*, 4662–4671. [CrossRef]
26. Cvetanovic, R.; Bonanno, G.; Comacchio, A.; Abedini, H.; Biadene, D.; Mattavelli, P. High Frequency Passivity Properties of Grid-Connected Admittance with Double-Sampling Asymmetric Dual-Edge Modulator. *IEEE Open J. Power Electron.* **2022**, *3*, 856–865. [CrossRef]
27. da Silva Carvalho, S.; Halamíček, M.; Vukadinović, N.; Prodić, A. Digital PWM for Multi-Level Flying Capacitor Converters with Improved Output Resolution and Flying Capacitor Voltage Controller Stability. In Proceedings of the 2018 IEEE 19th Workshop on Control and Modeling for Power Electronics (COMPEL), Padova, Italy, 25–28 June 2018; pp. 1–7. [CrossRef]
28. Corradini, L.; Maksimović, D.; Mattavelli, P.; Zane, R. *Digital Control of High-Frequency Switched-Mode Power Converters*; Wiley: Hoboken, NJ, USA, 2015; pp. 1–342. [CrossRef]
29. Ripamonti, G.; Saggini, S.; Corradini, L.; Rizzolatti, R.; Faccio, F.; Michelis, S.; Koukab, A.; Kayal, M. A Dual-Edge Pulsewidth Modulator for Fast Dynamic Response DC-DC Converters. *IEEE Trans. Power Electron.* **2019**, *34*, 28–32. [CrossRef]
30. Huang, Y.; Cheung, C.; Jayaprakash, K.V.A. Small signal modeling of dual-edge PWM modulator with fixed clock frequency. In Proceedings of the 2017 IEEE Applied Power Electronics Conference and Exposition (APEC), Tampa, FL, USA, 26–30 March 2017; pp. 1047–1053. [CrossRef]

electronics

MDPI

Article

Achieving Low-Latency, High-Throughput Online Partial Particle Identification for the NA62 Experiment Using FPGAs and Machine Learning †

Pierpaolo Perticaroli [1,*], Roberto Ammendola [2], Andrea Biagioni [1], Carlotta Chiarini [1,3], Andrea Ciardiello [3], Paolo Cretaro [1], Ottorino Frezza [1], Francesca Lo Cicero [1], Michele Martinelli [1], Roberto Piandani [4], Luca Pontisso [1], Mauro Raggi [1,3], Cristian Rossi [1,3], Francesco Simula [1], Matteo Turisini [1,‡], Piero Vicini [1] and Alessandro Lonardo [1,*]

1 Sezione di Roma, Istituto Nazionale di Fisica Nucleare, P.le Aldo Moro, 2, 00185 Rome, Italy; andrea.biagioni@roma1.infn.it (A.B.); carlotta.chiarini@uniroma1.it (C.C.); paolo.cretaro@gmail.com (P.C.); ottorino.frezza@roma1.infn.it (O.F.); francesca.locicero@roma1.infn.it (F.L.C.); michele.martinelli@roma1.infn.it (M.M.); luca.pontisso@roma1.infn.it (L.P.); mauro.raggi@uniroma1.it (M.R.); cristian.rossi@uniroma1.it (C.R.); francesco.simula@roma1.infn.it (F.S.); m.turisini@cineca.it (M.T.); piero.vicini@roma1.infn.it (P.V.)

2 Sezione di Roma Tor Vergata, Istituto Nazionale di Fisica Nucleare, Via della Ricerca Scientifica 1, 00133 Rome, Italy; roberto.ammendola@roma2.infn.it

3 Dipartimento di Fisica, Università Sapienza di Roma, P.le Aldo Moro 2, 00185 Rome, Italy; andrea.ciardiello@uniroma1.it

4 Instituto de Física, Universidad Autónoma de San Luis Potosí, San Luis Potosí 78000, Mexico; roberto.piandani@cern.ch

* Correspondence: pierpaolo.perticaroli@roma1.infn.it (P.P.); alessandro.lonardo@roma1.infn.it (A.L.)

† This article is a revised and expanded version of a paper Perticaroli, P.; Ammendola, R.; Biagioni, A.; Chiarini C.; Ciardiello, A.; Cretaro, P.; Frezza, O.; Lo Cicero F.; Martinelli, M.; Piandani, R.; et al; FPGA-RICH: A low-latency, high-throughput online particle identification system for the NA62 experiment. In Proceedings of the 27th Conference on Computing in High Energy and Nuclear Physics (CHEP 2024), Krakow, Poland, 19–25 October 2024.

‡ Current address: Consorzio Interuniversitario del Nord-Est per il Calcolo Automatico (CINECA), Via dei Tizii 6/B, 00185 Rome, Italy.

Abstract: FPGA-RICH is an FPGA-based online partial particle identification system for the NA62 experiment employing AI techniques. Integrated between the readout of the Ring Imaging Cherenkov detector (RICH) and the low-level trigger processor (L0TP+), FPGA-RICH implements a fast pipeline to process in real-time the RICH raw hit data stream, producing trigger primitives containing elaborate physics information—e.g., the number of charged particles in a physics event—that L0TP+ can use to improve trigger decision efficiency. Deployed on a single FPGA, the system combines classical online processing with a compact Neural Network algorithm to achieve efficient event classification while managing the challenging ∼10 MHz throughput requirement of NA62. The streaming pipeline ensures ∼1 µs latency, comparable to that of the NA62 detectors, allowing its seamless integration in the existing TDAQ setup as an additional detector. Development leverages High-Level Synthesis (HLS) and the open-source hls4ml package software–hardware codesign workflow, enabling fast and flexible reprogramming, debugging, and performance optimization. We describe the implementation of the full processing pipeline, the Neural Network classifier, their functional validation, performance metrics and the system's current status and outlook.

Keywords: FPGA-based systems; real-time particle identification; neural network acceleration; high-level synthesis; Cherenkov detectors; low-latency trigger systems; high-energy physics experiments; online data processing; quantized neural networks; high-throughput computing

1. Introduction

NA62 is a fixed target experiment in the North Area of the SPS complex at CERN [1] which aims at measuring the branching ratio of the ultra-rare $K^+ \rightarrow \pi^+ \nu\bar{\nu}$ decay with 10% precision [2]. The expected branching ratio is of the order of $O(10^{-10})$. To achieve the required precision, NA62 must collect $O(10^{13})$ kaon decays, accompanied by a rejection factor of $O(10^{12})$ to suppress the huge background from other kaon decays. Part of this suppression must be made during the online data acquisition stage in order to reduce the amount of data that needs to be stored and analyzed offline. For this reason, the NA62 Trigger and Data Acquisition system (TDAQ) [3] is equipped with a two-stage data selection system, called the trigger system. The first trigger stage—denoted as Level 0 (L0)—is implemented in hardware and works on filtering background events to reduce their full rate of order 10 MHz by a factor 10. Here, we refer to an "event" as the instantaneous physical situation or occurrence associated with a point in spacetime (typically with a fundamental interaction between particles that results in the creation of other particles), gleaned from the TDAQ system by the output provided by several different detectors. Data are delivered at 1 MHz ($\sim$10 GB/s bandwidth) to an online farm of commodity processors (PC farm) that implements the L1 trigger stage, where selections are performed in software, bringing the final event rate to about 100 kHz ($\sim$2 GB/s bandwidth since an average NA62 complete event size is $\sim$20 kB [3]). L0 relies on an FPGA-based Level Zero Trigger Processor (L0TP+) [4] communicating with the readout boards of all the experiment sub-detectors. The readout boards temporarily store event data (for up to $\approx$ 1 ms), waiting for a trigger decision signal from L0TP+ indicating whether an event needs to be sent to L1 or flushed. For each event, a sub-group of fast detectors sends minimal physics information to L0TP+ through a dedicated trigger flow (trigger primitives), and L0TP+ operates logical coincidences between them according to user-defined masks, determines whether the event is signal or background, and sends the trigger decision back to the detector readout boards through the NA62 common infrastructure, which distributes clock, trigger, backpressure, and reference signals to all detectors.

The NA62 detector receives the particles beam from the CERN SPS accelerator with bursts of a few seconds ($\sim$4–6 s) duration every 15–20 s. The time structure of bursts is roughly constant during each data-taking run of a few hours duration. So bursts naturally define coherent data-taking units, down to the level of a final data file for permanent storage, identified by a unique burst id. All electronics operate in a fully synchronized way thanks to the common distributed 40 MHz clock, which is also used for timestamping (32-bits with a resolution of 25 ns). To account for the fact that L0 trigger primitives relative to the same physical event are generated by the different sub-detectors with a different latency, and thus can arrive to L0TP+ with different timing, a timing protocol is imposed on the dispatch of trigger primitives from the sub-detectors. The sub-detectors are obliged to send primitives periodically in packets every 6.4 µs even if the packet contains no primitives. This way, the primitives delays can be defined in terms of an integer number of packets and compensated by the time-alignment logic of L0TP+, which relies on buffers to temporarily store the faster detectors' primitives.

One of the sub-detectors sending primitives to L0TP+ is a Ring Imaging Cherenkov detector (RICH), used for timing and particle identification (PID) purposes. The RICH operates by detecting Cherenkov photons emitted by charged particles traveling through a gas radiator; these photons form rings on an array of photodetectors (photomultiplier tubes, or PMTs), with the ring radius depending on the particle's momentum.

The RICH utilizes an array of up to 2048 PMTs, of which 1952 are currently in use. This array is split between two disks as shown in Figure 1, where an example RICH event is also presented. For the PMTs, a compact size Hamamatsu R7400 U-03 photomultiplier (PM) is used [5]. Its typical gain is 0.7×10^6 at 800 V and 1.5×10^6 at 900 V with the average charge generated by the electron multiplier for each photo-electron being 80 fC and 240 fC, respectively. The PM has a UV glass window and a bialkali cathode providing a 20% quantum efficiency at about $\lambda = 420$ nm and a sensitivity ranging from visible to near UV ($\lambda = 185 \div 690$ nm). The PM transit time spread is 0.28 ns. The input pulses from the 2048 PMT channels are read from the front-end (FE) electronics of the RICH, which is placed near the PMT disks and is comprised of 64 boards, each hosting 4 NINO chips. NINO is an 8-channel chip developed at CERN for the ALICE experiment for precision time measurement [6], which has an input signal range compatible with the RICH PMTs. Each NINO channel features an ultra-fast low-noise input amplifier followed by a discriminator stage and outputs a LVDS pulse proportional to the input charge. Moreover the NINO provides an 8-channel OR output which constitutes a RICH supercell and is used in the standard RICH L0 trigger primitive generation flow. The front-end boards are connected to the readout setup which relies on the TEL62 [7], a general-purpose Trigger and Data Acquisition board used by most sub-detectors of the experiment, which is in charge of data digitization, timestamping, buffering, and network forwarding. A TEL62 hosts four Time-to-Digital Converter Daughterboards (TDCBs), each of which can handle 128 TDC channels using the CERN high-performance time-to-digital converter (HPTDC) [8], for a total of 512 TDC channels per TEL62. Thus, in the case of the RICH PMTs, four TEL62s are needed to read out the full 2048 PMT channels.

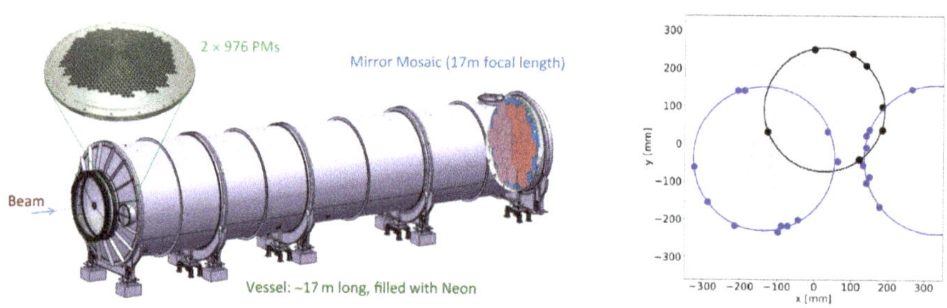

(a)

(b)

Figure 1. (**a**) The NA62 Ring Imaging Cherenkov detector. The Cherenkov light cones produced by charged particles crossing the neon in the vessel are reflected by a mirror mosaic onto two disks placed on the upstream side of the detector. Each disk houses 976 PMTs. Image from reference [1]. (**b**) An example RICH event with three charged particles.

In the baseline TDAQ configuration of the experiment, a fifth TEL62 is used to generate RICH trigger primitives for L0TP+ [9]: the fifth board reads the supercell signals from the main readout boards and performs time-clustering and the computation of cluster multiplicity and average time. This results in a trigger algorithm that provides L0 PMT-hit multiplicity at low granularity and no ring information. This setup does not take advantage of the PID capabilities of the RICH, which are only utilized during offline analysis.

FPGA-RICH aims at bringing some of the PID capabilities of the RICH into L0, processing raw PMT-hit data in real time at the full 10 MHz rate of the experiment: a Neural Network (NN) classifier extracts physics information which is then incorporated into enhanced trigger primitives sent to L0TP+ as shown in Figure 2. In its current implementation, the classifier extracts the number of Cherenkov rings (N_r), corresponding to the number of charged particles in the event. This information can be used in L0TP+ trigger masks to improve trigger selectivity. A key design goal is maintaining low latency ($O \sim 1$ μs), comparable to other sub-detectors sending primitives to L0TP+, in order to facilitate time alignment logic and buffering at L0TP+ level. An FPGA-based streaming solution is chosen for this purpose over a GPU-based one that we implement beforehand [10].

In collider physics experiments, the use of ML has been ubiquitous for many years in the context of offline data analysis, with increasing adoption in software-based online selection systems. Recent work has extended to the design of the low-level firmware-based implementation of ML algorithms aimed at ultra-low-latency triggers (e.g., [11–15]), especially in the context of the future High-Luminosity upgrade of the Large Hadron Collider at CERN [16], which will require new trigger methods for dealing with an increasing data rate.

This paper presents a mature system capable of ~1 μs scale latency and ~10 MHz throughput that is currently undergoing validation at the NA62 detector, and discusses the methods and strategies adopted for the integration of its streaming processing pipeline with the detector readout.

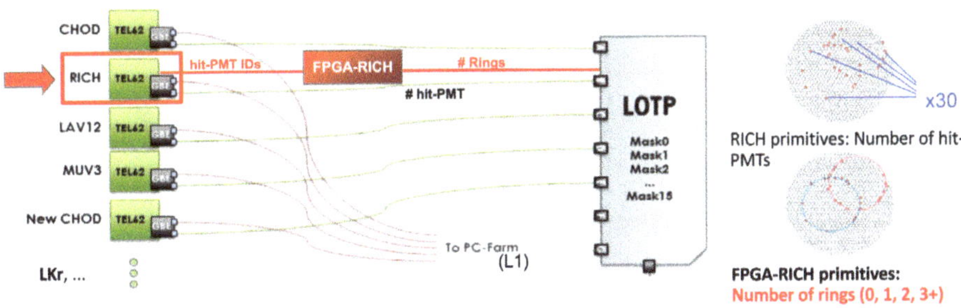

Figure 2. The placement of FPGA-RICH within the NA62 Trigger and Data Acquisition system, with its new stream of primitives.

2. Materials and Methods

FPGA-RICH receives detector event data from the RICH readout boards in the 32-bit multi-event packet format called MGP (Multi-event GPU Packet; the name originates from the previously adopted GPU solution [10]) shown in Figure 3.

Each MGP contains multiple events, where each event contains a timestamp and a variable number of hit PMT IDs belonging to those that detected photons; each ID is an integer ranging from 0 to 2047.

The hit PMT ID data are used as input features to the Neural Network classifier during online inference. For training the network offline, we use a dataset composed of 3.13 million events for training and 3.50 million for testing, extracted from the EOS [17] open-source distributed disk storage system at CERN. The datasets are collected during NA62 RUN 1 (2016–2018) and include both raw detector data and results processed by the experiment offline analysis reconstruction software. Specifically, a data item includes the raw PMT ID hit-list of the event and the Cherenkov Rings information, such as number of rings N_r, their centers and radii, and the number of electrons present as provided by two NA62 offline reconstruction algorithms [18]: one (called *RICHRECO*) relying solely on the RICH PMT hits geometry, while another (called *DownstreamTrack*) using the particles track information from the NA62 spectrometer as seed for ring identification. An example event with the information we extract from the NA62 reconstruction framework is shown in Figure 4.

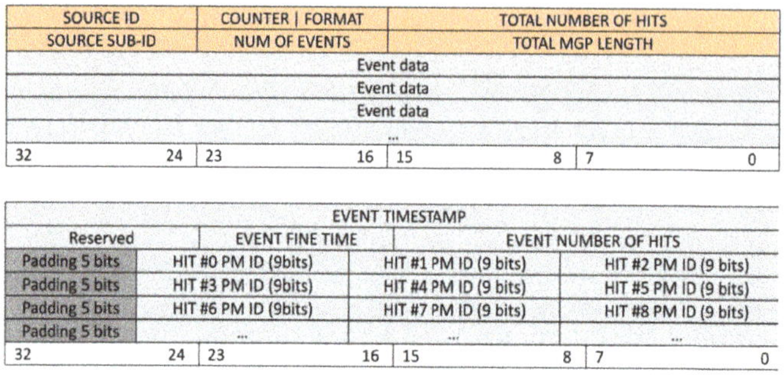

Figure 3. Multi-event MGP format above, with the "Event data" field expanded below. The ID in "HIT PM ID" uses a simple encoding: the real PMT ID (integer 0 to 2047) can be obtained concatenating the 9 bit-field (counting 0 to 511) to the "SOURCE SUB-ID" of the MGP header, which indicates the readout board number (0, 1, 2 or 3) that sent the event fragment.

```
 31daf85         7       220 20    2  -80.1   109.5 182.981   8.94    14 769 580 581 1401
 1373 1284 1280 126 64 43 41 33 32 409
 31daf85         7       220 30  0.000
 31daf85         7       220 40 -0.155  0.217 33.120 33.121  0.008  2.192
 31daf85         7       220 50  1.000
 31daf85         7       220 60  0.000
 31daf85         7       220 21    0  -80.1   109.5 182.948   0.75    14  409 1284  581
126   64    43    41    33    32   769   580 1401 1373 1280
 31daf85         7       220 21    0 -285.2   -35.6 175.964   1.00     7  281 1993 1500
711 1987 1984  920
 31daf85         7       220 22    1      0       1       0       0   28
 31daf85         7       220 23    2      0       0       0       0   28  769  711  580
581 1127 1197 1196 1401 1373 1284 1280 1284 1500 1710 1682 1993 1987 1984  126   64
 43   41   33   32  309  281  409  920
```

Figure 4. Example of an event from a file extracted from the NA62 reconstruction framework. The first two columns of each row are the timestamp and the burst ID of the event (the burst is a periodic window lasting $\sim$5 s when accelerated particles are made to collide and the detector is active), while the third is a generic event ID given by the reconstruction method. In the fourth column, there is a tag defining the information contained in the rest of each line: (tag 20) summary of the parameters of a reconstructed ring, such as the coordinates of the center (sixth and seventh columns), the ring radius (eighth column), the likelihood (ninth column), the number of PMTs used for the reconstruction (tenth column) and their list of IDs (from column eleven onward), obtained by the DownstreamTrack reconstruction algorithm; (tag 40) direction and module of the momentum of the track reconstructed in NA62 spectrometer; (tag 50, tag 60, tag 30) other physics information; (tag 21) same information as tag 20, but for a RICHRECO reconstructed ring; (tag 22) summary of the parameters coming from the DownstreamTrack method, like the number of rings reconstructed (fifth column); (23) summary of the parameters coming from the RichReco method, like the number of rings reconstructed (fifth column) plus the number of hit PMTs in the event (tenth column) and their list of IDs (from column eleven onward). In this example, the event DownstreamTrack identifies only one ring, while RichReco identifies two.

The benefit of using experimental data, rather than Monte Carlo simulations, is that we account for all biases due to electronic noise and physics background.

Figure 5 shows the distribution of the number of PMT hits and number of rings in the events of the training dataset.

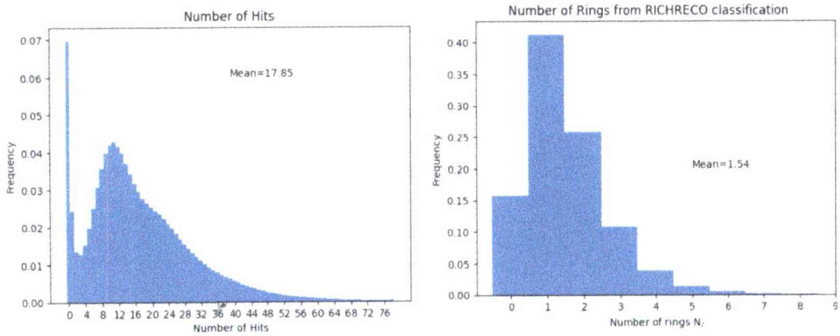

Figure 5. Distributions on the 3.13 million events training dataset: left, number of PMT hits per event; right, number of rings from the offline trackless reconstruction algorithm (RICHRECO).

2.1. The FPGA-RICH Streaming Pipeline

The FPGA-RICH methodology is based on a streaming processing pipeline that features a single FPGA device (AMD™ Xilinx Versal VCK190) interfaced upstream with the RICH readout and downstream with L0TP+. A scheme is presented in Figure 6.

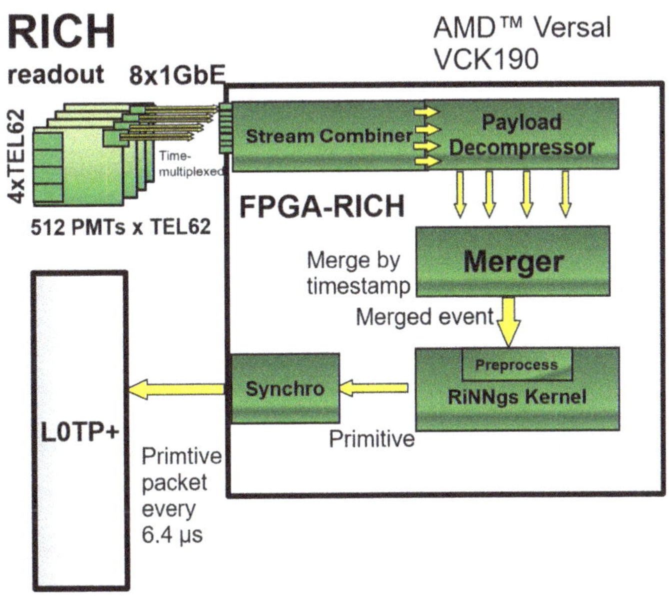

Figure 6. Scheme of the FPGA-RICH pipeline integrated with the RICH readout and L0TP+.

The RICH uses four TEL62 data-acquisition boards to handle the readout of its 2048 PMT channels, each board managing 512 PMT channels. Custom firmware is implemented in the TEL62s to provide a dedicated trigger flow to FPGA-RICH, separate from the baseline flow based on the hit-multiplicity mentioned in Section 1: the firmware aims at delivering individual PMT-channels hit-data to FPGA-RICH in a convenient format. The PMT channel hits clustered around a specific timestamp are collected to build an event fragment, and subsequently, multiple event fragments are put into an MGP packet. MGPs are sent out through UDP. Each board sends an MGP packet to FPGA-RICH periodically every 12.8 µs, beginning with the start-of-burst signal and relying on two 1 GbE ethernet links used with time-multiplexing [9] (alternatively on and off in time). If no event fragments are present, an empty MGP is sent.

Within FPGA-RICH, the first step of the pipeline takes care of combining the two time-multiplexed streams from each board into a single stream, making for four streams in total, one per board. Afterwards, a *decompressor* decodes the MGP packets data encapsulated in the UDP packets payload for each stream, arranging them into separate paths, one for the header—incorporating events timestamp and meta-data information—and one for the events hit-data (64 bits for header and 128 bits for data). Since the event fragments from each board carry only a fourth of the full PMT readout information, they have to be merged to build a complete physics event: a *merger* module handles this process. It manages each of the four MGP streams through a FIFO (First In First Out buffer) interface. By construction, each MGP contains a 12.8 µs window of digitized detector measurements, but each MGP can contain a variable number of events, with different timestamps, and this is true both across the same stream MGPs and across different streams MGPs, simply because of how physics events are distributed in time and in space among the TEL62s (one board might be more active than another), so the merger has to time align the event fragments. The merging process is started after a configurable number of packets are received in the FIFO streams. Merged events are built in the following way: the timestamps of the input events at the head of each stream are compared, and the smallest timestamp is taken as base T_b. All other streams events are checked, and if their timestamp T_x belongs to a fixed time window W above the base time $T_b \leq T_x \leq T_b + W$ (where W is set at 25 ns), the events are extracted from the FIFOs for merging, and their PMT hit-data are gathered. This process is repeated by extracting events from the streams until timestamps at the head of all four streams are not in the time window. Then, the merged event is complete and it can be streamed out, while the building of the next merged event starts.

The single merged events are produced in a 128-bit format called M^{2}EGP (Multi Merged Event Packet) shown in Figure 7, and are streamed via AXI4-Stream to the kernel implementing the Neural Network, called RiNNgs (Rings Neural Network). The M^{2}EGP format uses a header with timestamp and number of hits information, and multiple data words carrying the PMT hit IDs of the event. Each data word can contain up to 8 PMT hit IDs.

Hdr	STR 3 MGP	STR 2 MGP	STR 1 MGP	STR 0 MGP	STR 3 HITS	STR 2 HITS	STR 1 HITS	STR 0 HITS
	STR 1; HIT 1		STR 1; HIT 0		STR 0; HIT 5		STR 0; HIT 4	
	STR 2; HIT 0		STR 1; HIT 8		STR 1; HIT 7		STR 1; HIT 6	
	STR 3; HIT 3		STR 3; HIT 2		STR 3; HIT 1		STR 3; HIT 0	
	PADDED BITS							
Bits	127...120	119...112	111...104	103...96	95...88	87...80	79...72	71...64

	RESERVED	WINDOW	TOT HITS	TIMESTAMP				FT
	STR 0; HIT 3		STR 0; HIT 2		STR 0; HIT 1		STR 0; HIT 0	
	STR 1; HIT 5		STR 1; HIT 4		STR 1; HIT 3		STR 1; HIT 2	
	STR 2; HIT 4		STR 2; HIT 3		STR 2; HIT 2		STR; HIT 1	
	PADDED BITS		STR 3; HIT 6		STR 3; HIT 5		STR 3; HIT 4	
...	63...56	55...48	47...40	39...32	31...24	23...16	15...8	7...0

Figure 7. The M^{2}EGP (Multi Merged Event Packet) data format. It represents a single event as it comes streamed in input to the Neural Network kernel. The header contains the timestamp (which has a resolution of 25 ns) and finetime (FT, which allows a maximum resolution of 100 ps) of the event and some metadata information; the following words carry the PMT Hit IDs of the event, at most 8 per word. STR i indicates that prior to the merging, the hit belonged to the i-th readout board stream.

The RiNNgs kernel employs a preprocessing stage to build the input vector for the Neural Network from the stream of 128-bit words composing the M^2EGP (as will be described in Section 2.3), then it classifies the event with respect to the number of Cherenkov rings (N_r) and sends the N_r information along with the event timestamp to a *synchronizer*. The synchronizer standardizes the FPGA-RICH trigger primitive flow with the L0TP+ protocol, which expects primitives delivered in packets every 6.4 µs from all sub-detectors. It groups FPGA-RICH primitives into 6.4 µs windows, sending empty packets when no primitives are present. The synchronizer uses an internal time counter, triggered by the start of burst signal that FPGA-RICH receives from the NA62 common timing, trigger and control (TTC) infrastructure [9] alongside the common 40 MHz clock.

2.2. The Rings Neural Network IP (RiNNgs) Development Workflow

The FPGA-RICH pipeline is described in Hardware Description Language (VHDL), with the exception of the RiNNgs kernel, which relies on a multi-stage, iterative workflow based on High-Level Synthesis (HLS). The HLS programming paradigm allows translation of a high-level description of a design (C++ in our case) into a Register Transfer Level (RTL) hardware description, through the use of a tool (we use Xilinx^{TM} Vitis 2022.2) leveraging directives, or pragmas, provided in the high-level code—such as loop unrolling and pipelining—to optimize the generated RTL code. RiNNgs development workflow is schematized in Figure 8.

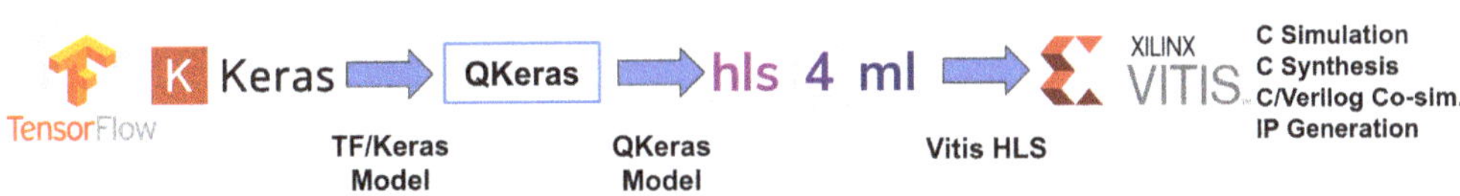

Figure 8. Software to hardware codesign workflow for the Rings Neural Network (RiNNgs) IP.

Here, we describe this workflow at a high level; the details of the Neural Network models implemented with it are provided in Section 2.3.

The open-source machine learning framework Tensorflow, with the Keras API, is used to design the Neural Network model architecture (number and kind of layers) and the input representation and preprocessing, and to define training strategies such as class balancing and hyperparameters tuning (batch size, optimizer choice, learning rate, etc.). Training is performed with full numerical precision (32-bit floating-point) in Keras.

Afterwards, the QKeras python library [19] is used to transform the model layers into a quantized version that uses variable fixed-point precision for the weights, biases and activations, and to train the model in a quantization-aware fashion. The quantization optimizes resource consumption and computational efficiency of the FPGA implementation. Through iterative training runs, the aim is to find the minimal fixed-point data size (and best partitioning between integral and fractional widths) that does not degrade classification performance with respect to the un-quantized Keras model.

After this step, the High-Level Synthesis for Machine Learning (hls4ml v0.7) [20] python library from CERN is used to convert the Neural Network layers defined in QKeras into an HLS implementation. In particular, the hls4ml library implements a series of custom tuneable parameters to configure the Neural Network HLS implementation, in terms of dataflow and resource usage. In terms of dataflow, either a parallel or a streaming implementation can be set (with the *IOType* parameter), determining the type of data structure used for the Neural Network inputs, intermediate activations between layers, and outputs. In the parallel case, arrays are used, which are typically implemented in RAM and, in principle, can be fully unrolled (implemented on separate RAM units) at the cost of FPGA memory. In the stream case, HLS streams are used, which are a more efficient and scalable mechanism to represent data that are produced and consumed in a sequential manner, and are typically implemented with FIFO buffers instead of RAMs. This is the ideal approach for the online RICH data processing and is what we use for our models.

For what concerns parallelization and resource reuse, hls4ml offers a *ReuseFactor* parameter that configures how often a particular hardware resource (like a multiplier) is reused during computation. Low *ReuseFactor* means more dedicated resources for independent computations, for a typically faster but resource-consuming implementation. In this context (in hls4ml v0.7), an optimization parameter called *Strategy* can be set to either *Latency* to optimize for latency and maximum parallelization, or *Resource*, which assumes a ReuseFactor higher than one and uses less parallelization.

The final workflow step is the synthesis of the HLS model into an FPGA bitstream through the Xilinx Vivado tool (v2022.2). For verification of the HLS model classification performance, the emulation offered by hls4ml, which is a bit-accurate software simulation of the design, is used, while for verification of the model performance in terms of throughput, latency and resource consumption, the estimates provided by the Vivado C/RTL co-simulation, which is a simulation of the RTL generated by HLS that uses a C testbench as stimuli, are used.

Throughout all the steps described above, the design targets of Neural Network classification accuracy, throughput, latency and FPGA resource usage have to be verified. The key challenge for our work is managing the 10 MHz event throughput of NA62, which restricts the RiNNgs Neural Network to an Initiation Interval (II)—in HLS terminology, the number of clock cycles required between the beginning of an algorithm's processing on one data sample and the beginning on the following data sample. Assuming a reference clock of 150 MHz, this corresponds to an upper limit of 15 cycles. This limits the complexity of the Neural Network models that can be deployed with a single FPGA as a target, given the existing trade-off between model size, II, and FPGA resources consumption. In particular, for our system, we test fully connected and Convolutional Neural Network models. In fully connected (fc) networks, a layer's computation consists of the $input\text{-}vector \times weight\text{-}matrix$ multiplication, requiring $M_l \times N_l = d_l$ multiply–accumulate operations, where M_l and N_l are the input and output dimensions of layer l. Since multiple layers are implemented as stages of a pipeline, the II is ultimately limited by the layer with the largest II and thus d_l. The *ResourceFactor* can be configured to employ multiple multiplier units in parallel and improve II but at the cost of many resources if the layers are large. For two-dimensional Convolutional Neural Network (CNN) layers, the streaming implementation made by hls4ml (version 0.7) [21] relies on a stream to process the input layer feature map of $height \times width \times channels = H \times W \times C$. Each item of the stream is an array of size C, so there are actually HW items that are streamed to the layer, one per clock cycle. This sequential processing is optimized to reach $\sim$1 μs latency [21] and to consume few FPGA memory resources, as it does not build and keep in memory the whole input–tensor matrix and kernel–weight matrix to perform matrix multiplication as is typically done in general matrix multiplication algorithms [22] but only buffers temporarily in FIFOs the input items that need to be reused while the convolutional sliding window moves through the feature map. However, in the hls4ml version that we use, it costs at least HW clock cycles in terms of II since a whole input feature map has to be streamed item by item (or pixel by pixel for single channel images), before the next feature map can be processed.

2.3. The RiNNgs Neural Network Models Architecture

We test different variants for the RiNNgs model architecture that we call 8×8-fc, 16×16-fc, and 16×16-CNN.

The 8×8-fc model is illustrated in Figure 9: it is composed of 3 fully connected layers with, respectively, 64, 16, and 4 output neurons. The first two layers are activated by ReLu functions, while a simple argmax is applied after the last layer. The event is classified in one of four N_r classes for 0, 1, 2, or 3 or more rings.

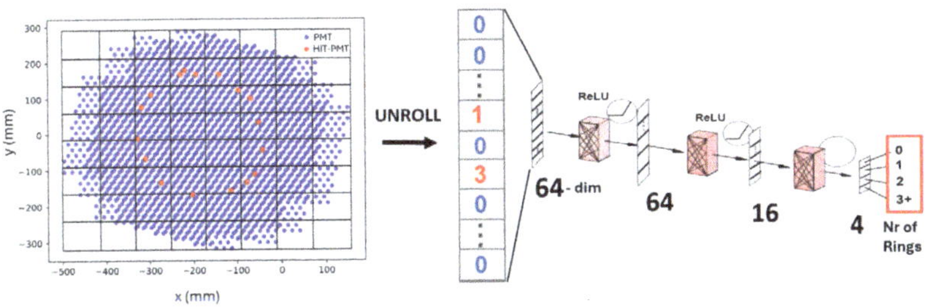

(a)

```
Layer (type)                  Output Shape              Param #
================================================================
input1 (InputLayer)           [(None, 64)]              0
fc1 (Dense)                   (None, 64)                4160
act1 (Activation)             (None, 64)                0
fc2 (Dense)                   (None, 16)                1040
act2 (Activation)             (None, 16)                0
fc3 (Dense)                   (None, 4)                 68
================================================================
Total params: 5268
```

(b)

Figure 9. (**a**) Scheme of the architecture and preprocessing of the 8×8-fc model. The RICH disk plane is discretized in 8×8 cells. The value in each cell is the number of hit PMTs in the cell. The 64 values obtained are used as input for the fc model (**b**) Layer specification in Keras and parameters of the 8×8-fc model. The Output Shape column indicates the (*Batch size*, *Output size*) of each layer (the *Batch size* is unspecified at model definition). The Activation layers are Rectified Linear Unit (ReLU) layers.

The 64-dimensional linear input is obtained from the preprocessing procedure illustrated in Figure 9: the RICH disk plane containing the PMTs is treated similarly to an image and discretized into 8 × 8 cells or bins containing a variable number of PMTs, the maximum number of PMTs in the most populated cell being 55. A look-up table is used to map each hit-PMT ID in an event to a cell, and the 64-dimensional input to the NN is obtained by "unrolling" the discretized image into a linear vector, where each cell contains the number of hit PMTs in that cell; on average, only ∼2–3 PMT-hits are found in a hit cell. After NN quantization, we use 6 integer bits for the input representation, <8,1> fixed-point representation for the weights and biases of all layers, and <16,5> for activations. Given the pair <x,y>, x is the size in bits of the integer part, and y is the same quantity for the fractional part of the fixed-point number of size x+y bits. The *Strategy* parameter of the hls4ml library is set to *Latency*, the *ReuseFactor* parameter is set to 8, and the *IOtype* parameter is set to *Streaming*.

The 16×16-fc model is a variant of the 8×8-fc model that uses a finer 16 × 16 grid for the input preprocessing stage. The input layer size thus grows to 16 × 16 = 256. To keep the II below 15 clock cycles at 150 MHz, the first layer has to be reduced compared to the 8×8-fc variant, from size 64 to size 32, and the *ReuseFactor* has to be halved to 4.

The 16×16-CNN model architecture is illustrated in Figure 10.

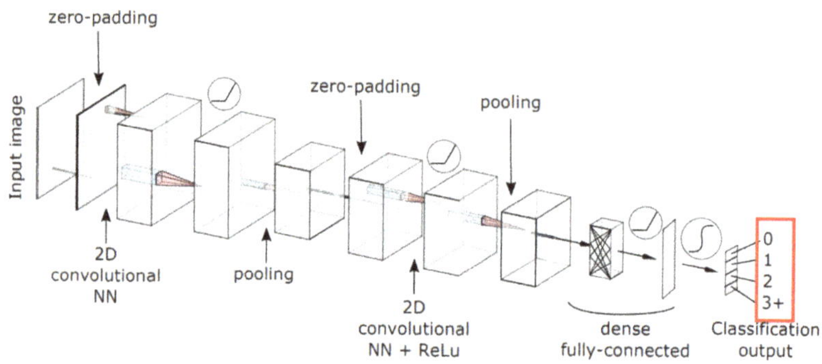

(**a**)

```
Layer (type)                Output Shape           Param #
==============================================================
input1 (InputLayer)         [(None, 16, 16, 1)]    0
conv1 (Conv2D)              (None, 16, 16, 8)      80
act1 (Activation)           (None, 16, 16, 8)      0
maxp1 (MaxPooling2D)        (None, 8, 8, 8)        0
conv2 (Conv2D)              (None, 8, 8, 8)        584
act2 (Activation)           (None, 8, 8, 8)        0
maxp2 (MaxPooling2D)        (None, 4, 4, 8)        0
flatten (Flatten)           (None, 128)            0
fc3 (Dense)                 (None, 16)             2064
act3 (Activation)           (None, 16)             0
fc4 (Dense)                 (None, 4)              68
softmax (Activation)        (None, 4)              0
==============================================================
Total params: 2796
```

(**b**)

Figure 10. (**a**) Scheme of the architecture of the 16×16-*CNN* model. (**b**) Layers specification in Keras and parameters of the 16×16-*CNN* model. The Output Shape column indicates the (*Batch size*, Image *x-dim size*, Image *y-dim size*, *Number of channels*) in output to each layer. Activation layers are ReLUs, except for the Softmax layer at the end. The two Conv2D layers use *filters* = 8, *kernel_size* = 3 and *padding* = *same*. The MaxPooling layers use *pool_size* = 2, *stride* = 2 and *padding* = *same*.

It is a compact model using two convolutional layers ($filters = 8$, $kernel\ size = 3$) with ReLU and Max Pooling ($poolsize = 2$, $stride = 2$), and two fully connected layers from 128 to 16 and from 16 to 4. Similarly to the 16×16-fc model case, the input preprocessing involves the creation of a compressed image of size 16×16, but in this case, the image is not unrolled before being input to the NN. Example images are shown in Figure 11. The quantization uses <8,1> fixed-point representation for the weights and biases and <16,6> for input and activations. The $Strategy$ parameter is set to $Latency$, the $ReuseFactor$ is set to 1, and the $IOtype$ is set to $Streaming$.

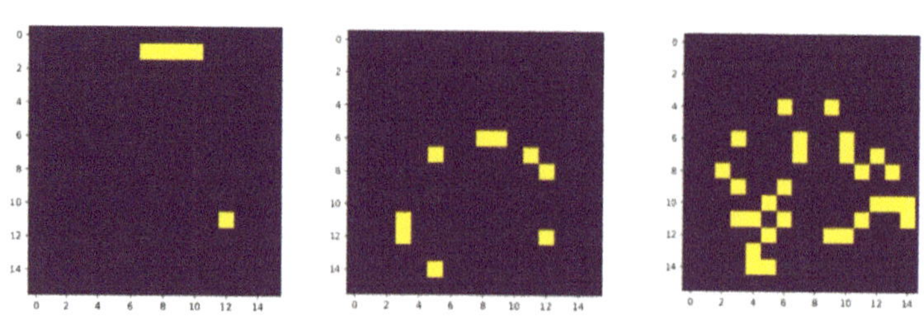

Figure 11. Examples of 16×16 images generated in the preprocessing stage in the 16×16-*CNN* model with 0, 1, and 2 rings.

As described above, all three model variants require a similar preprocessing stage to build the NN input from the PMT hits. This preprocessing stage (called '*imagify*') has to be implemented in hardware to integrate the RiNNgs kernel inside the FPGA-RICH pipeline, where it receives the hits through the stream of M^2EGP words. It is written in HLS and works as a simple state machine, processing one word of the M^2EGP packet at a time. In the first state, it reads an M^2EGP header from the stream, and it extracts the total number of hits in the event and computes the total number of M^2EGP data words that it has to process (each data word contains up to 8 hits). Then, in the second state, it receives the data words from the stream: for each one, it reads in parallel all the PMT ID hits and maps them to a corresponding position of the NN input array, using the look-up table that is obtained from the PMT disk plane discretization procedure in Python (v. 3.8.12) and is now synthesized on the FPGA internal memory. When it is finished processing all data words, the state machine goes back to the previous stage, waiting for the next header.

2.4. Functional and Performance Validation Methodology of the Full FPGA-RICH Pipeline

To perform functional validation and a preliminary assessment of the throughput performance of the FPGA-RICH pipeline in the laboratory, we developed a firmware for a separate FPGA board sporting four 1GbE ports to deliver synthetic data to FPGA-RICH over ethernet: stored event data packets (MGPs) are sent over four links every 12.8 µs, emulating the timing and protocol of the TEL62 streams. Then, for the full validation of the system, FPGA-RICH is integrated in parasitic mode (i.e., without affecting the standard experiment data-taking) with the RICH readout at NA62.

3. Results

The performance of the three RiNNgs model variants described above is presented in Table 1, in terms of $efficiency$ (or $recall = \frac{TruePositives}{TruePositives+FalseNegatives}$) and $purity$ (or $precision = \frac{TruePositives}{TruePositives+FalsePositives}$) of the classification for the different N_r classes obtained on the 3.5 million events test dataset, averaged over five training runs.

Table 1. Classification performance (%) of different RiNNgs Neural Network model variants, for the quantized versions.

Efficiency	8×8-fc	16×16-fc	16×16-CNN
0 ring(s)	88.88 ± 0.28	88.86 ± 0.10	88.40 ± 0.25
1 ring(s)	88.90 ± 0.24	88.94 ± 0.24	88.53 ± 0.22
2 ring(s)	76.34 ± 0.87	77.82 ± 0.64	78.31 ± 0.43
3+ ring(s)	77.12 ± 0.55	77.06 ± 0.76	74.29 ± 0.58
Purity	**8×8-fc**	**16×16-fc**	**16×16-CNN**
0 ring(s)	95.04 ± 0.23	94.92 ± 0.16	95.42 ± 0.26
1 ring(s)	86.48 ± 0.24	87.22 ± 0.19	87.30 ± 0.25
2 ring(s)	72.22 ± 0.35	72.66 ± 0.41	70.34 ± 0.33
3+ ring(s)	84.62 ± 0.41	84.94 ± 0.42	85.10 ± 0.36

The table reports the performance of the quantized QKeras version of the models. We do not notice a significant difference with the performance of the HLS software emulated version as can be seen in Figure 12, which shows inference performance of the 8×8-fc architecture on the test dataset with the Receiver Operating Characteristic (ROC) curves for the different precision versions of the model: 32-bit Keras, quantized QKeras, and the bit-accurate software emulation of the quantized HLS version provided by hls4ml.

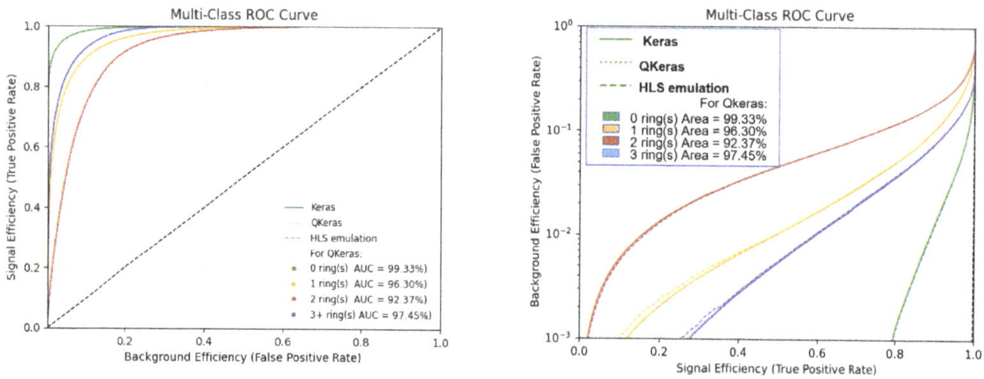

(a) (b)

Figure 12. ROC curves for the 8×8-*fc* model. The different colors refer to different number-of-rings classes, while the different line styles refer to different precision versions for the model: the 32-bit Keras version, the quantized QKeras version, and a software emulation of the quantized HLS version provided by hls4ml. The area under curve refers to the QKeras version. (**a**) The standard ROC-curves visualization. (**b**) A semi log-scale visualization with inverted axes of the same ROC curves, which best highlights the minimal separation between the different precision versions of the model.

Table 2 presents FPGA resources utilization, II, and latency for the different model variants after synthesis.

Table 2. Performance and utilization * after synthesis of the RiNNgs Neural Network model variants.

NN Variant	LUT	Flip-Flop	DSP	BRAM	II (Cycles)	Latency (Cycles)	Clock (MHz)
8×8-*fc*	65k 7.3%	40k 2.2%	145 7.4%	0 0.0%	5	18	150
16×16-*fc*	118k 13.2%	94k 5.2%	230 11.7%	244 25.2%	12	26	150
16×16-*CNN*	51k 5.7%	29k 1.6%	282 14.4%	1 0.1%	369	388	220

* On a Xilinx Versal VCK190 FPGA.

Tables 1 and 2 show that the finer grid of the 16×16-fc variant does not help the network learn significantly better than the 8×8-fc variant, while the cost difference in terms of FPGA resources and II is significant. The 16×16-CNN variant is light on resources but requires a very large number of II cycles ($II = 369$, throughput 0.7 MHz) by nature of the previously described hls4ml streaming implementation requiring at least one clock cycle per pixel. It has to be noted that the latest versions of the hls4ml package (v 0.8.1+) have introduced an updated streaming implementation for convolutional layers, allowing a larger portion of the input image (related to the convolutional kernel size) to be processed per clock cycle. Adopting this feature in future FPGA-RICH models could improve II performance, though it is unlikely that the II of fully connected models could be matched.

For the current FPGA-RICH implementation, we choose to prioritize the advantage of low II granted by the 8×8-fc version, whose classification performance ($efficiency \approx 83\%$ and $purity \approx 85\%$ on the four classes average) is satisfactory for L0TP+ masks, and can be further adjusted to favor purity or efficiency where it best suits the trigger selectivity strategy, using the ROC curves and changing classification thresholds.

The II values reported in Table 2 are relative to the Neural Network algorithm that starts when an input vector is received and do not include the preprocessing stage. Since this stage operates on the M^2EGP words which can contain 8 PMT hits at most, and it takes one clock cycle to read a word, the II of this stage is variable and it depends on the number of hits in the event. We measure an II = 2–15 cycles at 150 MHz clock (throughput = 75–10 MHz), where 15 cycles are required for an extremely unlikely scenario where the events received contain 13 words (97-104 PMT hits). For average NA62 events with 3 words ($\sim$18 hits, see Figure 5), the II of the preprocessing stage is equal to 3 cycles, so it does not compromise throughput and the Neural Network stage is the bottleneck with its 5 cycles, which correspond to a 30 MHz throughput. This is comfortably above the L0 10 MHz requirement, so the RiNNgs stage of the FPGA-RICH pipeline satisfies the throughput.

The Validation of the Full FPGA-RICH Pipeline

The full FPGA-RICH pipeline integrating the 8×8-fc variant of the NN is synthesized with a 150 MHz clock. The resource usage is LUT = 127,777 (14.2%), Flip-Flop = 107,981 (6.0%), DSP = 146 (7.4%), and BRAM = 25 (2.6%).

The pipeline is tested with synthetic MGP packets, in input to FPGA-RICH every 12.8 μs from four streams, emulating the TEL62s of the RICH readout. In this scenario, the effective event throughput seen by FPGA-RICH can be controlled by setting the number of events in a packet on the sender side. However, a realistic timing structure depends also on how many and how the events hits are split across the different TEL62s streams and how well their timestamps are aligned. In particular, these parameters affect the throughput performance of the FPGA-RICH *merger*, which has a budget of $\sim$2000 clock cycles at 150 MHz to perform the merging of the events inside the four streams' packets. The cycles spent increase if there are more hits in an event but also if the hits are less distributed among streams since this reduces the amount of parallelization achievable in the merging operation. Reproducing the exact experimental pattern of MGP packets is challenging, but we use the artificially controlled setup to estimate a bottom limit on achieved throughput of 9.375 MHz under the following test scenario: 120 events time aligned across the streams and carrying a total of 18 hits (average-event hits number) balanced across the streams. More stringent tests with this simple packet structure, just adding events, are limited by the 1500 bytes cap on the ethernet frame size that the system uses.

For what concerns the latency of the full pipeline, a measurement is obtained with the Vivado Integrated Logic Analyzer, and it is well within the $\sim$1 μs target: the time from the first set of events input to the *decompressor* to the time of the first RiNNgs-primitive input to the synchronizer is $\approx$900 ns, to which a variable component has to be added since the *synchronizer* sends out a packet of primitives every 6.4 μs.

Rather than pushing in the synthetic data direction, we have decided to finalize validation directly on real data by integrating FPGA-RICH with the RICH readout in parasitic mode. In parallel, we complete a synthesis of the full pipeline at 300 MHz clock, which if needed will increase the *merger* effective clock cycles budget. The pipeline is currently under validation at the experiment. It is tested during NA62 Run 2 (in 2024). It collects data successfully for about a fourth of the $\sim$5 s periodic data collection window of the experiment (the burst), after which it overflows because of a leftover issue related not to the pipeline itself but to the custom TEL62 firmware: corrupted MGP packets with misaligned timestamps among the four TEL62 streams are created, and this increases the effective throughput seen by the *merger* above 10 MHz because same-time events that should be merged show up as separate events.

The solution of adjusting the TEL62 firmware while the experiment is taking data is not ideal, but development is undergoing to work around the issue downstream at the

FPGA-RICH level by flushing corrupted events. This will allow us to keep up with the throughput at the cost of some event-classification accuracy.

4. Discussion

We have developed FPGA-RICH, an FPGA-based system designed to implement real-time AI-based partial particle identification within the strict latency and throughput constraints of the NA62 low-level trigger system. The system combines traditional data processing techniques with modern machine learning approaches, classifying events by number of charged particles with performance suitable for trigger selectivity improvement, while maintaining the required 10 MHz throughput and 1 μs scale latency. The use of High-Level Synthesis allows for relatively easy reprogrammability, which has been beneficial for development in iteratively testing different Neural Network solutions, and will be beneficial as the system impact on trigger efficiency is evaluated and which will possibly motivate adjustments.

This work shows the effectiveness and maturity of modern programming paradigms and machine learning algorithms even within the challenging context of High Energy Physics experiments' online data acquisition and analysis. As a future step, we envision the transfer of the current implementation of FPGA-RICH from an independent FPGA device to the one hosting L0TP+ itself. L0TP+ is deployed on a Xilinx VCU118 board, using only a small fraction of FPGA resources (30% BRAM, 20% of LUT , 1% DSP). Furthermore, the board setup sports a consistent number of available high-speed links [23]. This scheme of integration allows a direction for development, where we collect primitive data from other NA62 sub-detectors at L0TP+ level, for instance energy from the calorimeter, and use it to produce even more refined physics trigger primitives at L0, such as the number of electrons, highlighting the versatility granted by the input–output and logic re-programmability of an FPGA-based Trigger and Data Acquisition system and how it can allow elaborate data analysis pipelines at the lowest hardware level.

Author Contributions: Conceptualization, A.L., P.V., P.C., R.A., O.F., L.P., M.T. and A.C.; methodology, A.L., L.P., P.C., M.T., C.R., P.P. and A.C.; Hardware block design: R.A., A.B., P.C., O.F., F.L.C. and P.V.; software, M.T., P.C., P.P., C.R., L.P., A.C. and M.M.; validation, P.P., M.T., P.C., A.L., A.B., L.P., P.V. and C.C.; Formal analysis: A.C., A.L., P.P., L.P., M.T. and C.R.; data curation, M.T. and R.P.; writing—original draft preparation, P.P.; writing—review and editing, A.L., L.P., C.R., A.C., R.P., R.A., F.S. and O.F.; supervision, A.L.; project administration, A.L. and M.R.; funding acquisition, A.L., P.V. and M.R. All authors have read and agreed to the published version of the manuscript.

Funding: This research was founded by INFN Scientific Committees 1 (NA62 experiment) and 5 (APEIRON experiment), by the EuroHPC-JU TEXTAROSSA project G.A. n.956831, and by Italian PNRR MUR project CUPI53C22001400006-FAIR (funded by NextGenerationEU).

Data Availability Statement: A reduced set of the original data presented in this study, along with the software described, are openly available at https://baltig.infn.it/ape-lab/fpgarich.git, accessed on 4 May 2025. The full dataset is available upon reasonable request, due to the NA62 experiment-data-sharing policy.

Acknowledgments: Pierpaolo Perticaroli is a PhD student enrolled in the National PhD program in Artificial Intelligence, XXXIX cycle, course on Health and life sciences, organized by Università Campus Bio-Medico di Roma. This article is a revised and expanded version of a paper entitled *FPGA-RICH: A low-latency, high-throughput online particle identification system for the NA62 experiment* [24], which was presented at *Conference on Computing in High Energy and Nuclear Physics (CHEP2024)*, in the AGH University of Kraków, Institute of Nuclear Physics Polish Academy of Sciences and Jagiellonian University, 19–25 October 2024.

Conflicts of Interest: The authors declare no conflicts of interest.

Abbreviations

The following abbreviations are used in this manuscript:

FPGA	Field Programmable Gate Array
RICH	Ring Imaging Cherenkov Detector
L0TP	Level 0 Trigger Processor
TDAQ	Trigger and Data Acquisition
HLS	High-Level Synthesis
NN	Neural Network
PMT	Photo-Multiplier Tube
CNN	Convolutional Neural Network
FC	Fully Connected
RiNNgs	Rings Neural Network
MGP	Multi-event GPU Packet
M^2EGP	Multi Merged Event Packet

References

1. Gil, E.C.; Albarrán, E.M.; Minucci, E.; Nüssle, G.; Padolski, S.; Petrov, P.; Szilasi, N.; Velghe, B.; Georgiev, G.; Kozhuharov, V.; et al. The beam and detector of the NA62 experiment at CERN. *J. Instrum.* **2017**, *12*, P05025. [CrossRef]
2. Cortina Gil, E.; Jerhot, J.; Lurkin, N.; Numao, T.; Velghe, B.; Wong, V.W.S.; Bryman, D.; Hives, Z.; Husek, T.; Kampf, K.; et al. Observation of the $K^+ \to \pi^+ \nu\bar{\nu}$ decay and measurement of its branching ratio. *J. High Energy Phys.* **2025**, *2025*. [CrossRef]
3. Cortina Gil, E.; Kleimenova, A.; Minucci, E.; Padolski, S.; Petrov, P.; Shaikhiev, A.; Volpe, R.; Numao, T.; Petrov, Y.; Velghe, B.; et al. Performance of the NA62 trigger system. *JHEP* **2023**, *03*, 122.
4. Ammendola, R.; Biagioni, A.; Ciardiello, A.; Cretaro, P.; Frezza, O.; Lamanna, G.; Lo Cicero, F.; Lonardo, A.; Martinelli, M.; Piandani, R.; et al. Progress report on the online processing upgrade at the NA62 experiment. *J. Instrum.* **2022**, *17*, C04002. [CrossRef]
5. Anzivino, G.; Barbanera, M.; Bizzeti, A.; Brizioli, F.; Bucci, F.; Cassese, A.; Cenci, P.; Ciaranfi, R.; Duk, V.; Engelfried, J.; et al. Light detection system and time resolution of the NA62 RICH. *J. Instrum.* **2020**, *15*, P10025. [CrossRef]
6. Anghinolfi, F.; Jarron, P.; Krummenacher, F.; Usenko, E.; Williams, M. NINO, an ultra-fast, low-power, front-end amplifier discriminator for the Time-Of-Flight detector in ALICE experiment. In Proceedings of the 2003 IEEE Nuclear Science Symposium. Conference Record (IEEE Cat. No.03CH37515), Portland, OR, USA, 19–25 October 2003; Volume 1, pp. 375–379. [CrossRef]
7. Spinella, F.; Angelucci, B.; Lamanna, G.; Minuti, M.; Pedreschi, E.; Pinzino, J.; Piandani, R.; Sozzi, M.; Venditti, S. The TEL62: A real-time board for the NA62 Trigger and Data AcQuisition. Data flow and firmware design. In Proceedings of the 2014 19th IEEE-NPSS Real Time Conference, Nara, Japan, 26–30 May 2014; pp. 1–2. [CrossRef]
8. Christiansen, J. *HPTDC High Performance Time to Digital Converter*; Technical report; Version 2.2 for HPTDC version 1.3.; CERN: Geneva, Switzerland, 2004.
9. Ammendola, R.; Angelucci, B.; Barbanera, M.; Biagioni, A.; Cerny, V.; Checcucci, B.; Fantechi, R.; Gonnella, F.; Koval, M.; Krivda, M.; et al. The integrated low-level trigger and readout system of the CERN NA62 experiment. *Nucl. Instruments Methods Phys. Res. Sect. A Accel. Spectrometers Detect. Assoc. Equip.* **2019**, *929*, 1–22. [CrossRef]
10. Cretaro, P.; Biagioni, A.; Frezza, O.; Cicero, F.L.; Lonardo, A.; Martinelli, M.; Paolucci, P.S.; Pontisso, L.; Simula, F.; Vicini, P.; et al. NaNet: A Reconfigurable PCIe Network Interface Card Architecture for Real-time Distributed Heterogeneous Stream Processing in the NA62 Low Level Trigger. *PoS* **2019**, *TWEPP2018*, 118. [CrossRef]
11. Nottbeck, N.; Schmitt, D.C.; Büscher, P.D.V. Implementation of high-performance, sub-microsecond deep neural networks on FPGAs for trigger applications. *J. Instrum.* **2019**, *14*, P09014. [CrossRef]
12. Iiyama, Y.; Cerminara, G.; Gupta, A.; Kieseler, J.; Loncar, V.; Pierini, M.; Qasim, S.R.; Rieger, M.; Summers, S.; Van Onsem, G.; et al. Distance-Weighted Graph Neural Networks on FPGAs for Real-Time Particle Reconstruction in High Energy Physics. *Front. Big Data* **2021**, *3*, 598927. [CrossRef] [PubMed]
13. Bortolato, G.; Cepeda, M.; Heikkilä, J.; Huber, B.; Leutgeb, E.; Rabady, D.; Sakulin, H.; on behalf of the CMS collaboration. Design and implementation of neural network based conditions for the CMS Level-1 Global Trigger upgrade for the HL-LHC. *J. Instrum.* **2024**, *19*, C03019. [CrossRef]
14. Migliorini, M.; Pazzini, J.; Triossi, A.; Zanetti, M.; Zucchetta, A. Muon trigger with fast Neural Networks on FPGA, a demonstrator. *J. Phys. Conf. Ser.* **2022**, *2374*, 012099. [CrossRef]

15. Govorkova, E.; Puljak, E.; Aarrestad, T.; James, T.; Loncar, V.; Pierini, M.; Pol, A.A.; Ghielmetti, N.; Graczyk, M.; Summers, S.; et al. Autoencoders on field-programmable gate arrays for real-time, unsupervised new physics detection at 40 MHz at the Large Hadron Collider. Autoencoders on FPGAs for real-time, unsupervised new physics detection at 40 MHz at the Large Hadron Collider. *Nat. Mach. Intell.* **2022**, *4*, 154–161.
16. Aberle, O.; Béjar Alonso, I.; Brüning, O.; Fessia, P.; Rossi, L.; Tavian, L.; Zerlauth, M.; Adorisio, C.; Adraktas, A.; Ady, M.; et al. *High-Luminosity Large Hadron Collider (HL-LHC): Technical Design Report*; CERN Yellow Reports: Monographs; CERN: Geneva, Switzerland, 2020. [CrossRef]
17. Peters, A.; Sindrilaru, E.; Adde, G. EOS as the present and future solution for data storage at CERN. *J. Phys. Conf. Ser.* **2015**, *664*, 042042. [CrossRef]
18. NA62 Collaboration. *2017 NA62 Status Report to the CERN SPSC*; Technical report; CERN: Geneva, Switzerland, 2017.
19. Coelho, C.N.; Kuusela, A.; Li, S.; Zhuang, H.; Ngadiuba, J.; Aarrestad, T.K.; Loncar, V.; Pierini, M.; Pol, A.A.; Summers, S. Automatic heterogeneous quantization of deep neural networks for low-latency inference on the edge for particle detectors. *Nat. Mach. Intell.* **2021**, *3*, 675–686. [CrossRef]
20. Duarte, J.; Han, S.; Harris, P.; Jindariani, S.; Kreinar, E.; Kreis, B.; Ngadiuba, J.; Pierini, M.; Rivera, R.; Tran, N.; et al. Fast inference of deep neural networks in FPGAs for particle physics. *JINST* **2018**, *13*, P07027.
21. Aarrestad, T.; Loncar, V.; Ghielmetti, N.; Pierini, M.; Summers, S.; Ngadiuba, J.; Petersson, C.; Linander, H.; Iiyama, Y.; Di Guglielmo, G.; et al. Fast convolutional neural networks on FPGAs with hls4ml. *Mach. Learn. Sci. Technol.* **2021**, *2*, 045015. [CrossRef]
22. Vasudevan, A.; Anderson, A.; Gregg, D. Parallel Multi Channel convolution using General Matrix Multiplication. In Proceedings of the 2017 IEEE 28th International Conference on Application-specific Systems, Architectures and Processors (ASAP), Seattle, WA, USA, 10–12 July 2017; pp. 19–24. [CrossRef]
23. Ammendola, R.; Biagioni, A.; Chiarini, C.; Cretaro, P.; Frezza, O.; Lo Cicero, F.; Lonardo, A.; Martinelli, M.; Perticaroli, P.; Piandani, R.; et al. The new hardware trigger processor at NA62 experiment: Status of the System and First Results. In Proceedings of the 27th Conference on Computing in High Energy and Nuclear Physics (CHEP 2024), Krakow, Poland, 21–25 October 2024.
24. Perticaroli, P.; Ammendola, R.; Biagioni, A.; Chiarini, C.; Ciardiello, A.; Cretaro, P.; Frezza, O.; Lo Cicero, F.; Martinelli, M.; Piandani, R.; et al. FPGA-RICH: A low-latency, high-throughput online particle identification system for the NA62 experiment. In Proceedings of the 27th Conference on Computing in High Energy and Nuclear Physics (CHEP 2024), Krakow, Poland, 19–25 October 2024.

electronics

MDPI

Article

Enhancing Radiation Resilience and Throughput in Spaceborne RS(255,223) Encoder via Interleaved Pipelined Architecture

Xufeng Li [1,2], Li Zhou [1,*] and Yan Zhu [1]

1 National Space Science Center, Chinese Academy of Sciences, Beijing 100190, China; lixufeng21@mails.ucas.ac.cn (X.L.); zhuyan@nssc.ac.cn (Y.Z.)

2 School of Computer Science and Technology, University of Chinese Academy of Sciences, Beijing 100190, China

* Correspondence: zhouli@nssc.ac.cn

Abstract: The error correction capability of the RS(255,223) code has been significantly enhanced compared to that of the RS(256,252) code, making it the preferred choice for the next generation of onboard solid-state recorders (O-SSRs). With the application of non-volatile double data rate (NV-DDR) interface technology in O-SSRs, instantaneous transmission rates of up to 1 Gbps per data I/O interface can be achieved. This development imposes higher requirements on the encoding throughput of RS encoders. For RS(255,223) encoders, throughput improvement is limited by the structures of serial architectures. The algorithm's inherent characteristics restrict the depth of pipelining. In contrast, parallel solutions face bottlenecks in resource efficiency. To address these challenges, an interleaved pipelined architecture is proposed. By integrating interleaving technology within the pipeline, the structure overcomes the limitations of serial architectures. Using this architecture, a 36-stage pipelined RS(255,223) encoder is implemented. The throughput is greatly enhanced, and the radiation tolerance is also improved due to the application of interleaving techniques. The RS(255,223) encoder performance was evaluated on the Xilinx XC7K325T platform. The results confirm that the proposed architecture can support high data rates and provide effective error correction. With an 8-bit symbol size, a single encoder achieved throughput of 3.043 Gbps, making it highly suitable for deployment in future space exploration missions.

Keywords: solid-state recorder; error correction code; Reed–Solomon code; FPGA-based architecture; pipeline; interleave; bit upset

1. Introduction

As the central hub of the spacecraft data management system, the onboard solid-state recorder (O-SSR) [1–4] plays a critical and irreplaceable role in modern space missions. It must efficiently collect, classify, store, and schedule data from multiple sources in real time. At the same time, data integrity and reliability must be ensured under extreme space environments [5].

As spacecraft systems become more complex, modern O-SSRs face unprecedented technical challenges. Large volumes of high-data-rate information must be processed. These data streams come from dozens or even hundreds of sources, including scientific payloads [6,7], platform subsystems [8], and environmental monitoring instruments [9]. Additionally, long-term reliable storage must be maintained for deep space exploration and other specialized missions.

From a system-level perspective, storage performance has become a key factor limiting overall spacecraft capabilities. Recent technological advancements show clear asymmetry.

The storage density has improved significantly with 3D NAND stacking technology [10], reaching the terabyte level. However, progress in radiation resistance and high-speed access remains slow. These factors directly impact the spacecraft operational lifespan and scientific observation capabilities. In deep space exploration, O-SSR reliability is often the decisive factor in mission success or failure.

NAND flash is widely used as the core storage medium in O-SSRs. Its performance has been greatly improved with advancements in non-volatile double data rate (NV-DDR) interface technology [11]. The latest spaceborne NAND flash storage interfaces support reference clock frequencies of up to 500 MHz. Using double data rate technology, each data I/O interface can achieve instantaneous transfer speeds of up to 1000 Mbps.

In the harsh space radiation environment, data reliability is severely threatened. Single-event effects (SEEs) [12] are the main causes of data errors in O-SSRs. To protect data integrity, error correction coding (ECC) [13] is widely used in spaceborne storage systems. Currently, ECC methods for space applications mainly include Reed–Solomon (RS) codes [14,15], Hamming codes [16], and low-density parity check (LDPC) codes [17]. RS codes are commonly chosen due to their strong error correction capabilities and efficient implementation.

The RS(256,252) and RS(255,223) codes have been used in space missions. RS(256,252) is valued for its low algorithmic complexity and simple implementation. It supports a maximum operating frequency of 400 MHz [18], making it suitable for high-speed data transmission. However, it can only correct two symbol errors, which limits its effectiveness in high-radiation environments. RS(255,223) offers much better error correction, correcting up to 16 symbol errors. This makes it ideal for space missions that require high reliability. However, its higher algorithmic complexity reduces its maximum operating frequency to only 120 MHz [19]. As a result, it cannot meet the speed requirements of NV-DDR high-speed storage interfaces.

To improve both radiation resistance and high-speed access in O-SSRs, further research is urgently needed. The RS(255,223) encoder architecture must be optimized. The data processing speed should be increased, enabling its application in NV-DDR storage systems.

In response to these bottlenecks, recent research has achieved progress in addressing the following issues:

- In the field of RS(255,223) encoder architecture optimization, an innovative coefficient-by-coefficient update architecture was proposed by Silva et al. [19]. This method introduced a parameter pre-computation mechanism. First, intermediate parameters were generated using input symbols and the least significant coefficient. Then, a distributed update strategy was applied, dividing the coefficient update process into parallel operations across 32 registers. Through logic restructuring, the critical path delay was significantly reduced. As a result, an operating frequency of 120 MHz was achieved, doubling the performance of traditional architectures. However, as the interface rates in modern O-SSRs continue to reach the tens-of-Gbps range, this performance level remains insufficient for practical applications.
- To address this challenge, a parallel processing architecture based on algorithm simplification was proposed by Zhan [20]. This approach employed a timing compression technique to merge multi-cycle operations into a single clock cycle. At the same time, spatial parallelism was used to enhance the system throughput. When the bit width was expanded to 256 bits (with 32 parallel lanes), a theoretical throughput of 8.192 Gbps was achieved. However, several design challenges arose. Increased routing congestion caused timing degradation. Logic resource consumption grew at a super-linear rate. More importantly, the clock frequency decreased as parallelism increased.

This limitation makes bit-width expansion alone an unsustainable solution in meeting performance requirements.

These research findings highlight the core challenges in optimizing RS encoders. Serial architectures are inherently constrained by their algorithmic structures, limiting the degree of pipelining that can be applied, while parallel solutions face resource efficiency bottlenecks.

To overcome these limitations and enhance the radiation resistance, a novel interleaved pipelined architecture is proposed in this study for the implementation of the RS(255,223) encoder. Significant performance improvements have been achieved through both algorithmic optimization and structural innovation.

At the algorithmic level, interleaving techniques [21] are introduced to enable the RS encoder to protect against multi-bit upset (MBU) [22]. This mechanism ensures that MBU-induced burst errors are dispersed across multiple parity sequences, significantly enhancing the system's radiation resistance.

On the architectural side, the limitations of traditional RS encoders are successfully overcome. The interleaving technique is integrated into the pipeline. As a result, the pipeline is extended to 36 stages without causing any stalls. A dynamic parameter-switching mechanism allows a single encoding module to efficiently process four interleaved parity sequences. Each pipeline stage is configured with four identical computation parameters, enabling automatic switching between different parity sequences after processing each input symbol. As a result, the processing interval between adjacent symbols is extended to three clock cycles, ensuring sufficient timing margins for deep pipeline construction. Additionally, a continuous data flow is maintained, preventing pipeline stalls. Within a single encoding module, 4 × 223 symbols are continuously input, with every two symbols per three-symbol interval mapped to an RS codeword. Ultimately, four interleaved parity sequences are alternately output, achieving both enhanced performance and improved reliability.

In summary, both the operating frequency of the encoder and the radiation resistance of the encoded data are significantly improved in this study. In contrast to traditional approaches, where interleaving operations are performed only after encoding, the interleaving technique is innovatively integrated into the pipelining process. Consequently, a 36-stage pipeline is successfully developed. By dispersing multi-bit upsets across multiple parity sequences, the interleaving approach is shown to dramatically enhance the data radiation resistance.

Experimental results indicate that, with an 8-bit symbol size, an operating frequency of 450 MHz is achieved by a single encoder, with the data processing rate reaching 3.03 Gbps. Theoretical analysis suggests that this hybrid encoding strategy can improve the error correction capability by approximately four times.

The remainder of this paper is organized as follows. Section 1 provides a detailed review and description of RS(255,223), including its algorithmic foundations and a basic hardware implementation. Section 2 presents the proposed 36-stage pipelined architecture with interleaving techniques. Section 3 discusses the experimental results, and Section 4 concludes the paper.

2. Related Work

In this section, the mathematical foundations of the RS(255,223) code [23,24] are first reviewed to establish the theoretical basis for the subsequent hardware implementation. A commonly used reference architecture [14,19,25,26] is then introduced to illustrate how the RS(255,223) encoder can be implemented using digital circuits. This conventional architecture is employed as the foundation for the proposed design. Building upon this foundation, a deeply pipelined version of the encoder is presented, resulting in a significant improvement in the operating frequency and throughput.

2.1. Reed–Solomon Algorithm

RS codes are a type of block code. They are used to introduce redundancy, allowing errors to be detected and corrected during data transmission or storage. The encoding process is based on Galois Field (GF) operations. Polynomial division is used to generate check symbols, which are then added to form the final codeword. An RS code is typically represented as an (n, k) code. Here, n is the total number of symbols in a codeword, and k is the number of information symbols, which corresponds to the original data length. The number of redundancy check symbols is given by $r = n - k$. The maximum number of correctable symbol errors is $t = r/2$. Each symbol belongs to the finite field $GF(2^m)$.

The information data can be represented as a polynomial over the finite field:

$$I(x) = I_0 + I_1x + I_2x^2 + \cdots + I_{k-1}x^{k-1} \quad (1)$$

where I_i is an element of $GF(2^m)$. The goal of encoding is to construct a codeword polynomial:

$$C(x) = I(x) + P(x) \quad (2)$$

This polynomial must have specific mathematical properties to enhance the error detection and correction capabilities. A generator polynomial $g(x)$ is used for encoding. It is a minimal polynomial over the finite field and is defined as

$$g(x) = (x - \alpha^1)(x - \alpha^2)\cdots(x - \alpha^r) \quad (3)$$

Here, α is a primitive element of $GF(2^m)$. The coefficients of $g(x)$ also belong to $GF(2^m)$. For an RS(255, 223) code, the codeword length n is 255, the number of information symbols k is 223, the number of check symbols r is 32, and the maximum number of correctable symbol errors t is 16. Assuming that the code is computed over $GF(2^8)$, each symbol consists of 8 bits. This finite field contains 256 elements, with each symbol represented by one byte. The primitive polynomial used in this field is

$$P(x) = x^8 + x^4 + x^2 + x^1 + 1 \quad (4)$$

The generator polynomial $g(x)$ is constructed using 32 consecutive powers of the finite field element α, where α is the primitive element of $GF(2^8)$. If 223 symbols are given, they can be represented as an information polynomial:

$$I(x) = I_0 + I_1x + I_2x^2 + \cdots + I_{222}x^{222} \quad (5)$$

where I_i is an element of $GF(2^8)$. To allocate space for the check symbols, the information polynomial is shifted left by 32 positions:

$$I'(x) = I_x x^{32} \quad (6)$$

This operation is equivalent to appending 32 zeros to the end of the data, serving as placeholders for the check symbols. The check symbols are then computed using polynomial division:

$$P(x) = I'(x) \bmod g(x) \quad (7)$$

where $g(x)$ is the generator polynomial of length 32. The remainder $P(x)$ is also a polynomial of length 32, representing the check symbols. The final codeword $C(x)$ consists of both the information symbols and the check symbols:

$$C(x) = I_x x^{32} + P(x) \tag{8}$$

Upon expansion, the first 223 symbols correspond to the original information symbols, while the last 32 symbols represent the check symbols.

2.2. Widely Adopted Hardware Architecture

In Figure 1, the commonly used RS(255,223) encoding process is illustrated. Initially, an 8-bit-wide symbol I_i is received. The bitwise XOR operation is then performed between I_i and R_{32} to obtain the variable F. The intermediate encoding variables R_i ($i = 0$ to 32) are stored with an 8-bit width, all initialized to zero. The value of R_0 remains fixed at zero.

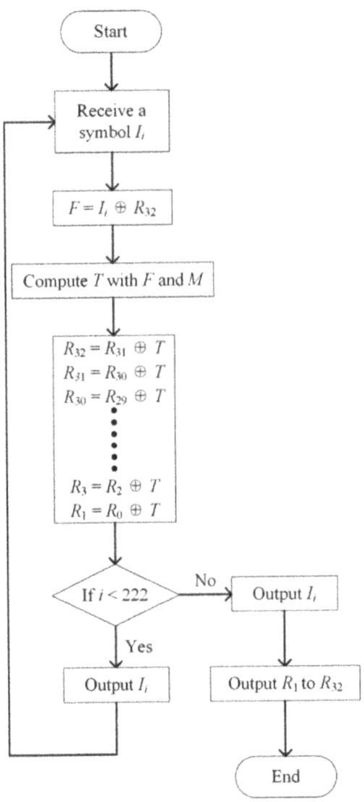

Figure 1. Example of widely adopted RS(255,223) hardware architecture. This figure illustrates the operational flow of a traditional architecture.

After computing F, the variable T is derived using F and a constant matrix M. The matrix M consists of eight 8-bit-wide hexadecimal constants: "EE", "77", "F8", "7C", "3E", "1F", "CC", and "66". The indices i and j are used to refer to the row and column positions of matrix M, respectively, where $M[i][j]$ denotes the j-th bit of the i-th row in binary form. For example, $M[0]$ corresponds to the hexadecimal value "EE", which, in binary, is 11101110. Thus, $M[0][1]$ refers to the second bit of "EE" (from left to right), which is 1. The computation of T follows columnwise logic. For each bit $T[j]$ in the output vector T, where $j \in \{0, 1, \ldots, 7\}$, the value is computed through the following steps. Each bit $F[i]$ in the vector F is bitwise ANDed with the corresponding bit $M[i][j]$. This operation acts as a filter. The matrix element $M[i][j]$ is included in the result only if $F[i] = 1$. Otherwise, it contributes nothing to the computation. The eight intermediate values, $F[0]$ and $M[0][j]$ through $F[7]$ and $M[7][j]$, are then combined using a bitwise XOR operation. This XOR step determines the parity of the selected bits. If an odd number of the selected $M[i][j]$ values contain ones, then $T[j]$ is set to 1. Otherwise, it is set to 0. From a linear algebra perspective, this computation resembles vector–matrix multiplication. However, the conventional multiply–add operation is replaced with AND-XOR logic. The selection of matrix elements is determined by bitwise AND operations, while addition is performed using bitwise XOR, implementing modulo-2 addition, which ensures parity checking. Consequently, each bit of T can be expressed according to Equation (9):

$$T[j] = \bigoplus_{i=0}^{7} (F[i] \wedge M[i][j]), \quad \text{where } j \in \{0, 1, \ldots, 7\} \tag{9}$$

Once T is computed, the intermediate variable R_i is updated. The updates occur in parallel. Each R_i is derived from R_{i-1}, which comes from the previous update. During the first update, all R_{i-1} values are reset to zero. If fewer than 223 symbols are received, only the received symbols are output. Otherwise, the received symbols are output first, followed by the sequential output of the intermediate variables R_i in increasing order. Finally, the algorithm terminates, and all variables are reset.

This method is computationally simple and easy to implement. However, it exhibits strict data dependencies, making it challenging to apply in a multi-stage pipelined architecture. In each iteration, when computing the parameter F, the value of R_{32} is derived from the result of the previous iteration. The update rule for R_{32} is defined as the XOR operation between R_{31} and T. The computation of R_{32} depends on the previous value of T, and T is determined by F, while F is influenced by R_{32}. This creates a long dependency chain. As a result, the effective overlapping of computations cannot be achieved without pipeline stalls.

3. Interleaved Pipelined Architecture

In traditional architectures, long dependency chains limit the ability to divide the pipeline into more stages. This results in a longer critical path, making it difficult to use higher clock frequencies and ultimately reducing the throughput.

To improve both the radiation tolerance and throughput, interleaving techniques have been introduced into the RS encoder. In the conventional design, the steps of receiving the input symbol I_i, computing parameter F, computing parameter T, and updating the parameter matrix R are handled in separate pipeline stages. However, there is a four-cycle dependency between parameter F and matrix R. These cycles include the computation of F, the computation of T, the update of R, and the write-back of R_{32} to the first stage for the next F computation. As a result, the pipeline has to be stalled to wait for R_{32} to be written back, which negatively impacts the performance.

To solve this problem, interleaving is applied to the pipeline design. The input sequence I_j (where $j = 0$ to 891) is divided into four interleaved sequences:

$$I_j = \{I_1^0, I_2^0, I_3^0, I_4^0, I_1^1, I_2^1, I_3^1, I_4^1, \ldots, I_1^{222}, I_2^{222}, I_3^{222}, I_4^{222}\}.$$

These interleaved sequences are then sequentially fed to the encoder for parallel processing. By interleaving the data, independent input streams are introduced into the pipeline. This allows the encoder to continue working on other data while waiting for dependencies to be resolved, reducing the idle time caused by the delay in writing back R_{32}. Each of the four interleaved streams I_1, I_2, I_3, and I_4 takes turns passing through the pipeline stages. This arrangement ensures that, for any given stream I_k (where $k = 1, 2, 3, 4$), there is a three-cycle interval between the processing of two consecutive symbols, I_{k_n} and $I_{k_{n+1}}$. When one stream reaches the stage that requires the updated R_{32}, the three-cycle gap guarantees that R_{32} has already been updated and written back to the input stage of the pipeline. For example, when I_4^4 is at the stage of updating matrix R, I_3^4 is in the stage of computing parameter T, I_2^4 is computing parameter F, and I_1^4 is receiving the input symbol. At the next active clock edge, I_4^4, I_3^4, I_2^4, and I_1^4 are advanced to the next pipeline stage. Meanwhile, the updated R_{32} is written back to the first stage, and I_4^5 is introduced into the pipeline. At this point, I_4^5 uses the returned R_{32} from the later stage. This staggered scheduling hides the delay between F and R, allowing the pipeline to run without stalling and improving the throughput. Since the interleaved streams are independent, the pipeline can be made deeper, and the system can run at a higher clock frequency. As a result, the overall data processing speed increases.

Radiation tolerance is also improved through this interleaved design. In conventional schemes, only up to 16 consecutive symbol errors can be corrected. However, in the proposed approach, the encoder output is interleaved across four error-correcting sequences, allowing up to 64 consecutive symbol errors to be corrected simultaneously. Although the RS(255,223) code itself is capable of correcting up to 16 symbol errors, the interleaved pipeline structure is designed to map each input stream into four separate RS codewords. As a result, even if a burst of 64 consecutive symbols is affected by a multi-bit upset, data recovery can still be achieved, provided that no individual codeword exceeds its 16-symbol correction threshold. As shown in Figure 2, a total of 892 symbols are input into the proposed architecture. Subsequently, 892 information symbols and 128 parity symbols are output. The output symbols are distributed among four error-correcting sequences, which are indicated in red, green, blue, and yellow, respectively. It can be observed that the input sequence is interleaved and partitioned into four distinct error-correcting streams.

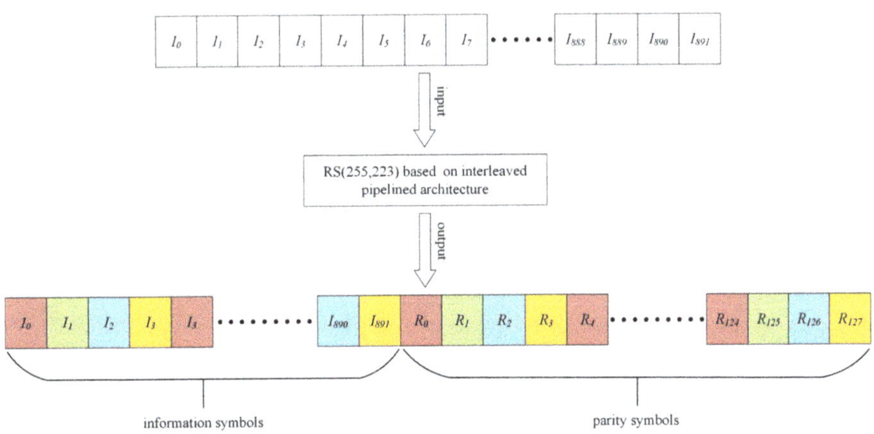

Figure 2. Interleaved distribution of output symbols in the proposed RS(255,223) encoder. A total of 892 input symbols are divided into four interleaved sequences, each assigned a distinct color corresponding to separate error-correcting codewords.

As shown in Figure 3, the interleaved pipelined architecture is proposed. Each segment between two dashed lines in Figure 3 is used to represent a single pipeline stage, with the stage number indicated between the lines. The logic of pipeline stages 1 through 6 and stage 36 is illustrated in detail. The stages from 7 to 35 are implemented by replicating the logic of stage 6 and are represented by ellipses for brevity. This architecture is composed of 36 pipeline stages. In the first stage, the input symbol I_j is received. After each symbol is received, a 2-bit counter, which is initialized to zero, is incremented. This counter is used to indicate which of the four error-correcting sequences—I_1, I_2, I_3, or I_4—the symbol I_j belongs to. A 1-bit valid signal is also used. It is initialized to 0 and is set high when a valid symbol is received. Both the valid and counter signals are passed along the pipeline together with the input symbol. At each pipeline stage, the valid signal is checked to determine whether the stage should be activated. Specifically, the registers located along the dashed lines are designated as inter-stage registers, which are used to control the operation of the pipeline. Each stage's inter-stage register is enabled for writing by the output of the valid register from the preceding stage. When a valid symbol is received, the valid register is set high. This valid signal is successively passed along the pipeline, activating the corresponding inter-stage registers and enabling the pipelined processing of the input data.

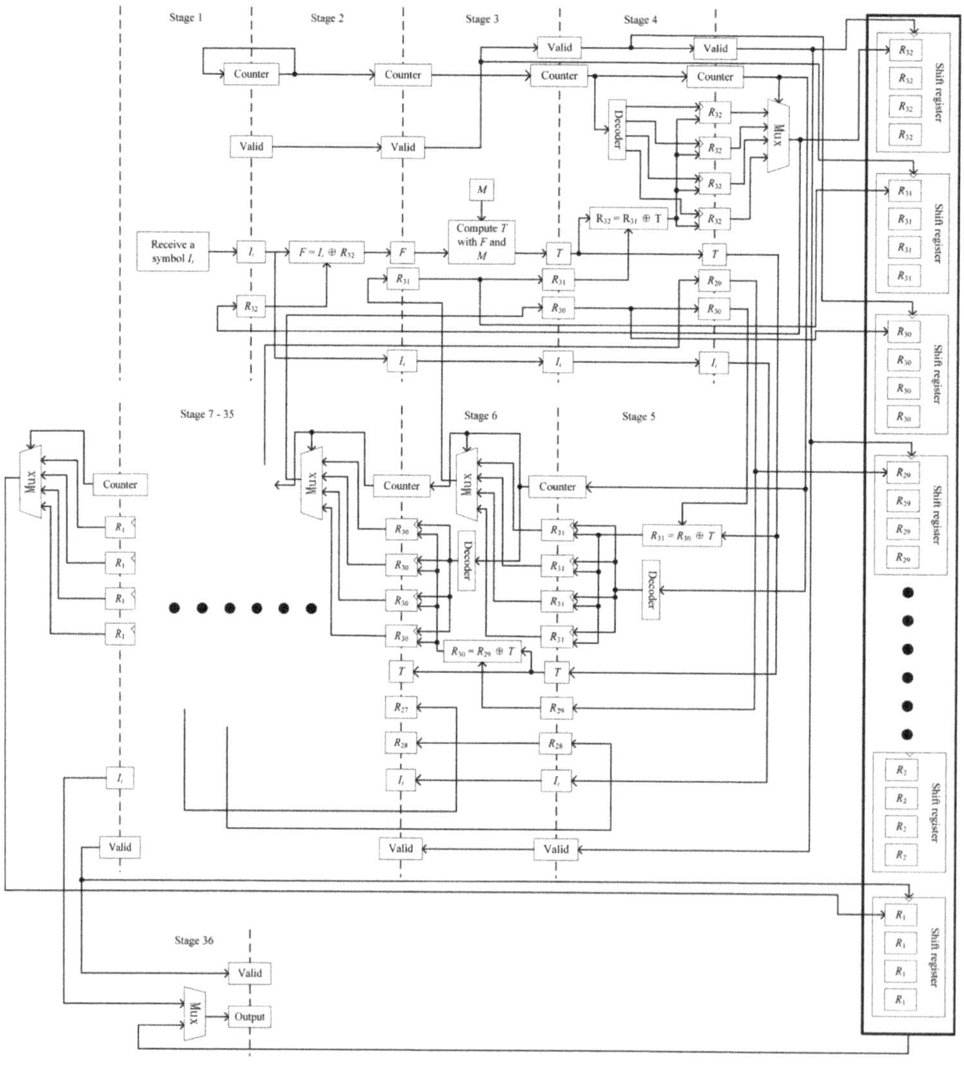

Figure 3. Implementation of the RS(255,223) algorithm in a interleaved pipelined architecture. A detailed view of the 36-stage pipeline structure is shown in this figure.

The counter is used to determine the interleaved sequence to which the symbol belongs, ensuring that the appropriate inter-stage register group is selected and updated accordingly. Each inter-stage register is composed of four identical sets of parameters, corresponding to the four error-correcting sequences. The counter ensures that data are written to the correct parameter group. An additional register, used for storing the parameter R_{32}, is included in the first pipeline stage. This register is updated by the fourth stage and is used in subsequent computations.

In the second stage, parameter F is calculated by performing a bitwise XOR between I_i and R_{32}. In this stage, the parameter R_{32} is supplied from stage 4 and is bypassed through intermediate pipeline stages to reach the current stage. In addition to being used in the computation, I_i is also written into the inter-stage register of the subsequent pipeline stage for further propagation.

In the third stage, parameter T is computed according to Equation (9). Within this stage, the parameter matrix M, which stores a set of constants, is utilized. The parameter R_{32} is bypassed through this stage and forwarded to the next pipeline stage. Beginning from the third stage, the valid signal is not only used as the write-enable signal for the inter-stage registers but is also employed as both the shift and write-enable control signal for the shift registers.

From stage 4 to stage 35, the parameters R are updated sequentially, with one parameter updated per stage in reverse index order. This staged distribution is intentionally designed to facilitate a narrow and elongated physical layout during hardware placement and routing. By structuring the pipeline in this way, several advantages are realized. First, the routing complexity is significantly reduced. Since each stage handles a smaller, isolated portion of the logic, shorter and more localized signal paths can be achieved. This minimizes the need for long interconnects across wide areas of the chip, which often lead to increased delays and timing violations in dense designs. Second, the narrow geometry allows for easier replication of the encoder module in systems requiring parallel processing. When multiple encoder instances are placed side by side, the elongated structure ensures that horizontal wiring between shared control signals, inputs, and outputs remains manageable. As a result, the design is better suited for high-throughput applications that require wide-bit or multi-channel parallelism.

From stage 4 to stage 35, the parameters R_i ($i = 1$ to 32) in the parameter matrix R are updated sequentially, with one parameter updated at each stage. Identical logic is applied across all stages. Initially, all parameters in matrix R are set to zero. In each stage, the updated value of R_i is computed by performing a bitwise XOR operation between T and R_{i-1}. Following each update, a 2-to-4 decoder is employed to generate four write-enable signals based on the value of a 2-bit counter. The 2-bit input signal is translated into a 4-bit one-hot output, in which exactly one bit is high, while the others remain low. This one-hot encoding feature enables the 2-bit counter to control four register write-enable signals. Each state of the counter activates the corresponding register, allowing the computed result to be stored separately for the four interleaved error-correcting sequences. The appropriate parameter register is selected based on the current counter value, and the updated result is written accordingly. This mechanism ensures that the results for all four sequences are correctly maintained in parallel throughout the pipeline.

In stage 5, once R_{32} has been updated, a 4-to-1 multiplexer (Mux) is employed to select one of the four outputs corresponding to the four interleaved error-correcting sequences. This multiplexer receives four candidate values as inputs, each representing the most recent result of R_{32} from one of the sequences. The selection signal is provided by the 2-bit counter, which determines the currently active sequence. Based on the counter value, one of the four inputs is routed through the multiplexer to the output. The selected value is then fed back to stage 1, where it is used in the encoding of the next input symbol that belongs to the same error-correcting sequence. At the same time, the selected value is written into a shift register specifically associated with R_{32}. After each write operation, the shift register is shifted by one symbol width to accommodate the next value. Once 892 shifts have been performed—corresponding to the total number of input symbols—the final computed values for all four sequences are retained within the shift register, completing the encoding process.

A similar procedure is followed for the remaining parameters R_{31} through R_1. After each parameter R_i is updated in stage n, the value is written into the designated register using the decoder. In stage $n+1$, the value is passed through a Mux and routed to stage $n-4$, where it is used for the next symbol encoding. In stage $n-3$, the value is written into its corresponding shift register. In stage 36, the final parameter R_1 is selected via a Mux and written directly into its shift register. As long as the number of processed symbols does not exceed 892, the input symbols I_i are output directly. Once all 892 symbols have been output, the contents of the 32 shift registers, comprising 128 parameters, are sequentially output. The 32 shift registers are interconnected as a unified structure. During the parameter update phase, shift operations are performed independently within each register. However, during the output phase, all shift registers are treated as a single logical unit. A unified shift is performed across all registers, shifting by one symbol width per clock cycle. This ensures that all encoded parameters are output sequentially and in the correct order.

Figure 4 illustrates the operational timing of the pipeline. During the first 892 clock cycles, one symbol is input at each cycle. A total of 892 symbols are processed, corresponding to four interleaved error-correcting sequences, with 223 symbols assigned to each sequence. Each input symbol is propagated through the pipeline and is output 35 clock cycles after it is received.

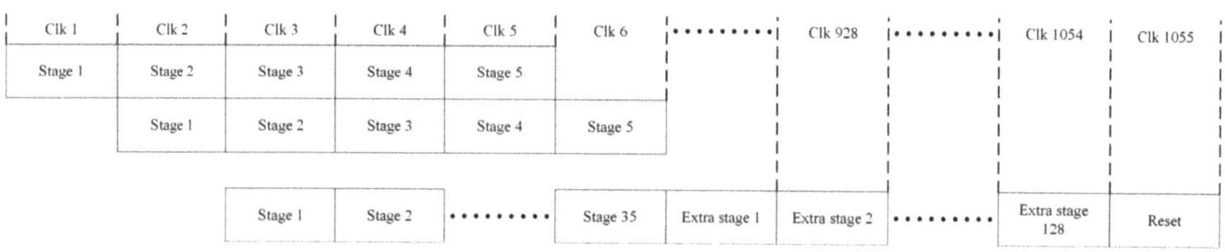

Figure 4. Timing diagram illustrating the processing and output of the interleaved pipelined architecture.

Once the final input symbol has exited the pipeline, 128 parity symbols are output sequentially. The "extra stage" shown in the figure refers to the stages responsible for outputting these parity symbols, which are generated from the shift operations performed by the 32 shift registers included in the architecture.

Following the completion of parity output, a one-cycle reset is performed to return all pipeline registers to their initial states, preparing the system for the next encoding operation. Including this reset cycle, the total number of clock cycles required to complete the encoding of one full data group 892 symbols is 1055.

Assuming an 8-bit symbol width and an operating frequency of 450 MHz, the theoretical throughput can be calculated as

$$\frac{892 \times 8 \text{ bits}}{1055 \text{ cycles}} \times 450 \text{ MHz} \approx 3.043 \text{ Gbps}$$

This value reflects the maximum effective throughput of the pipeline, taking into account the one-cycle reset. In practice, the reset operation requires four clock cycles to complete. In the first cycle, stage 1 to stage 5 and the shift registers from R_{32} to R_{23} are reset. In the second cycle, stage 6 to stage 16 and the shift registers from R_{22} to R_{13} are reset. In the third cycle, stage 17 to stage 25 and the shift registers from R_{12} to R_4 are reset. Finally, in the fourth cycle, stage 26 to stage 36 and the shift registers from R_3 to R_1 are reset. Although the reset process spans four clock cycles, only the first cycle impacts the pipeline data processing. As soon as the first reset cycle is completed, the pipeline is ready to receive new data. Therefore, only one clock cycle is effectively counted toward the reset in the throughput calculation.

4. Validation and Analysis

The RS(255,223) encoder based on the proposed interleaved pipelined architecture was implemented using the Xilinx XC7K325TFFG900-2 FPGA [27]. This device features 203,800 lookup tables (LUTs), 407,600 flip-flops, and 19.16 Mb of block RAM (BRAM). The validation and analysis are focused on two key aspects: the system's bit flip recovery capabilities and its overall performance.

4.1. Bit Flip Recovery Capabilities

Bit flips can occur in two forms: single-bit upsets (SBUs) and multi-bit upsets (MBUs). SBUs are observed at a much higher frequency than MBUs. RS coding is known to effectively prevent errors caused by SBUs. However, MBUs present a more complex challenge. Under different radiation intensities, various flip patterns can be observed [28–30]. A single-event upset that causes two consecutive bits to flip is classified as a double-bit upset (DBU). Similarly, when three consecutive bits flip, it is defined as a triple-bit upset (TBU); four consecutive flips result in a quadruple-bit upset (QDBU); and five consecutive flips are referred to as a quintuple-bit upset (QTBU). Other potential patterns exist but are considered negligible based on empirical observations.

In Figure 5, a representative data pattern stored in flash memory is presented. The red-marked section indicates an MBU—specifically, the most severe case of a QTBU. In this instance, three bit flips occurred in the third error-correcting sequence, resulting in two symbol errors. Meanwhile, two bit flips were observed in the fourth sequences, each also resulting in two symbol errors. Since RS(255,223) is capable of correcting up to 16 symbol errors, each sequence was able to correct its respective errors successfully. This scenario represents the most extreme case.

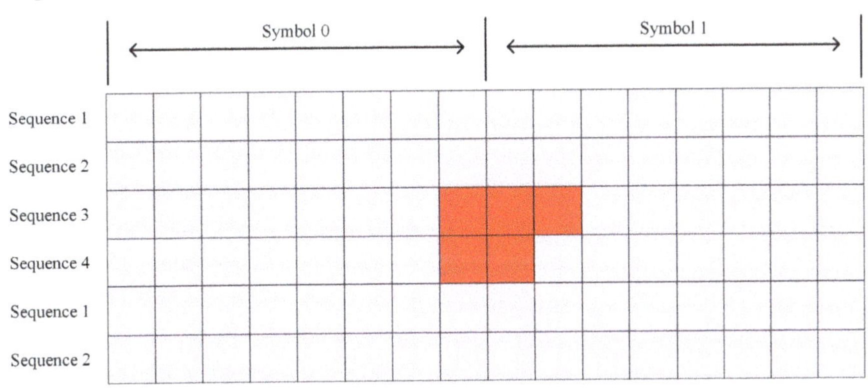

Figure 5. Flash memory data pattern with the red highlighted region indicating a severe QTBU case.

In the proposed design, the interleaved pipelined architecture ensures that the distance between two adjacent symbols in the same error-correcting sequence is at least three symbol periods. As a result, if any of the specified upset patterns occur, the erroneous symbols are distributed across different sequences. At most, one symbol error occurs per sequence, keeping the errors within the correction capability of each RS code. A single RS(255,223) code is capable of correcting up to 16 symbol errors. By interleaving four such error-correcting sequences, an error correction block is formed. This block can correct up to 64 consecutive errors. Even when spatially consecutive MBU events are present, data integrity can still be maintained by the proposed design.

To verify the system's recovery capability against bit flips, an error injection method was employed. A set of correct data was generated and written to the flash memory. Errors were then injected externally using debugging techniques. The corrupted data were subsequently read out and corrected. A comparison was made between the corrected output and the originally written data. If the data matched, it was concluded that the proposed architecture successfully mitigated the injected errors. The experimental results confirmed that all injected error patterns were fully corrected, verifying the system's robustness against both single-bit and multi-bit upsets.

4.2. Performance Evaluation

Evaluating the performance of a single module alone cannot accurately reflect its operating frequency within a complete O-SSR system. This is because the frequency is affected by the overall resource utilization on the FPGA. A single module requires only minimal resources, and this abundance may lead to an unrealistically high operating frequency. To obtain a more realistic assessment, the module was instantiated within a complete O-SSR system. Its resource utilization and operating frequency were then measured under actual operating conditions. The proposed architecture utilized 1728 slice LUTs—324 as memory and 1404 as logic—and a total of 7064 slice Registers. No additional FPGA resources were used. A clock frequency of 450 MHz was achieved by this architecture after applying triple modular redundancy (TMR).

To further highlight the advantages of the proposed architecture in terms of particle-induced bit flip resistance and encoding efficiency, a comprehensive comparison with several recently proposed schemes is presented in Table 1. The selected comparison schemes were all implemented within the O-SSR system or systems with similar architectures. Evaluations were based on three key metrics: the operating frequency, throughput, and radiation resistance capability. The encoding efficiency was assessed through the measurement of the operating frequency and throughput, while radiation tolerance was evaluated by examining the types of bit flip patterns that could be corrected.

Table 1. A comparison between the existing architectures and our proposed architecture. SBU: Single-Bit Upset, MBU: Multi-Bit Upset, DBU: Double-Bit Upset.

Architecture	Technology	Frequency	Throughput	Radiation Resistance	Year
[31]	M2S150TS	100 MHz	0.32 Gbps	All SBU	2017
[25]	XC4VSX55	100 MHz	0.42 Gbps	All SBU and Limited DBU	2017
[32]	5CGXFC7D7F31C8	120 MHz	0.17 Gbps	All SBU	2018
[33]	XC5VLX330	100 MHz	0.30 Gbps	All SBU and Limited MBU	2020
[20]	M2S150TS	125 MHz	0.80 Gbps	All SBU and All DBU	2021
[34]	XC5VFX130T	100 MHz	1.14 Gbps	All SBU and Most MBU	2024
[18]	XC7K325T	400 MHz	3.10 Gbps	All SBU and Most MBU	2024
Proposed	XC7K325T	450 MHz	3.04 Gbps	All SBU and Most MBU	2025
	XC4VSX55	290 MHz	1.95 Gbps		

To ensure fairness and consistency in the throughput comparison, all values reported in Table 1 reflect the performance of a single encoder module. Although it is technically feasible to enhance the effective throughput by replicating the encoder modules in a multi-core architecture, such an approach significantly increases the resource consumption and can artificially inflate the throughput figures. Therefore, throughput results derived from multi-core replication were deliberately excluded from our analysis. This methodology enabled a more accurate and meaningful assessment of the architectural merits of each design, free from the confounding effects of hardware scaling.

The proposed system achieved operating frequencies that were 3.60 to 4.50 times higher than those of all other schemes, with the exception of [18], with the throughput improved by factors ranging from 2.66 to 17.88. Additionally, the highest level of radiation tolerance was achieved. In contrast, works such as [31,32] employed only Hamming code-based methods, resulting in limited radiation resistance. The approach in [25] combined RS codes with LDPC codes but was only capable of mitigating DBU events. In [33], two different radiation-hardening strategies were selectively applied based on data criticality, where most data were only protected against SBU events, and a small portion of critical data were protected against MBUs. In [20], a strategy was introduced in which data from the same parity sequence were distributed across different memory regions, effectively preventing all DBU events. Meanwhile, [34] proposed an iterative interleaving method based on LDPC encoding, significantly enhancing the radiation resistance. However, this method led to high resource consumption and reduced throughput due to its computational complexity and iterative decoding process.

When compared to the proposed architecture, the design presented in [18] was found to operate at a clock frequency of 50 MHz lower, but with throughput that was 0.06 Gbps higher. This method was also capable of mitigating all SBU events and most MBU events. RS(256,252) codes were employed, and pipelining was utilized to accelerate the RS encoder, enabling operating frequencies and throughput levels comparable to those of the proposed system. Although interleaving techniques were adopted in both schemes, the proposed method integrates interleaving directly into the pipeline, whereas, in [18], a single interleaving module was implemented after the encoder to perform simple post-encoding interleaving.

The slightly lower throughput observed in the proposed system compared to [18] can be attributed to the adoption of a more complex encoding algorithm, RS(255,223), which necessitated the generation of 32 parity symbols per codeword. In contrast, only four parity symbols were required in their RS(256,252) scheme. This variation in algorithm complexity also led to differences in error correction capabilities. While both designs were capable of mitigating most MBU events, the maximum number of correctable errors differed substantially. In the worst-case scenario, up to 64 consecutive erroneous symbols could be corrected by the proposed method, whereas the method in [18] was limited to correcting only eight such symbols.

To account for the influence of the device technology on the performance, a new implementation of the proposed encoder was carried out on the XC4VSX55 platform 90 nm process [35]. This allowed for a direct comparison with earlier architectures implemented on platforms such as M2S150TS and 5CGXFC7D7F31C8, which utilize similar process technologies. It was observed that, even on this legacy device, the proposed architecture maintained superior throughput and radiation tolerance compared to prior methods. This demonstrates that the reported performance benefits are not solely the result of advanced hardware but are attributable to the underlying architectural enhancements.

5. Conclusions

The interleaved pipelined architecture proposed in this study is designed to effectively address the challenges associated with deploying the RS(255,223) encoder. The serial implementation of RS(255,223) has been constrained by its inherent algorithmic structure, which limits the depth of pipelining that can be achieved. These issues are mainly caused by long dependency chains between computation parameters. Parallel implementations, on the other hand, have been hindered by resource inefficiencies.

To overcome these constraints, an interleaving technique was incorporated into the pipelined structure. By enabling the encoder to alternate among four parity codewords, a four-cycle latency window was created for parameters with interdependencies. Consequently, a 36-stage pipeline was implemented. Through this design, a substantial increase in throughput was achieved, allowing performance levels that typically require extensive parallelism to be reached with significantly reduced parallel scaling. Additionally, the introduction of interleaving was found to inherently enhance the system's radiation tolerance.

The proposed architecture was thoroughly evaluated on the Xilinx XC7K325T platform, with specific attention given to throughput and error correction capabilities. It was analytically and experimentally verified that the system was capable of correcting all classified error types, demonstrating its effectiveness in recovering from both SBUs and MBUs. The results confirmed that high data rates can be supported while maintaining strong error correction performance. Although the achieved throughput was found to be slightly lower than that of the most advanced existing solution, a significantly higher level of radiation tolerance was demonstrated. As such, the proposed architecture is considered well suited for future deployment in space exploration missions where both high throughput and robust radiation resistance are critical.

The design was validated through extensive error injection experiments, which confirmed its resilience against a variety of bit flip patterns. However, it should be acknowledged that the radiation resilience was evaluated using fault injection, which serves as an indirect method of validation. Real-space or radiation chamber testing was not conducted in this study. As such, future work will include physical radiation testing to further substantiate the fault-tolerant capabilities of the proposed architecture under actual space or radiation-rich conditions. This step is expected to enhance the credibility and applicability of the design for space-grade and safety-critical systems.

While the current evaluation was conducted on a single module, potential scalability in system-level integration scenarios has also been taken into account. Due to its modular and pipelined structure, the proposed architecture is considered inherently suitable for deployment in multi-core encoder systems. Under high-traffic conditions, multiple encoder instances may be instantiated and operated in parallel, with efficiency maintained through appropriate scheduling and load-balancing mechanisms. Nonetheless, scalability challenges, such as interconnect bottlenecks and shared resource contention, may be encountered and will need to be carefully addressed in future multi-core system implementations. In future work, these multi-encoder configurations will be explored in greater depth, with the goal of optimizing the encoder performance in large-scale, high-throughput applications.

Author Contributions: Software, X.L.; validation, X.L.; formal analysis, X.L.; investigation, X.L.; writing—original draft, X.L.; writing—review and editing, X.L. and L.Z.; supervision, L.Z.; project administration, X.L.; funding acquisition, Y.Z. All authors have read and agreed to the published version of the manuscript.

Funding: This research was funded by the Science Foundation of the Chinese Academy of Sciences, grant number E4GZ120503.

Data Availability Statement: The raw data supporting the conclusions of this article will be made available by the authors on request.

Conflicts of Interest: The authors declare no conflicts of interest.

References

1. Song, Q.; Li, S.; Zhu, Y.; An, J.S. Design and Research of Multiple Data Channels in Solid State Recorder of the Satellite SJ-10. *Adv. Mater. Res.* **2015**, *1073*, 1977–1981 . [CrossRef]
2. Fabiano, M.; Furano, G. NAND flash storage technology for mission-critical space applications. *IEEE Aerosp. Electron. Syst. Mag.* **2013**, *28*, 30–36. [CrossRef]
3. Khaled, A.; Zhang, Q. An Energy Aware Mass Memory Unit for Small Satellites Using Hybrid Architecture. In Proceedings of the 2017 IEEE International Conference on Computational Science and Engineering (CSE) and IEEE International Conference on Embedded and Ubiquitous Computing (EUC), Guangzhou, China, 21–24 July 2017; Volume 1, pp. 210–213. [CrossRef]
4. Tu, S.; Wang, H.; Huang, Y.; Jin, Z. A spaceborne advanced storage system for remote sensing microsatellites. *Front. Inf. Technol. Electron. Eng.* **2024**, *25*, 600–615. [CrossRef]
5. Höeffgen, S.K.; Metzger, S.; Steffens, M. Investigating the effects of cosmic rays on space electronics. *Front. Phys.* **2020**, *8*, 318. [CrossRef]
6. Li, X.; Wen, X.; Xiong, S.; An, Z.; Xu, Y.; Liang, X.; Liu, X.; Yang, S.; Zhang, F.; Sun, X.; et al. Introduction to the SATech-01 satellite HEBS (GECAM-C). *Exp. Astron.* **2025**, *59*, 1–22. [CrossRef]
7. Jia, S.m.; Song, L.m.; Li, C.k.; Zhao, H.S.; Zhang, J.; Guan, J.; Ou, G.; Wang, J. The operation and data processing of the Einstein Probe FXT science data center. In *Radiation Detection Technology and Methods*; Springer: Berlin/Heidelberg, Germany, 2025; pp. 1–7.
8. Tian, S.; Li, C.; Zhao, L.; Yan, G.; Luo,W.; Gao, Y. Information Processing Technology of Housekeeping Subsystem for BJ-3A/B Satellites. *Spacecr. Eng.* **2023**, *32*, 85–92.
9. Ribet, M.; Sabatini, M.; Lampani, L.; Gasbarri, P. Monitoring of a controlled space flexible multibody by means of embedded piezoelectric sensors and cameras synergy. *J. Intell. Mater. Syst. Struct.* **2018**, *29*, 2966–2978. [CrossRef]
10. Aritome, S. *NAND Flash Memory Technologies*; John Wiley & Sons: New York, NY, USA, 2015.
11. Open NAND Flash Interface Workgroup. *Open NAND Flash Interface Specification*, 5.1 ed.; Open NAND Flash Interface Workgroup: Arlington, VA, USA, 2022.
12. Gonzales, L.; Danzeca, S.; Fiore, S.; Kramberger, I. Mixed-Field Radiation of 3-D MLC Flash Memories for Space Applications. *IEEE Trans. Nucl. Sci.* **2024**, *71*, 2400–2408. [CrossRef]
13. Peterson, W.W.; Weldon, E.J. *Error-Correcting Codes*, 2nd ed.; MIT Press: Cambridge, MA, USA, 1972.
14. Garg, D.; Sharma, C.P.; Chaurasia, P.; Chowdhury, A.R. High throughput FPGA implementation of Reed-Solomon Encoder for Space Data Systems. In Proceedings of the 2013 Nirma University International Conference on Engineering (NUiCONE), Ahmedabad, India, 28–30 November 2013; pp. 1–5. [CrossRef]
15. Samanta, J.; Bhaumik, J.; Barman, S. FPGA based area efficient RS (23, 17) codec. *Microsyst. Technol.* **2017**, *23*, 639–650. [CrossRef]
16. Rurik, W.; Mazumdar, A. Hamming codes as error-reducing codes. In Proceedings of the 2016 IEEE Information Theory Workshop (ITW), Cambridge, UK, 11–14 September 2016; pp. 404–408. [CrossRef]
17. Ge, G.; Yin, L. LDPC coding scheme for improving the reliability of multi-level-cell NAND flash memory in radiation environments. *China Commun.* **2017**, *14*, 10–21. [CrossRef]
18. Li, X.; Zhou, L.; Zhu, Y. A Novel Architecture for Addressing the Throughput Bottleneck in Spaceborne Solid-State Recorder for Electromagnetic Spectrum Sensors. *Remote Sens.* **2025**, *17*, 138. [CrossRef]
19. Silva, M.G.; Silvano, G.L.; Duarte, R.O. RTL development of a parameterizable Reed–Solomon Codec. *IET Comput. Digit. Tech.* **2021**, *15*, 143–159.
20. Zhang, X. Research of High Speed Synchronous NAND FLASH Spaceborne Storage Technology. Master's Thesis, University of Chinese Academy of Sciences (National Space Science Center of Chinese Academy of Sciences), Beijing, China, 2020.
21. Bartz, H.; Puchinger, S. Fast decoding of lifted interleaved linearized Reed–Solomon codes for multishot network coding. *Des. Codes Cryptogr.* **2024**, *92*, 2379–2421. [CrossRef]
22. Gil-Tomás, D.; Saiz-Adalid, L.J.; Gracia-Morán, J.; Carlos Baraza-Calvo, J.; Gil-Vicente, P.J. A Hybrid Technique Based on ECC and Hardened Cells for Tolerating Random Multiple-Bit Upsets in SRAM Arrays. *IEEE Access* **2024**, *12*, 70662–70675. [CrossRef]
23. Geisel, W.A. *Tutorial on Reed-Solomon Error Correction Coding*; National Aeronautics and Space Administration, Lyndon B. Johnson Space Center: Houston, TX, USA, 1990; Volume 102162.
24. Wolf, J.K. An introduction to Reed-Solomon Codes. Course Notes. 2020. Available online: http://pfister.ee.duke.edu/courses/ecen604/rspoly.pdf (accessed on 4 January 2021).
25. Xu, Z. Research on Solid-State Storage Technology for Spaceborne Integrated Electronic Systems. Ph.D. Thesis, University of Chinese Academy of Sciences (National Space Science Center, Chinese Academy of Sciences), Beijing, China, 2017.
26. Dayal, P.; Patial, R.K. Implementation of Reed-Solomon CODEC for IEEE 802.16 network using VHDL code. In Proceedings of the 2014 International Conference on Reliability Optimization and Information Technology (ICROIT), Faridabad, India, 6–8 February 2014; pp. 452–455. [CrossRef]
27. Xilinx. *Kintex-7 FPGAs Data Sheet(DS182)*, 2.17 ed.; Xilinx: San Jose, CA, USA, 2019.

28. Radaelli, D.; Puchner, H.; Wong, S.; Daniel, S. Investigation of multi-bit upsets in a 150 nm technology SRAM device. *IEEE Trans. Nucl. Sci.* **2005**, *52*, 2433–2437. [CrossRef]
29. Zhang, Z.; Liu, J.; Hou, M.; Sun, Y.; Hong, S.U.; Geng, C.; Yao, H.; Luo, J.; Duan, J.; Dan, M.O. Investigation of Multiple-bit Upsets in Anisotropic SRAM Device. *Nucl. Phys. Rev.* **2014**, *31*, 195–200. [CrossRef]
30. Chabot, A.; Alouani, I.; Niar, S.; Nouacer, R. A New Memory Reliability Technique for MULTIPLE Bit Upsets Mitigation. In Proceedings of the 16th ACM International Conference on Computing Frontiers, Alghero, Italy, 30 April–2 May 2019; pp. 145–152. [CrossRef]
31. Zhongjie, W. Research of On-board Data Routing Multiplexing and Storage. Master's Thesis, Harbin Institute of Technology, Harbin, China, 2016.
32. Pan, L. Research of Key Technologies of Onboard Mass Storage Base Done MMC. Master's Thesis, Harbin Institute of Technology, Harbin, China, 2017.
33. Qingan, L. Virtual Multichannel Storage Technology for Large Capacity Spaceborne Data. Master's Thesis, Huazhong University of Science and Technology, Wuhan, China, 2019.
34. Hao, Z. Research on LDPC Coding and Onboard Multi-Channel Storage System. Master's Thesis, Hunan University of Technology, Zhuzhou, China, 2024. [CrossRef]
35. Xilinx. *Virtex-4 Family Overview(DS112)*, 3.1 ed.; Xilinx: San Jose, CA, USA, 2010.

electronics

MDPI

Article

Scalable AI + DSP Compute Frameworks Using AMD Xilinx RF-SoC ZCU/VCU Platforms for Wireless Testbeds for Scientific, Commercial, Space, and Defense Applications

Buddhipriya Gayanath *, Gayani Rathnasekara, Kasun Karunanayake and Arjuna Madanayake

Department of Electrical and Computer Engineering, Florida International University, Miami, FL 33174, USA; grath003@fiu.edu (G.R.); kkaru003@fiu.edu (K.K.); amadanay@fiu.edu (A.M.)
* Correspondence: bgaya003@fiu.edu

Abstract

This paper describes recent engineering designs that allow full-duplex SerDes connectivity between a number of cascaded Xilinx radio frequency system-on-chip (RF-SoC) and VCU FPGA systems. The design allows for unlimited scalability with all-to-all connectivity across FPGA systems and RF-SoCs that allow for bidirectional data transport in streaming mode at a capacity of 50 Gbps per ADC-DAC channel. A custom massively parallel systolic-array architecture supporting 8 parallel data streams from time-interleaved ADC/DACs allow real-time matrix–vector-multiplication (MVM). The MVM can be $8 \times 8, 8 \times 16, \ldots, 8 \times 1024$ in supported matrix size, and is demonstrated in real time sustained throughput of 1 TeraMAC/second, for matrix size 8×512. The MVM is the building block supporting machine learning and filtering, with the computational graph split across FPGA systems using the SerDes connections. The RF data processed by the FPGA chain can be further utilized for higher-level AI workloads on an NVIDIA DGX Spark platform connected to the system. We demonstrate two platforms in which ZCU111 and ZCU1285 RF-SoC boards perform direct-RF data acquisition, while compute engines operating in real time on VCU128 and VCU129 FPGA boards showcase both digital beamforming and polyphase FIR filterbanking in a real-time bandwidth of 1.0 GHz.

Keywords: Aurora 64B/66B; DGX Spark; matrix–vector multiplier; RF-SoC; radio frequency machine learning; SerDes; wireless testbeds

1. Introduction

Emerging artificial intelligence (AI) enabled next-generation wireless testbeds require custom compute architectures mapped to field programmable logic array (FPGA) fabrics. While radio frequency system-on-chip (RF-SoC) platforms, such as the Xilinx ZCU111 and ZCU1285, integrate high-speed data converters capable of multi-GS/s operation, their on-chip programmable logic resources are limited compared to large standalone FPGAs [1,2]. This motivates heterogeneous integration of multiple RF-SoCs with downstream FPGA accelerators that provide significantly greater logic capacity, thereby enabling complex digital signal processing (DSP) pipelines at the radio edge.

1.1. SerDes Technology and Multi-Gigabit Transceivers

Serializer/deserializer (SerDes) technology forms the foundation of high-speed interconnects in modern digital communication systems [3]. As the demand for ever-higher throughput grows in both electrical and optical domains, advanced SerDes transceivers now deliver multi-gigabit-per-second (Gbps) data rates to support high-performance computing, cloud datacenters, and next-generation wireless communication networks [4–8]. A SerDes architecture converts wide parallel data streams into high-speed serial bit streams for transmission over differential signaling links, such as low-voltage differential signaling (LVDS) or other high-speed physical layers. At the receiver, the data is deserialized into parallel form for subsequent DSP. This conversion reduces interconnect complexity and mitigates high-frequency signal integrity challenges, making SerDes a crucial technology for scalable and reliable high-speed communication links. In FPGA-based systems, multi-gigabit transceivers (MGTs) serve as the SerDes blocks capable of operating at data rates in the multi-gigabit range enabling board-to-board communication, high-speed memory access, and network interface connectivity [3,9–12].

1.2. The Need for Scalable Compute Frameworks for Wireless Communication

Next-generation wireless systems including massive multiple-input multiple-output (MIMO) systems [13–17], terahertz band communication links [18–21], integrated sensing and communications (ISAC) [22–25], and AI-native physical-layer signal processing [26–29] demand unprecedented computational throughput at the radio edge. These systems must process multi-gigahertz bandwidth streams from massive antenna arrays, resulting in high-dimensional spatio-temporal data that must be handled in real time. While both traditional and modern RF-SoC platforms provide significantly enhanced sampling rates (often operating in the multi-GS/s range), they remain constrained by the limited on-chip processing density for advanced signal processing and AI inference workloads [30–32]. Therefore, scalable compute frameworks that partition workloads across heterogeneous devices are essential, with RF-SoCs responsible for high-speed direct-RF sampling, and downstream FPGA accelerators and graphics processing unit (GPU) clusters performing large-scale digital signal processing to satisfy real-time latency and throughput requirements.

1.3. Contribution of the Paper

This paper focuses on engineering design aspects for implementation of heterogeneous multi-FPGA systems, highlighting approaches to FPGA partitioning, high-speed streaming, and SerDes-based interconnects. We demonstrate two fully realized testbeds in which ZCU111 and ZCU1285 RF-SoC platforms (from AMD Xilinx, San Jose, CA, USA) are interconnected with Xilinx VCU128 and VCU129 FPGA accelerator boards (from AMD Xilinx, San Jose, CA, USA) over multiple 25 Gbps and 20 Gbps links, achieving maximum sustained real-time transfer rates of up to 50 Gbps per ADC–DAC channel. On the downstream VCU128/VCU129 platforms, FPGA-based MVM hardware cores are implemented using 8-phase polyphase decomposition, and the processed data are streamed back to the RF-SoCs for high-speed digital-to-analog converter (DAC) output. Additionally, we demonstrate system-level integration with an NVIDIA DGX Spark platform (from NVIDIA Corporation, Santa Clara, CA, USA), enabling higher-level AI/ML processing on the RF data as part of a scalable, AI-enabled wireless compute framework. The results showcase the potential of SerDes-enabled multi-FPGA frameworks as flexible, real-time DSP platforms for next-generation RF and AI-RF applications.

1.4. Organization of the Paper

The remainder of this paper is structured as follows. Section 2 provides a comprehensive review of related work on multi-FPGA platforms, including large-scale cloud and datacenter-scale deployments, wireless communication and RF testbeds, and distributed AI accelerators. Section 3 introduces the proposed scalable AI + DSP compute framework, discussing the theoretical background of the MVM core and the integration of the NVIDIA DGX Spark platform into the testbed. In Section 4, we describe the digital design aspects

https://doi.org/10.3390/electronics15020445

of the realized prototype testbed in detail, covering the soft IPs utilized, the RF-SoC and FPGA platforms employed, the associated hardware and IP configurations, and the overall system-level dataflow architecture. Section 5 presents the experimental setups and results for both configurations, including transmission coefficient measurements that demonstrate the practical viability of the testbed. Section 6 provides a detailed discussion of the implementation challenges encountered during system realization, along with the practical workarounds adopted to address them. Finally, Section 7 discusses the implications of the proposed architecture and outlines potential directions for future research.

2. Review

Recent advances in multi-FPGA platforms, particularly those interconnected through high-speed multi-gigabit transceivers, have enabled scalable and high-performance processing architectures that are increasingly essential for next-generation RF signal processing, wireless communication, and AI-accelerated systems. Prior work in this area can be broadly categorized into (i) cloud- and datacenter-scale FPGA deployments, (ii) multi-FPGA wireless communication and RF testbeds, and (iii) distributed FPGA accelerators for AI and signal processing. This section reviews representative efforts in each category and highlights the limitations that motivate the proposed scalable AI + DSP compute framework.

2.1. Cloud and Datacenter-Scale FPGA Platforms

Several notable efforts have demonstrated the deployment of reconfigurable logic at cloud and datacenter-scale. Microsoft's Catapult project [33,34] integrates FPGAs directly into datacenter servers to accelerate large-scale workloads such as web search, machine learning inference, and network processing. The Catapult fabric interconnects Altera Stratix V D5 FPGAs in a 6×8 two-dimensional torus topology using custom lightweight serial links providing up to 20 Gbps bidirectional bandwidth over FMC and PCIe interfaces. Similarly, Amazon EC2 F2 instances [35] deploy up to eight AMD Virtex UltraScale+ HBM VU47P FPGAs per node, interconnected via PCIe Gen3, enabling cloud based development and deployment of reconfigurable hardware accelerators. Furthermore, earlier large-scale efforts such as the Reconfigurable Computing Cluster (RCC) project [36] explored petascale computing using network of Xilinx Virtex FPGAs interconnected through custom RocketIO MGT links operating at approximately 2.5 Gbps and employing Aurora 8B/10B protocol cores. While these platforms demonstrate impressive scalability, they primarily target cloud workloads and lack direct integration with high-speed RF data converters or real-time wireless signal processing pipelines.

2.2. Multi-FPGA Wireless Communication and RF Testbeds

In the context of wireless communication testbeds, several multi-FPGA platforms have been proposed to address scalability and real-time processing challenges. The FPGA-based digital wireless channel emulator [37] distributes signal processing workloads across multiple interconnected Xilinx Virtex FPGA nodes to emulate large-scale wireless networks with up to 1250 devices at 1.9 MHz per-channel bandwidth. Inter-FPGA communication is achieved using GTX transceivers with 8B/10B encoding, providing 4 Gbps per lane. In a related effort, the authors in [38] present a scalable clock-synchronization and data-communication framework for quantum-domain experiments, enabling deterministic clock distribution and fiber-based data transfer across multiple RF-SoC and FPGA boards. Their architecture relies on the Aurora 64B/66B protocol for high-speed optical communication, demonstrated using ZCU216 RF-SoC platforms. Similarly, Ref. [39] introduces a modular multi-FPGA wireless MIMO-OFDM testbed based on CompactPCI hardware and interconnected Xilinx XC2V6000 FPGAs, enabling evaluation of spatial multiplexing and

https://doi.org/10.3390/electronics15020445

diversity techniques. While these platforms demonstrate distributed RF and baseband processing, they typically operate at relatively narrow bandwidths and do not explicitly address heterogeneous RF-SoC–FPGA partitioning for multi-gigahertz, AI-enabled wireless workloads.

2.3. Distributed FPGA Accelerators for AI and Signal Processing

Multi-FPGA acceleration has also been explored in the context of AI workloads. The authors in [40] propose multi-chip convolutional neural network (CNN) accelerators that partition computation across several FPGA devices interconnected via the Aurora protocol, demonstrated on Xilinx ZCU102 and VU19P platforms. These works highlight the potential of FPGA clusters for scalable AI inference and training. However, they are not integrated with direct-RF data acquisition and real-time wireless signal processing.

In contrast to prior work, the proposed compute framework tightly integrates direct-RF RF-SoC platforms with high-capacity downstream FPGA accelerators using multi-lane 20–25 Gbps SerDes links, enabling sustained real-time data rates of up to 50 Gbps per ADC-DAC channel. Unlike cloud-centric FPGA clusters or narrowband wireless testbeds, this work focuses on multi-gigahertz bandwidth RF data streaming, hardware-partitioned DSP pipelines, and closed-loop RF processing, while also supporting system-level integration with GPU-based AI platforms such as NVIDIA DGX Spark, for higher-level learning and inference. Therefore, the proposed testbed bridges a critical gap between scalable multi-FPGA compute architectures and AI-native, real-time wireless experimentation.

3. Proposed Testbed Architecture

In this section, we present an overview of the proposed multi-FPGA DSP framework, including its distributed computation architecture, the implementation of the MVM core used for real-time digital signal processing, and integration of NVIDIA DGX Spark platform, which will be leveraged in future work to execute higher-level AI algorithms on the processed RF data.

3.1. Overview of the Proposed Scalable AI + DSP Compute Framework

We envisage a scalable compute framework that leverages the heterogeneous integration of RF-SoCs and high-performance multi-FPGA platforms to enable AI-driven wireless testbeds. The proposed framework is illustrated in Figure 1. In this architecture, the RF-SoCs perform direct RF data acquisition and transmission through their integrated data converters, while the compute-intensive DSP and AI workloads are transferred to downstream FPGAs with significantly greater logic, memory, and DSP resources. The high-speed direct RF sampling rates require the support for both massive parallelism and multi-rate signal processing using polyphase digital systolic arrays [41]. The illustration depicts a subset of DSP and layers of a large multi-layer neural network implemented across multiple FPGA platforms in order to process the incoming polyphase ADC samples in training or inference. Due to the compute limitations in the RF-SoC, only a subset of the neural network layers is implemented, and the remaining layers are executed on the high-performance VCU128/VCU129 boards. Therefore, the output data of the RF-SoC implemented layers is transported through multiple 25 Gbps MGT links, which are realized across the selected FPGA platforms.

A single-layer implementation corresponds to multiple 8×8 MVM implementations. Each MVM core represents an 8 point convolution operation using 8 polyphase decomposition. Here, $f(x)$ is the activation function, which is ReLU/Sigmoid, etc. Each activation outputs are fully connected with the nodes in the subsequent layer. Furthermore, during training stages, feedback information can be transferred to the preceding layers

https://doi.org/10.3390/electronics15020445

implemented on the upstream FPGA platforms through the same MGT links. Finally, the computed results can be routed back to the RF-SoC via the duplex MGT channels and output through the DAC, thereby enabling a closed-loop, real-time wireless testbed capability.

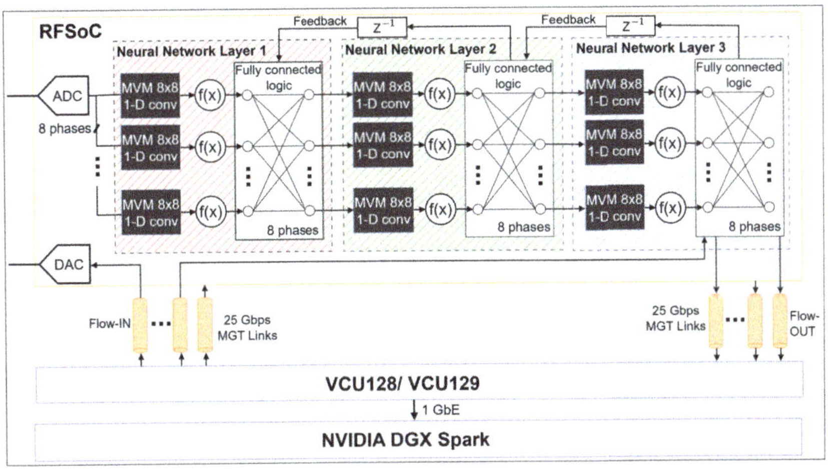

Figure 1. Proposed scalable AI + DSP compute framework.

As an extension to the testbed, the DGX Spark platform is connected to the FPGA system via a 1 GbE interface to retrieve processed RF data for executing more advanced AI algorithms.

3.2. Matrix–Vector Multiplier (MVM) Core

The hardware realized MVM core is a fully parallel multiply–accumulate (MAC) engine tailored for high-speed RF/AI applications. It is built upon an 8×8 block of input samples together with an 8×1 weight vector and performs one length-8 dot product at each FPGA fabric clock cycle. Notably, it performs a real-time convolution operation,

$$y(n) = h(n) * x(n) = \sum_{l=0}^{L-1} h(l)\, x(n-l) \tag{1}$$

where $h(n)$ denotes the convolution kernel used in AI/ML systems such as CNNs, $x(n)$ is a multi-GHz-rate wideband input signal, and L is the length of the sequence $h(n)$. This generic atomic unit can be realized on time-multiplexed or instantiated in parallel for higher-order matrix–vector operations, dense neural networks, and in polyphase finite impulse response (FIR) filters. In addition, the 8×8 MVM core can be used as a reconfigurable processing element (PE) in a tile-based AI + DSP compute fabric as proposed in this framework as illustrated in Figure 1.

In order to achieve higher bandwidths, the MVM core is designed as a M-phase polyphase architecture. Accordingly, M parallel samples are produced per FPGA fabric clock cycle. If the FPGA clock index is q, $n(k,q) = Mk + q$ for which $q = 0, 1, \ldots, M-1$ represents the effective high-rate sample index associated with the q-th interleaved ADC and DAC paths. Accordingly, the q-th output sample for each FPGA clock cycle k is

$$y_q(k) = \sum_{l=0}^{L-1} h(l)\, x(Mk - l - q). \tag{2}$$

https://doi.org/10.3390/electronics15020445

In the prototype, the number of parallel phases is set to $M = 8$ and length of sequence $L = 512$. To support the required 512×8 polyphase convolution operation, the architecture instantiates 64 parallel copies of the 8×8 MVM cores. This parallelization enables the system to compute all $M = 8$ convolution outputs per FPGA clock cycle while sustaining the full $L = 512$ tap processing requirement. The MVM architecture was designed using the Xilinx System Generator (SysGen) tool box in MATLAB R2020a [42] to enable efficient development, verification, and seamless hardware realization. Once the design is simulated and verified, the complete MVM core was exported as a synthesizable SysGen IP. The generated SysGen IP was incorporated into the AMD Xilinx Vivado IP Integrator flow [43] using Vivado v2020.2 to construct the complete digital system and interface with the remaining IP blocks in the design. This IP-centric workflow enables tight coupling between high-level DSP design and the low-level hardware infrastructure, ensuring efficient utilization of FPGA resources. As a result, the prototyped MVM core performs 4096 MACs/clock cycle in a single data path, resulting in real-time operations across 8 parallel data paths processing at 250 MHz on digital fabric, leading to 1 TeraMAC/s throughput. For detailed implementation specifics, the reader is referred to our prior work [44].

3.3. *Integration of NVIDIA DGX Spark Platform*

The NVIDIA DGX Spark platform is introduced as a compact AI supercomputing solution aimed at individual developers, researchers, and students, addressing the traditional barrier of limited access to large-scale datacenter computation, which is implemented as a mini PC [45]. It is based on the Grace Blackwell GB10 superchip, which combines an Arm-based Grace CPU and a Blackwell-class GPU within a single package. This tightly coupled CPU-GPU architecture enables high AI computation throughput up to the petaFLOP scale within a constrained power envelope, making it suitable for laboratory-scale deployment alongside FPGA-based RF systems. The system provides a 128 GB unified memory space shared between the CPU and GPU, which facilitates efficient handling of large datasets and model parameters during training and fine-tuning, while the network connectivity is provided through an integrated high-speed Ethernet interface, enabling consistent data exchange with the FPGA testbed.

In addition to high-speed data converters, Xilinx Zynq UltraScale+ RF-SoC platforms such as the ZCU111 and ZCU216 integrate embedded ARM Cortex-A53 cores, tightly coupled with programmable logic (PL) on a single chip. Using the PYNQ framework [46,47], the hardware is exposed through Python and Jupyter notebook interfaces, enabling researchers and designers to capture and process the acquired RF data in a flexible, software-driven environment. Within this experimental framework, the NVIDIA DGX Spark platform serves as a complementary "AI brain in the lab", providing the heavy offline and near-real-time computational capability required for training neural receivers, channel models, synchronizer, and resource-allocation policies, as well as for conducting large-scale simulations, hyperparameter tuning, and architecture search on the acquired RF data using the PYNQ framework. The trained and optimized models can then be quantized and mapped back onto the multi-FPGA platform for inference, so that advanced AI-driven algorithms, developed using the computational power of DGX Spark, can be executed in real time over the air RF data on the proposed wireless testbed.

4. Digital Design Architecture

In this section, we discuss the digital design aspects of the realized multi-FPGA prototype testbed, detailing the soft IP cores employed in the system, as well as the hardware configuration of the RF-SoC and FPGA development boards. The overall platform is described in two architectural configurations: (i) an interconnected ZCU111-VCU128-VCU129

https://doi.org/10.3390/electronics15020445

system linked through multiple 25 Gbps links, and (ii) an interconnected ZCU1285-VCU128 system operating over multiple 20 Gbps links. In addition, we outline the specialized cabling and hardware interfaces required to implement these high-speed connections in practice, which will help mitigate common challenges in digital-RF system integration for the broader research community.

4.1. A Starting Point to MGTs in Xilinx FPGAs

During our preliminary MGT configuration process, the Xilinx LogiCORE Integrated Bit Error Ratio Test (IBERT) IP for UltraScale/UltraScale+ GTY transceivers was employed to evaluate and monitor the high-speed serial links used in our system. This provides a reliable starting point for configuring MGT links. The IBERT core provides built-in pattern generators and checkers, enabling link verification through pseudo-random binary sequence (PRBS) testing and link status monitoring [48]. We utilized this IP primarily to configure the PLLs, determine the correct clocking configurations, including reference clock sources and reference clock rates for a desired line rate, and to identify the specific GTY transceiver quads on each board for the targeted interfaces, following the XmYn naming convention where m and n represent its (x,y) coordinates of the transceiver location out of the available transceivers. Furthermore, the IBERT design aids hardware-level debugging and validation of GTY transceiver configurations by enabling eye diagram visualization and link status monitoring for established serial connections. This ensured valid transceiver configurations, facilitating reliable point-to-point and loopback connectivity across the multi-FPGA platform.

4.2. Aurora 64B/66B IP Core

To facilitate the implementation of multi-gigabit transceivers for Xilinx FPGAs, Xilinx has developed the Aurora 64B/66B protocol IP, offering a scalable, lightweight, link-layer protocol for high-speed serial communication. As its name suggests, the protocol employs 64B/66B encoding, which achieves very low transmission overhead and improves line efficiency. It supports data lanes with throughput ranging from 0.5 Gbps to 400 Gbps and is capable of both full-duplex and simplex configurations based on user requirements [49]. The Aurora 64B/66B IP core supports the AXI4-Stream user interface, and its simple framing structure can be easily adapted to encapsulate user-specific data or even the data from other protocols, such as gigabit ethernet. Because of its low resource cost, scalable throughput, and flexible user interface, it is well-suited to chip-to-chip, board-to-board, and backplane links, as well as streaming applications [49]. It is designed to automatically initialize and maintain channel integrity by transmitting idle sequences in the absence of user payload, thereby ensuring continuous link activity while reducing design complexity for system integration.

To implement the proposed architecture, we employed the ZCU111, ZCU1285, VCU128, and VCU129 FPGA platforms, each equipped with GTY transceivers. The Aurora 64B/66B IP core is used to leverage these transceiver lanes for data transport at the designated line rates. The core's compatibility with AMD UltraScale+ and AMD Zynq device families enables seamless deployment across the selected platforms.

4.3. Multi-FPGA Prototype Testbed

We envision a scalable data processing pipeline that integrates multiple AMD Zynq UltraScale+ RF-SoCs with high-performance Xilinx FPGA platforms to serve as an emerging AI-native testbed.

The AMD Zynq UltraScale+ RF-SoC ZCU111 and ZCU1285 evaluation kits are employed as the primary RF data acquisition platforms in the proposed testbed. The ZCU111 provides eight 12-bit ADCs operating at up to 4.096 GSPS and eight 14-bit DACs at up to

https://doi.org/10.3390/electronics15020445

6.554 GSPS, whereas the ZCU1285 extends this capability to sixteen ADC and DAC channels with comparable resolution but a reduced ADC sampling rate of 2.220 GSPS [50,51]. Despite the high RF sampling capability, the ZCU111 and ZCU1285 are constrained by relatively limited on-chip logic and DSP resources, with only 930 K system logic cells and 4272 DSP slices, which restrict their ability to implement complex AI-driven DSP workloads. To address this limitation, the acquired RF data is streamed to downstream FPGA platforms with substantially greater compute capacity. In particular, the AMD Virtex UltraScale+ VU37P FPGA on the VCU128 platform provides a significant increase in logic density, offering 2853 K system logic cells, 340.9 Mb of on-chip memory, and 9024 DSP slices, complemented by 8 GB of integrated high-bandwidth memory (HBM), thereby enabling efficient execution of compute-intensive DSP and matrix-based operations [52]. This capability is further extended by the AMD Virtex UltraScale+ VU29P FPGA on the VCU129 platform, which delivers even greater compute capacity with 3780 K system logic cells, 454.5 Mb of on-chip memory, and 12,288 DSP slices, supporting deeper processing pipelines and larger-scale parallel architectures [53]. Together, this heterogeneous architecture provides a flexible and scalable foundation for AI-native RF testbeds, where the RF-SoCs act as high-speed data acquisition front-ends and the VCU128/VCU129 platforms serve as powerful compute back-ends capable of sustaining real-time multi-gigabit dataflows.

4.4. Aurora 64B/66B IP Configuration

When working with the Aurora 64B/66B IP, proper IP configuration and the supporting logic are essential for the reliable establishment of MGT links across FPGA platforms. In our designs, the Aurora core manages GTY transceiver initialization, control character encoding and decoding, error detection, channel bonding, lane monitoring, AXI4-Stream data interfacing, and clock compensation, thereby ensuring reliable high-speed operation.

In each design, the Aurora IP was instantiated with GTY transceivers configured for the respective line rate and a lane count of four. To achieve the interested line rates of 25 Gbps and 20 Gbps, a GT reference clock of 156.25 MHz was used across all FPGA platforms, while the `INIT_clk` was configured at 250 MHz. Each channel was set in duplex mode with the framing interface enabled, and the supporting logic, including clocking and reset modules, was implemented following the guidelines of the provided example design of the Aurora 64B/66B IP.

In addition to these settings, the starting GT quad, GT lane parameter selection, and reference clock assignment should be carefully performed based on the target FPGA platform. A summary of such board-specific settings are shown in Tables 1 and 2 based on the setup.

Table 1. Board-specific Aurora 64B/66B IP configuration settings related to transceiver location for ZCU111-VCU128-VCU129 setup.

FPGA Platform	GT Connector Interface	Starting GT Quad	Starting GT Lane	GT Reference Clock
ZCU-111	SFP28	Quad X0Y1	X0Y4	MGTREFCLK1 128
VCU-128	QSFP28	Quad X0Y7	X0Y28	MGTREFCLK0 131
VCU-129	SFP28	Quad X1Y2	X1Y8	MGTREFCLK0 226

Table 2. Board-specific Aurora 64B/66B IP configuration settings related to transceiver location for ZCU1285-VCU128 setup.

FPGA Platform	GT Connector Interface	Starting GT Quad	Starting GT Lane	GT Reference Clock
ZCU-1285	Bullseye	Quad X0Y1	X0Y4	MGTREFCLK0 128
VCU-128	FMCP-HSCP	Quad X0Y0	X0Y0	MGTREFCLK0 124

https://doi.org/10.3390/electronics15020445

4.5. Hardware Configuration

The prototype testbed is realized in two distinct configurations, which are differentiated by their operating line rates of 25 Gbps and 20 Gbps. The corresponding system-level dataflow architectures for the interconnected ZCU111–VCU128–VCU129–DGX Spark platform and ZCU1285–VCU128 platform are illustrated in Figure 2 and Figure 3, respectively.

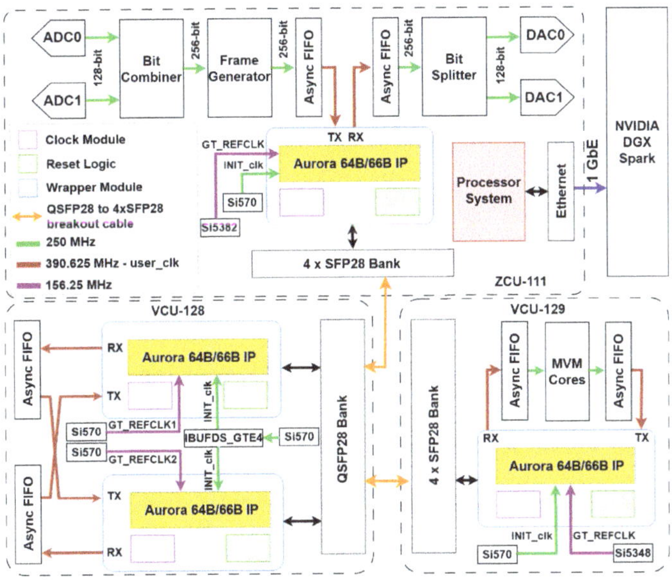

Figure 2. System-level dataflow architecture of the multi-FPGA DSP testbed incorporating the ZCU111, VCU128, VCU129, and DGX Spark platforms.

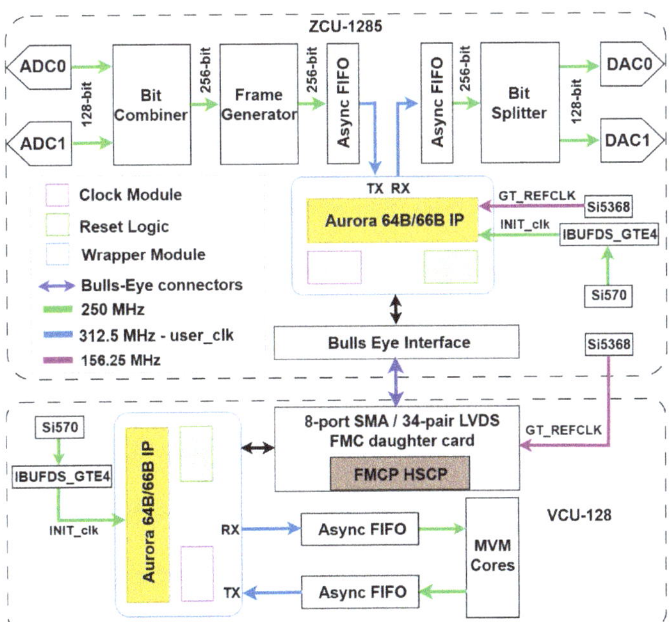

Figure 3. System-level dataflow architecture of the interconnected ZCU1285 and VCU128 platforms.

4.5.1. ZCU111–VCU128–VCU129 Platform: Interconnected at 25 Gbps

In this setup, two ADC/DAC pairs of the ZCU111 were configured with a sampling rate of 4.0 GSa/s. We employed a decimation/interpolation factor of 2, providing an effective instantaneous RF bandwidth of 1.0 GHz for each channel. The number of phases was set to 8, producing a 128-bit output word from each ADC at a 250 MHz FPGA fabric clock. These two 128-bit words, corresponding to the outputs of the two ADC channels, were repacked into a single 256-bit word. This aggregated data stream was then passed to a custom frame generator module, which generated the `_tlast` and `_tkeep` signals to define frame boundaries and formatted the output bus to comply with the AXI4-Stream protocol required by the Aurora IP. Based on the target line rate of 25 Gbps, the user logic interfacing with the Aurora core must operate at a clock frequency of 390.625 MHz. Therefore, an asynchronous first-in–first-out (FIFO) buffer configured in packet mode was employed to manage the clock domain crossing (CDC), with three CDC synchronization stages to ensure reliable data transfer. With the Aurora IP configured in a four-lane full-duplex architecture, where each lane operates at 25 Gbps, the interface achieves a combined throughput of 256 bits at 390.625 MHz, corresponding to an effective bit rate of 100 Gbps (i.e., 4 × 25 Gbps across the four lanes).

The sample data captured from the ZCU111 was then transmitted through its SFP28 interface using a 0.5 m Cisco QSFP-4SFP25G-CU50CM-compatible breakout cable (100G QSFP28 to 4 × 25G SFP28 passive direct-attach copper cables from FS.com Inc., New Castle, DE, USA), and it was received at the QSFP28 interface of the VCU128. The VCU128 design comprised two Aurora IP instances to facilitate connectivity with both ZCU111 and VCU129 platforms. In this configuration, the first Aurora instance received the incoming data, which was subsequently passed through to the second Aurora instance for transmission. Since the `user_clk` signals for the two Aurora instances were generated from independent clock sources, asynchronous FIFOs were inserted between them to ensure reliable duplex operation across the channel.

From the VCU128, the data was further transmitted to the VCU129 board via a similar QSFP28-to-SFP28 breakout cable connected to the SFP28 interface bank. On the VCU129, the AXI4-Stream data bus was routed to the DSP logic (referred to here as MVM cores) and its output is connected to the transmit interface of the Aurora IP instance, enabling the data to traverse the same boards in the reverse direction and return to the ZCU111 RF-SoC for DAC reconstruction.

In addition, the NVIDIA DGX Spark platform communicates with the ZCU111 over high-speed Ethernet using standard networking protocols (e.g., UDP/TCP sockets) through PYNQ framework to exchange RF data and control information, thereby enhancing the overall capability and flexibility of the testbed.

4.5.2. ZCU1285–VCU128 Platform: Interconnected at 20 Gbps

This setup exploits the GTY transceivers available in the ZCU-1285 RF-SoC interfacing through Samtec Bullseye connectors (Samtec RSP-200723-02-BEYE cable assembly from Samtec Inc., New Albany, IN, USA). On the VCU128 side, an 8-port SMA/34-pair LVDS FPGA Mezzanine Connector (FMC) daughter card (from HiTech Global, LLC, San Jose, CA, USA) is employed, connected through the FPGA Mezzanine card plus high serial pin count (FMCP HSCP) connector interface, which provides access to 8 serial transceivers, with the SMA cables from the RF-SoC connected to this module.

From the RF data converter side, two ADC/DAC pairs were configured with a sampling rate of 2.0 GSa/S with an effective instantaneous RF bandwidth of 1.0 GHz for each channel. The line rate was set to 20 Gbps, as the 25 Gbps configuration resulted in insufficient eye opening with the existing physical connections. As a result, the core operation frequency is 312.5 MHz. With the Aurora IP configured in a four-lane full-duplex architecture, where each lane operates at 20 Gbps, the interface achieves a combined throughput of 256 bits at 312.5 MHz, corresponding to an effective bit rate of 80 Gbps. The digital design components used in this configuration were similar to those in the previous setup, including bit combiners/splitters, frame generators, and FIFO buffers. The captured RF data are transported to the VCU128 FPGA and fed to the MVM cores, after which the resulting output is returned to the ZCU1285 and transmitted through the DAC.

5. Experiment Setup and Results

Figure 4 compares the measured eye diagrams obtained using the IBERT eye scan utility under different physical interconnects and line rates. As shown in Figure 4a, the 25 Gbps Bullsye-to-FMC connection shows a severely constrained eye opening, with an open-UI of 0%, indicating insufficient timing margin for reliable operation at this line rate. In contrast, reducing the line rate to 20 Gbps for the same Byllsye-to-FMC path, as shown in Figure 4b, significantly improves the signal integrity showing an open-UI of 44.44% and a comparatively larger open area, enabling stable link operation. Figure 4c demonstrates that for the SFP28 based interconnect, the 25 Gbps configuration achieves a considerably wider eye opening with an open-UI of 55.56%, confirming that the SFP28 based physical channel provides better signal integrity than Bullseye-to-FMC interconnect. These measurements further validate that the Bullseye-to-FMC path is the primary limiting factor at higher line rates, thereby motivating the use of reduced line rate of 20 Gbps for the ZCU1285–VCU128 platform for robust and reliable operation.

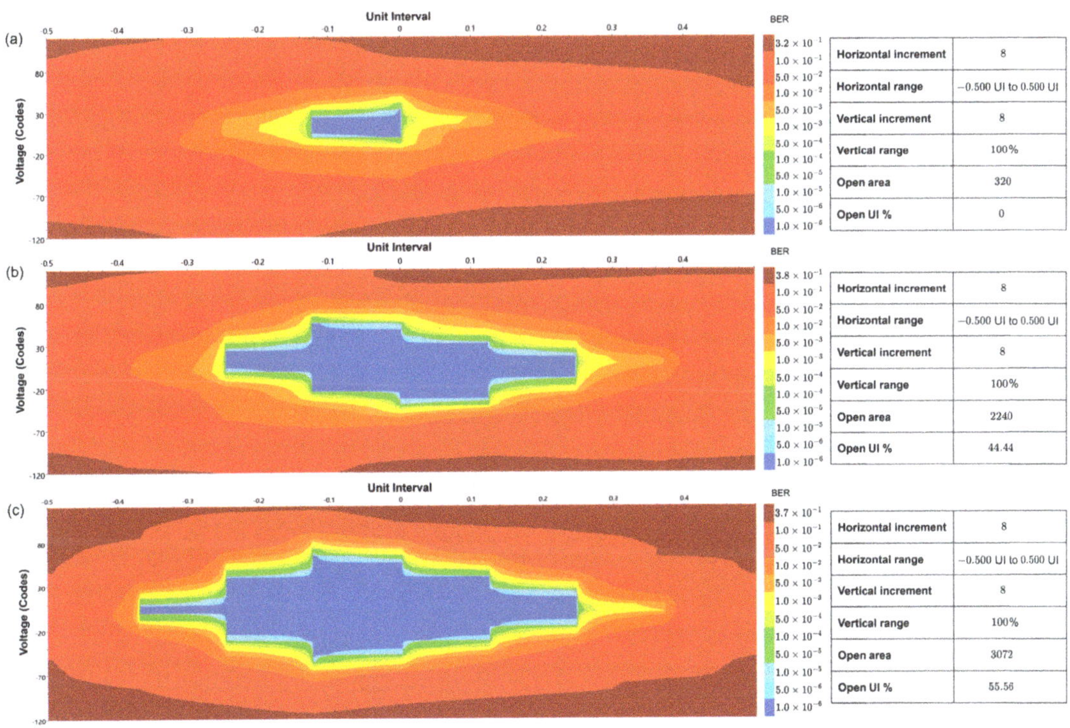

Figure 4. Integrated Bit Error Ratio Test (IBERT) eye diagram comparison for different physical interconnects and line rates: (**a**) 25 Gbps Bullseye-to-FMC connection, (**b**) 20 Gbps Bullseye-to-FMC connection, and (**c**) 25 Gbps SFP28-based connection.

https://doi.org/10.3390/electronics15020445

Figure 5a presents the experimental setup of the ZCU111–VCU128–VCU129 platform interconnected via QSFP28-to-4×SFP28 breakout cables, with the DGX Spark connected through a 1-GbE link. For demonstration, the 512-tap MVM core, configured as a bandpass filter, is implemented on VCU-129 FPGA, with a single ADC sample data stream routed through the entire testbed. The demonstrated bandpass filter's impulse response $h(n)$ is designed using Equation (3).

$$h[n] = 0.974^n \cos\left(\frac{\pi(n-1)}{3}\right) \cdot \frac{\sin(0.15\pi(n-1)/4 + 0.01)}{0.5(\pi(n-1)/4 + 0.01)} \tag{3}$$

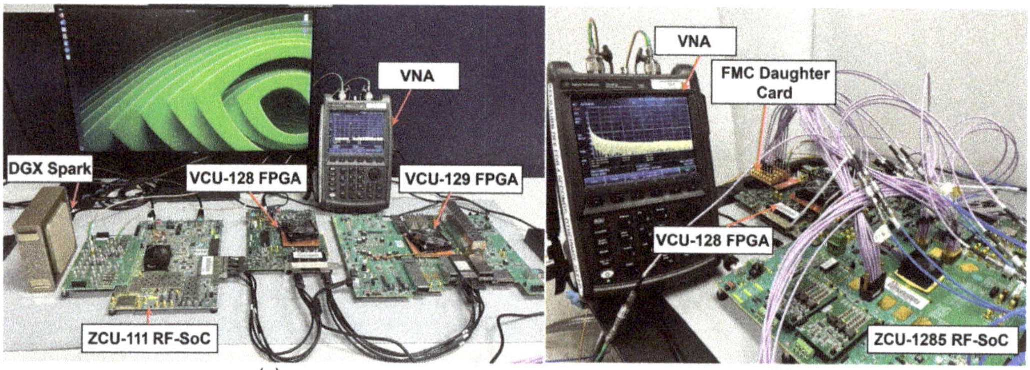

Figure 5. (**a**) Experimental setup of the ZCU111–VCU128–VCU129 platforms interconnected via QSFP28-to-4×SFP28 breakout cables, with DGX Spark connected over 1-GbE. (**b**) ZCU1285–VCU128 setup using Bullseye cables and an FMC daughter card for SMA interfacing.

The transmission coefficient ($S_{21}(dB)$) between the ADC and DAC ports was measured using an Agilent FieldFox N9923A (6 GHz) RF vector network analyzer (from Agilent Technologies, Santa Clara, CA, USA) calibrated up to 1 GHz with 10,001 points. Furthermore, the DGX Spark unit is connected to the ZCU111 with 1 GbE connection as illustrated. Figure 6a shows the normalized S_{21} magnitude response of the implemented bandpass filter. The result illustrates a sharply defined passband over the 320–360 MHz frequency range and strong attenuation across the stopband.

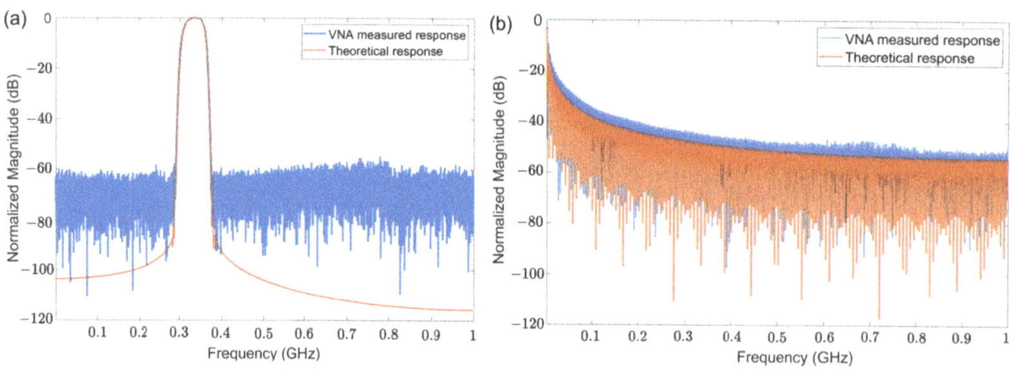

Figure 6. (**a**) Normalized measured S_{21} response of the ZCU111–VCU128–VCU129 setup, with the bandpass filter implemented on the VCU129, shown alongside the theoretical bandpass filter response. (**b**) Normalized theoretical versus measured response of the moving average filter implemented on the VCU128 in the ZCU1285–VCU128 setup.

https://doi.org/10.3390/electronics15020445

Figure 5b depicts the corresponding setup for the ZCU1285–VCU128 platform where the MVM core configured as a moving average low-pass filter is implemented on VCU128. The low-pass filter is implemented with $h(n) = 0.9999$ using the 512-tap MVM core. Figure 6b shows the resulting normalized S_{21} magnitude response of the entire setup. Both measured responses exhibit close alignment with the MATLAB-simulated theoretical response across the full 1 GHz bandwidth. These results collectively confirm the correct operation and practical feasibility of the proposed scalable AI + DSP compute framework across the full RF bandwidth.

In addition, system-level integration of the DGX Spark platform with the proposed testbed was experimentally validated by transferring captured RF samples from the ZCU111 to the DGX Spark unit via the PYNQ framework. This integration confirms the feasibility of extending the testbed toward an AI-native architecture capable of supporting higher-level learning and inference on captured and processed RF data. While this work establishes the end-to-end dataflow and system integration, comprehensive evaluation of advanced learning and inference algorithms on the DGX Spark platform is reserved for future work.

6. Implementation Challenges and Practical Workarounds

The realization of this scalable, multi-FPGA AI + DSP computational framework using RF-SoC and high-performance FPGA platforms presents several nontrivial engineering challenges. This section discusses the key implementation issues encountered during system development, along with the solutions and workarounds adopted. These insights are intended to aid practitioners in reproducing and extending similar high-speed, SerDes-enabled RF systems.

6.1. *Identification of Correct MGT Interfaces and GTY Quad Selection*

A fundamental challenge during implementation was the correct identification of the MGT interfaces and their corresponding GTY quads for each FPGA platform. Each physical connector (i.e., SFP28, QSFP28, FMC, and Bullseye) maps to specific GTY transceiver locations following the Xilinx XmYn naming convention. Based on this convention, accurate selection of the starting GT quad and lane is essential for successful Aurora IP configuration. This required careful cross-referencing of FPGA evaluation board user guides [50–53] and its schematic documents provided on the Xilinx product pages. To validate the correctness of the selected interfaces, the IBERT example design [54] was extensively used. IBERT enabled verification of link establishment through lane and channel status indicators and facilitated confirmation of the correct XmYn mappings for the target interfaces. To assist readers in reproducing the design, Tables 1 and 2 under Section 4.4 list the connector interfaces, corresponding GTY quads, and starting lane selections for each RF-SoC and FPGA platform employed in this testbed.

6.2. *Clocking Configuration*

Selecting appropriate clocking configurations is one of the most critical aspects for stable operation of the Aurora 64B/66B IP at the target line rates. Two primary clock domains must be correctly defined: the GT reference clock and the system clock (`INIT_clk`).

For the evaluated line rates of 25 Gbps and 20 Gbps, a GT reference clock frequency of 156.25 MHz was selected across all platforms. This choice was motivated by three factors: (i) it is the default reference clock supported by the GTY transceivers on the evaluated boards, (ii) the required clock files are readily available through the system controller resources provided by the vendors, and (iii) the same reference clock configuration is recommended in IBERT reference designs for reliable high-speed operation. The specific GT reference clock sources used for each platform are listed in Tables 1 and 2 (Section 4.4).

https://doi.org/10.3390/electronics15020445

The Aurora core additionally requires a free-running system clock (`INIT_clk`) for its initialization which can be sourced either from a dedicated FPGA fabric clock pin or from a reference clock input associated with one of the GTY transceivers. In this work, a 250 MHz `INIT_clk` was used, which consistently resulted in reliable lane initialization and channel bring-up. In cases where sufficient FPGA fabric clock pins were unavailable (specifically on the VCU128 platform), unused transceiver reference clocks were reused as the free-running system clocks. These clocks cannot be directly connected to fabric logic and must instead be routed through appropriate `IBUFDS_GTE*` primitives and constrained correctly in the Xilinx Design Constraints (XDC) file, as described in Ref. [55].

6.3. AXI4-Stream-Compliant RTL Modules

Another significant challenge involved ensuring correct AXI4-Stream protocol [56] compliance across custom digital modules used in the data path, including frame generators, and MVM core modules. Reliable inter-FPGA RF data transport requires strict adherence to AXI4-Stream protocol, particularly the correct alignment and timing of `_tvalid`, `_tdata`, `_tkeep`, and `_tlast` signals. Early design issues were addressed by updating the custom modules to ensure that the `_tvalid` signal was asserted only alongside valid data and by introducing packet-aware buffering using FIFOs configured in packet mode. These changes were essential for achieving stable, continuous data streaming across multiple FPGA devices at multi-gigabit rates.

6.4. Handling Non-Sequential GTY Lane Connectivity on QSFP28 Interfaces on VCU129

An additional practical consideration arose when configuring the Aurora 64B/66B IP on the VCU129 platform using QSFP28 interfaces. The QSFP28 connector maps to multiple GTY quads (Quads 124–127); however, within each quad, only a subset of the GTY lanes are physically connected. For instance, in Quad 124, only GTY0 and GTY2 are routed to the connector, while GTY1 and GTY3 are unconnected.

This non-sequential lane connectivity complicates GUI-based Aurora IP configuration, which typically assumes contiguous lane assignments. To address this limitation, explicit lane selection was performed during I/O planning, ensuring that only physically connected GTY lanes were enabled in the Aurora configuration. This approach is documented in the Xilinx I/O planning guidelines [57,58] and enabled successful 128-bit data transmission using multiple non-contiguous lanes within the same quad.

7. Discussion

Emerging AI-driven RF systems demand increasingly complex computational tasks, requiring scalable and efficient DSP frameworks. In this work, we present a scalable DSP compute framework tailored for AI-native RF testbeds by leveraging interconnected Xilinx multiple FPGA platforms through multi-gigabit transceiver links. We validated the implementation of the platform through two experimental setups. The ZCU111–VCU128–VCU129 platform achieves a combined throughput of 100 Gbps, corresponding to 50 Gbps per ADC stream, whereas the ZCU1285-VCU128 platform provides a slightly lower combined throughput of 80 Gbps, corresponding to 40 Gbps per ADC stream. Integrating both these configurations yields a fully interconnected, all-to-all wireless testbed that enables rapid prototyping of real-time wireless communication systems and beyond-5G/6G baseband pipelines, including higher-order modulation and demodulation schemes, polyphase filtering, real-time spectrum sensing, beamforming, and MIMO testbeds, as well as AI-assisted PHY and MAC-layer algorithms tightly coupled to high-speed RF front-ends. The experimental validation using real-time transfer function measurements across 1 GHz of instantaneous RF bandwidth, combined with the implementation of the

https://doi.org/10.3390/electronics15020445

MVM core on high-performance FPGA platforms, further demonstrates the viability of the proposed AI + DSP computing testbed for broader scientific, commercial, space, and defense applications. Moreover, the integration with the NVIDIA DGX Spark platform provides a path toward executing higher-level AI algorithms on the RF data processed by the multi-FPGA system, enhancing its capability as a next-generation AI-enabled wireless research testbed.

Compared to prior multi-FPGA and wireless testbeds, the proposed system uniquely combines direct-RF RF-SoC front-ends with high-capacity downstream FPGA accelerators and GPU-based AI platforms using sustained multi-lane 20–25 Gbps SerDes links, enabling real-time processing of multi-gigahertz RF bandwidths that exceed the capabilities of existing implementations. Current limitations arise primarily from physical interconnect constraints at the highest line rates, specifically with the ZCU1285-VCU128 platform, while full-scale AI learning evaluations are reserved for future work.

The authors plan to expand the platform by interconnecting a ZCU216 RF-SoC evaluation kit and a Stratix-10 AX FPGA development kit to support wider-band, higher-channel-count heterogeneous RF acquisition. This expanded architecture will enable the generation of advanced, high-fidelity RF datasets that will be highly valuable to the AI-enabled wireless research community.

Author Contributions: Conceptualization and system design by A.M. Multi-FPGA platform implementation and digital designs incorporating Aurora 64B/66B IP by B.G. Digital design and implementation of MVM core architecture by G.R. Integration of digital system with hardware–software co-design using the PYNQ platform and the DGX Spark by K.K. All authors have read and agreed to the published version of the manuscript.

Funding: This work was supported by NSF (under the grant DHARMA.AI 2509389).

Data Availability Statement: All original contributions from this study are documented within the article. For further details, please contact the corresponding author.

Conflicts of Interest: The authors declare no conflicts of interest.

Abbreviations

The following abbreviations are used in this manuscript:

ADC	Analog-to-digital converter
AI	Artificial Intelligence
CDC	Clock domain crossing
CNN	Convolutional neural network
CPU	Central processing unit
DAC	Digital-to-analog converter
DSP	Digital signal processing
FIFO	First-in-first-out
FIR	Finite impulse response
FMC	FPGA Mezzanine Connector
FMCP HSCP	FPGA Mezzanine Card Plus High Serial Pin Count
FPGA	Field Programmable Logic Array
GbE	Gigabit Ethernet
Gbps	Gigabits per second
GPU	Graphics Processing Unit
GT	Gigabit transceiver
HBM	High-bandwidth memory
IBERT	Integrated Bit Error Ratio Tester
IP	Intellectual Property

https://doi.org/10.3390/electronics15020445

ISAC	Integrated Sensing and Communications
LVDS	Low-voltage differential signaling
MAC	Multiply–accumulate
MGTs	Multi-gigabit transceivers
MIMO	Multiple-input multiple-output
MVM	Matrix–vector multiplication
OFDM	Orthogonal frequency division multiplexing
PLL	Phase-locked loop
PR	Processing element
PRBS	Pseudo-random binary sequence
QSFP	Quad Small Form-factor Pluggable
RAM	Random access memory
RCC	Reconfigurable computimg cluster
ReLU	Rectified linear unit
RF	Radio Frequency
SerDes	Serializer/deserializer
SFP	Small Form-factor Pluggable
SoC	System-on-chip
UI	Unit interval
XDC	Xilinx Design Constraints

References

1. De Silva, U.; Silva, H.; Madanayake, A. Augmented Envelope Neural Networks on RF-SoC for Digital Self-Interference Cancellation. *IEEE Access* **2024**, *12*, 44091–44103. [CrossRef]
2. Weerasooriya, H.; Rathnasekara, G.; Restuccia, F.; Madanayake, A. RF-SoC Platforms for RF-AI Spectrum Perception. In Proceedings of the 2024 International Applied Computational Electromagnetics Society Symposium (ACES), Orlando, FL, USA, 19–22 May 2024; pp. 1–2.
3. Athavale, A.; Christensen, C. *High-Speed Serial I/O Made Simple—A Designers' Guide, with FPGA Applications*; Xilinx Connectivity Solutions: San Jose, CA, USA , 2005.
4. Stauffer, D.R.; Mechler, J.T.; Sorna, M.A.; Dramstad, K.; Ogilvie, C.R.; Mohammad, A.; Rockrohr, J.D. *High Speed Serdes Devices and Applications*; Springer Science & Business Media: New York, NY, USA, 2008.
5. Lee, S.L.; Chen, J.; Liu, S.I.; Yang, C.F.; Tsao, H.W.; Hsu, S.H.; Lin, C.C.; Yang, C.L.; Zhang, Z.J.; Fu, K.L.; et al. Development of 400 Gb/s optical transceivers for SMF based datacenter optical interconnect. In Proceedings of the 2018 27th Wireless and Optical Communication Conference (WOCC), Hualien, Taiwan 30 April–1 May 2018; pp. 1–4. [CrossRef]
6. Tang, M.; Zhu, H.; Zhu, Y.; Wang, S. Research of 800 Gbit/s OSFP DR8 Silicon Photonics Optical Transceiver Module. In Proceedings of the 2024 4th International Conference on Electronic Information Engineering and Computer Communication (EIECC), Wuhan, China, 27–29 November 2024; pp. 187–191. [CrossRef]
7. Suzuki, N.; Miura, H.; Mochizuki, K.; Matsuda, K. Simplified digital coherent-based beyond-100G optical access systems for B5G/6G [Invited]. *J. Opt. Commun. Netw.* **2022**, *14*, A1–A10. [CrossRef]
8. Suzuki, N.; Miura, H.; Matsuda, K.; Matsumoto, R.; Motoshima, K. 100 Gb/s to 1 Tb/s Based Coherent Passive Optical Network Technology. *J. Light. Technol.* **2018**, *36*, 1485–1491. [CrossRef]
9. Cho, H.; Ha, U.; Roh, T.; Kim, D.; Lee, J.; Oh, Y.; Yoo, H.J. 1.2 Gb/s 3.9 pJ/b mono-phase pulse-modulation inductive-coupling transceiver for mm-range board-to-board communication. In Proceedings of the 2013 IEEE International Solid-State Circuits Conference Digest of Technical Papers, San Francisco, CA, USA, 17–21 February 2013; pp. 202–203. [CrossRef]
10. De Silva, U.P.; Lokumarambage, A.; Malavipathirana, H.; Mohottala, C.; Thayaparan, S. IEEE 802.3 100Gbps Ethernet PCS IP design challenges and solutions. In Proceedings of the 2016 IEEE Symposium on Computer Applications & Industrial Electronics (ISCAIE), Penang, Malaysia, 30–31 May 2016; pp. 21–25. [CrossRef]
11. Mansour, W.; Janvier, N.; Fajardo, P. FPGA Implementation of RDMA-Based Data Acquisition System Over 100-Gb Ethernet. *IEEE Trans. Nucl. Sci.* **2019**, *66*, 1138–1143. [CrossRef]
12. Ruiz, M.; Sidler, D.; Sutter, G.; Alonso, G.; López-Buedo, S. Limago: An FPGA-Based Open-Source 100 GbE TCP/IP Stack. In Proceedings of the 2019 29th International Conference on Field Programmable Logic and Applications (FPL), Barcelona, Spain, 8–12 September 2019; pp. 286–292. [CrossRef]
13. Marzetta, T.L. Massive MIMO: An Introduction. *Bell Labs Tech. J.* **2015**, *20*, 11–22. [CrossRef]
14. Maruta, K.; Falcone, F. (Eds.) *Massive MIMO Systems*; MDPI: Basel, Switzerland, 2020.

https://doi.org/10.3390/electronics15020445

15. Abood, T.; Hburi, I.; Khazaal, H.F. Massive MIMO: An Overview, Recent Challenges, and Future Research Directions. In Proceedings of the 2021 International Conference on Advance of Sustainable Engineering and its Application (ICASEA), Wasit, Iraq, 27–28 October 2021; pp. 43–48. [CrossRef]
16. Nayebi, E.; Ashikhmin, A.; Marzetta, T.L.; Yang, H. Cell-Free Massive MIMO systems. In Proceedings of the 2015 49th Asilomar Conference on Signals, Systems and Computers, Pacific Grove, CA, USA, 8–11 November 2015; pp. 695–699. [CrossRef]
17. Björnson, E.; Sanguinetti, L. Scalable Cell-Free Massive MIMO Systems. *IEEE Trans. Commun.* **2020**, *68*, 4247–4261. [CrossRef]
18. Akyildiz, I.F.; Jornet, J.M.; Han, C. Terahertz band: Next frontier for wireless communications. *Phys. Commun.* **2014**, *12*, 16–32. [CrossRef]
19. Akyildiz, I.F.; Han, C.; Hu, Z.; Nie, S.; Jornet, J.M. Terahertz Band Communication: An Old Problem Revisited and Research Directions for the Next Decade. *IEEE Trans. Commun.* **2022**, *70*, 4250–4285. [CrossRef]
20. Petrov, V.; Pyattaev, A.; Moltchanov, D.; Koucheryavy, Y. Terahertz band communications: Applications, research challenges, and standardization activities. In Proceedings of the 2016 8th International Congress on Ultra Modern Telecommunications and Control Systems and Workshops (ICUMT), Lisbon, Portugal, 18–20 October 2016; pp. 183–190. [CrossRef]
21. Song, H.J.; Lee, N. Terahertz Communications: Challenges in the Next Decade. *IEEE Trans. Terahertz Sci. Technol.* **2022**, *12*, 105–117. [CrossRef]
22. Lu, S.; Liu, F.; Li, Y.; Zhang, K.; Huang, H.; Zou, J.; Li, X.; Dong, Y.; Dong, F.; Zhu, J.; et al. Integrated Sensing and Communications: Recent Advances and Ten Open Challenges. *IEEE Internet Things J.* **2024**, *11*, 19094–19120. [CrossRef]
23. Sivasankar, S.; Kumarasiri, U.; Lawrance, K.; Karunanayake, K.; Sen, P.; Cintra, R.J.; Madanayake, A. Joint Communication and Sensing at D-Band SDR and at 5.8 GHz via Multibeam Arrays. *IEEE Trans. Microw. Theory Tech.* **2025**, *73*, 3236–3249. [CrossRef]
24. Elbir, A.M.; Mishra, K.V.; Chatzinotas, S.; Bennis, M. Terahertz-Band Integrated Sensing and Communications: Challenges and Opportunities. *IEEE Aerosp. Electron. Syst. Mag.* **2024**, *39*, 38–49. [CrossRef]
25. Pin Tan, D.K.; He, J.; Li, Y.; Bayesteh, A.; Chen, Y.; Zhu, P.; Tong, W. Integrated Sensing and Communication in 6G: Motivations, Use Cases, Requirements, Challenges and Future Directions. In Proceedings of the 2021 1st IEEE International Online Symposium on Joint Communications & Sensing (JC&S), Dresden, Germany, 23–24 February 2021; pp. 1–6. [CrossRef]
26. Wang, C.X.; Renzo, M.D.; Stańczak, S.; Wang, S.; Larsson, E.G. Artificial Intelligence Enabled Wireless Networking for 5G and Beyond: Recent Advances and Future Challenges. *arXiv* **2020**. [CrossRef]
27. Katsaros, K.; Mavromatis, I.; Antonakoglou, K.; Ghosh, S.; Kaleshi, D.; Mahmoodi, T.; Asgari, H.; Karousos, A.; Tavakkolnia, I.; Safi, H.; et al. AI-Native Multi-Access Future Networks—The REASON Architecture. *IEEE Access* **2024**, *12*, 178586–178622. [CrossRef]
28. Xu, S.; Kurisummoottil Thomas, C.; Hashash, O.; Muralidhar, N.; Saad, W.; Ramakrishnan, N. Large Multi-Modal Models (LMMs) as Universal Foundation Models for AI-Native Wireless Systems. *IEEE Netw.* **2024**, *38*, 10–20. [CrossRef]
29. Poddar, A.K.; Mayank, A.; Prabhu, A.S.; Krishan, G.D.; Kasyap P, A. A Survey on Distributed AI Systems: Architectures, Strategies, and Applications. In Proceedings of the 2025 International Conference on Intelligent and Secure Engineering Solutions (CISES), Greater Noida, Gautam Buddha Nagar, U.P., India, 11–13 August 2025; pp. 291–298. [CrossRef]
30. Glover, L.; Maguire, S.; Kerr, J. Software Defined Radio with Zynq UltraScale+ RFSoC. 2024. Available online: https://www.rfsocbook.com (accessed on 24 November 2025).
31. Chu, O. The Future of Radar Technology—Integrating RFSoC with Reconfigurable Computing for Reconfigurable Radar Systems. In Proceedings of the 2024 IEEE 4th International Conference on Electronic Technology, Communication and Information (ICETCI), Changchun, China, 24–26 May 2024; pp. 609–615. [CrossRef]
32. Enbin, W.; Zhaojian, J.; Zhifeng, M.; Deshe, W.; Qiongzhi, W. AI Heterogeneous Radar Digital Back-end Platform Based on RFSoC. In Proceedings of the 2022 IEEE 6th Advanced Information Technology, Electronic and Automation Control Conference (IAEAC), Beijing, China, 3–5 October 2022; pp. 1885–1889. [CrossRef]
33. Putnam, A.; Caulfield, A.M.; Chung, E.S.; Chiou, D.; Constantinides, K.; Demme, J.; Esmaeilzadeh, H.; Fowers, J.; Gopal, G.P.; Gray, J.; et al. A Reconfigurable Fabric for Accelerating Large-Scale Datacenter Services. *IEEE Micro* **2015**, *35*, 10–22. [CrossRef]
34. Ovtcharov, K.; Ruwase, O.; Kim, J.Y.; Fowers, J.; Strauss, K.; Chung, E. Toward Accelerating Deep Learning at Scale Using Specialized Hardware in the Datacenter. In Proceedings of the 27th IEEE HotChips Symposium on High-Performance Chips (HotChips 2015), Cupertino, CA, USA, 22–25 August 2015.
35. Amazon Web Services (AWS). Amazon EC2 F2 Instances. 2025. Available online: https://aws.amazon.com/ec2/instance-types/f2/ (accessed on 24 November 2025).
36. Sass, R.; Kritikos, W.V.; Schmidt, A.G.; Beeravolu, S.; Beeraka, P. Reconfigurable Computing Cluster (RCC) Project: Investigating the Feasibility of FPGA-Based Petascale Computing. In Proceedings of the 15th Annual IEEE Symposium on Field-Programmable Custom Computing Machines (FCCM 2007), Napa, CA, USA, 23–25 April 2007; pp. 127–140. [CrossRef]
37. Buscemi, S.; Kritikos, W.; Sass, R. A Range and Scaling Study of an FPGA-Based Digital Wireless Channel Emulator. In Proceedings of the 2013 IEEE 21st Annual International Symposium on Field-Programmable Custom Computing Machines, Seattle, WA, USA, 28–30 April 2013; pp. 137–144. [CrossRef]

https://doi.org/10.3390/electronics15020445

38. Xu, Y.; Rajagopala, A.D.; Fruitwala, N.; Huang, G. Multi-FPGA Synchronization and Data Communication for Quantum Control and Measurement. *arXiv* **2025**. [CrossRef]
39. Wouters, M.; Bourdoux, A.; Derore, S.; Janssens, S.; Derudder, V. An approach for real time prototyping of MIMO-OFDM systems. In Proceedings of the 2004 12th European Signal Processing Conference, Vienna, Austria, 6–10 September 2004; pp. 689–692.
40. Park, G.; Taing, T.; Kim, H. High-Speed FPGA-to-FPGA Interface for a Multi-Chip CNN Accelerator. In Proceedings of the 2023 20th International SoC Design Conference (ISOCC), Jeju, Republic of Korea, 25–28 October 2023; pp. 333–334. [CrossRef]
41. Gayanath, B.; Karunanayake, K.; Mohammad, H.; Venkatakrishnan, S.B.; Alwan, E.A.; Jornet, J.; Singh, A.; Madanayake, A. D-Band SDR with 64 GHz B/W on COTS Chiplets. In Proceedings of the 2025 International Applied Computational Electromagnetics Society Symposium (ACES), Orlando, FL, USA, 18–21 May 2025; pp. 1–2. [CrossRef]
42. Advanced Micro Devices, Inc. Introduction to System Generator. In *Vivado Design Suite Tutorial: Model-Based DSP Design Using System Generator (UG948)*; Advanced Micro Devices, Inc.: Santa Clara, CA, USA, 2020.
43. Advanced Micro Devices, Inc. Getting Started with Vivado IP Integrator. In *Vivado Design Suite User Guide: Designing IP Subsystems Using IP Integrator (UG994)*; Advanced Micro Devices, Inc.: Santa Clara, CA, USA, 2025.
44. Rathnasekara, G.; Madanayake, A. A Systolic Array Matrix Multiplier on RF-SoC for Wireless AI Applications. In Proceedings of the IEEE Radio and Wireless Week (RWW), Los Angeles, CA, USA, 18–21 January 2026.
45. NVIDIA Corporation. DGX Spark User Guide. 2025. Available online: https://docs.nvidia.com/dgx/dgx-spark/index.html (accessed on 24 November 2025).
46. AMD. PYNQ: Python Productivity for Zynq. 2025. Available online: https://www.pynq.io/ (accessed on 23 November 2025).
47. Karunanayake, K.; Singh, A.; Jornet, J.; Madanayake, A. PanTera: RF-SoC Testbed using PYNQ Platform for 147 GHz SDR with 64 Mbps at up to 2 km. In Proceedings of the MILCOM 2024—2024 IEEE Military Communications Conference (MILCOM), Washington, DC, USA, 28 October–1 November 2024; pp. 111–116. [CrossRef]
48. Xilinx. *IBERT for UltraScale GTY Transceivers v1.3—LogiCORE IP Product Guide*; 4 February 2021. Document No: PG196; Xilinx: San Jose, CA, USA, 2021.
49. AMD. *Aurora 64B/66B v13.0—LogiCORE IP Product Guide*; 11 December 2024. Document No: PG074 (v13.0); AMD: Santa Clara, CA, USA, 2024.
50. Xilinx, Inc. *ZCU111 Evaluation Board User Guide*; UG1271 (v1.2), 2 October 2018; Xilinx: San Jose, CA, USA, 2018.
51. Xilinx, Inc. *ZCU1285 Characterization Board User Guide*; UG1348 (v1.0), 16 July 2019; Xilinx: San Jose, CA, USA, 2019.
52. Xilinx, Inc. *VCU128 Evaluation Board User Guide*; UG1302 (v1.0), 21 December 2018; Xilinx: San Jose, CA, USA, 2018.
53. Xilinx, Inc. *VCU129 Evaluation Board User Guide*; UG1238 (v1.0), 21 June 2017; Xilinx: San Jose, CA, USA, 2017.
54. Advanced Micro Devices, Inc. *Generating and Implementing the IBERT Example Design*; Vivado Design Suite User Guide: Programming and Debugging (UG908); Advanced Micro Devices, Inc.: Santa Clara, CA, USA, 2025.
55. AMD—Adaptive SoC & FPGA Support. *67029—Using a Transceiver Reference Clock as System Clock for a Debug Core Such as IBERT*; 23 September 2021. Knowledge Article; AMD: Santa Clara, CA, USA, 2021.
56. AMD. How AXI4-Stream Works. In *Vitis High-Level Synthesis User Guide (UG1399), Section "How AXI4-Stream Works"*; AMD: Santa Clara, CA, USA, 2025.
57. Xilinx, Inc. *Vivado Design Suite User Guide—I/O and Clock Planning*; UG899 (v2022.1), 4 May 2022; Xilinx: San Jose, CA, USA, 2022.
58. AMD Adaptive Support Community. How to Configure Aurora 64B/66B IP on VCU129 Board with Nonsequential GTY Transceiver Connections for 128 bit Data Transmission. 2026. Available online: https://adaptivesupport.amd.com/s/question/0D54U00008fGDekSAG/how-to-configure-aurora-64b66b-ip-on-vcu129-board-with-nonsequential-gty-transceiver-connections-for-128bit-data-transmission?language=en_US (accessed on 8 January 2026).

https://doi.org/10.3390/electronics15020445

electronics

MDPI

Article

Attention Distribution-Aware Softmax for NPU-Accelerated On-Device Inference of LLMs: An Edge-Oriented Approximation Design

Sanoop Sadheerthan [1,2], Min-Jie Hsu [3], Chih-Hsiang Huang [2] and Yin-Tien Wang [1,*]

[1] Department of Artificial Intelligence, Tamkang University, New Taipei City 251301, Taiwan; 613835031@o365.tku.edu.tw

[2] Innodisk Corporation, New Taipei City 221006, Taiwan; allen_huang@innodisk.com

[3] Department of Electrical Engineering, National Taiwan Normal University, Taipei 106308, Taiwan; mjhsu@ntnu.edu.tw

[*] Correspondence: ytwang@mail.tku.edu.tw

Abstract

Low-power NPUs enable on-device LLM inference through efficient integer and fixed-point algebra, yet their lack of native exponential support makes Transformer softmax a critical performance bottleneck. Existing NPU kernels approximate e^x using uniform piecewise polynomials to enable O(1) SIMD indexing, but this wastes computation by applying high-degree arithmetic indiscriminately in every segment. Conversely, fully adaptive approaches maximize statistical fidelity but introduce pipeline stalls due to comparator-based boundary search. To bridge this gap, we propose an attention distribution-aware softmax that uses Particle Swarm Optimization (PSO) to define non-uniform segments and variable polynomial degrees, prioritizing finer granularity and lower arithmetic complexity in attention-dense regions. To ensure efficiency, we snap boundaries into a 128-bin LUT, enabling O(1) retrieval of segment parameters without branching. Inference measurements show that this favors low-degree execution, minimizing exp-kernel overhead. Using TinyLlama-1.1B-Chat as a testbed, the proposed weighted design reduces cycles per call exp kernel (CPC) by 18.5% versus an equidistant uniform Degree-4 baseline and 13.1% versus uniform Degree-3, while preserving ranking fidelity. These results show that grid-snapped, variable-degree approximation can improve softmax efficiency while largely preserving attention ranking fidelity, enabling accurate edge LLM inference.

Keywords: Large Language Models (LLMs); softmax approximation; Multi-Objective Optimization (MOO); Edge AI; distribution-aware optimization; Neural Processing Units (NPUs) acceleration

1. Introduction

Large language models (LLMs) are increasingly moving from cloud-only deployment to practical edge execution because on-device inference improves privacy, latency, and availability [1–4] and aligns with the broader push toward trustworthy and privacy-preserving AI infrastructures for resource-constrained edge/IoT systems [5,6]. Transformer architectures make this possible through attention, as formalized by Vaswani et al. [7], and later scaled to efficient foundation models such as LLaMA [8]. However, bringing Transformer attention onto edge accelerators introduces a mismatch: NPUs are optimized for dense linear algebra and high-throughput tensor kernels [2–4], while attention includes nonlinear functions that must be computed repeatedly at scale.

Edge NPUs and DSP-class vector engines are designed around integer/fixed-point arithmetic, which aligns naturally with quantization toolchains such as integer-only inference training and deployment methods [9] and practical quantization frameworks like AIMET [10]. This design focus is also why many NPUs do not provide native transcendental units for $\exp(\cdot)$, instead relying on approximation kernels to implement these operators efficiently. In Transformer attention, this limitation is most visible in softmax, which transforms logits into a probability distribution and therefore requires repeated exponentiation and normalization.

Softmax is a core attention primitive introduced with the Transformer formulation [7] and is computed for every head in every layer. Given an attention score vector z, softmax is defined as

$$\text{Softmax}(z_i) = \frac{\exp(z_i)}{\sum_j \exp(z_j)} \tag{1}$$

Even with the standard stabilization step $z \leftarrow z - \max(z)$, the kernel must evaluate many exponentials and a normalization term. In TinyLlama-1.1B-Chat [11], attention is executed across 22 layers and 32 heads, which yields $22 \times 32 = 704$ softmax evaluations per forward pass; this high call frequency makes softmax one of the most repeatedly executed transcendental operators in the model's inference graph. This motivates treating softmax approximation as a first-order systems problem rather than a minor numerical detail.

Recent work on accelerating the softmax bottleneck in attention largely falls into two approximation families. The first—still the most common in deployed accelerators—uses uniform segmentation with a fixed approximation form, because equidistant bins enable constant-time indexing and predictable control flow that maps well to SIMD kernels. This lineage traces back to classical results on piecewise polynomial approximation and joint placement, which highlight the accuracy–complexity tension that often pushes implementations toward uniform joints for determinism [12–19]. Modern uniform designs for DNN softmax include hardware-aware piecewise linear or low-order polynomial approximations [13,18], LUT-centric and piecewise-constant formulations that replace arithmetic with table gathers [14,19], and integer-only range-reduction schemes that reuse a single low-degree polynomial over repeated uniform tiles (e.g., ln2-based decomposition) [15,16]. Large-scale evaluations further confirm that uniform grids are attractive in practice because they simplify indexing (often to shifts/bit slicing) and make performance predictable across inputs [20].

A second line of work targets non-uniform or variable-structure approximations to better match the non-uniform statistics of activations and attention. These approaches allocate resolution unevenly, either by using configurable/non-uniform function generators, multi-LUT factorization, or piecewise schemes whose segment widths (and sometimes polynomial structure) are not fixed [21–26]. This category includes parameterized activation function engines intended to trade LUT size against arithmetic under non-uniform partitioning [23,24], LUT-based softmax variants that introduce irregular segmentation or multi-stage indexing [25], and recent non-uniform approximation units that explicitly optimize the piecewise structure for transformer nonlinearities or general activation acceleration [21,26]. Among these, PACE [21] and Flex-SFU [26] are especially relevant because they demonstrate the benefit of flexible non-uniform approximation, but they do so through dedicated approximation hardware support. PACE integrates a polynomial approximation engine as an ISA extension and uses a comparator-based Part Detector for partition selection, while Flex-SFU adds a dedicated special-function unit whose address decoder performs BST-like breakpoint traversal using SIMD comparisons. Such designs im-

https://doi.org/10.3390/electronics15061312

prove approximation efficiency, but their reliance on comparator-driven partition selection, irregular control flow, or architectural extensions makes direct integration into existing fixed-function NPU inference paths less straightforward. In contrast, our work targets a more deployment-constrained setting: we seek a distribution-aware approximation that can be integrated into the existing inference flow without requiring BST traversal, comparator arrays, or ISA extensions.

This work targets the gap between these two extremes: we aim to preserve the deterministic indexing advantages of uniform designs while capturing the statistical efficiency benefits of non-uniform allocation. We learn non-uniform segments and assign a variable polynomial degree per segment using Particle Swarm Optimization (PSO) [27,28]. To make the learned segmentation deployable in SIMD-friendly kernels, we quantize ("snap") the learned boundaries onto a fixed 128-bin grid, enabling O(1) bin indexing while retaining the benefits of a distribution-aware partition.

Contributions:

- Distribution-aware segmentation: We learn per-head non-uniform segment boundaries that allocate finer resolution to attention-dense regions and coarser resolution to the sparse tail, using PSO-driven optimization.
- Variable-degree polynomial exp: We assign a per-segment polynomial degree (0–5), so most runtime evaluations use low-degree Horner chains, reducing multiply–accumulate work versus fixed Degree-3/Degree-4 baselines.
- Hardware-friendly deterministic indexing: We snap boundaries to a LUT128 grid over $[-20, 0]$ and use a bin-to-segment mapping table for O(1), branch-free segment selection—avoiding a comparator-heavy boundary search (e.g., BST) that is expensive in SIMD NPU kernels.
- Measured efficiency gains: On TinyLlama-1.1B-Chat (704 heads per forward pass), our weighted variable-degree design reduces exp-kernel CPC by 18.5% versus uniform 16-segment Degree-4 and 13.1% versus uniform 16-segment Degree-3, and improves MPS throughput by up to 24.1% and 30.9%, respectively, across large vector lengths, while preserving attention ranking fidelity.

2. Related Work

2.1. Uniform and Fixed-Structure Approximations

Uniform approximation of transcendental functions—most notably e^x—remains the prevailing strategy in hardware implementations because it offers a predictable balance between numerical error and implementation cost. A foundational theoretical perspective is provided by Pavlidis and Maika (1974) [12], who study piecewise polynomial approximation when the segment joints (boundaries) are treated as optimization variables. While variable joints can reduce approximation error, practical accelerators frequently avoid boundary optimization at inference time because it complicates indexing and control, motivating the continued dominance of uniform segmentation (fixed, equidistant joints) in throughput-oriented designs. In other words, many hardware kernels prefer deterministic, constant-time indexing over the additional accuracy that boundary flexibility can provide.

In deep neural network accelerators, this preference appears prominently in hardware-aware softmax designs that approximate e^x using uniformly segmented, fixed-structure approximators. Geng et al. (2019) [13] exemplify this approach by replacing exponentiation with a piecewise linear function (PLF)—a Degree-1 approximation implemented as a small set of linear segments defined over uniform intervals. The primary advantage is hardware efficiency: evaluation reduces to a small number of multiply–add operations and a simple segment index computation. The limitation is that the approximation resolution is "one-size-fits-all": the same uniform step size is applied regardless of how attention logits (or

https://doi.org/10.3390/electronics15061312

intermediate activations) are statistically distributed, which can lead to over-allocation of resources in low-impact regions and insufficient fidelity where curvature is highest.

This uniform-segmentation philosophy also appears in more recent Transformer-specific accelerators. Kim et al. (2025) [17] implement a dedicated hardware block where the exponential is approximated via piecewise linear approximation (PLA) with a configurable uniform interval length. Although such configurability enables design-time tuning of memory-versus-error trade-offs, the runtime segmentation remains strictly uniform over a fixed domain (e.g., $[-16, 16]$) and therefore cannot adapt its resolution to head-specific sparsity patterns or to the empirically observed concentration of stabilized attention logits near zero.

A second uniform family eliminates polynomial arithmetic entirely in favor of LUT-driven (Degree-0) designs. Vasyltsov and Chang (2021) [14] propose memory-centric softmax approximations—such as reciprocal-exponentiation schemes and LUT-based normalization—that replace expensive exponentiation/division circuitry with table indexing and multiplication by precomputed factors. These approaches are attractive for edge-class accelerators because they minimize control and arithmetic complexity. However, their accuracy depends critically on how the input range is discretized and whether the runtime dynamic range matches the assumed stabilization window; coarse uniform binning can degrade distribution fidelity when the attention-logit statistics deviate from the design assumptions. Complementing these method proposals, Leiva-Valverde et al. (2025) [18] systematically evaluate approximation families, demonstrating that low-degree polynomials (Degree-1 and Degree-2) frequently underfit the exponential curve; while higher-order polynomials are required to mitigate this accuracy loss, implementing them within the preferred uniform, power-of-two sampling grids—chosen to simplify addressing via bit-shifts—forces the hardware to incur high arithmetic costs globally, even where such precision is unnecessary.

A parallel line of work achieves uniformity through range reduction, reusing a single low-degree polynomial over repeated tiles of the domain. I-BERT (2021) [15] popularized an integer-only exponential approximation by decomposing inputs into quotient and remainder such that the remainder lies in a fixed interval of width $\ln 2$, approximating e^p on that interval with a Degree-2 polynomial, and implementing the scaling term as a power-of-two shift. SoftmAP (2024) [16] adopts a closely related integer-only formulation for associative processors. These methods are compelling because they provide stable, end-to-end integer dataflow, but they still apply an identical approximation structure across all tiles, although softmax tails often require far less precision than logits near the maximum. Finally, IntAttention (2025) [19] proposes an integer attention pipeline that uses LUT-based exponentiation and introduces sparsity-aware clipping; however, within the retained active range, its mapping remains a uniform, table-indexed mechanism.

Overall, uniform approximation methods dominate because they map naturally to constant-time indexing and SIMD-friendly kernels, making them strong baselines for NPU softmax implementations. Their shared limitation is the inability to allocate approximation resolution in proportion to the non-uniform statistics of stabilized attention logits—motivating distribution-aware methods that preserve hardware-friendly indexing while tailoring segments and computational effort to observed attention distributions.

2.2. Hardware-Specific Modifications and Softmax Replacements

To circumvent the computational cost of the natural exponential function (e^x), alternative approaches modify the softmax operator itself, either by changing the mathematical base or replacing the function entirely. Several works [29–31] have proposed substituting base-e with base-2 (2^x) or employing "Pseudo-Softmax" log-domain simplifications, which

https://doi.org/10.3390/electronics15061312

allow exponentiation to be performed via efficient hardware bit-shifts. More recently, specialized VLSI designs [20,32] have introduced hardware-friendly alternatives that replace exponentials with simpler algebraic operations: Squaremax uses squaring (x^2) instead of exp(x), while other designs exploit Leading-One Detectors (LODs) and bit-shift operations to minimize critical path delay. While these modifications successfully reduce area and power, they fundamentally alter the mathematical definition of the attention mechanism, typically creating a "fidelity gap" that necessitates model retraining or fine-tuning. In contrast, our work targets the standard base-*e* definition to ensure drop-in compatibility with pretrained LLM weights without requiring access to the training pipeline.

2.3. Non-Uniform and Variable-Degree Approximations

To address the inefficiency of uniform segmentation, recent research has pivoted towards distribution-aware strategies that adapt the approximation complexity to the function's curvature or input distribution. This paradigm—allocating finer resolution to complex regions and coarser resolution to linear ones—has been explored across diverse domains, ranging from FPGA generators to secure multi-party computation (MPC).

In the domain of hardware generation, early works like NnCore (2017) [23] introduced automated tools for creating floating-point operators. NnCore employs a "Segment Search Algorithm" to place boundaries based on error thresholds and utilizes "outlier handling" to split segments requiring large coefficients. While effective for generating high-precision operators, resolving these arbitrary boundaries at runtime necessitates a binary search module built from comparators, increasing logic depth. To mitigate this cost, González-Díaz et al. (2021) [24] proposed a hardware-based Activation Function-Core (AFC) optimized for resource-constrained FPGAs. Instead of arbitrary boundaries, AFC restricts segment limits to linear combinations of powers-of-two, allowing a "wordlength-efficient decoder" to identify segments using simple bitwise logic. Similarly, Dong et al. (2019) [25] employed a magnitude-based segmentation for softmax, partitioning the domain into logarithmic categories (e.g., $[-10, -1]$ vs. $[-0.0001, 0]$) to index a Degree-0 LUT. While computationally efficient, these rule-based segmentation schemes are static and fail to adapt to the dynamic probability distributions of attention heads.

In the realm of secure MPC (multi-party computation), Nimbus [22] demonstrated that a distribution-aware segmentation could maintain high fidelity using variable-degree polynomials (e.g., cubic in the "head" and linear in the "tail") by shrinking the active interval to fit the input density. Although theoretically sound, this method optimizes for cryptographic ring sizes and communication bandwidth rather than NPU cycle counts, making its segmentation logic ill-suited for the execution pipelines of edge accelerators.

State-of-the-art accelerators have sought to combine the accuracy of adaptive segmentation with hardware efficiency. Flex-SFU (2025) [26] introduces a "binary-tree search" (BST) hardware unit to support fully non-uniform piecewise interpolation, utilizing an offline SGD-based optimization to place breakpoints. Similarly, PACE (2025) [21] proposes a "Polynomial Approximation Compute Engine" capable of executing arbitrary degrees and partitions, using a hardware "Part Detector" that performs parallel comparisons against learned breakpoints to select polynomial coefficients at runtime. However, PACE is evaluated in floating-point precision and does not target integer-only (INT) execution.

While these architectures achieve high accuracy, they suffer from a common limitation: they require specialized hardware units (e.g., BSTs or comparator arrays) that are not present in standard integer NPUs. Implementing Flex-SFU or PACE logic on a commodity DSP would require software branching or vector-divergent comparisons, destroying SIMD throughput. Our work bridges this gap. Unlike Flex-SFU and PACE, which rely on hardware comparators to handle non-uniform boundaries, we propose a software-defined

https://doi.org/10.3390/electronics15061312

approach that maps learned, variable-degree segments onto a "snapped" integer grid. This allows us to capture the benefits of distribution-aware approximation (like Nimbus) while retaining the O(1) deterministic indexing of uniform LUTs, enabling high-fidelity inference on standard integer architectures without specialized ISA extensions.

3. Methodology

3.1. Workflow Overview: Attention Distribution-Aware Softmax Approximation

The overall workflow can be categorized into two phases:

1. Offline calibration stage that learns per-head approximation configurations.
2. Online inference stage that executes the resulting softmax efficiently on the NPU.

3.1.1. Phase 1: Offline Calibration Stage (Figure 1)

We run representative forward passes and collect per-layer, per-head pre-softmax attention logits $z = (QK^{\top})/\sqrt{d} + \text{mask}$, represented in the same integer domain as the target deployment. Numerical stabilization is then applied directly in the quantized domain via row-wise maximum subtraction, and the stabilized logits are clamped to a real interval $[-20, 0]$ to define a bounded approximation interval that captures the numerically relevant softmax region. Next, we run Particle Swarm Optimization (PSO) [27,28] to search head-specific, non-uniform segment boundaries and segment-wise polynomial degrees for $S \in \{4, 8, 12, 16\}$, producing a small set of candidate configurations per head. The final configuration is selected using a Pareto-style trade-off between approximation fidelity (KL divergence against a floating-point reference) and estimated kernel cost, after which the selected boundaries are snapped to the nearest LUT-aligned grid to enable hardware-friendly indexing. Finally, we generate the per-segment polynomial coefficients offline and export them as compact tables for deployment.

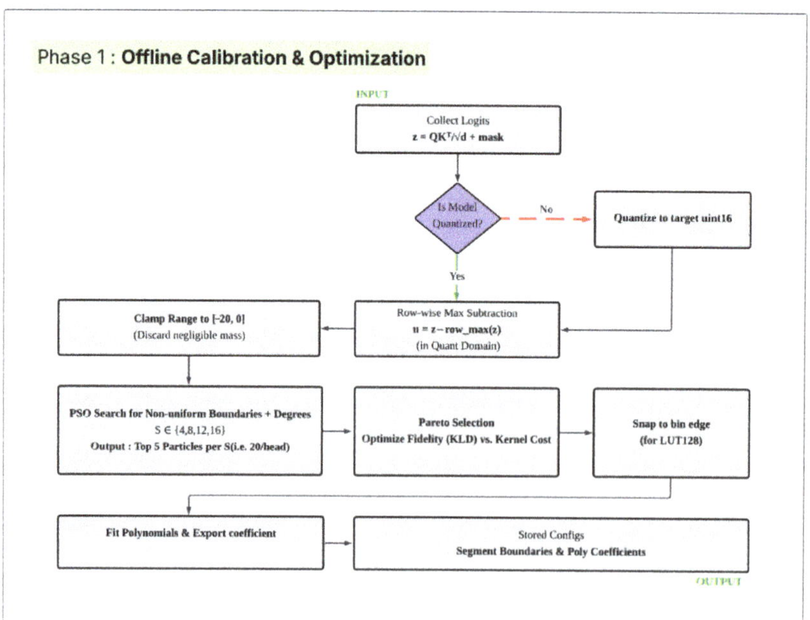

Figure 1. Phase 1 offline workflow.

https://doi.org/10.3390/electronics15061312

3.1.2. Phase 2: Online Inference Stage (Figure 2)

During inference, each stabilized logit is mapped to its corresponding segment using LUT-based indexing. The kernel then evaluates the segment's polynomial approximation of $\exp(\cdot)$ using Horner's rule in fixed-point arithmetic. Finally, softmax normalization is performed to produce approximate attention probabilities in the target quantized format, while maintaining NPU-friendly control flow and arithmetic throughout.

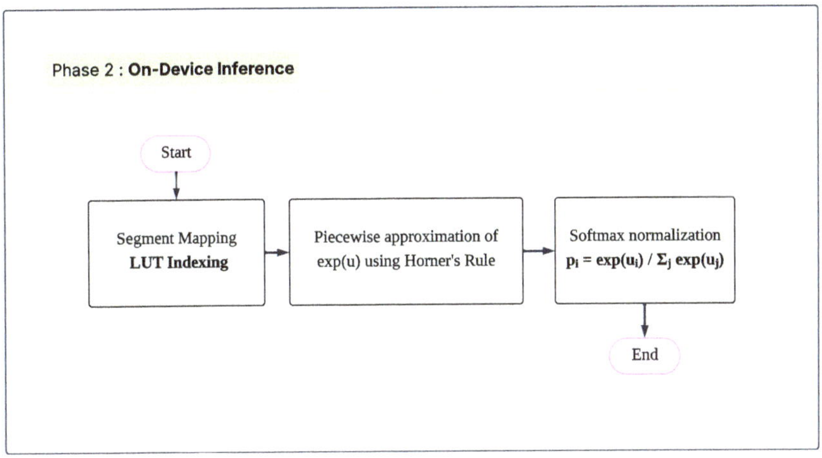

Figure 2. Phase 2 online workflow.

3.2. Detailed Methodology of the Proposed Workflow

3.2.1. Attention Score Data Collection and Statistical Characterization—Phase 1

To design an approximation that matches the statistics encountered during inference, we collect attention score tensors at the exact point where softmax is applied in Transformer attention. For each layer ℓ and head h, we record the masked, scaled dot-product logits

$$z_{\ell,h} = \frac{QK^{\top}}{\sqrt{d}} + M, \tag{2}$$

where M denotes the causal and padding mask (additive form) consistent with the deployment implementation. Data collection is performed on a representative text corpus to ensure realistic token distributions and attention patterns; in our experiments we use WikiText prompts, but the procedure is model- and dataset-agnostic.

Because the target NPU kernel operates in fixed-point arithmetic, the captured logits are represented in the same numerical domain used at deployment. If the model is already quantized, logits are obtained in the quantized representation; otherwise (FP32/BF16), logits are quantized to an affine unsigned 16-bit integer format using the activation encoding parameters (scale and offset) from the deployment toolchain. We then apply the standard numerically stable softmax transform by subtracting the row-wise maximum in the quantized domain:

$$u_{l,h} = z_{l,h} - \max_{\text{row}}(z_{l,h}), \tag{3}$$

so that $u_{\ell,h} \leq 0$ elementwise. To focus approximation capacity on the region that materially contributes to the softmax denominator, we clamp the stabilized logits to a bounded interval $[L, 0]$ (with $L = -20$ in this work):

$$\tilde{u}_{\ell,h} = \text{clip}(u_{\ell,h}, L, 0), \tag{4}$$

motivated by the fact that $\exp(u)$ becomes negligible for sufficiently negative u(e.g., $\exp(-20) \approx 2 \times 10^{-9}$). In addition to enabling a fixed approximation domain, clamping provides an explicit measure of "discarded mass," which we track as the fraction of values clipped at L.

Finally, we statistically characterize $\widetilde{u}_{\ell,h}$ to expose the non-uniform structure that motivates distribution-aware approximation. For each layer ℓ, we compute per-head normalized histograms (PDF estimates) and the corresponding CDFs over $[L, 0]$, and we additionally summarize head-to-head variability using boxplots of subsampled values. As illustrated by the per-head plots in Figure 3 (e.g., Layer 07), different heads can exhibit shifted modes, different tail behaviors, and varying dispersion even within the same layer, indicating that the "important" regions of the approximation interval are not uniform across heads. These empirical statistics provide the basis for allocating more, shorter segments to density-heavy regions and fewer, wider segments to sparse regions in the subsequent optimization stage.

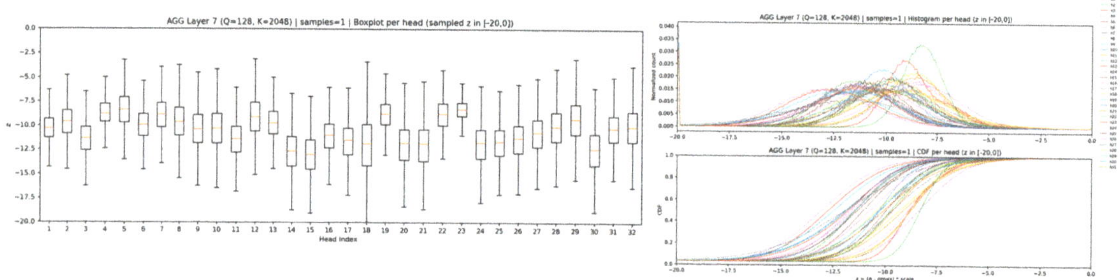

(a) (b)

Figure 3. Per-head statistical characterization of stabilized attention logits for TinyLlama-1.1B-Chat-v1.0 Layer 7 ($Q = 128$, $K = 2048$) after row-wise max subtraction and clamping to $[-20, 0]$: (**a**) boxplot of sampled z values per head; (**b**) normalized histogram (PDF) per head with the corresponding cumulative distribution function (CDF), highlighting head-dependent distribution shifts and tail behavior within the same layer.

3.2.2. PSO Optimization (Boundaries + Degree)—Phase 1

After collecting stabilized attention logits $\widetilde{u}_{\ell,h} \in [L, 0]$ (Section 3.2.1), we optimize a hardware-friendly piecewise polynomial approximation of $\exp(\cdot)$ for each (ℓ, h). The approximation interval $[L, 0]$ is partitioned into S non-uniform segments, and each segment is assigned a polynomial degree. We solve this joint design problem using Particle Swarm Optimization (PSO) because the search space is mixed (continuous boundaries + discrete degrees), non-convex, and the objective must be evaluated through the exact fixed-point inference pipeline.

Parameterization and Runtime-Consistent Segment Normalization:

For a chosen segment count S, each PSO particle encodes a set of segment boundaries $B = \{b_0, b_1, \ldots, b_S\}$ with fixed endpoints $b_0 = L$ and $b_S = 0$, and strictly increasing interior boundaries ($b_i < b_{i+1}$). It also encodes the per-segment polynomial degrees $d = \{d_0, \ldots, d_{S-1}\}$, constrained by an implementation-friendly maximum degree $d_{\max}$(e.g., $d_{\max} \leq 5$ during search, and later restricted to the deployed degree set).

Within each segment s, inputs are not fitted directly as raw $u \in [b_s, b_{s+1}]$. Instead, the kernel uses a segment-local normalized coordinate

$$t = \frac{u - \mathrm{mid}_s}{\mathrm{half}_s} \in [-1, 1], \quad \mathrm{mid}_s = \frac{b_s + b_{s+1}}{2}, \quad \mathrm{half}_s = \frac{b_{s+1} - b_s}{2}, \tag{5}$$

https://doi.org/10.3390/electronics15061312

which matches the runtime implementation that computes mid_s and half_s in fixed-point and maps each u into a bounded variable before polynomial evaluation, shown in Figure 4. Consequently, polynomial fitting is performed on $t \in [-1\ 1]$ to ensure that the learned coefficients are consistent with the runtime coordinate transform and avoid scale-induced conditioning issues.

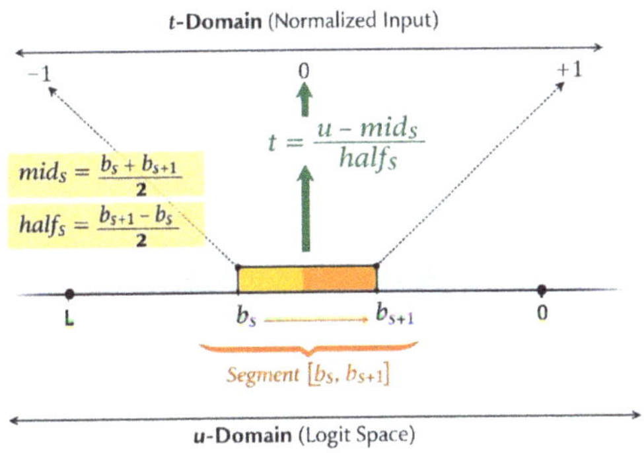

Figure 4. Runtime normalization: Segment mapping to $t \in [-1, 1]$.

To ensure deployability, boundaries are quantized to a fixed-point format (Q30) and forced to remain strictly increasing after quantization. Polynomial coefficients are quantized to the kernel coefficient format (Q31) and evaluated via Horner's rule using integer-like multiply–accumulate operations consistent with the target NPU/HVX kernel.

Two-Stage PSO Strategy:

Jointly optimizing boundaries (continuous) and degrees (discrete) is highly non-convex. As shown in Figure 5, PSO is performed in two stages to improve stability and convergence.

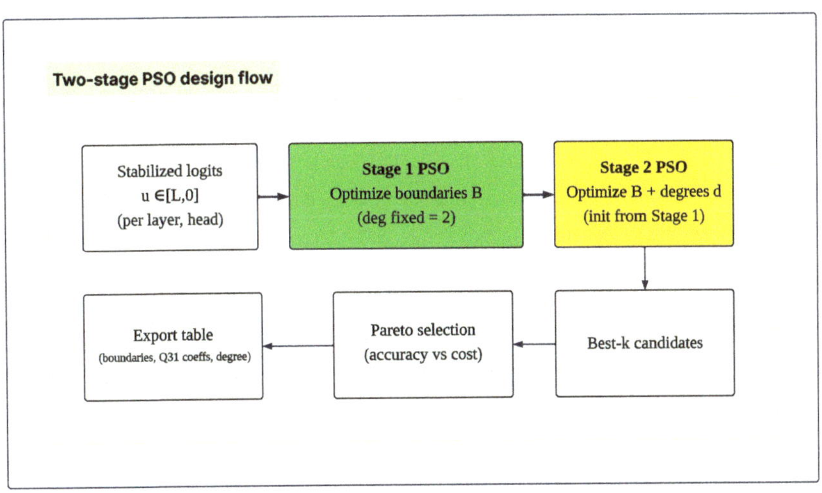

Figure 5. Two-stage PSO design flow diagram.

In Stage 1, we perform boundary optimization with a fixed Degree-2 polynomial in every segment: all segments share the same low-order approximation, and PSO searches only the boundary locations B. This stage quickly identifies a segmentation aligned with the empirical density of u and provides a strong initialization. In Stage 2, starting from

https://doi.org/10.3390/electronics15061312

the best boundary candidates from Stage 1, PSO jointly optimizes B and the per-segment degrees $d = \{d_0, \ldots, d_{S-1}\}$ (bounded by $d_{\max}$). This stage assigns higher degrees only to segments that require greater curvature fidelity, while keeping other segments low-degree to reduce compute cost.

Fitness Function Definition:

Each PSO candidate is scored using an exact evaluation pipeline that mirrors deployment arithmetic and quantization effects. Given captured affine-uint16 pre-softmax tensors (logits in the deployment quantized form), the evaluator constructs a candidate piecewise polynomial $\widehat{\exp}(u)$, computes softmax probabilities in the same quantized output format, and measures divergence against a reference.

Reference ("gold") output: The gold softmax is computed from the same stabilized-and-clipped logits $\tilde{u}$ by dequantizing to real values, applying a numerically stable floating-point softmax, and re-quantizing to uint16 probabilities (deployment scale/offset).

Approximate output: The candidate approximation uses: (i) boundary quantization (Q30), (ii) segment mapping via the same LUT-based indexing used at inference, (iii) runtime-consistent normalization $t \in [-1, 1]$, (iv) fixed-point Horner evaluation of $\widehat{\exp}(u)$ producing Q31 exponent values, and (v) quantized normalization to uint16.

Objective Function:

The PSO fitness is formulated to jointly balance approximation accuracy, robustness, and hardware cost, while explicitly penalizing degenerate segmentations. For each candidate particle, we compute the per-row KL divergence between the quantized gold reference distribution and the approximated distribution, and aggregate robustness statistics across rows, including the mean $\mathrm{KL}_{\mathrm{mean}}$, a high-percentile term (e.g., KL_{p95}) to capture tail behavior, and optionally the maximum $\mathrm{KL}_{\max}$.

To reflect deployment constraints, we add regularizers that discourage pathological solutions. A density penalty promotes non-collapsing segment utilization by penalizing deviations of the segment mass distribution m from uniformity (e.g., via $\mathrm{KL}(\mathrm{Uniform} \parallel m)$), improving stability across heads. An expected-compute term estimates the arithmetic cost as $\mathbb{E}[\cos \mathrm{t}] = \sum_{s=0}^{S-1} m_s \cdot d_s^p$, where $p \in \{1, 2\}$ controls whether degree scales linearly or disproportionately penalizes higher degrees. We further include a flip penalty for cases where the reference quantizes to zero, but the approximation yields a non-zero probability, since this can distort sparsity patterns and ranking under low-bit outputs. Finally, a tiny-width penalty discourages segments below a minimum width (unfavorable for LUT indexing and prone to ill-conditioned scaling), and a degeneracy penalty rejects invalid runtime parameterizations (e.g., segments that quantize to zero half-width and produce invalid inverse scaling values). The final minimized objective takes the form (terms explained in Table 1):

$$\mathcal{L} = \mathbf{KL_{mean}} + \lambda_{\mathbf{rob}} \mathbf{KL}_{p95} + \lambda_{\mathbf{maxKL_{max}}} + \lambda_{\mathbf{dens}} \mathbf{KL}(\mathbf{Uniform} \| m) + \lambda_{\mathbf{cost}} \sum_s m_s d_s^p + \lambda_{\mathbf{flip}} \cdot \mathbf{FlipRate} + \lambda_{\mathbf{tiny}} \cdot \mathbf{TinyWidthPenalty} + \lambda_{\mathbf{bad}} \cdot \mathbf{BadFrac}. \quad (6)$$

Table 1. Fitness terms used in PSO optimization and their roles.

Symbol/Term	Measurement/Definition	Motivation	Impact on Optimization
$\mathrm{KL}_{\mathrm{mean}}$	Mean row-wise KL divergence between gold and approximate softmax	Primary fidelity objective	Improves average probability accuracy
$\lambda_{\mathrm{rob}} \cdot \mathrm{KL}_{\mathrm{p95}}$	Robust tail error (e.g., 95th percentile KL)	Prevents rare but severe failures that can destabilize attention	Reduces worst-case rows; increases stability

https://doi.org/10.3390/electronics15061312

Table 1. *Cont.*

Symbol/Term	Measurement/Definition	Motivation	Impact on Optimization
$\lambda_{max} \cdot KL_{max}$	Maximum KL across rows (optional)	Additional safeguard if outliers must be strictly controlled	Strongly penalizes catastrophic cases
λ_{dens} KL(Uniform ‖ m)	Divergence between uniform mass target and observed segment masses m (on train)	Discourages pathological boundary collapse and encourages well-conditioned segmentation	Produces balanced segment usage; improves robustness
$\lambda_{cost} \cdot \sum_s m_s d_s^p$	Expected compute proxy (usage-weighted degree), p∈{1,2}	Encodes hardware efficiency directly into the search	Favors low-degree where possible; limits expensive segments
λ_{flip} · FlipRate	Rate where gold quantizes to 0 but approx yields > 0	Prevents quantization-induced "spurious mass" that can inflate KL and alter ranking	Preserves sparsity/near-zero behavior
λ_{tiny} · TinyWidthPenalty	Penalty for segments with width < w_{min}	Avoids ill-conditioned normalization and unstable inverse-half scaling,	Prevents boundary collapse during LUT128 snapping
λ_{bad} · BadFrac	Fraction of segments producing invalid runtime params (e.g., zero half-width after quantization)	Ensures deployability and prevents kernel corner cases	Filters out non-implementable candidates

Outputs for Downstream Selection:

For each (l, h) and each $S \in \{4, 8, 12, 16\}$, PSO returns the top-k candidates (e.g., $k = 5$) together with their segment boundaries B (in both floating-point and quantized Q30 form) and degree vector d. Each candidate is also accompanied by accuracy summaries (KL_{mean}, KL_{p95}, and optionally KL_{max}), an efficiency proxy (expected degree), and validity indicators from the tiny-width and degeneracy checks. These candidates are then passed to Section 3.2.3 for Pareto-style configuration selection.

3.2.3. Pareto-Style Configuration Selection—Phase 1

For each attention head (ℓ, h), the PSO stage produces a small candidate pool of segment/degree configurations by running optimization under multiple segment budgets $S \in \{4, 8, 12, 16\}$ and retaining the top-ranked solutions per S. Each candidate c is defined by its segment boundaries $B = \{b_0, \ldots, b_S\}$, per-segment degrees $d = \{d_0, \ldots, d_{S-1}\}$, and the corresponding fixed-point polynomial tables used by the runtime kernel. Because the selection must jointly satisfy accuracy and deployability/efficiency constraints, we treat configuration choice as a two-objective decision: minimize approximation error while minimizing a lightweight proxy for kernel cost.

Accuracy (safety-first filtering): Each candidate is evaluated using the same quantized pipeline as deployment, producing integer softmax outputs that are compared against a floating-point reference. We summarize per-row divergence using a robust KL statistic (e.g., KL_{p95}) and apply a hard safety cutoff:

$$\mathrm{KL}(c) \le \tau_{\mathrm{KL}}, \tag{7}$$

discarding candidates that exceed τ_{KL} as shown in Figure 6. This prevents selecting configurations that may be fast but exhibit rare, high-impact errors in a subset of rows—an important failure mode for attention.

https://doi.org/10.3390/electronics15061312

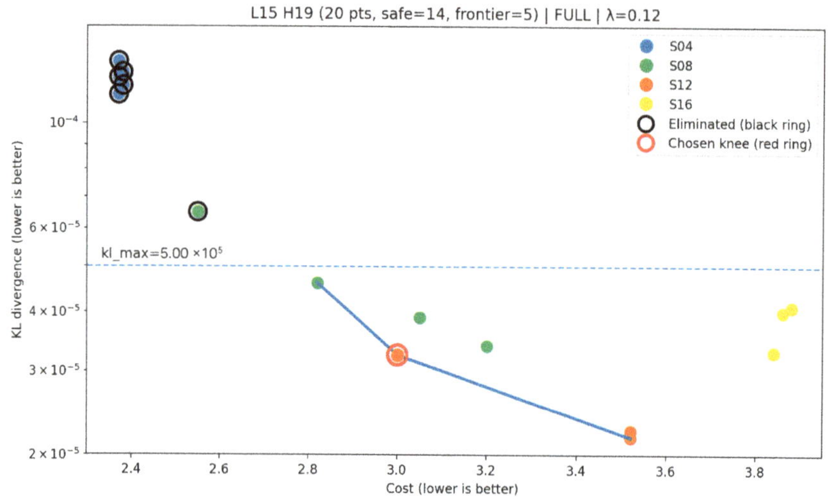

Figure 6. Pareto-style configuration selection for attention head (Layer 15, Head 19) showing candidate designs across segment counts S = 4, 8, 12, 16 in the cost–KL plane (λ = 0.12).

Cost proxy: Among safe candidates, we compute a scalar cost that approximates runtime complexity and control overhead.

$$\mathrm{Cost}(c) \;=\; \mathbb{E}[d] \;+\; \lambda\, S. \tag{8}$$

Here $\mathbb{E}[d] = \sum_{s=0}^{S-1} m_s d_s$ is the usage-weighted expected polynomial degree, where m_s denotes the fraction of stabilized logits that fall into segment s(estimated from the calibration samples). The term λS penalizes larger segment counts, capturing additional boundary checks, table footprint, and control flow overhead. The hyperparameter λ controls the accuracy–efficiency trade-off and can be tuned to a target kernel budget.

Pareto frontier and knee selection: Safe candidates are projected into the $(\mathrm{Cost}, \mathrm{KL})$ plane and reduced to a Pareto frontier (non-dominated set). We compute the frontier efficiently by sorting candidates by increasing cost and retaining only those that strictly decrease the best KL observed so far. From this frontier, we select a single "knee" configuration that achieves most of the attainable KL reduction before diminishing returns set in. Concretely, for consecutive frontier points (c_{i-1}, c_i), we define the marginal gain:

$$g_i \;=\; \frac{\mathrm{KL}(c_{i-1}) - \mathrm{KL}(c_i)}{\mathrm{Cost}(c_i) - \mathrm{Cost}(c_{i-1})}, \tag{9}$$

and choose the last point before the gain drops sharply (e.g., below a fixed fraction of the previous gain). This rule prefers solutions that are meaningfully more accurate per unit cost, rather than simply selecting the most accurate (often most expensive) configuration.

Fallback policy: If no candidate satisfies the safety threshold for a given head, we fall back to the candidate with the minimum KL (and, secondarily, lower cost). This ensures every head receives a deployable configuration while preserving the conservative bias toward accuracy.

3.2.4. LUT128 Boundary Quantization (Snap to LUT Bin's Edge)—Phase 1

To reduce runtime control overhead and enable fast segment mapping, the selected per-head segmentation can be aligned to a uniform LUT128 grid (Figure 7) over the stabilized logit interval $[L, 0]$ (with $L = -20$ in our implementation). We define LUT

https://doi.org/10.3390/electronics15061312

edges $\{e_0, \ldots, e_{128}\}$ with spacing $\Delta = (0 - L)/128 = 20/128$, and quantize each optimized boundary b_i to its nearest LUT edge,

$$\hat{b}_i = \arg \min_{e \in \{e_0, \ldots, e_{128}\}} \mid b_i - e \mid, \tag{10}$$

with endpoints fixed to $\hat{b}_0 = L$ and $\hat{b}_S = 0$. This representation enables constant-time LUT indexing to determine the segment, avoiding per-element boundary search. This is important on NPUs, where compare-heavy control flow (e.g., BST-based boundary search) can be disproportionately expensive due to branching, reduced SIMD utilization, and pipeline disruption in fixed-function kernels.

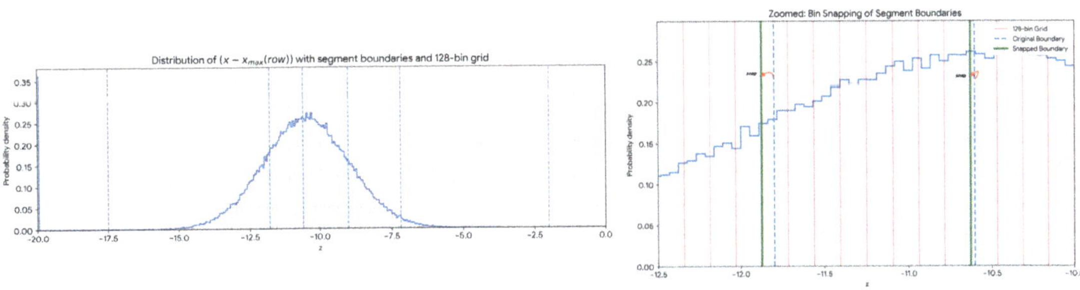

(**a**) (**b**)

Figure 7. Segment boundary snapping visualization. (**a**) Distribution overview showing the 128-bin grid (red) and calculated boundaries (blue). (**b**) Zoomed detail illustrating the snapping of boundaries to the nearest hardware bin edge (green).

The quantitative accuracy impact of this snapping step is reported later in Section 5.2.

Boundary collision handling:

A key risk in grid snapping is boundary collision, where two adjacent interior boundaries fall within the same LUT bin and become indistinguishable after quantization. We incorporate LUT feasibility directly into the offline PSO search by enforcing a minimum effective segment width equal to the LUT resolution. Concretely, PSO includes a tiny-width penalty that discourages any segment width $w_s = b_{s+1} - b_s$ smaller than $\Delta = 20/128$. By penalizing $w_s < \Delta$, the search avoids configurations that would collapse under LUT128 snapping, ensuring that the snapped boundary indices remain strictly increasing and that LUT-based segment mapping remains unambiguous at runtime.

3.2.5. Fixed-Point Coefficient Generation—Phase 1

After boundary snapping (Section 3.2.4, Boundary snapping and collision handling), we generate segment-wise polynomial coefficients for approximating $\exp(u)$ in a form that is runtime-compatible with the NPU kernel. The central goal is to avoid a fit–deploy mismatch: coefficients are not fit in an idealized continuous domain, but instead in the same normalized variable that the kernel computes using integer midpoints, half-widths, and fixed-point scaling.

Runtime-consistent segment normalization:

For each attention head, the finalized boundary vector $B = \{b_0, \ldots, b_S\}$ is converted to Q30:

$$b_i^{(Q30)} = \text{round}\left(b_i \cdot 2^{30}\right). \tag{11}$$

https://doi.org/10.3390/electronics15061312

For each segment $s \in \{0, \ldots, S-1\}$, the kernel operates using an integer midpoint and half-width

$$\text{mid}_s^{(Q30)} = \left\lfloor \frac{b_s^{(Q30)} + b_{s+1}^{(Q30)}}{2} \right\rfloor, \text{half}_s^{(Q30)} = \left\lfloor \frac{b_{s+1}^{(Q30)} - b_s^{(Q30)}}{2} \right\rfloor, \tag{12}$$

and a reciprocal for normalization (guarded against $\text{half}_s^{(Q30)} = 0$):

$$\text{invHalf}_s^{(Q48)} = \left\lfloor \frac{2^{48}}{\text{half}_s^{(Q30)}} \right\rfloor. \tag{13}$$

Given a stabilized/clipped input $u^{(Q30)}$ inside the segment, runtime computes a normalized coordinate $t \in [-1,1]$ in Q15 (with rounding/saturation). We fit using the same mapping,

$$t^{(Q15)} = \text{clip}\left(\text{sign}(\delta) \cdot \left\lfloor \frac{|\,\delta\,| \cdot \text{invHalf}_s^{(Q48)}}{2^{48}} \right\rfloor, -2^{15}, 2^{15}-1\right), \delta = \left(u^{(Q30)} - \text{mid}_s^{(Q30)}\right) \cdot 2^{15}, \tag{14}$$

and use $t = t^{(Q15)}/2^{15}$ as the regressor variable during coefficient synthesis.

Segment-wise sampling and polynomial fitting:

For each segment s, we generate sample points using Chebyshev nodes over $[-1,1]$, which reduces oscillations and improves stability for polynomial approximation. These nodes are mapped into the segment using the integer midpoint/half-width:

$$u_k^{(Q30)} = \text{round}(\text{mid}_s^{(Q30)} + \text{half}_s^{(Q30)} \cdot t_k), t_k \in [-1,1]. \tag{15}$$

Targets are computed in real space:

$$y_k = \exp\left(\frac{u_k^{(Q30)}}{2^{30}}\right), \tag{16}$$

while the input to fitting is the runtime-derived t_k obtained from the Q15 normalization path above. A per-segment polynomial of degree d_s (selected by PSO/Pareto) is fitted in the power basis:

$$P_s(t) = \sum_{i=0}^{d_s} c_{s,i} t^i, \tag{17}$$

using standard least-squares fitting on the generated samples. Degenerate cases are handled conservatively: if $d_s = 0$ or $\text{half}_s^{(Q30)} \leq 0$, the segment uses a constant midpoint approximation

$$P_s(t) = \exp\left(\frac{\text{mid}_s^{(Q30)}}{2^{30}}\right). \tag{18}$$

Coefficient quantization and export:

The fitted floating-point coefficients are quantized to Q31 for direct use in fixed-point Horner evaluation:

$$c_{s,i}^{(Q31)} = \text{sat}\left(\text{round}\left(c_{s,i} \cdot 2^{31}\right)\right), \text{sat}(\cdot) \in \left[-2^{31}, 2^{31}-1\right]. \tag{19}$$

The resulting per-head table stores the finalized LUT-aligned boundaries, the per-segment degrees $\{d_s\}$, and the corresponding per-segment coefficient vectors $\left\{c_{s,0}^{(Q31)}, \ldots, c_{s,d_s}^{(Q31)}\right\}$. These

https://doi.org/10.3390/electronics15061312

tables are exported as compact JSON artifacts or in a suitable format and can be loaded directly by the deployment kernel, ensuring that the offline approximation is consistent with runtime scaling, normalization, and fixed-point arithmetic.

3.2.6. Runtime Execution of the Distribution-Aware Softmax On-Device—Phase 2

At deployment time, the proposed method replaces the floating-point softmax inside attention with a table-driven, fixed-point kernel parameterized by the offline outputs from Section 3.2.5. The kernel consumes stabilized attention logits and produces quantized attention probabilities using only NPU-friendly integer arithmetic and constant-time table lookup.

Runtime inputs and stabilization (integer-domain):

Given the masked attention score matrix $z = QK^{\top}/\sqrt{d} + \text{mask}$, we apply per-row stabilization by subtracting the row maximum, $u = z - \max(z)$, which guarantees $u \le 0$. We then clamp u to the approximation domain via $u \leftarrow \text{clip}(u, [L, 0])$, with $L = -20$ in our implementation. This bounds the approximation to the numerically relevant region where the softmax probability mass concentrates.

Segment mapping using LUT128 (no boundary search, no int64 required):

To avoid compare-heavy boundary search (e.g., BST), the runtime kernel uses a uniform LUT128 grid over $[L, 0]$. Let LUT edges (e_j) be

$$e_j = L + j\Delta, \;\; j \in \{0, \ldots, 128\}, \;\; \Delta = \frac{0 - L}{128}. \tag{20}$$

Each stabilized element $u \in [L, 0]$ is mapped to a LUT bin index(b):

$$b = \text{clip}\left(\left\lfloor \frac{u - L}{\Delta} \right\rfloor, 0, 127\right). \tag{21}$$

Key deployment detail: After the snapping step in Section 3.2.4, all segment boundaries align with LUT bin edges, eliminating the need to store floating-point boundaries (or int64 values) for runtime selection. Instead, we use a compact lookup table $bin\_to\_seg[128]$ that maps each LUT bin b directly to a segment ID $s \in \{0, \ldots, S-1\}$. This design enables $O(1)$ per-element segment selection, is branch-free and SIMD-friendly, and does not rely on int64 support.

Normalized coordinate per segment (Q15), using precomputed mid/half tables:

For the selected segment s, the kernel approximates $\exp(u)$ using a polynomial evaluated on a canonical variable $t \in [-1, 1]$. Runtime uses the per-segment precomputed constants mid_s, half_s, and invHalf_s, derived from the snapped LUT indices, and computes $t^{(Q15)}$ using the same fixed-point mapping (rounding/saturation) as in Section 3.2.5 (conceptually, $t \approx \frac{u - \text{mid}_s}{\text{half}_s}$ scaled to Q15 and saturated to $[-2^{15}, 2^{15} - 1]$).

Implementation note: Because mid and half are derived from LUT bin edges, they can be represented compactly and computed using 32-bit arithmetic. Consequently, the inference kernel avoids Q30 int64 operations and requires only the LUT bin index b, the corresponding segment ID s, and the precomputed per-segment mid/half/reciprocal tables.

Fixed-point polynomial evaluation of $\exp(\cdot)$ using Horner's rule (Q31 $\times$ Q15 $\rightarrow$ Q31):

For each segment s, the offline generator produces the selected degree d_s and the corresponding coefficient set $\{c_{s,0}, \ldots, c_{s,d_s}\}$, quantized to signed Q31 and stored as int32. The polynomial is

$$P_s(t) = c_{s,0} + c_{s,1}t + \ldots + c_{s,d_s}t^{d_s}, t \in [-1, 1]. \tag{22}$$

https://doi.org/10.3390/electronics15061312

Runtime evaluates it in Horner form:

$$\hat{\exp}(u) = P_s(t) = (\ldots((c_{s,d_s}t + c_{s,d_s-1})t + \ldots)t + c_{s,1})t + c_{s,0}. \tag{23}$$

Horner step in fixed-point:

Let t be Q15 (int16) and the accumulator y be Q31 (int32). Each step performs one multiply–accumulate:

$$y \leftarrow \mathrm{sat}_{32}\left(\mathrm{rnd}\left(\frac{y \cdot t^{(Q15)}}{2^{15}}\right) + c_{s,k}^{(Q31)}\right), k = d_s - 1, \ldots, 0 \tag{24}$$

here, $\mathrm{rnd}(\cdot)$ denotes integer rounding applied before the shift, and $\mathrm{sat}_{32}(\cdot)$ denotes saturation to the signed 32-bit range.

This structure matches the HVX-style implementation pattern (coefficient lookup + Horner MAC chain) while keeping arithmetic in 16/32-bit lanes, which is preferred for NPU/DSP vector kernels.

Softmax normalization in quantized domain:

After computing $\hat{\exp}(u)$ for all elements in a row, the kernel completes softmax with integer normalization:

$$\hat{p}_i = \frac{\hat{\exp}(u_i)}{\sum_j \hat{\exp}(u_j)}. \tag{25}$$

The result is then quantized to the deployment probability format (e.g., u16 "counts" using the target softmax scale/offset), using integer division with rounding.

3.2.7. Runtime Table Storage and Deployment Footprint

At deployment time, the proposed kernel stores only compact integer runtime tables; floating-point boundaries are not retained. For each head, the runtime state consists of the bin_to_seg [128] lookup table, the per-segment degree metadata, the per-segment normalization constants (mid, half, and invHalf), and the per-segment Q31 polynomial coefficients Table 2. The values mid, half, and invHalf are stored explicitly rather than derived online. This choice is intentional: while mid and half are derivable from snapped segment boundaries, invHalf requires a reciprocal/division operation, which is comparatively expensive in the target fixed-point kernel. Precomputing and storing these terms, therefore, reduces runtime arithmetic and keeps the normalization path simple and predictable.

Table 2. Runtime storage breakdown per head for the proposed table-driven kernel (variable segment count S).

Item	Entries per Head	Type	Bytes per Entry	Bytes per Head
bin_to_seg [128]	128	uint8	1	128
Per-segment degree	S	uint8	1	S
Per-segment mid	S	int32	4	$4S$
Per-segment half	S	int32	4	$4S$
Per-segment invHalf	S	int32	4	$4S$
Per-segment polynomial coefficients $c_{s,i}$	$\sum_{s=0}^{S-1}(d_s+1)$	int32	4	$4\sum_{s=0}^{S-1}(d_s+1)$
Total	—	—	—	$128 + 13S + 4\sum_{s=0}^{S-1}(d_s+1)$

For the 16-segment configuration used in our experiments, the storage expression reduces to $336 + 4\sum_{s=0}^{15}(d_s+1)$ bytes per head. If all heads in TinyLlama-1.1B-Chat (704 heads total) are instantiated as 16-segment heads, the overall runtime table storage is approxi-

https://doi.org/10.3390/electronics15061312

mately 374 KB when the observed weighted-average degree is used as a practical proxy, and 462 KB in the fixed Degree-4 upper-bound case. This confirms that the total deployment footprint of the proposed per-head tables remains compact for edge-oriented inference. Although our implementation and measurements were carried out on a v73 Hexagon Tensor Processor platform, this storage formulation is not specific to one vendor or device family; it follows directly from the generic table-driven fixed-point runtime design. On the representative v73-class platform considered here, the reported memory hierarchy includes an L1 data cache of at least 32 KB, an L2 cache of at least 512 KB, and 8 MB of tightly coupled memory (TCM) [33]. Under these reference capacities, the full 374–462 KB table footprint exceeds L1 capacity but remains within the scale of L2 and is small relative to TCM, while the active per-head working set is substantially smaller. The exact residency of these tables within the memory hierarchy depends on the runtime's allocation and scheduling policy.

4. Experimental Setup

4.1. Hardware and Deployment Environment

We evaluate the proposed distribution-aware softmax in a mixed workflow that mirrors the practical constraints of deploying custom attention operators on edge NPUs.

Phase 1 (offline, x86 Linux):

All offline steps—attention-logit collection, PSO-based segmentation/degree search, Pareto-style configuration selection, LUT128 boundary snapping, and Q-format coefficient generation—are executed on an x86 Linux platform. This phase produces per-layer/per-head kernel parameters (LUT-aligned boundaries, per-segment degrees, and quantized polynomial coefficients).

Phase 2 (deployment-oriented, mixed device + on-device benchmarking):

We use a mixed setup consisting of a Qualcomm IQ9 Series development platform (Qualcomm Technologies, Inc., San Diego, CA, USA) together with x86 fixed-point simulations. This mixed approach is necessary because Qualcomm AI Engine Direct SDK (Qualcomm Technologies, Inc., San Diego, CA, USA) [34] is closed-source, and direct custom-op support for generative-model attention/softmax kernels is limited. We validate runtime feasibility and performance primarily through the direct on-device HTP-v73 benchmarking toolchain, ensuring the full runtime path is implementable using only integer operations consistent with HVX/HTP support (int16/int32 arithmetic, saturating behavior, and vector-friendly control flow).

4.2. Model and Workloads

We use TinyLlama/TinyLlama-1.1B-Chat-v1.0 [11], a LLaMA-family [8] decoder-only Transformer. The model configuration includes 22 Transformer layers, hidden size 2048, 32 attention heads, 4 key/value heads (GQA), intermediate size 5632, vocabulary size 32,000, and maximum positional embeddings of 2048.

To match the fixed-shape execution constraints commonly required by NPUs, we evaluate attention softmax using a context length $K = 2048$ and a fixed chunk (query) length $Q = 128$. This corresponds to the common "prefill + chunked decode" pattern, where the softmax shape during the chunk phase is $[B, H, Q, K]$ with $Q = 128$, $K = 2048$.

Data for attention-logit collection:

To obtain realistic long-form text for collecting attention logits, we draw passages from the Wikimedia Wikipedia dataset hosted on Hugging Face [35]. We use a fixed language snapshot specified by the dataset configuration (default: `20231101.en`, i.e., the English

https://doi.org/10.3390/electronics15061312

Wikipedia dump dated 1 November 2023). Passages are extracted from the dataset's train split in standard mode to simulate a continuous data ingestion pipeline.

Clamp Range Selection:

In the subsequent approximation experiments, the lower clamp bound was fixed to $L = -20$ based on the observed stabilized-logit distributions across heads in TinyLlama, balancing tail coverage against unnecessary expansion of the approximation domain.

Generality Across Workloads

To examine whether the learned segmentation transfers beyond the calibration workload, we additionally evaluated the proposed approximation on two domain-shifted text sources: a coding corpus [36] and a biomedical corpus [37]. Table 3 summarizes the results across all 704 attention heads. In both cases, the proposed method preserved perfect Top-1 agreement with the gold softmax while maintaining high top-k overlap and low KL divergence. This indicates that the learned segmentation transfers well under moderate workload shift and does not require mandatory recalibration for general-purpose deployment.

Table 3. Cross-workload transfer of the learned segmentation (vs. FP32 softmax).

Workload	Dataset	Top-1 Match Rate (p50/p95)	Top-k Overlap Mean (p50/p95)	$KL_{gold \to approx} Mean$ $(p50/p95)$
Coding	The Stack [36]	1.000/1.000	0.9961/0.9991	$6.19 \times 10^{-5}/3.42 \times 10^{-3}$
Biomedical	PubMedQA [37]	1.000/1.000	0.9959/0.9991	$5.99 \times 10^{-5}/2.10 \times 10^{-3}$

More detailed comparisons against baselines are in the Results Section.

This behavior is consistent with the structure of the learned approximation: attention-dense regions are assigned narrower segments with predominantly lower polynomial degree, while sparse-tail regions are covered by wider segments with relatively higher degree. As a result, the approximation remains accurate not only in high-probability regions but also in lower-probability regions that may become more relevant under shifted workloads. In practice, recalibration is therefore optional for general use but remains preferable for specialized domains when maximizing low-degree utilization and efficiency is the primary goal.

4.3. *PSO Configuration Search and Selection*

In our experiments, segment boundaries and per-segment polynomial degrees are optimized per (ℓ, h) using a two-stage Particle Swarm Optimization (PSO) search. For each query attention head, PSO consumes the recorded stabilized-logit distribution together with activation quantization parameters from the model encodings produced by Qualcomm's AIMET [10]. We run PSO independently for each segment count $S \in \{4, 8, 12, 16\}$ with maximum polynomial degree $d_{\max} = 5$. Stage-1 performs global exploration with 40 particles for 200 iterations (global-best PSO, c1 = 1.4, c2 = 1.4, w = 0.7); Stage-2 refines by re-initializing 40 particles from Stage-1 outputs and continuing for 300 iterations with the same hyperparameters.

Each particle minimizes the fitness $\mathcal{L}$ defined in Section 3.2.2, i.e., a weighted sum of fidelity/robustness and hardware-aware regularizers, parameterized in our runs as follows:

$$\lambda_{\text{rob}} = 10.0,\ p_{\text{rob}} = 95.0,\ \lambda_{\max} = 5.0,\ \lambda_{\text{cost}} = 0.001, \text{P}(\textit{in cost term}) = 1,\ \lambda_{\text{flip}} = 10.0\ \lambda_{\text{dens}} = 0.01,\ \lambda_{\text{tiny}} = 10.0$$

https://doi.org/10.3390/electronics15061312

These weights are tunable hyperparameters: increasing λ_{rob}, λ_{max}, or λ_{dens} biases PSO toward higher accuracy/robustness, while increasing λ_{cost}(and λ_{tiny}) pushes the search toward lower-compute, LUT-friendly solutions with potentially larger approximation error.

In our current implementation, using PySwarms (version 1.3.0) [38] on an AMD Ryzen 9 CPU (Advanced Micro Devices, Inc., Santa Clara, CA, USA) with parallel job assignment, the offline PSO search for 12 heads required approximately 12–13 min on average while evaluating all $S \in \{4, 8, 12, 16\}$. For TinyLlama-1.1B-Chat, this corresponds to 704 heads and 2816 optimization jobs in total, giving an overall one-time calibration cost of roughly 49 h under the same setup. This cost reflects the current prototype implementation and could likely be reduced through faster search libraries, improved parallelization, or GPU acceleration.

Sensitivity to λ_{rob} and λ_{cost}

We performed a small sensitivity study on Layer 10, Heads 0–31, by varying λ_{rob} and λ_{cost} while keeping all other PSO settings fixed. Figure 8 shows that the selected expected degree changes predictably with the intended fidelity–efficiency trade-off. At fixed $\lambda_{cost} = 0.001$, increasing λ_{rob} (Figure 8) raises the mean expected degree from 1.79 to 1.91 while reducing the mean KL p95 from 3.34×10^{-5} to 1.77×10^{-5}. At fixed $\lambda_{rob} = 10$, increasing λ_{cost} (Figure 8) lowers the mean expected degree from 2.56 to 0.99, but increases the mean KL p95 from 1.20×10^{-5} to 3.92×10^{-5}. This indicates that the final expected degree is robust in the sense that it follows a consistent and interpretable trade-off, rather than being highly unstable to small hyperparameter changes.

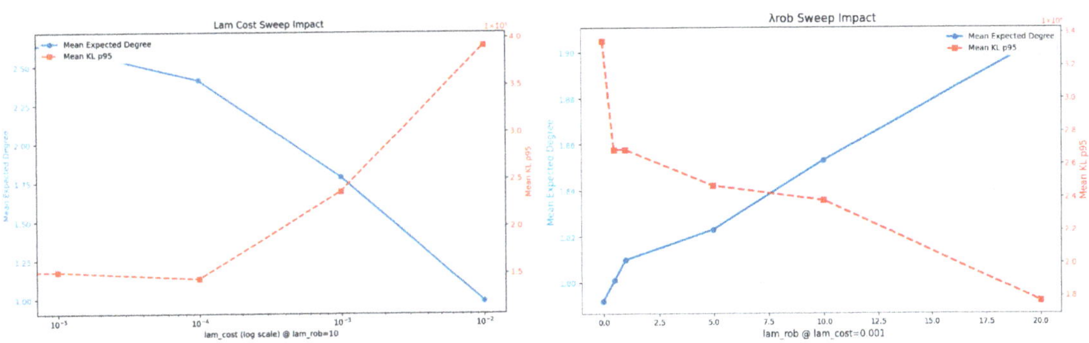

(a) (b)

Figure 8. Sensitivity of the Pareto-selected design to hyperparameter variation: (**a**) impact of sweeping λ_{cost}, and (**b**) impact of sweeping λ_{rob}.

The setting used in this work ($\lambda_{rob} = 10, \lambda_{cost} = 0.001$) was selected as a balanced operating point after Pareto selection. More generally, users may tune these weights according to deployment priorities: higher λ_{rob} favors robustness and accuracy, whereas higher λ_{cost} favors lower arithmetic cost and lower expected degree.

4.4. Baselines for Comparison

Baseline 1 (Exact/"Gold"): FP32 softmax

Standard floating-point softmax serves as the accuracy reference.

Baseline 2 (Standard approximation): Uniform piecewise polynomial

We compare against uniform fixed-structure baselines with 16 equidistant segments and fixed Degree-3 or Degree-4 polynomials, since this design is a widely used deployment-oriented standard in DSP/NPU softmax kernels due to its deterministic $O(1)$ indexing,

SIMD-friendly execution, robust behavior, and strong approximation fidelity [13,14,18]. Prior work and quantitative evaluations also show that higher-order polynomial approximations better capture softmax curvature and preserve attention-ranking fidelity under quantization, making 16-segment Degree-3 and Degree-4 strong practical references [18]. These baselines are also the most appropriate matched comparisons for our method because they belong to the same piecewise-polynomial exp-approximation family and share the same kernel-level deployment assumptions. We note that I-BERT [15] and SoftmAP [16] are important related public references and among the closest available designs to our setting; however, they are not directly comparable to our main numerical evaluation, since I-BERT uses a range-reduced single second-order polynomial in an end-to-end integer-only Transformer pipeline, while SoftmAP targets a software–hardware co-design for associative processors. Therefore, uniform 16-segment Degree-3 and Degree-4 were chosen both because they provide the fairest matched comparison and because they represent robust practical reference designs for evaluating the benefit of our distribution-aware variable-degree method.

4.5. Evaluation Metrics

We group metrics into Algorithm Quality and hardware efficiency to separately evaluate preservation of model softmax behavior and compute cost reduction respectively.

4.5.1. Algorithm Quality Metrics

1. Perplexity (PPL):

We measure end-to-end generation quality by computing perplexity on a held-out token stream, comparing FP32 vs. approximated softmax paths. (In our evaluation pipeline, only the fixed-shape attention softmax calls for the chunk phase are replaced; all other operations remain identical.)

2. Attention ranking fidelity:

Ranking fidelity is evaluated per attention row and then aggregated across rows, heads, and layers. We report the Top-1 match rate, defined as the fraction of rows for which $\arg\max p_{\text{approx}} = \arg\max p_{\text{fp32}}$, and the Top-$K$ overlap (with $K = 50$), measured as the set overlap between the FP32 and approximate top-K index sets (e.g., intersection-over-union or an equivalent overlap ratio).

3. Distributional divergence (KLD—Kullback–Leibler Divergence):

We compute KL divergence between FP32 and approximate softmax output distribution (after both are normalized):

$$D_{\text{KL}}\left(p_{\text{\_fp32}} \;\|\; p_{\text{\_approx}}\right) = \sum_j \text{p\_fp32}(j) \log \frac{p_{\text{\_fp32}(j)}}{p_{\text{\_approx}(j)}}. \quad (26)$$

We report tail statistics (e.g., p95) to capture worst-case rows.

4.5.2. Hardware Efficiency Metrics

These measurements are directly obtained using Qualcomm's Hexagon SDK 6.4.0.1 (Qualcomm Technologies, Inc., San Diego, CA, USA) [39] with the HTP (Hexagon Tensor Processor) v73 benchmark tool. We report CPC (cycles per call), measured by the HTP benchmarking tool (on-device) as the total cycle count required to execute a single kernel invocation at a given vector length, and CPE/CPM (cycles per element/member), which normalizes the cycle count by the number of processed elements to enable fair comparison across different vector sizes. In addition, we also report throughput in terms of MPS (million executions per second), which provides a complementary view of practical execution-rate improvement on-device. Finally, to place the exp-kernel gains in a broader deployment context, we include a rough on-device estimate of the overall softmax-stage cost by combining the measured exp results with benchmark-derived or inferred costs for reciprocal, reduction, and scaling.

5. Results

5.1. Offline Optimization Outcomes

5.1.1. PSO Output

Across 704 heads, PSO consistently converges to low expected polynomial degree, indicating that most heads do not require uniformly high-degree exp approximations. In Table 4, the mean expected degree stays ~1.79–1.83 across ranks, with p95 $\approx$ 2.22, suggesting higher degrees are rarely dominant. PSO also favors moderate-to-high segmentation: Table 5 shows S12 and S16 account for ~82–86% of candidate solutions across ranks, while S04 is ~2%, implying coarse segmentation is usually insufficient. The per-head distribution plots (Figure 9) qualitatively align with this trend: PSO places finer segmentation around the attention-dense region near 0 (after max-subtraction) and coarser coverage in the negative tail, enabling accuracy with lower average degree (Tables 4 and 5, Figure 9).

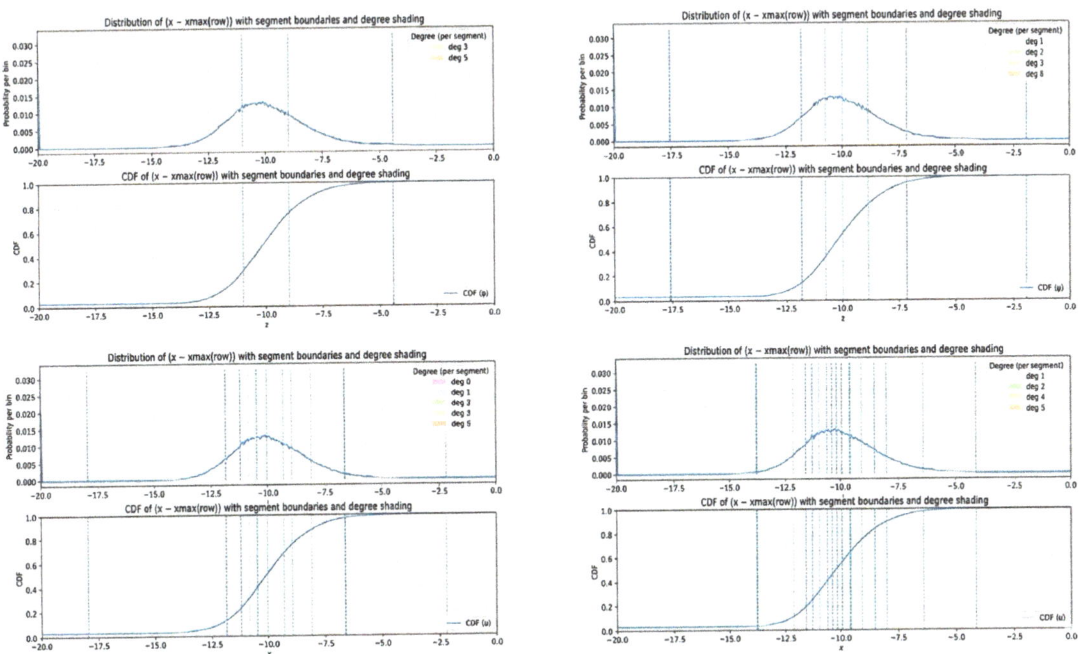

Figure 9. PSO Rank 1 outputs for TinyLlama-1.1B-Chat-v1.0 Layer 03 head 16 for $S = 4, 8, 12, 16$.

Table 4. PSO output—Expected degree summary by rank.

Rank	Heads	Expected Degree (Mean)	Expected Degree (p50)	Expected Degree (p95)
1	704	1.7901	1.8405	2.2195
2	704	1.8124	1.8525	2.2198
3	704	1.8144	1.8688	2.2330
4	704	1.8258	1.8760	2.2425
5	704	1.8347	1.8904	2.2330

https://doi.org/10.3390/electronics15061312

Table 5. PSO output—Segment choice distribution by rank.

Rank	Heads	S04 (%)	S08 (%)	S12 (%)	S16 (%)
1	704	1.99	15.20	31.82	50.99
2	704	1.99	14.49	33.95	49.57
3	704	2.41	14.35	31.68	51.56
4	704	1.85	12.50	33.52	52.13
5	704	1.85	14.49	32.95	50.71

5.1.2. Pareto Selection Output

Since PSO produces multiple candidates per head (5 ranks × 4 segment counts = 20 candidates), Pareto selection chooses one deployable configuration per head. Table 6 shows selections are concentrated in top ranks (Rank 1: 44.6%, then Rank 2/3), indicating strong solutions appear early. Segment choices shift toward a practical trade-off: S08 and S12 dominate (~38% each), with S16 at 22.9% and S04 nearly unused (0.43%) (Table 6). The final selected set yields an overall expected degree mean ≈ 2.04 (p95 ≈ 2.70) (Table 7), reflecting a controlled increase relative to raw PSO candidates to improve robustness while still keeping computation far below uniform high-degree baselines (Tables 6 and 7).

Table 6. Pareto frontier—Rank and segment selection summary.

Category	Item	Count	Share (%)
Rank chosen	Rank 1	314	44.60
	Rank 2	141	20.03
	Rank 3	108	15.34
	Rank 4	82	11.65
	Rank 5	59	8.38
Segment chosen	S04	3	0.43
	S08	269	38.21
	S12	271	38.49
	S16	161	22.87

Table 7. Expected degree summary (overall).

N	Expected Degree (Mean)	Expected Degree (p50)	Expected Degree (p95)
704	2.044349	2.043064	2.695313

5.2. Pre-Deployment Boundary Quantization (Snapping to Bin Edge) Effects

Snapping Pareto-selected boundaries to the LUT128 grid causes negligible accuracy loss (Table 8). Top-1 match rate stays at 1.0000 across p50–p99, so argmax decisions are unchanged. Top-k = 50 overlap is effectively identical (no change up to p95; only a tiny drop at p99 of -1.52×10^{-4}). For distribution fidelity, KL(Gold || Approx) shows only a small median increase ($+3.05 \times 10^{-6}$ at p50, $+5.92 \times 10^{-6}$ at p75), while p95 and p99 improve slightly. Overall, LUT128 snapping preserves ranking fidelity and distribution fidelity.

Table 8. Accuracy impact of 128-bin snapping (Proposed-Pareto frontier, n = 704 heads).

Metric	Percentile	Before Snap	After Snap	Δ (After − Before)
Top-1 match rate	p50	1.0000	1.0000	0.0000
	p75	1.0000	1.0000	0.0000
	p95	1.0000	1.0000	0.0000
	p99	1.0000	1.0000	0.0000

https://doi.org/10.3390/electronics15061312

Table 8. *Cont.*

Metric	Percentile	Before Snap	After Snap	Δ (After − Before)
Top-k = 50 overlap mean	p50	0.995938	0.995938	0.000000
	p75	0.997812	0.997812	0.000000
	p95	0.999219	0.999219	0.000000
	p99	0.999839	0.999687	−0.000152
KL(Gold‖Approx) mean	p50	4.51425×10^{-5}	4.81967×10^{-5}	$+3.0542 \times 10^{-6}$
	p75	9.94484×10^{-5}	1.05373×10^{-4}	$+5.9246 \times 10^{-6}$
	p95	1.48090×10^{-3}	1.39199×10^{-3}	-8.8910×10^{-5}
	p99	2.80421×10^{-2}	2.78062×10^{-2}	-2.3590×10^{-4}

5.3. *Final Accuracy vs. Baselines*

5.3.1. Perplexity

All methods are extremely close in end-to-end language modeling quality. The uniform baselines (16 segments, deg-3/deg-4) are nearly identical to FP32, and the proposed weighted configuration shows only a small increase in PPL (7.0983 vs. 7.0904 FP), shown in Table 9. This indicates that the variable-degree, distribution-aware approximation preserves the downstream generation behavior under the fixed-length attention workload.

Table 9. Perplexity comparison table.

Method	PPL	Avg NLL	Tokens
FP (gold)	7.09042	1.95874	339456
Uniform 16-seg, deg-4 [13,14,18]	7.09177	1.95893	339456
Uniform 16-seg, deg-3 [13,14,18]	7.09155	1.95890	339456
Proposed (avg degree, weighted)	7.09827	1.95985	339456

5.3.2. Attention Rank Fidelity

Ranking is preserved at the most critical level: Top-1 match is 1.0 across all percentiles (p50–p99) for both baselines and the proposed method (Table 10).

Table 10. Attention rank fidelity—Top-1 match rate (per head).

Method	*n* (Heads)	p50	p75	p95	p99
Uniform 16-segment, Degree-4 [13,14,18]	704	1.0000	1.0000	1.0000	1.0000
Uniform 16-segment, Degree-3 [13,14,18]	704	1.0000	1.0000	1.0000	1.0000
Proposed average degree (weighted)	704	1.0000	1.0000	1.0000	1.0000

For Top-k (k = 50), the proposed method remains extremely high (p50 = 0.9959, p95 = 0.9992) but is slightly below the uniform baselines—especially deg-4, which is near-perfect (Table 11). Practically, this suggests the proposed method maintains the argmax, and top mass remains almost identical.

Table 11. Attention rank fidelity—Top-k = 50 overlap mean (per head).

Method	*n* (Heads)	p50	p75	p95	p99
Uniform 16-segment, Degree-4 [13,14,18]	704	0.9998438	1.0000	1.0000	1.0000
Uniform 16-segment, Degree-3 [13,14,18]	704	0.9984375	0.9990625	0.9996875	0.9998438
Proposed average degree (weighted)	704	0.9959375	0.9978125	0.9992188	0.9996875

https://doi.org/10.3390/electronics15061312

5.3.3. Distributional Divergence (Kullback–Leibler Divergence)

Table 12 shows that our method exhibits a higher $KL(Gold\|Approx)$ than the uniform 16-segment baselines, particularly in the upper tail (p99). This behavior is expected and does not contradict the strong ranking fidelity observed in Tables 10 and 11. KL divergence is highly sensitive to small absolute-probability differences distributed across many low-mass entries, so coarse approximation in the far-negative "tail" of the stabilized logits can inflate KL even when the top-ranked tokens remain unchanged. This interpretation is also supported by the perplexity results in Table 9: although the proposed method shows larger KL upper-tail values, the downstream language modeling impact remains very small, with perplexity increasing only from 7.09042 (gold) to 7.09827 (proposed). This suggests that the elevated KL is dominated mainly by discrepancies in low-mass tail probabilities rather than errors in the dominant attention entries that most directly affect next-token prediction. This is consistent with prior findings that attention probability mass is typically concentrated in a small subset of "heavy hitter" tokens, with the remaining entries contributing negligibly to the final distribution [40]. Moreover, several studies attribute large-magnitude negative logits and "systematic outliers" to softmax range expansion and note that these tail regions are primarily problematic for quantization—rather than semantically important—making them suitable targets for clipping or low-precision treatment [41]. Related analysis on quantizable attention similarly argues that extreme values often correspond to "do-nothing" or near-no-op head behavior, suggesting that exact exponential fidelity in all tail regions is less critical than preserving the dominant attention structure [42].

Table 12. KL divergence—KL (Gold || Approx) mean (per head).

Method	*n* (Heads)	p50	p75	p95	p99
Uniform 16-segment, Degree-4 [13,14,18]	704	5.8380×10^{-7}	1.7642×10^{-5}	2.5454×10^{-4}	5.7168×10^{-4}
Uniform 16-segment, Degree-3 [13,14,18]	704	9.5414×10^{-6}	2.9664×10^{-5}	2.6727×10^{-4}	5.9334×10^{-4}
Proposed average degree (weighted)	704	4.8197×10^{-5}	1.0537×10^{-4}	1.3920×10^{-3}	2.7806×10^{-2}

In our case, PSO intentionally prioritizes accuracy where it matters most—the dense region near 0 where attention mass concentrates—and allocates lower polynomial degrees to the sparse tail to reduce compute. As a result, we preserve Top-1 agreement (Table 10) and maintain high Top-k overlap (Table 11), while accepting a comparatively higher KL that is dominated by tail discrepancies rather than errors in dominant tokens. This trade-off aligns with the deployment objective: minimize exp-kernel cost while retaining attention ranking behavior that most directly impacts downstream generation quality.

5.4. Final Compute Cost vs. Baselines

5.4.1. Baseline vs. Proposed Avg Degree Model

During a full forward pass, we see, as shown in Table 13, most exp evaluations fall into low-to-mid degrees: deg2 (35.50%) and deg3 (26.77%) dominate, while deg0 + deg1 already contribute ~28.65% of all calls. High-cost degrees are relatively rare (deg-4 6.80%, deg-5 2.28%). This confirms the core design objective: PSO shifts work toward cheaper polynomial orders in regions where attention scores concentrate, and reserves higher degrees only where needed. Table 14 and Figure 10 report the CPC per call for uniform baselines (single fixed degree for all segments: deg-3 or deg-4) and for our per-segment kernels (deg0–deg4). To estimate the end-to-end runtime cost of the proposed model, we compute a weighted-average CPC using the observed degree shares from Table 13:

$$\mathrm{CPC}_{\mathrm{avg}} = \sum_{d} p(d) \cdot \mathrm{CPC}(d)$$

https://doi.org/10.3390/electronics15061312

Table 13. Observed average degree usage during forward pass.

Degree	Count	Share (%)
deg0	25,786,200	13.97
deg1	27,086,745	14.68
deg2	65,515,000	35.50
deg3	49,405,466	26.77
deg4	12,548,381	6.80
deg5	4,207,584	2.28
Total	184,549,376	100.00

Table 14. On-device cycles per call (CPC) comparison: Existing vs. proposed.

Vector Length (N)	Existing: Uniform deg4 [13,14,18]	Existing: Uniform deg3 [13,14,18]	Proposed deg-0	Proposed deg-1	Proposed deg-2	Proposed deg-3	Proposed deg-4
3	399.3250	335.8287	341.9989	307.5472	325.3782	341.1928	380.0429
6	408.8030	333.0498	393.9897	433.9223	344.7052	372.0468	391.7174
21	432.2397	377.2180	346.7558	387.5393	376.8401	381.9031	389.5363
47	412.8360	346.5294	400.1823	445.3874	340.8204	374.7148	399.5101
103	761.2046	697.6511	736.8042	739.9724	700.8750	751.9182	795.0950
347	1671.1382	1568.3010	1675.5996	1665.7684	1634.9799	1648.6060	1871.2115
7381	26,856.3081	24,458.3473	12,398.4813	14,012.6216	23,477.0033	26,439.2541	27,366.1926
9396	25,833.6635	25,610.3980	13,213.8330	15,313.4047	23,101.1840	24,815.9886	25,602.3606
27,296	38,032.7271	36,168.2892	18,735.6174	22,873.7001	33,170.4274	36,142.4854	38,236.9382
60,128	60,189.0124	55,585.2256	30,111.9064	36,666.9100	51,389.4922	56,804.2415	61,702.9383
104,728	154,997.2576	145,480.8383	78,355.1687	92,846.7735	13,4861.7057	148,072.3513	157,135.5429

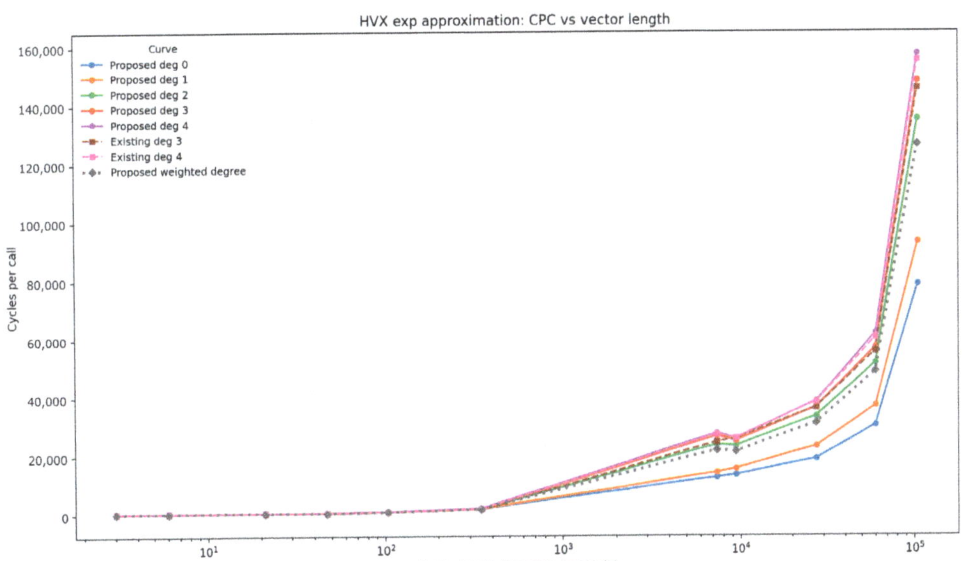

Figure 10. HVX exp() approximation cost across vector lengths (CPC vs. Vector length), cycles per call (CPC) on the Qualcomm IQ9 HTP v73 for uniform baselines (deg-3/deg-4) and proposed per-degree kernels (deg-0…deg-4), plotted against vector length on a log x-axis. The "proposed average degree" curve is a weighted mixture based on the measured degree distribution during the average attention forward pass (Table 13), illustrating how low-degree dominance translates into lower effective runtime cost at realistic sequence/context sizes.

https://doi.org/10.3390/electronics15061312

For realistic long vectors (where exp dominates runtime), the proposed weighted model is consistently cheaper than uniform baselines, shown in Table 15.

Table 15. Reduction in CPC at long vector lengths: Existing vs. proposed.

Vector Length (N)	Proposed Weighted avg CPC	Uniform deg-3 CPC [13,14,18]	Uniform deg-4 CPC [13,14,18]	Δ vs. deg-3	Δ vs. deg-4
27,296	30,897.9840	36,168.2892	36,168.2892	−14.6%	−18.8%
60,128	48,641.7277	55,585.2256	55,585.2256	−12.5%	−19.2%
104,728	126,358.9047	145,480.8383	145,480.8383	−13.1%	−18.5%

As the runtime workload is skewed toward deg0–deg3, the proposed distribution-aware configuration converts that skew directly into lower average CPC and CPM, as shown in Figures 10 and 11, while the uniform baselines pay the same high degree cost for every element regardless of where the probability mass lies.

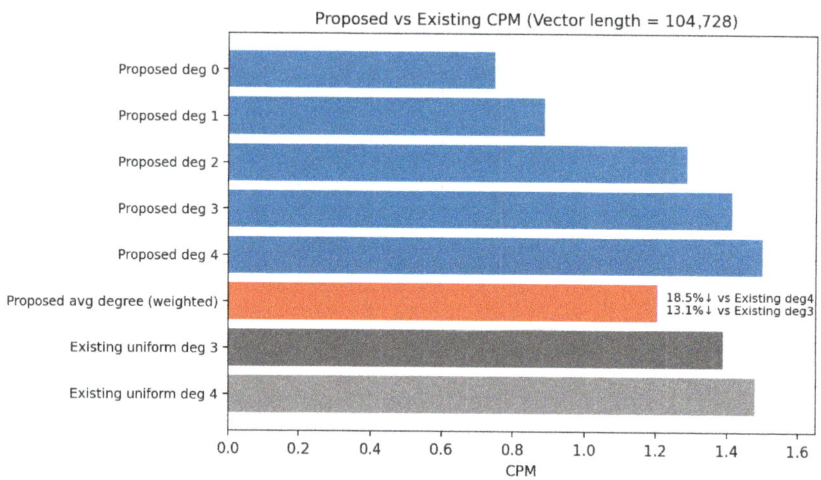

Figure 11. Summary cost at the largest benchmark point (CPM at N = 104,728). Cost-per-element (CPE) comparison at vector length 104,728 for uniform baselines and per-degree proposed kernels, including the weighted "proposed average degree" point. The proposed weighted design reduces exp-kernel compute cost by 18.5% vs. uniform deg-4 and 13.2% vs. uniform deg-3, consistent with the measured prevalence of low-degree segments in Table 13.

5.4.2. Throughput—Million Executions per Second (MPS)

As shown in Table 16, the proposed weighted design consistently improves execution throughput over the uniform baselines at large vector lengths. At $N = 27{,}296$, it achieves 0.0502 MPS, compared with 0.0404 for uniform Degree-3 and 0.0383 for uniform Degree-4, corresponding to gains of 24.1% and 30.9%, respectively. At $N = 60{,}128$, the proposed method reaches 0.0317 MPS versus 0.0263 and 0.0242, giving improvements of 20.4% and 30.8%. At the largest benchmarked length, $N = 104{,}728$, it attains 0.0120 MPS, while the uniform Degree-3 and Degree-4 baselines reach only 0.0099 and 0.0092, yielding gains of 20.8% and 30.0%.

These results show that the reduced expected compute of the proposed variable-degree design translates directly into higher on-device throughput in the long-vector regime most relevant to attention execution.

https://doi.org/10.3390/electronics15061312

Table 16. On-device throughput comparison in million executions per second (MPS) at large vector lengths.

Vector Length (N)	Proposed Weighted avg MPS	Uniform deg-3 MPS [13,14,18]	Uniform deg-4 MPS [13,14,18]	Δ vs. deg-3	Δ vs. deg-4
27,296	0.0502	0.0404	0.0383	+24.1%	+30.9%
60,128	0.0317	0.0263	0.0242	+20.4%	+30.8%
104,728	0.0120	0.0099	0.0092	+20.8%	+30.0%

5.4.3. Runtime Segment Indexing Cost: LUT128 vs. BST

To isolate segment selection overhead, we evaluate the Degree-0 configuration, where each segment computes a constant (i.e., polynomial cost is minimized and CPC is dominated by the indexing/control path). Table 17 shows that LUT128-based indexing consistently outperforms BST-based boundary search [26] across all vector lengths. For small vectors ($N \leq 103$), LUT128 already reduces CPC by ~5–12%, indicating lower per-call control overhead. As vector length grows, the gap widens substantially: at N = 104,728, LUT128 achieves a 1.88× speedup and 46.87% CPC reduction relative to BST.

Table 17. Deg-0 16 segment selection overhead: LUT128 vs. BST.

Vector Length (N)	CPC (BST) [26]	CPC (LUT128)	Speedup (BST/LUT)	CPC Reduction
3	326.0278	341.9989	0.9533×	−4.90%
6	365.0819	393.9897	0.9266×	−7.92%
21	396.3407	346.7558	1.1430×	12.51%
47	381.7663	400.1823	0.9540×	−4.82%
103	784.7727	736.8042	1.0651×	6.11%
347	1791.0647	1675.5996	1.0689×	6.45%
7381	25,005.0804	12,398.4813	2.0168×	50.42%
9396	26,350.0281	13,213.8330	1.9941×	49.85%
27,296	36,625.5212	18,735.6174	1.9559×	48.84%
60,128	55,434.4263	30,111.9064	1.8410×	45.68%
104,728 (Summary)	147,460.1100	78,355.1687	1.8819×	46.87%

This trend matches NPU kernel behavior: BST requires repeated comparisons and branch-heavy control, which scales poorly and disrupts SIMD utilization, whereas LUT128 segment mapping is constant-time and branch-free, using a simple bin index followed by a table lookup. In practice, this validates the deployment choice in Section 3.2.4: snapping boundaries to LUT edges enables deterministic indexing and removes a major runtime bottleneck that is orthogonal to polynomial degree.

5.4.4. Rough On-Device Estimate of Softmax-Stage Cost

The CPC/CPM improvements reported earlier are measured for the exp-approximation kernel itself which is the main direction of the research. To place these gains in a broader softmax context, we also provide a rough on-device estimate of the remaining softmax-stage cost for one representative row of length $K = 2048$. In our implementation, normalization is performed using one reciprocal per row followed by elementwise scaling, while the row-wise sum is treated separately. The reciprocal, reduction-proxy, and multiply costs used in this estimate were obtained or inferred from Hexagon SDK on-device benchmarking on the IQ9 platform with the v73 HTP. Combining these with the measured exp CPM values gives an estimated per-row softmax-stage cost of 3590.31 cycles for the proposed weighted design, compared with 3964.07 cycles for uniform Degree-3 and 4150.23 cycles for uniform Degree-4.

https://doi.org/10.3390/electronics15061312

This corresponds to a rough estimated reduction of about 9–11% versus uniform Degree-3 and about 13–15% versus uniform Degree-4. Under this decomposition, the exp stage still accounts for approximately 69–73% of the estimated softmax-stage cost, indicating that it remains the dominant optimization target. These values should be interpreted only as a rough on-device estimate, not as a real-time end-to-end deployment measurement.

6. Conclusions

This work addresses the softmax bottleneck in NPU-deployed Transformers by introducing a grid-snapped, attention distribution-aware approximation. By bridging statistical optimality with hardware constraints, we demonstrate that high-fidelity inference is achievable without applying uniform high-precision arithmetic across the entire domain.

6.1. Key Contributions

Our primary contribution synthesizes offline Particle Swarm Optimization (PSO) with hardware-compliant quantization. The PSO learns non-uniform segments favoring low-degree polynomials in attention-dense regions. Crucially, we introduced grid-snapping—quantizing boundaries to a 128-bin virtual grid—to enable O(1) deterministic indexing, effectively eliminating the control overhead of adaptive segmentation. Empirical validation on TinyLlama-1.1B-Chat confirms a 18.5% reduction in exponential-kernel CPC versus the uniform 16-segment Degree-4 baseline and 13.1% versus the uniform 16-segment Degree-3 baseline, together with MPS throughput gains of up to 30.9%, while maintaining attention ranking fidelity.

6.2. Limitations

This study operates within specific scopes of validity. First, while performance results are reported from on-device benchmarking on the Qualcomm Dragonwing IQ9 platform(Qualcomm Technologies, Inc., San Diego, CA, USA) with the v73 Hexagon Tensor Processor, fully integrated end-to-end LLM inference latency for the proposed custom softmax approximation is not yet available. In the current deployment setting, the available tooling does not provide a practical path for injecting and evaluating the custom kernel inside a complete generative inference pipeline [34,39]. Second, distributional metrics such as KL divergence remain sensitive to sparse tail discrepancies; however, in our experiments these deviations are concentrated in low-probability regions and do not materially degrade Top-1/Top-*k* ranking fidelity, while perplexity remains largely unchanged. Finally, the offline PSO search incurs a pre-processing cost; however, this is a one-time compilation overhead that is effectively amortized over the model's deployment lifetime, though scaling to larger models may benefit from smart swarm initializations.

6.3. Future Work

Subsequent investigations will target the validation of end-to-end wall-clock latency on physical hardware. Methodological enhancements will focus on the PSO algorithm, specifically the integration of tail-robustness constraints to minimize distributional outliers. Furthermore, the adoption of smart initialization strategies is proposed to accelerate swarm optimization, thereby facilitating the scalable deployment of this approximation technique across extensive large language models. In addition, reducing the number of fully independent per-head configurations to a smaller shared or clustered set is a promising deployment strategy, as it could substantially lower one-time calibration cost, simplify optimization, and improve scalability for large-model deployment. Another important direction is the analysis of runtime table residency, loading overhead, and cache/TCM behavior under practical deployment conditions.

https://doi.org/10.3390/electronics15061312

Author Contributions: Conceptualization, S.S. and M.-J.H.; methodology, S.S. and M.-J.H.; software, S.S.; validation, M.-J.H., C.-H.H. and Y.-T.W.; formal analysis, M.-J.H.; investigation, S.S.; resources, Y.-T.W. and C.-H.H.; data curation, S.S.; writing—original draft preparation, S.S.; writing—review and editing, M.-J.H.; visualization, S.S.; supervision, C.-H.H. and Y.-T.W.; project administration, C.-H.H.; funding acquisition, C.-H.H., Y.-T.W. and M.-J.H. All authors have read and agreed to the published version of the manuscript.

Funding: This work was supported by Innodisk Corporation, Taiwan; in part by the "Higher Education Sprout Project" of National Taiwan Normal University and the Ministry of Education (MOE), Taiwan; and in part by the National Science and Technology Council (NSTC), Taiwan, under Grant NSTC114-2221-E-003-036 and Grant NSTC114-2221-E-032-026.

Data Availability Statement: The original contributions presented in this study are included in the article. Further inquiries can be directed to the corresponding author.

Acknowledgments: The authors sincerely appreciate the constructive comments and valuable suggestions from the anonymous reviewers, which greatly improved the quality of this manuscript.

Conflicts of Interest: Sanoop Sadheerthan is an internship student at Innodisk Corporation. Chih-Hsiang Huang serves as an assistant manager at Innodisk Corporation. All other authors declare no conflicts of interest. The authors also declare that the supporting sources were not involved in the study design, collection, analysis, interpretation of data, the writing of this article or the decision to submit it for publication.

Abbreviations

The following abbreviations are used in this manuscript:

BST	Binary Search Tree
CPC	Clocks Per Call
CPE	Clocks Per Element
CPM	Clocks Per Member
DSP	Digital Signal Processor
FGPA	Field-Programmable Gate Array
HTP	Hexagon Tensor Processor
HVX	Hexagon Vector eXtension
ISA	Instruction Set Architecture
KL	Kullback–Leibler (divergence)
LUT	Look-Up Table
MAC	Multiply–Accumulate
PPL	Perplexity
PSO	Particle Swarm Optimization
QNN	Qualcomm Neural Network
SDK	Software Development Kit
SIMD	Single Instruction Multiple Data
TCM	Tightly Coupled Memory
NPU	Neural Processing Unit

References

1. Xu, D.; Zhang, H.; Yang, L.; Liu, R.; Huang, G.; Xu, M.; Liu, X. Fast On-Device LLM Inference with NPUs. *arXiv* **2024**, arXiv:2407.05858. [CrossRef]
2. Tan, T.; Cao, G. Efficient Execution of Deep Neural Networks on Mobile Devices with NPU. In Proceedings of the 20th International Conference on Information Processing in Sensor Networks (co-located with CPS-IoT Week 2021), Sydney, Australia, 21–24 April 2020; pp. 283–298. [CrossRef]
3. Li, J.; Xu, J.; Huang, S.; Chen, Y.; Li, W.; Liu, J.; Lian, Y.; Pan, J.; Ding, L.; Zhou, H.; et al. Large Language Model Inference Acceleration: A Comprehensive Hardware Perspective. *arXiv* **2025**, arXiv:2410.04466. [CrossRef]

4. Hao, Z.; Wei, J.; Wang, T.; Huang, M.; Jiang, H.; Jiang, S.; Cao, T.; Ren, J. Scaling LLM Test-Time Compute with Mobile NPU on Smartphones. *arXiv* **2025**, arXiv:2509.23324. [CrossRef]
5. Kumar, D.; Pramod Pawar, P.; Kumar Meesala, M.; Kumar Pareek, P.; Reddy Addula, S.; Shwetha, K.S. Trustworthy IoT Infrastructures: Privacy-Preserving Federated Learning with Efficient Secure Aggregation for Cybersecurity. In Proceedings of the 2024 International Conference on Integrated Intelligence and Communication Systems (ICIICS), Kalaburagi, India, 22–23 November 2024; pp. 1–8. [CrossRef]
6. Papaioannou, A.; Dimara, A.; Kouzinopoulos, C.S.; Krinidis, S.; Anagnostopoulos, C.-N.; Ioannidis, D.; Tzovaras, D. LP-OPTIMA: A Framework for Prescriptive Maintenance and Optimization of IoT Resources for Low-Power Embedded Systems. *Sensors* **2024**, *24*, 2125. [CrossRef] [PubMed]
7. Vaswani, A.; Shazeer, N.; Parmar, N.; Uszkoreit, J.; Jones, L.; Gomez, A.N.; Kaiser, L.; Polosukhin, I. Attention Is All You Need. *arXiv* **2023**, arXiv:1706.03762. [CrossRef]
8. Touvron, H.; Lavril, T.; Izacard, G.; Martinet, X.; Lachaux, M.-A.; Lacroix, T.; Rozière, B.; Goyal, N.; Hambro, E.; Azhar, F.; et al. LLaMA: Open and Efficient Foundation Language Models. *arXiv* **2023**, arXiv:2302.13971. [CrossRef]
9. Jacob, B.; Kligys, S.; Chen, B.; Zhu, M.; Tang, M.; Howard, A.; Adam, H.; Kalenichenko, D. Quantization and Training of Neural Networks for Efficient Integer-Arithmetic-Only Inference. In Proceedings of the 2018 IEEE/CVF Conference on Computer Vision and Pattern Recognition, Salt Lake City, UT, USA, 18–22 June 2018; pp. 2704–2713. [CrossRef]
10. Siddegowda, S.; Fournarakis, M.; Nagel, M.; Blankevoort, T.; Patel, C.; Khobare, A. Neural Network Quantization with AI Model Efficiency Toolkit (AIMET). *arXiv* **2022**, arXiv:2201.08442. [CrossRef]
11. Zhang, P.; Zeng, G.; Wang, T.; Lu, W. TinyLlama: An Open-Source Small Language Model. *arXiv* **2024**, arXiv:2401.02385. [CrossRef]
12. Pavlidis, T.; Maika, A.P. Uniform Piecewise Polynomial Approximation with Variable Joints. *J. Approx. Theory* **1974**, *12*, 61–69. [CrossRef]
13. Geng, X.; Lin, J.; Zhao, B.; Kong, A.; Aly, M.M.S.; Chandrasekhar, V. Hardware-Aware Softmax Approximation for Deep Neural Networks. In *Computer Vision—ACCV 2018, Proceedings of the 14th Asian Conference on Computer Vision, Perth, Australia, 2–6 December 2018*; Jawahar, C.V., Li, H., Mori, G., Schindler, K., Eds.; Lecture Notes in Computer Science; Springer International Publishing: Cham, Switzerland, 2019; Volume 11364, pp. 107–122. [CrossRef]
14. Vasyltsov, I.; Chang, W. Efficient Softmax Approximation for Deep Neural Networks with Attention Mechanism. *arXiv* **2021**, arXiv:2111.10770. [CrossRef]
15. Kim, S.; Gholami, A.; Yao, Z.; Mahoney, M.W.; Keutzer, K. I-BERT: Integer-Only BERT Quantization. *arXiv* **2021**, arXiv:2101.01321. [CrossRef]
16. Rakka, M.; Li, J.; Dai, G.; Eltawil, A.; Fouda, M.E.; Kurdahi, F. SoftmAP: Software-Hardware Co-Design for Integer-Only Softmax on Associative Processors. *arXiv* **2024**, arXiv:2411.17847. [CrossRef]
17. Kim, R.; Lee, D.; Kim, J.; Park, J.; Lee, S. Hardware Accelerator for Approximation-Based Softmax and Layer Normalization in Transformers. *Electronics* **2025**, *14*, 2337. [CrossRef]
18. Leiva-Valverde, A.; Elizondo-Fernández, F.; León-Vega, L.G.; Meinhardt, C.; Castro-Godínez, J. A Quantitative Evaluation of Approximate Softmax Functions for Deep Neural Networks. *arXiv* **2025**, arXiv:2501.13379. [CrossRef]
19. Zhong, W.; Feng, H.; Zhou, Z.; Peng, H.; Yu, S. IntAttention: A Fully Integer Attention Pipeline for Efficient Edge Inference. *arXiv* **2025**, arXiv:2511.21513. [CrossRef]
20. Kang, Y.; Wang, D. Hardware-Oriented Approximations of Softmax and RMSNorm for Efficient Transformer Inference. *Micromachines* **2026**, *17*, 84. [CrossRef]
21. Prasad, A.S.; İslamoğlu, G.; Bertaccini, L.; Rossi, D.; Conti, F.; Benini, L. PACE: An Optimal Piecewise Polynomial Approximation Unit for Flexible and Efficient Transformer Non-Linearity Acceleration. In Proceedings of the 2025 IEEE Computer Society Annual Symposium on VLSI (ISVLSI), Kalamata, Greece, 6–9 July 2025; pp. 1–6. [CrossRef]
22. Li, Z.; Yang, K.; Tan, J.; Lu, W.; Wu, H.; Wang, X.; Yu, Y.; Zhao, D.; Zheng, Y.; Guo, M.; et al. Nimbus: Secure and Efficient Two-Party Inference for Transformers. *arXiv* **2024**, arXiv:2411.15707. [CrossRef]
23. Ho, S.M.H.; So, H.K.-H. NnCore: A Parameterized Non-Linear Function Generator for Machine Learning Applications in FPGAs. In Proceedings of the 2017 International Conference on Field Programmable Technology (ICFPT), Melbourne, Australia, 11–13 December 2017; pp. 160–167. [CrossRef]
24. González-Díaz_Conti, G.; Vázquez-Castillo, J.; Longoria-Gandara, O.; Castillo-Atoche, A.; Carrasco-Alvarez, R.; Espinoza-Ruiz, A.; Ruiz-Ibarra, E. Hardware-Based Activation Function-Core for Neural Network Implementations. *Electronics* **2021**, *11*, 14. [CrossRef]
25. Dong, X.; Zhu, X.; Ma, D. Hardware Implementation of Softmax Function Based on Piecewise LUT. In Proceedings of the 2019 IEEE International Workshop on Future Computing (IWOFC), Hangzhou, China, 14–15 December 2019; pp. 1–3. [CrossRef]
26. Andri, R.; Reggiani, E.; Cavigelli, L. Flex-SFU: Activation Function Acceleration with Nonuniform Piecewise Approximation. *IEEE Trans. Comput.-Aided Des. Integr. Circuits Syst.* **2025**, *44*, 4236–4248. [CrossRef]

https://doi.org/10.3390/electronics15061312

27. Kennedy, J.; Eberhart, R. Particle Swarm Optimization. In Proceedings of the ICNN'95—International Conference on Neural Networks, Perth, Australia, 27 November–1 December 1995; Volume 4, pp. 1942–1948. [CrossRef]
28. Shi, Y.; Eberhart, R. A Modified Particle Swarm Optimizer. In Proceedings of the 1998 IEEE International Conference on Evolutionary Computation: IEEE World Congress on Computational Intelligence (Cat. No.98TH8360), Anchorage, AK, USA, 4–9 May 1998; pp. 69–73. [CrossRef]
29. Wei, Z.; Arora, A.; Patel, P.; John, L. Design Space Exploration for Softmax Implementations. In Proceedings of the 2020 IEEE 31st International Conference on Application-Specific Systems, Architectures and Processors (ASAP), Manchester, UK, 6–8 July 2020; pp. 45–52. [CrossRef]
30. Cardarilli, G.C.; Di Nunzio, L.; Fazzolari, R.; Giardino, D.; Nannarelli, A.; Re, M.; Spanò, S. A Pseudo-Softmax Function for Hardware-Based High Speed Image Classification. *Sci. Rep.* **2021**, *11*, 15307. [CrossRef]
31. Stevens, J.R.; Venkatesan, R.; Dai, S.; Khailany, B.; Raghunathan, A. Softermax: Hardware/Software Co-Design of an Efficient Softmax for Transformers. *arXiv* **2021**, arXiv:2103.09301. [CrossRef]
32. Hsieh, M.-H.; Li, X.-H.; Huang, Y.-H.; Kuo, P.-H.; Huang, J.-D. A Hardware-Friendly Alternative to Softmax Function and Its Efficient VLSI Implementation for Deep Learning Applications. In Proceedings of the 2024 IEEE International Symposium on Circuits and Systems (ISCAS), Singapore, 19–22 May 2024; pp. 1–5. [CrossRef]
33. Chips and Cheese. Qualcomm's Hexagon DSP, and now, NPU. Available online: https://chipsandcheese.com/p/qualcomms-hexagon-dsp-and-now-npu (accessed on 13 March 2026).
34. Qualcomm Technologies, Inc. Qualcomm AI Runtime (QAIRT) Documentation. Available online: https://docs.qualcomm.com/nav/home?product=1601111740010412 (accessed on 10 February 2026).
35. Wikimedia Foundation. Wikimedia/Wikipedia Dataset. Hugging Face Datasets. Available online: https://huggingface.co/datasets/wikimedia/wikipedia (accessed on 10 February 2026).
36. Hugging Face. The Stack. Available online: https://huggingface.co/datasets/bigcode/the-stack (accessed on 13 March 2026).
37. Hugging Face. PubMedQA. Available online: https://huggingface.co/datasets/qiaojin/PubMedQA (accessed on 13 March 2026).
38. PySwarms Developers. PySwarms Documentation. Available online: https://pyswarms.readthedocs.io/en/latest/ (accessed on 13 March 2026).
39. Qualcomm Technologies, Inc. Hexagon SDK Documentation. Available online: https://docs.qualcomm.com/nav/home?product=1601111740010422 (accessed on 10 February 2026).
40. Zhang, Z.; Sheng, Y.; Zhou, T.; Chen, T.; Zheng, L.; Cai, R.; Song, Z.; Tian, Y.; Ré, C.; Barrett, C.; et al. H_2O: Heavy-Hitter Oracle for Efficient Generative Inference of Large Language Models. *arXiv* **2023**, arXiv:2306.14048. [CrossRef]
41. An, Y.; Zhao, X.; Yu, T.; Tang, M.; Wang, J. Systematic Outliers in Large Language Models. *arXiv* **2025**, arXiv:2502.06415. [CrossRef]
42. Bondarenko, Y.; Nagel, M.; Blankevoort, T. Quantizable Transformers: Removing Outliers by Helping Attention Heads Do Nothing. *arXiv* **2023**, arXiv:2306.12929. [CrossRef]

https://doi.org/10.3390/electronics15061312

MDPI AG
Grosspeteranlage 5
4052 Basel
Switzerland
Tel.: +41 61 683 77 34

Electronics Editorial Office
E-mail: electronics@mdpi.com
www.mdpi.com/journal/electronics

www.ingramcontent.com/pod-product-compliance
Lightning Source LLC
Chambersburg PA
CBHW061444210926
51850CB00008B/1607